A Kodansha Comics Trade Paperback Original
Living-Room Matsunaga-san 6 copyright © 2019 Keiko Iwashita
English translation copyright © 2021 Keiko Iwashita

Published in the United States by Kodansha Comics, an imprint of
Kodansha USA Publishing, LLC, New York.

Publication rights for this English edition arranged through
Kodansha Ltd., Tokyo.

First published in Japan in 2019 by Kodansha Ltd., Tokyo
as *Living no Matsunaga-san*, volume 6.

ISBN 978-1-64651-055-9

Original cover design by Tomohiro Kusume and Hirotoshi Ikewaki (arcoinc)

Printed in the United States of America.

www.kodanshacomics.com

9 8 7 6 5 4 3 2 1
Translation: Ursula Ku
Lettering: Jan Lan Ivan Concepcion
Additional Lettering: Michael Martin
Editing: Kristin Osani and Tiff Ferentini
Kodansha Comics edition cover design by Phil Balsman

Publisher: Kiichiro Sugawara

Director of publishing services: Ben Applegate
Associate director of operations: Stephen Pakula
Publishing services associate managing editor: Madison Salters
Production managers: Emi Lotto, Angela Zurlo

MAGIC ☻ KNIGHT RAYEARTH

25TH ANNIVERSARY EDITION

CLAMP

A BELOVED CLASSIC MAKES ITS STUNNING RETURN IN THIS GORGEOUS, LIMITED EDITION BOX SET!

This tale of three Tokyo teenagers who cross through a magical portal and become the champions of another world is a modern manga classic. The box set includes three volumes of manga covering the entire first series of *Magic Knight Rayearth*, plus the series's super-rare full-color art book companion, all printed at a larger size than ever before on premium paper, featuring a newly-revised translation and lettering, and exquisite foil-stamped covers. A strictly limited edition, this will be gone in a flash!

KC/
KODANSHA
COMICS

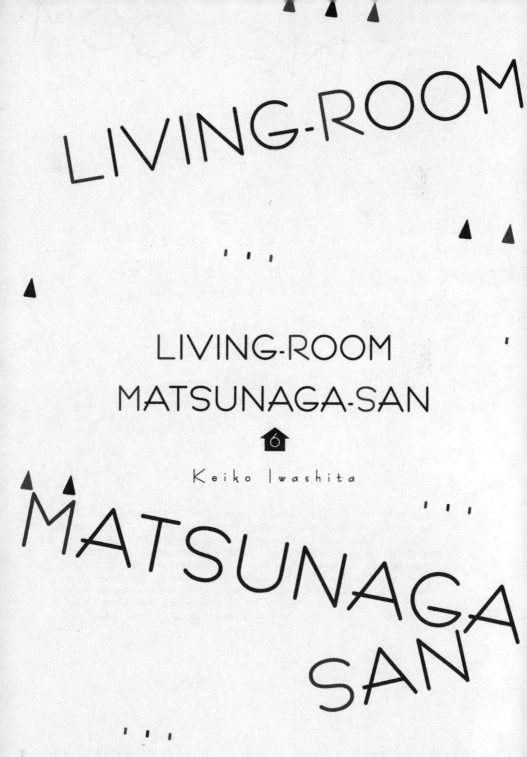

LIVING-ROOM

LIVING-ROOM
MATSUNAGA-SAN

6

Keiko Iwashita

MATSUNAGA
SAN

LIVING-ROOM

Contents

Story

Family circumstances have wrested Meeko from an ordinary family life to her uncle's boarding house, where her unrequited feelings for her house-mate Matsunaga-san only grow with each passing day. Not only do they spend a day at Kitneyland with each other, they unexpectedly spend a night at a...special...place, as well. Afterwards, while preparing for her school festival, Meeko learns that her homeroom teacher Kobayashi-sensei is the "Konatsu" of legend...and that she and Matsunaga-san used to be in a romantic relationship. As complications unfurl, a previously reluctant Matsunaga-san and Ryo-kun show up to Meeko's school festival...!

SAN

Characters

Boarding House

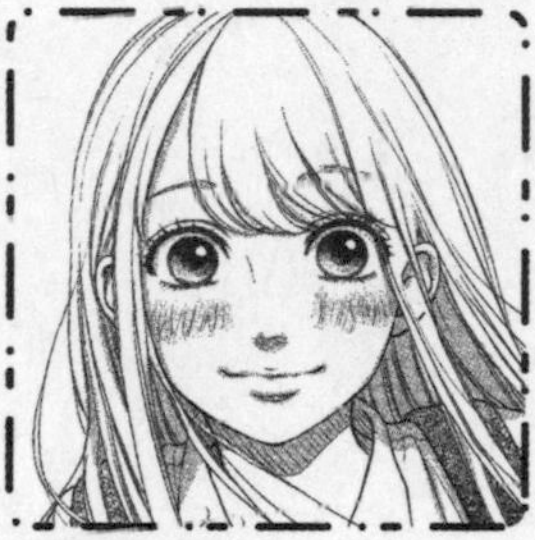

Miko Sonoda

A 17-year-old high school girl.
Only knows how to cook curry.
Pining for Matsunaga-san.

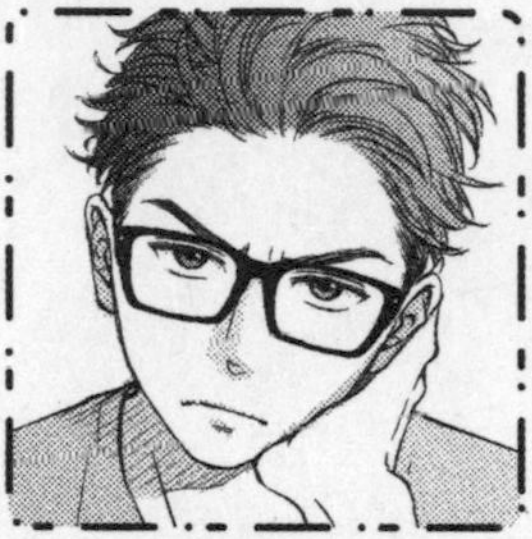

Jun Matsunaga

A designer who works from home.
28 years old.
Sharp-tongued but caring.

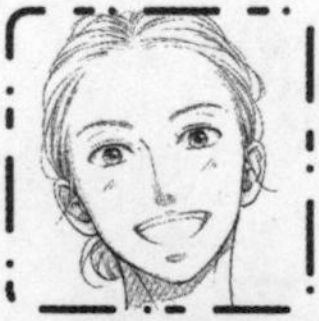

Kentaro Suzuki
A bartender.
Girl-crazy (?)

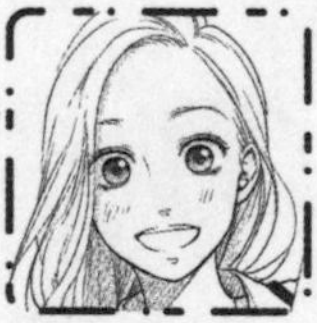

Asako Onuki
A nail artist.
Like a big sister.

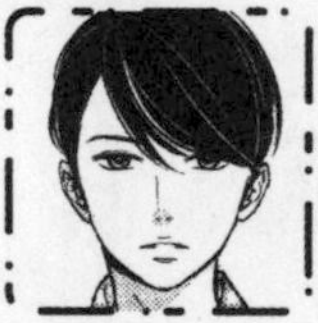

Ryo Hojo
A quiet college student.
Doesn't have a girlfriend.

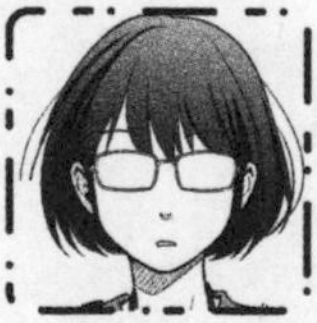

Akane Hattori
An enigma.
Actually has a boyfriend.

School

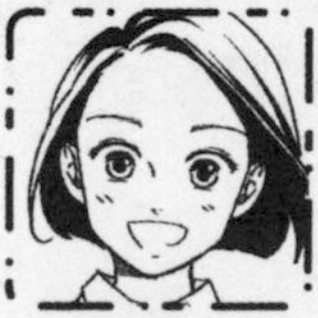

Ricchan
Meeko's friend.

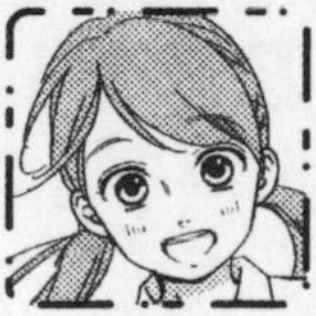

Maho
Meeko's friend.

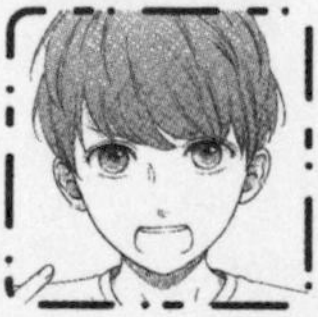

Natsumi Kobayashi
Meeko's homeroom teacher.

MATSUNAGA-

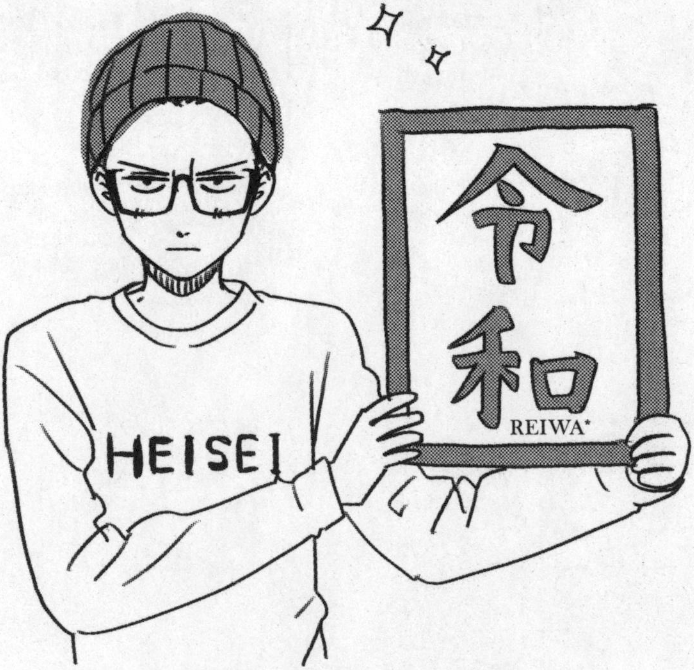
HEISEI
令和
REIWA*

*The Reiwa era of Japan began on May 1st, 2019,
marking the end of the Heisei era.

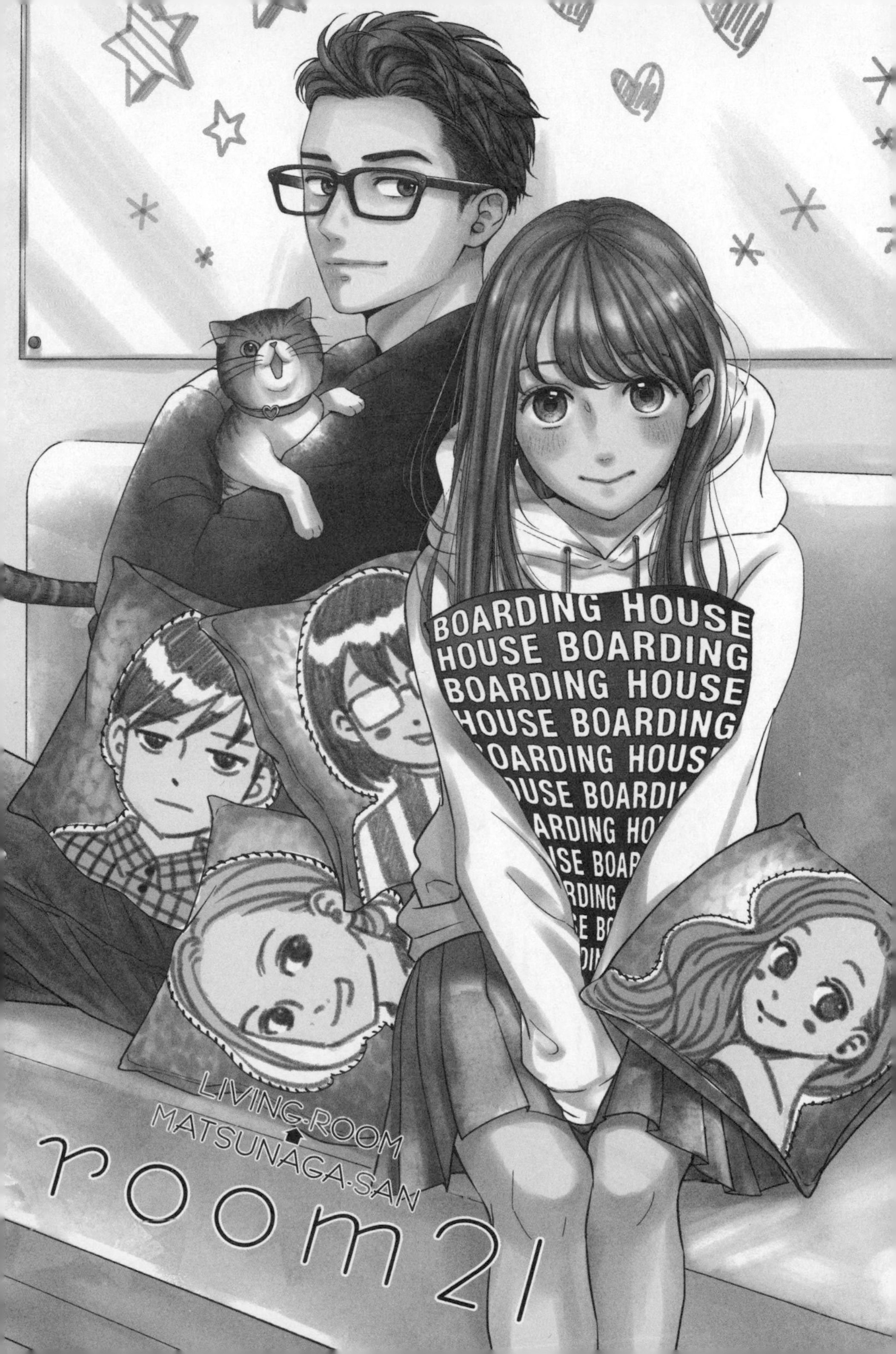
BOARDING HOUSE
HOUSE BOARDING
BOARDING HOUSE
HOUSE BOARDING
LIVING-ROOM
MATSUNAGA-SAN
room 21

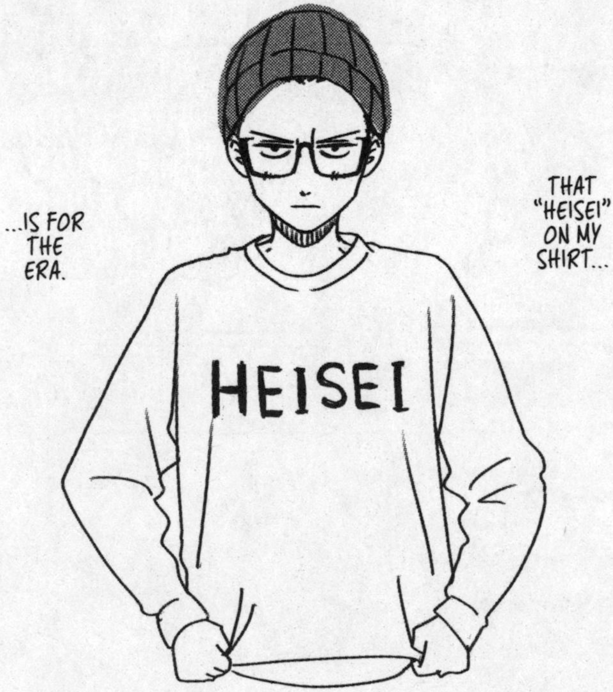
THAT "HEISEI" ON MY SHIRT...
HEISEI
...IS FOR THE ERA.

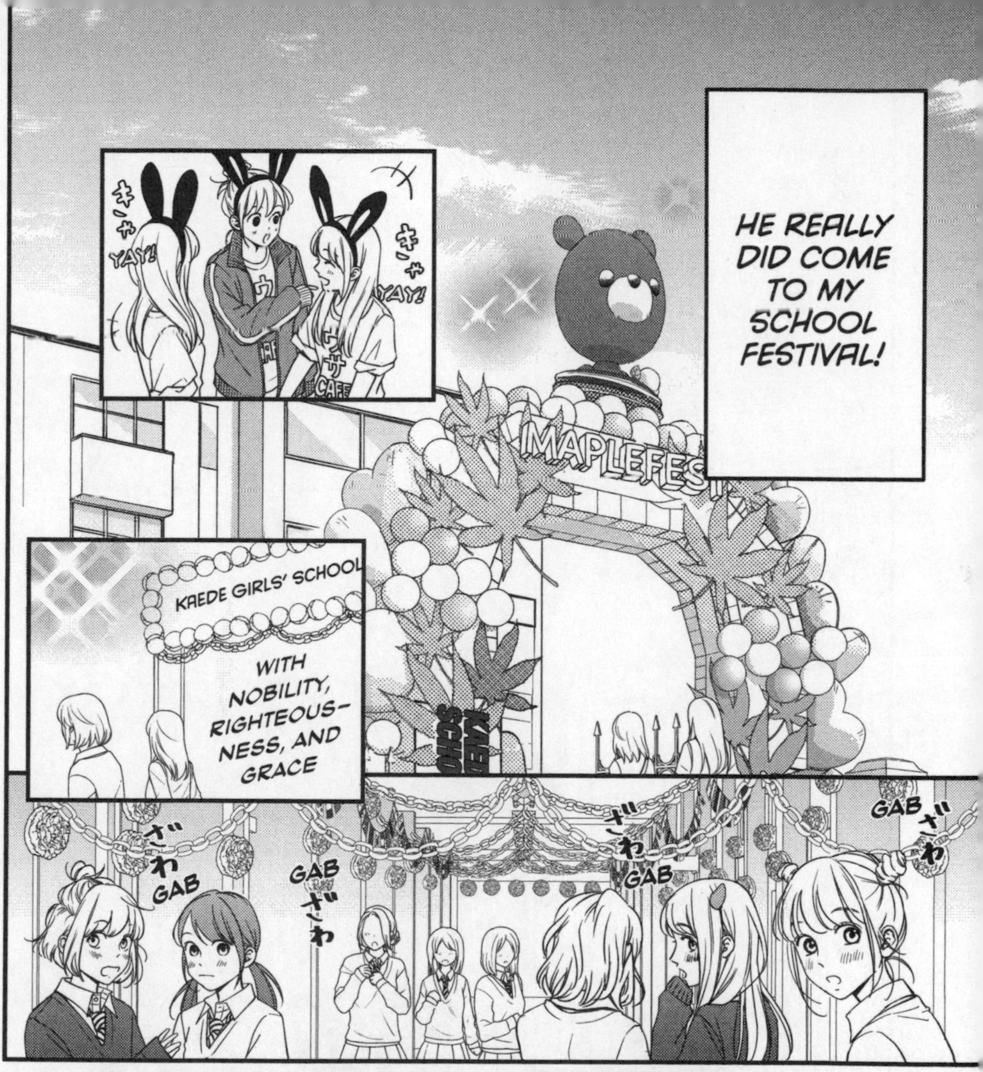
HE REALLY DID COME TO MY SCHOOL FESTIVAL!
キャ YAY!
キャ YAY!
ウサ CAFE
MAPLEFEST
KAEDE GIRLS' SCHOOL
WITH NOBILITY, RIGHTEOUSNESS, AND GRACE
GAB ざわ
ざわ GAB
GAB ざわ
ざわ GAB

KEN-CHAN'S EASY-PEASY QUIZ

Q1: WHY DIDN'T MIKO-CHAN INVITE ME TO THE SCHOOL FESTIVAL?

1: BECAUSE I'M TOO TRUSTWORTHY

2: BECAUSE I'M TOO HOT

3: BECAUSE I WOULD STEAL THE SHOW FROM JUN-KUN

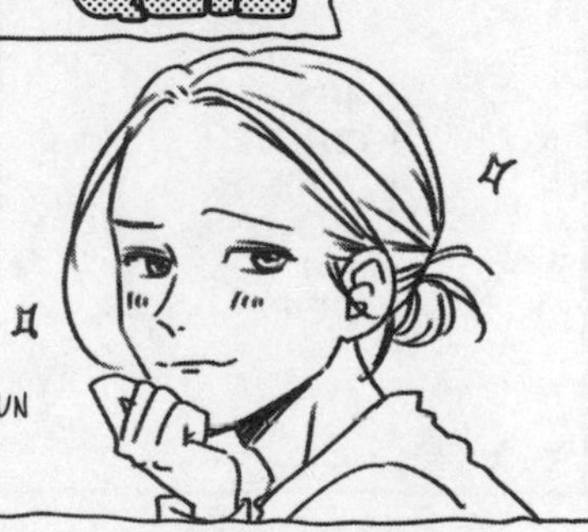

ANSWER: ALL OF THE ABOVE ♡

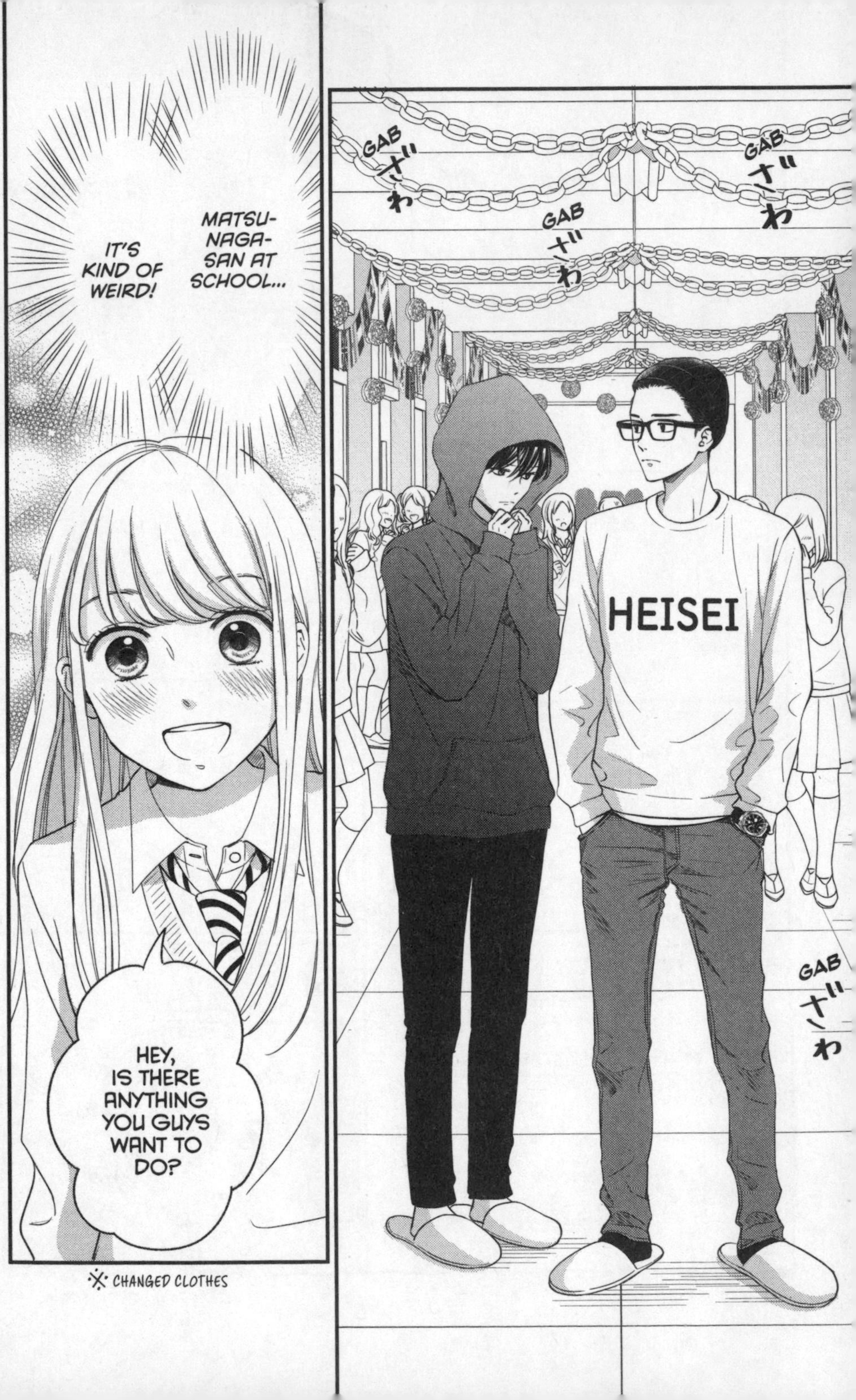
GAB ざわ
GAB ざわ
GAB ざわ
HEISEI
GAB ざわ
MATSU-NAGA-SAN AT SCHOOL...
IT'S KIND OF WEIRD!
HEY, IS THERE ANYTHING YOU GUYS WANT TO DO?

※ CHANGED CLOTHES

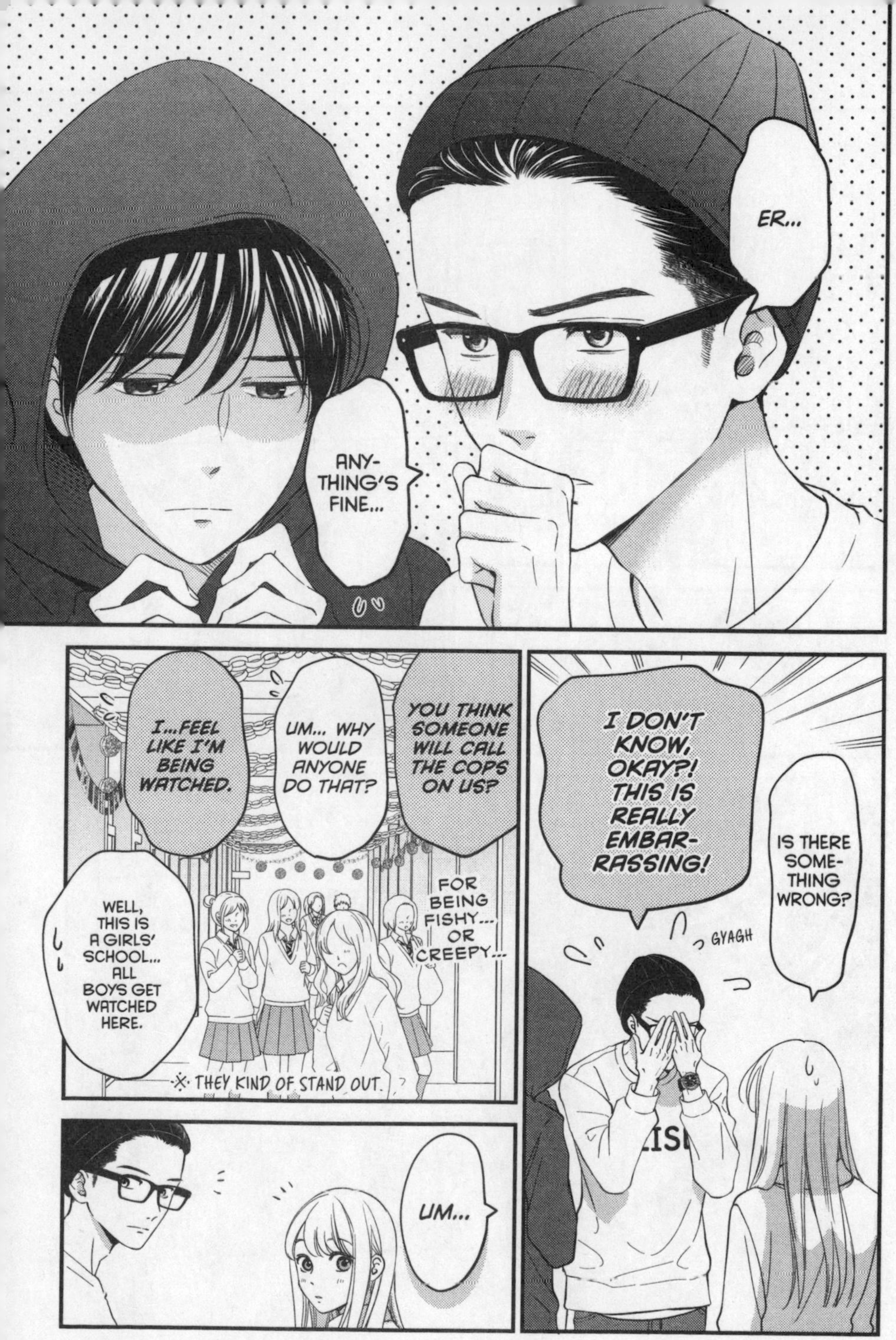

ER...
ANY-THING'S FINE...
IS THERE SOME-THING WRONG?
I DON'T KNOW, OKAY?! THIS IS REALLY EMBAR-RASSING!
GYAGH
YOU THINK SOMEONE WILL CALL THE COPS ON US?
UM... WHY WOULD ANYONE DO THAT?
I...FEEL LIKE I'M BEING WATCHED.
FOR BEING FISHY... OR CREEPY...
WELL, THIS IS A GIRLS' SCHOOL... ALL BOYS GET WATCHED HERE.
※THEY KIND OF STAND OUT.
UM...

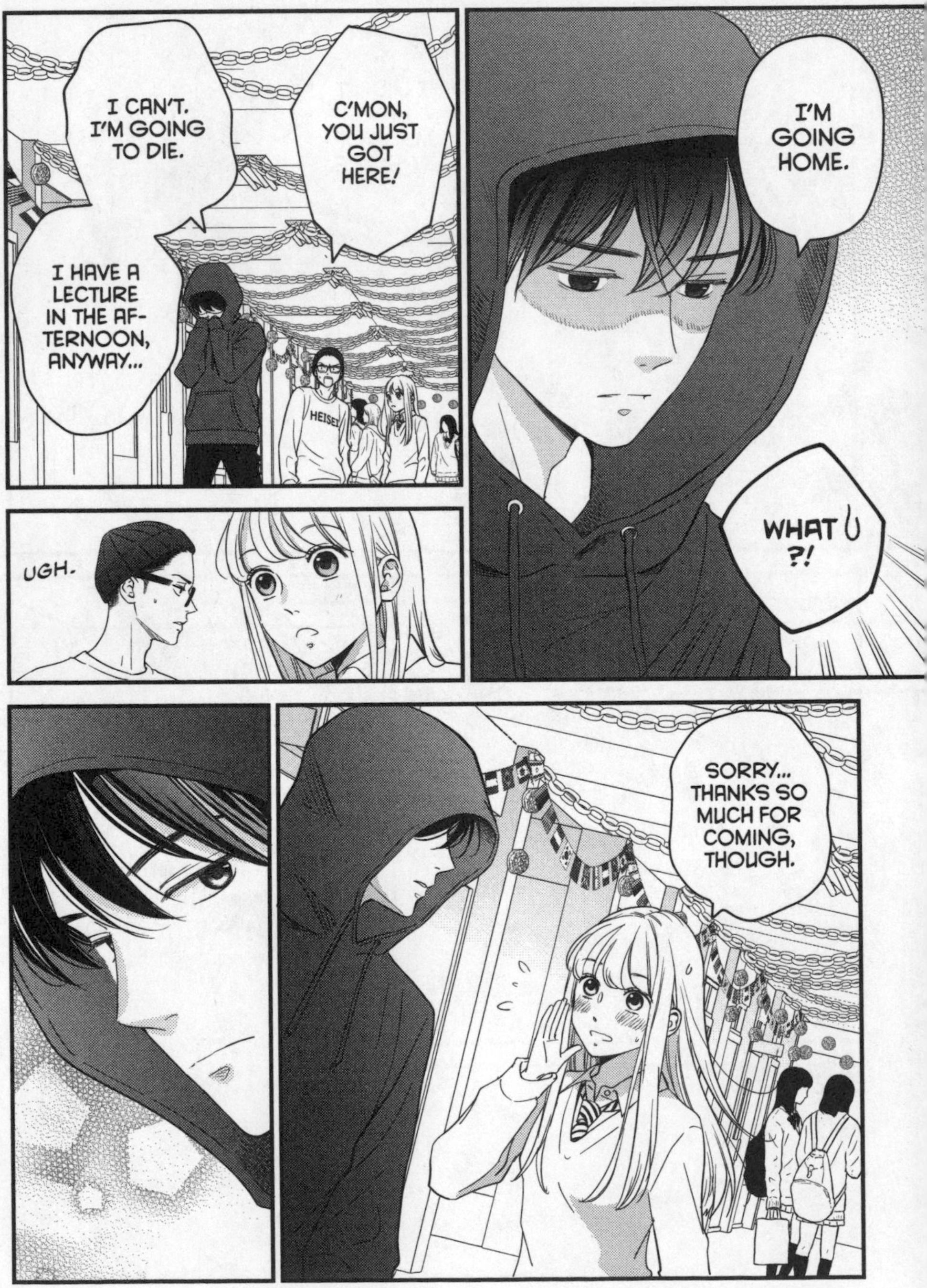
I'M GOING HOME.
WHAT?!
C'MON, YOU JUST GOT HERE!
I CAN'T. I'M GOING TO DIE.
I HAVE A LECTURE IN THE AF-TERNOON, ANYWAY...
UGH.
SORRY... THANKS SO MUCH FOR COMING, THOUGH.

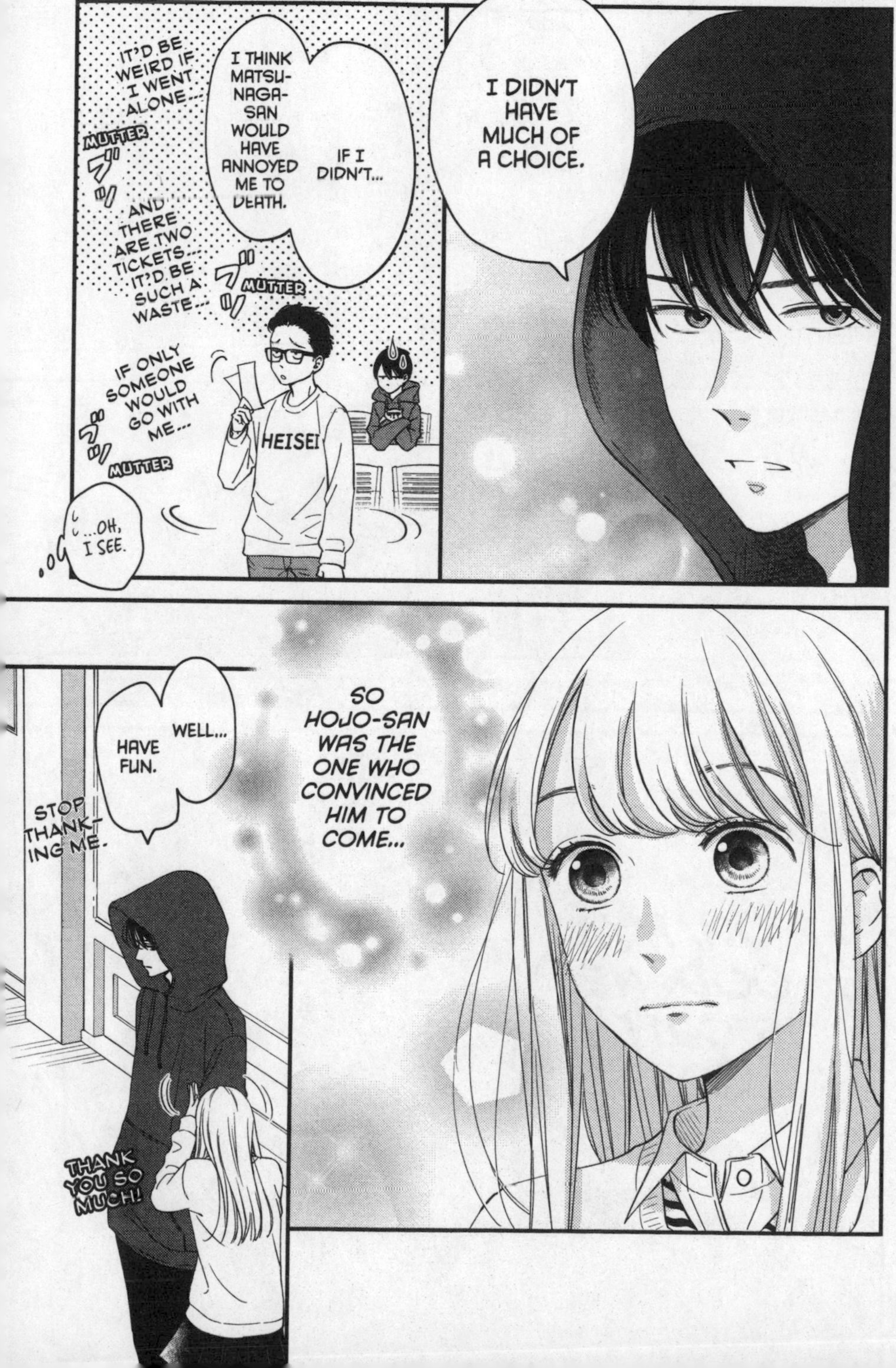
I DIDN'T HAVE MUCH OF A CHOICE.
IF I DIDN'T...
I THINK MATSU-NAGA-SAN WOULD HAVE ANNOYED ME TO DEATH.
IT'D BE WEIRD IF I WENT ALONE...
MUTTER
AND THERE ARE TWO TICKETS... IT'D BE SUCH A WASTE...
MUTTER
IF ONLY SOMEONE WOULD GO WITH ME...
MUTTER
...OH, I SEE.
SO HOJO-SAN WAS THE ONE WHO CONVINCED HIM TO COME...
WELL... HAVE FUN.
STOP THANKING ME.
THANK YOU SO MUCH!

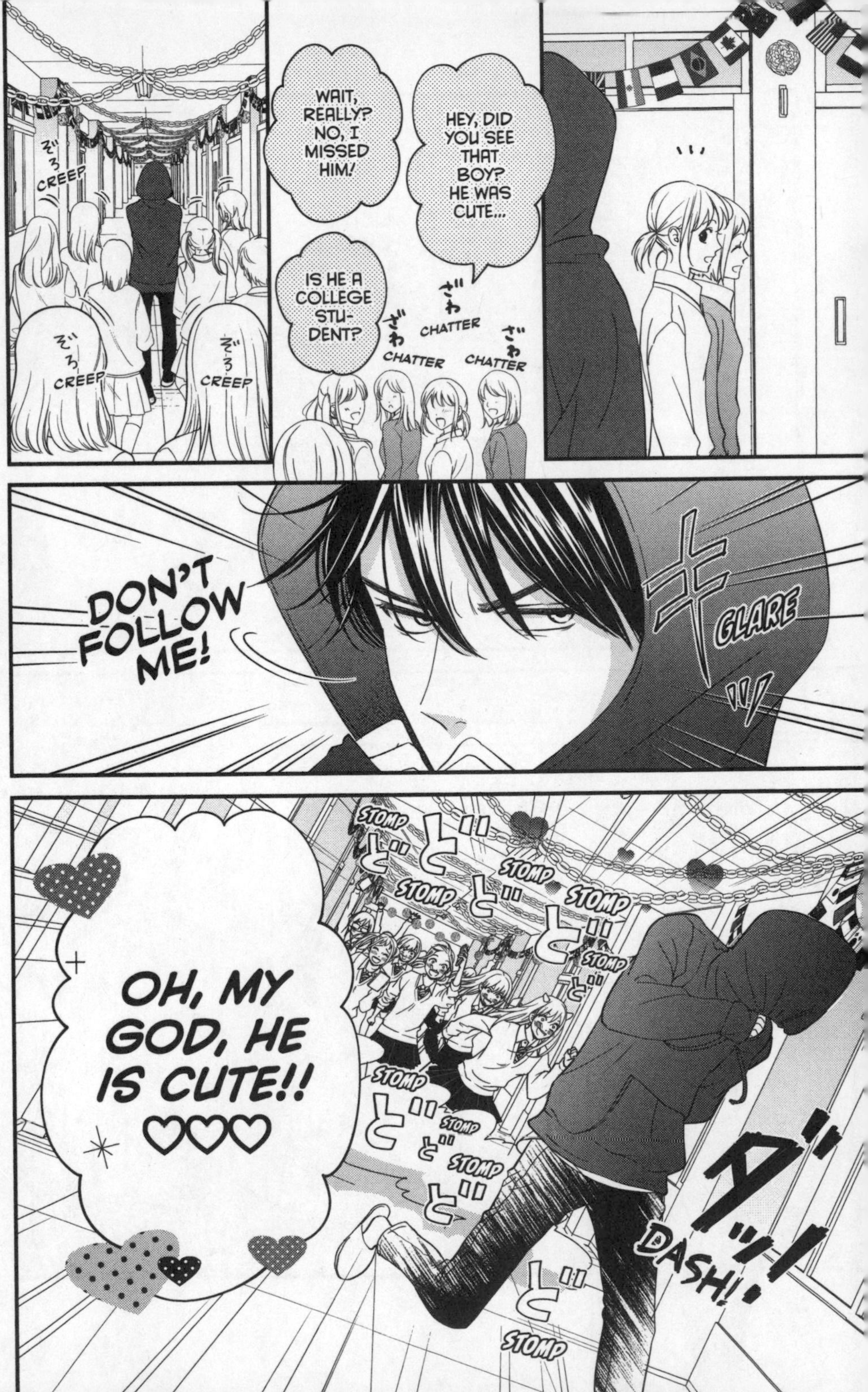
HEY, DID YOU SEE THAT BOY? HE WAS CUTE...
WAIT, REALLY? NO, I MISSED HIM!
ざわ CHATTER
ざわ CHATTER
IS HE A COLLEGE STU-DENT?
ざわ CHATTER
ぞろ CREEP
ぞろ CREEP
ぞろ CREEP
キ GLARE
DON'T FOLLOW ME!
ダッ! DASH!
ど STOMP
ど STOMP
ど STOMP
ど STOMP
ど STOMP
ど STOMP
ど STOMP
ど STOMP
ど STOMP
ど STOMP
OH, MY GOD, HE IS CUTE!! ♡♡♡

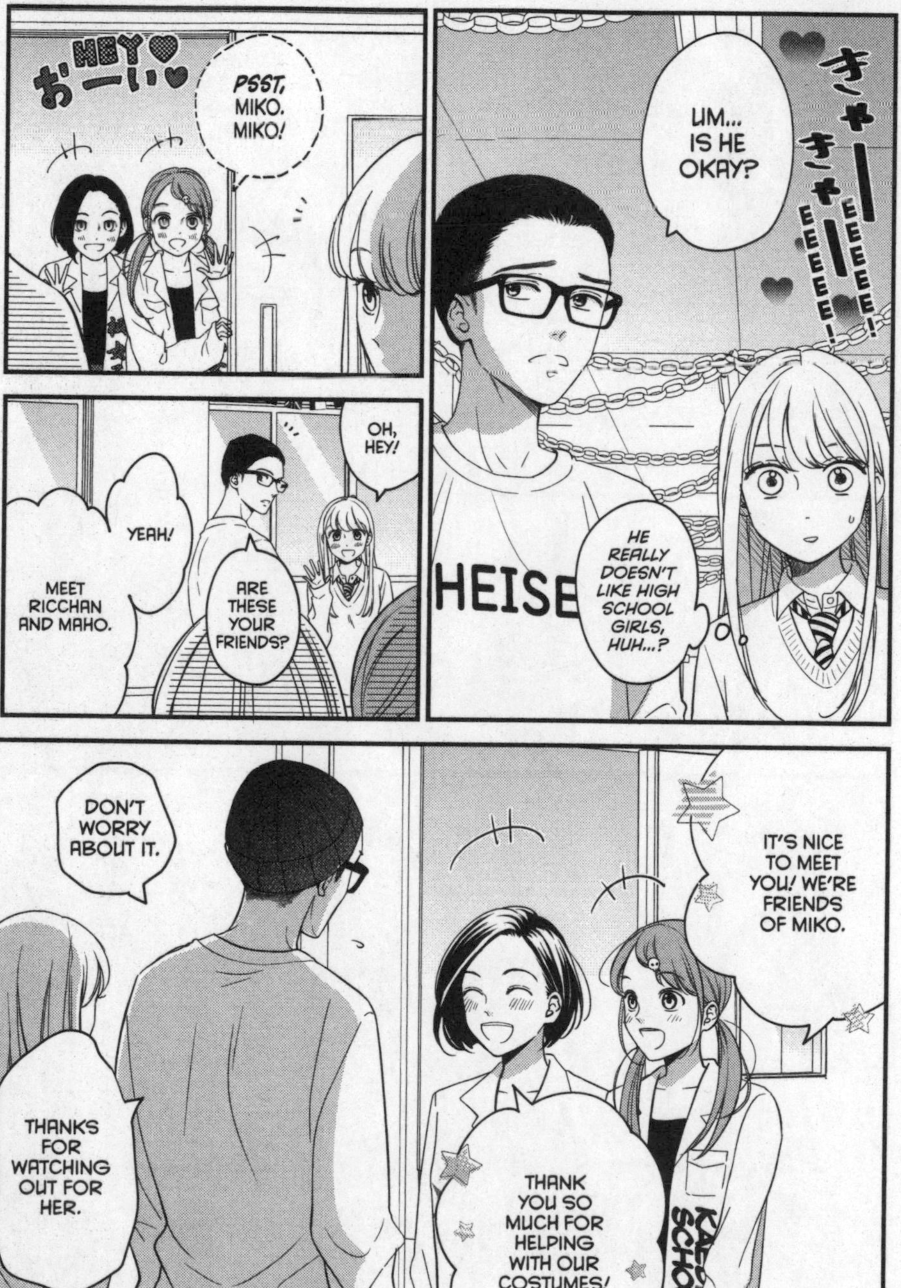
UM... IS HE OKAY?
きゃーきゃー
EEEEE! EEEEE!
HEISE
HE REALLY DOESN'T LIKE HIGH SCHOOL GIRLS, HUH...?
HEY♥ おーい♥
PSST, MIKO. MIKO!
OH, HEY!
ARE THESE YOUR FRIENDS?
YEAH!
MEET RICCHAN AND MAHO.
IT'S NICE TO MEET YOU! WE'RE FRIENDS OF MIKO.
THANK YOU SO MUCH FOR HELPING WITH OUR COSTUMES!
DON'T WORRY ABOUT IT.
THANKS FOR WATCHING OUT FOR HER.

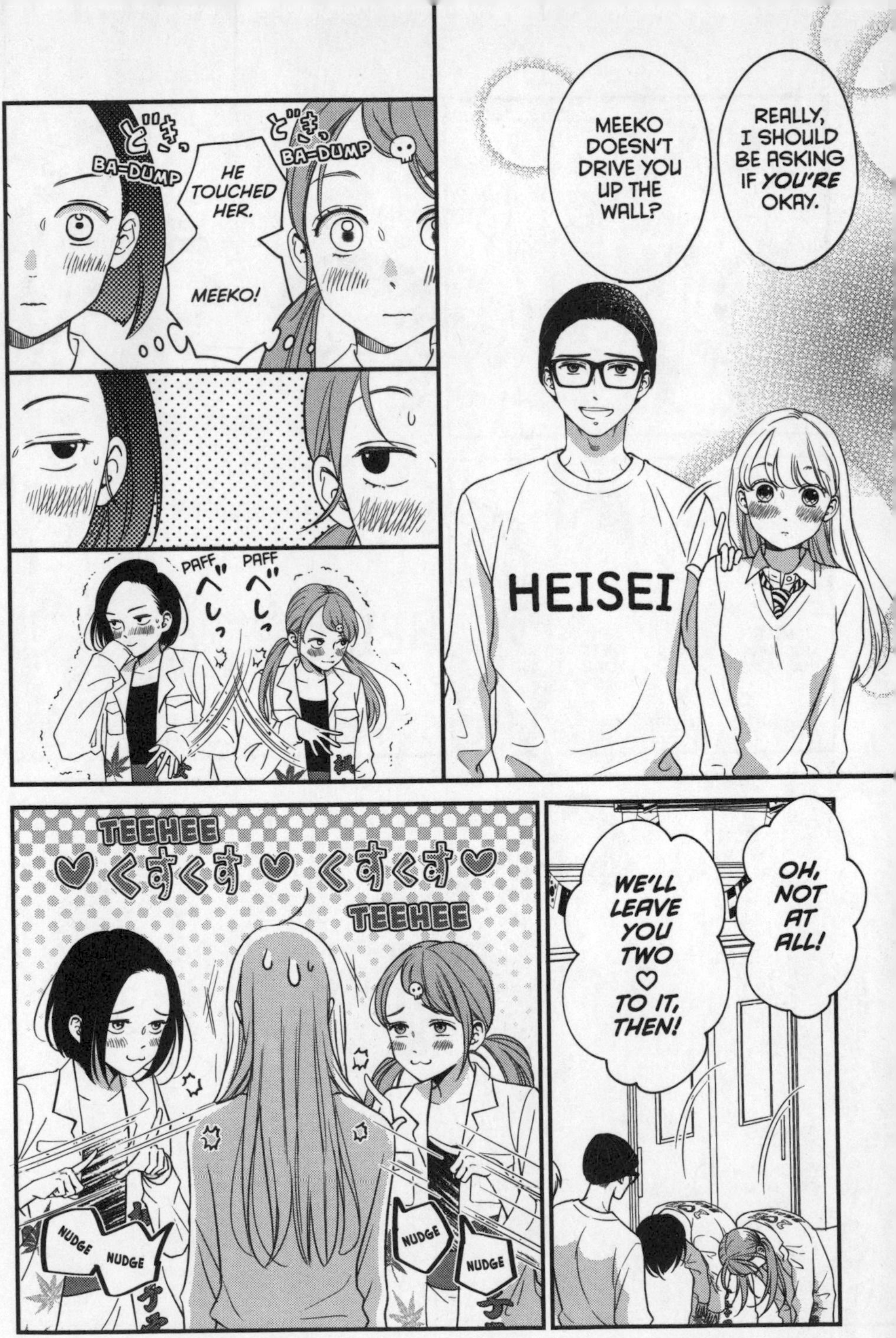
REALLY, I SHOULD BE ASKING IF *YOU'RE* OKAY.
MEEKO DOESN'T DRIVE YOU UP THE WALL?
HEISEI
どき、
BA-DUMP
どき、
BA-DUMP
HE TOUCHED HER.
MEEKO!
べしっ
PAFF
べしっ
PAFF
OH, NOT AT ALL!
WE'LL LEAVE YOU TWO ♡ TO IT, THEN!
♡くすくす♡くすくす♡
TEEHEE
TEEHEE
NUDGE
NUDGE
NUDGE
NUDGE

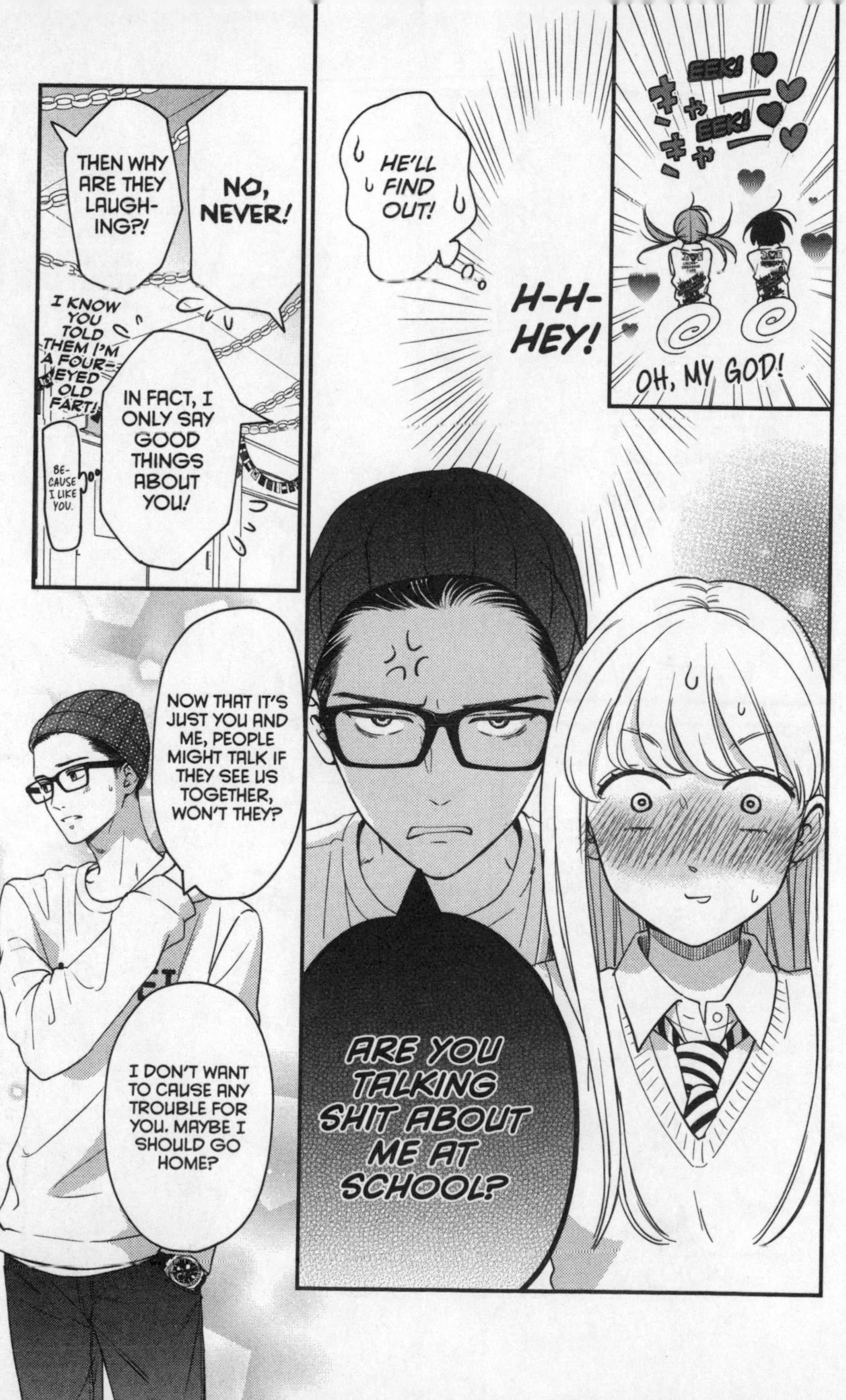

キャー EEK!
キャー EEK!
OH, MY GOD!
H-H-HEY!
HE'LL FIND OUT!
ARE YOU TALKING SHIT ABOUT ME AT SCHOOL?
NO, NEVER!
THEN WHY ARE THEY LAUGHING?!
IN FACT, I ONLY SAY GOOD THINGS ABOUT YOU!
I KNOW YOU TOLD THEM I'M A FOUR-EYED OLD FART!
BE-CAUSE I LIKE YOU.
NOW THAT IT'S JUST YOU AND ME, PEOPLE MIGHT TALK IF THEY SEE US TOGETHER, WON'T THEY?
I DON'T WANT TO CAUSE ANY TROUBLE FOR YOU. MAYBE I SHOULD GO HOME?

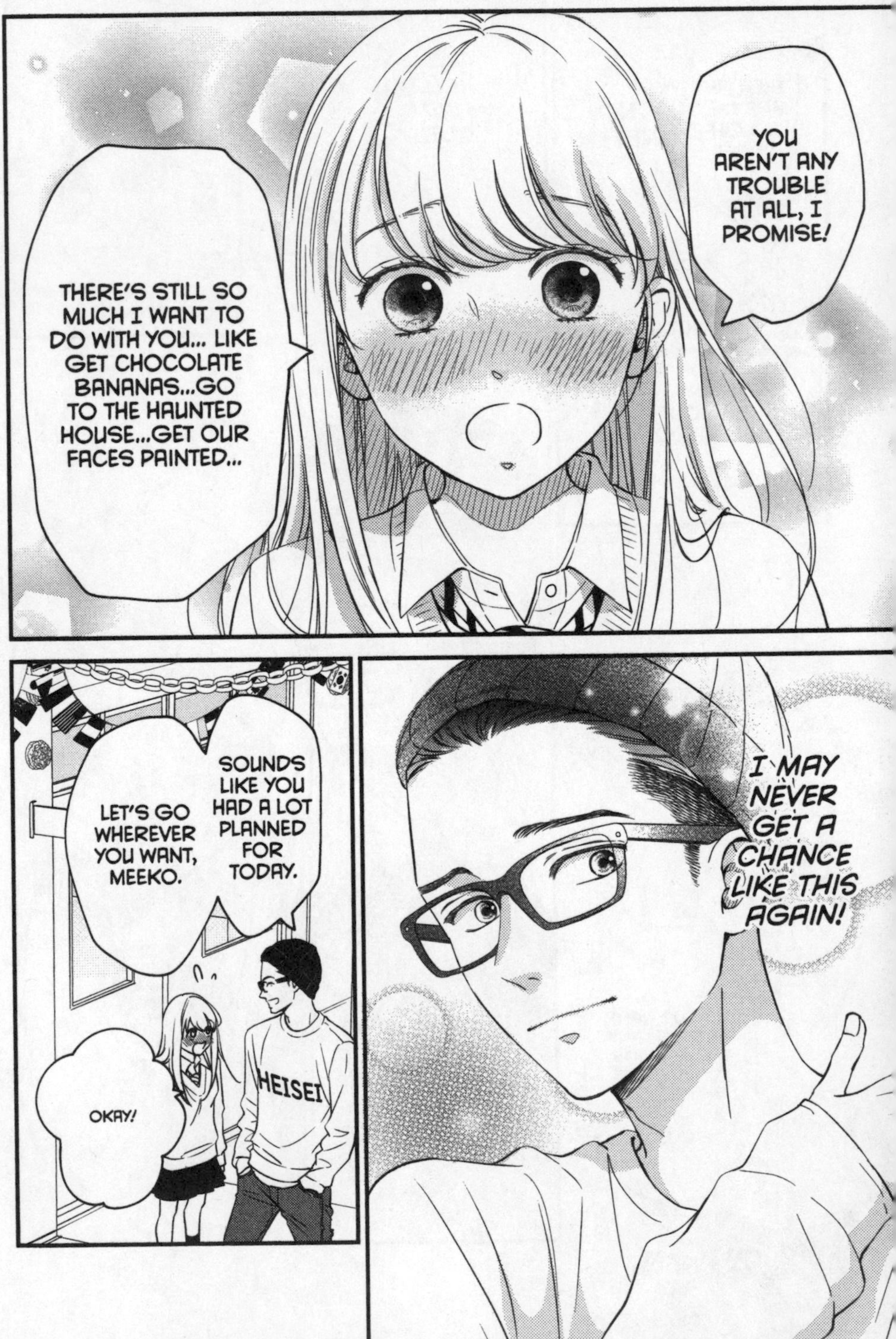
YOU AREN'T ANY TROUBLE AT ALL, I PROMISE!
THERE'S STILL SO MUCH I WANT TO DO WITH YOU... LIKE GET CHOCOLATE BANANAS...GO TO THE HAUNTED HOUSE...GET OUR FACES PAINTED...
I MAY NEVER GET A CHANCE LIKE THIS AGAIN!
SOUNDS LIKE YOU HAD A LOT PLANNED FOR TODAY.
LET'S GO WHEREVER YOU WANT, MEEKO.
HEISEI
OKAY!

*Haunted House

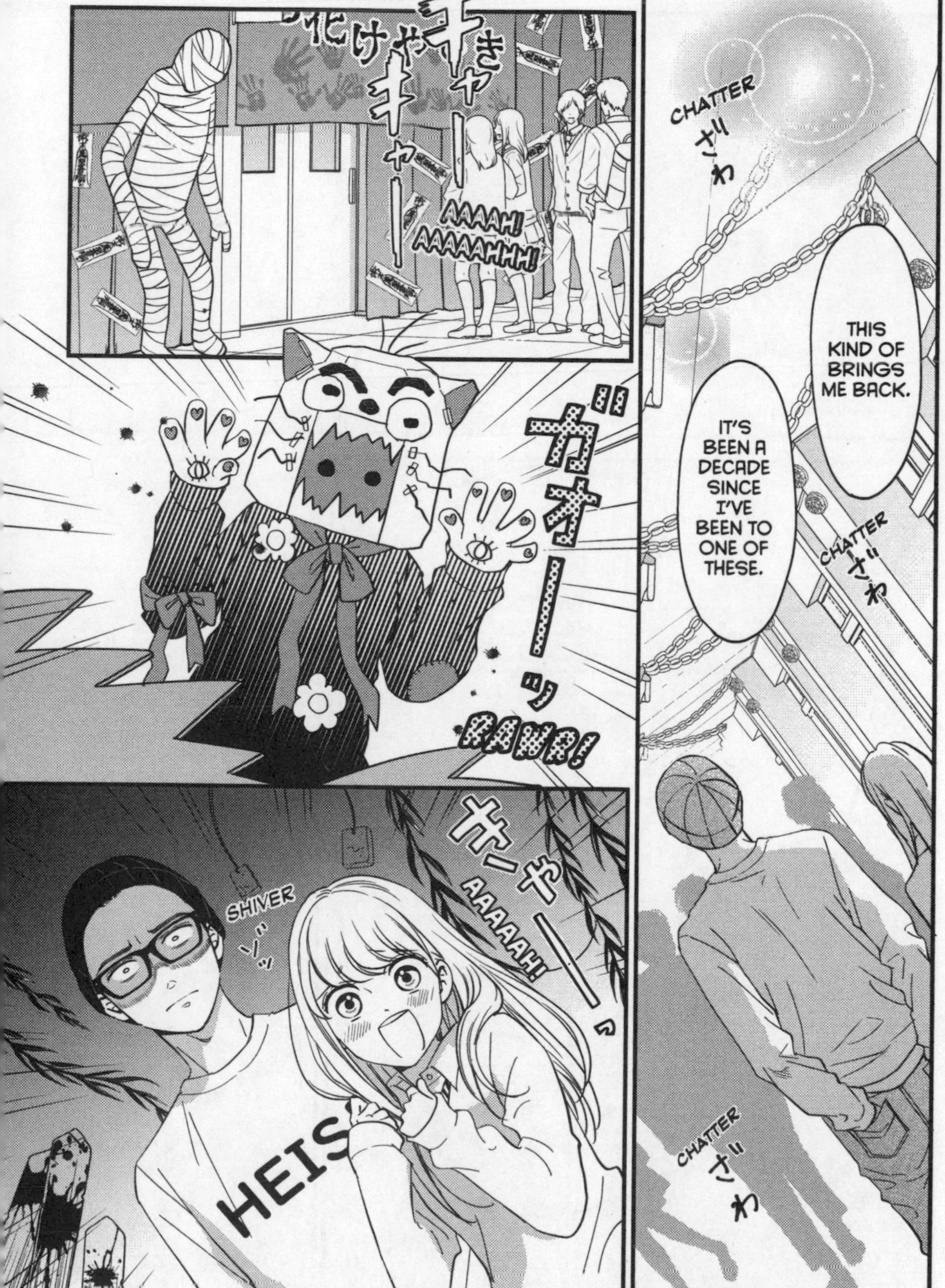
CHATTER
ざわ
THIS KIND OF BRINGS ME BACK.
IT'S BEEN A DECADE SINCE I'VE BEEN TO ONE OF THESE.
CHATTER
ざわ
CHATTER
ざわ
キャーキャーー
AAAAH! AAAAAHHH!
ガオーーッ
RAWR!
キャーー♪
AAAAAH!
SHIVER
HEIS

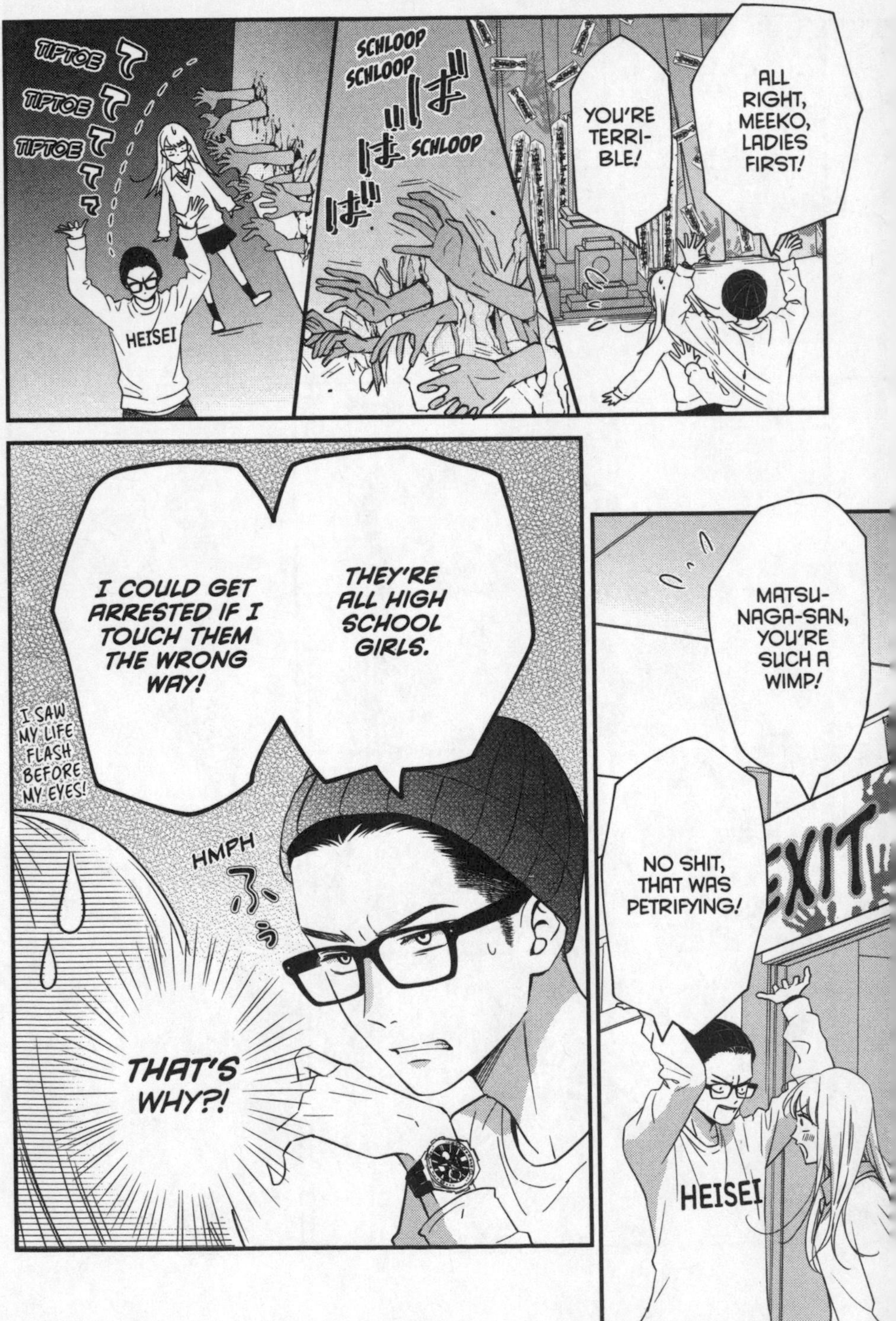

ALL RIGHT, MEEKO, LADIES FIRST!
YOU'RE TERRIBLE!
SCHLOOP
SCHLOOP
ば
ば
SCHLOOP
ば
TIPTOE
TIPTOE
TIPTOE
MATSU-NAGA-SAN, YOU'RE SUCH A WIMP!
NO SHIT, THAT WAS PETRIFYING!
EXIT
THEY'RE ALL HIGH SCHOOL GIRLS.
I COULD GET ARRESTED IF I TOUCH THEM THE WRONG WAY!
HMPH
ふぅ
THAT'S WHY?!
I SAW MY LIFE FLASH BEFORE MY EYES!

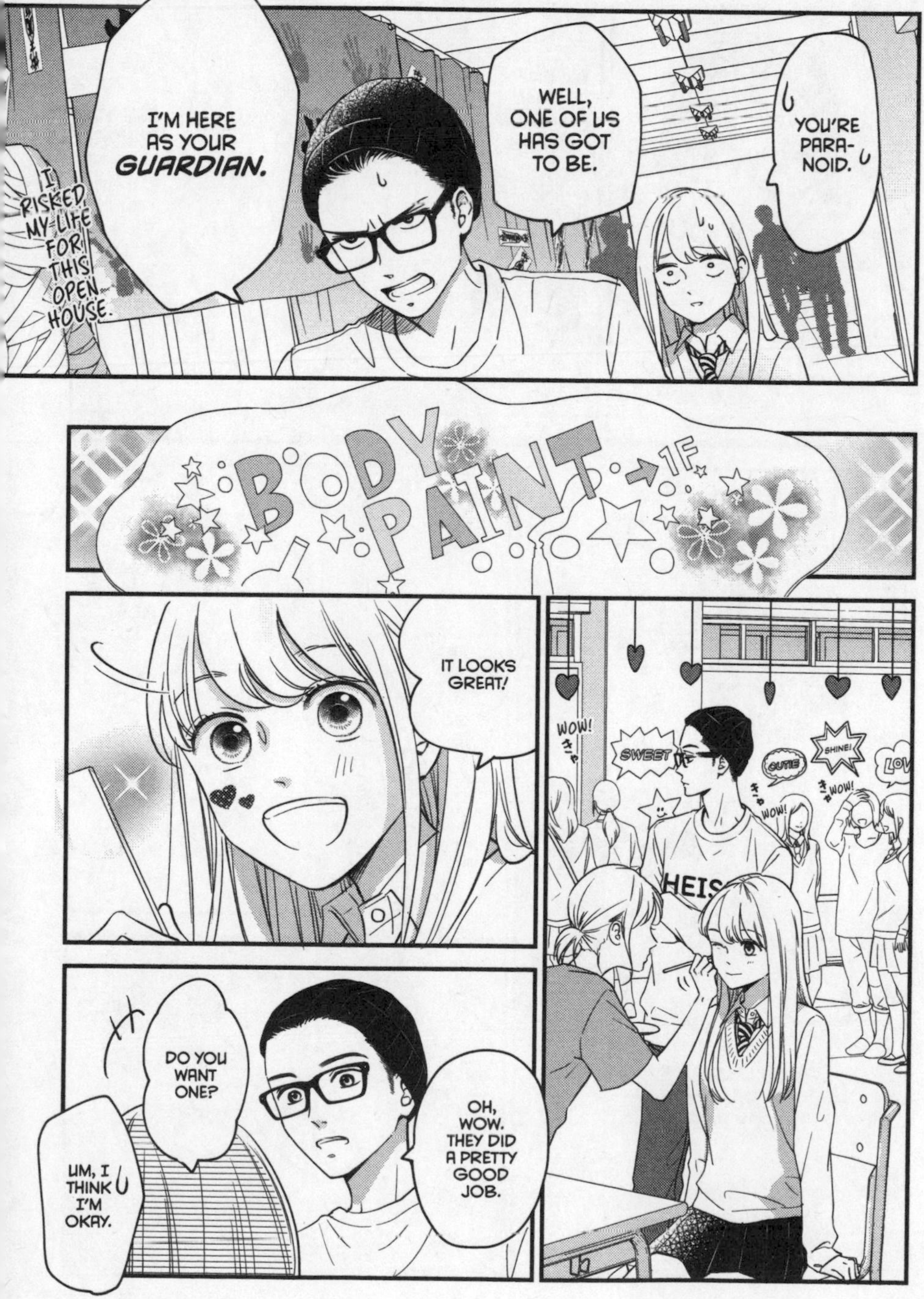
YOU'RE PARA-NOID.
WELL, ONE OF US HAS GOT TO BE.
I'M HERE AS YOUR *GUARDIAN.*
I RISKED MY LIFE FOR THIS OPEN HOUSE.
BODY PAINT → 1F
LOV
SHINE!
WOW!
CUTIE
WOW!
SWEET
WOW!
HEIS
IT LOOKS GREAT!
OH, WOW. THEY DID A PRETTY GOOD JOB.
DO YOU WANT ONE?
UM, I THINK I'M OKAY.

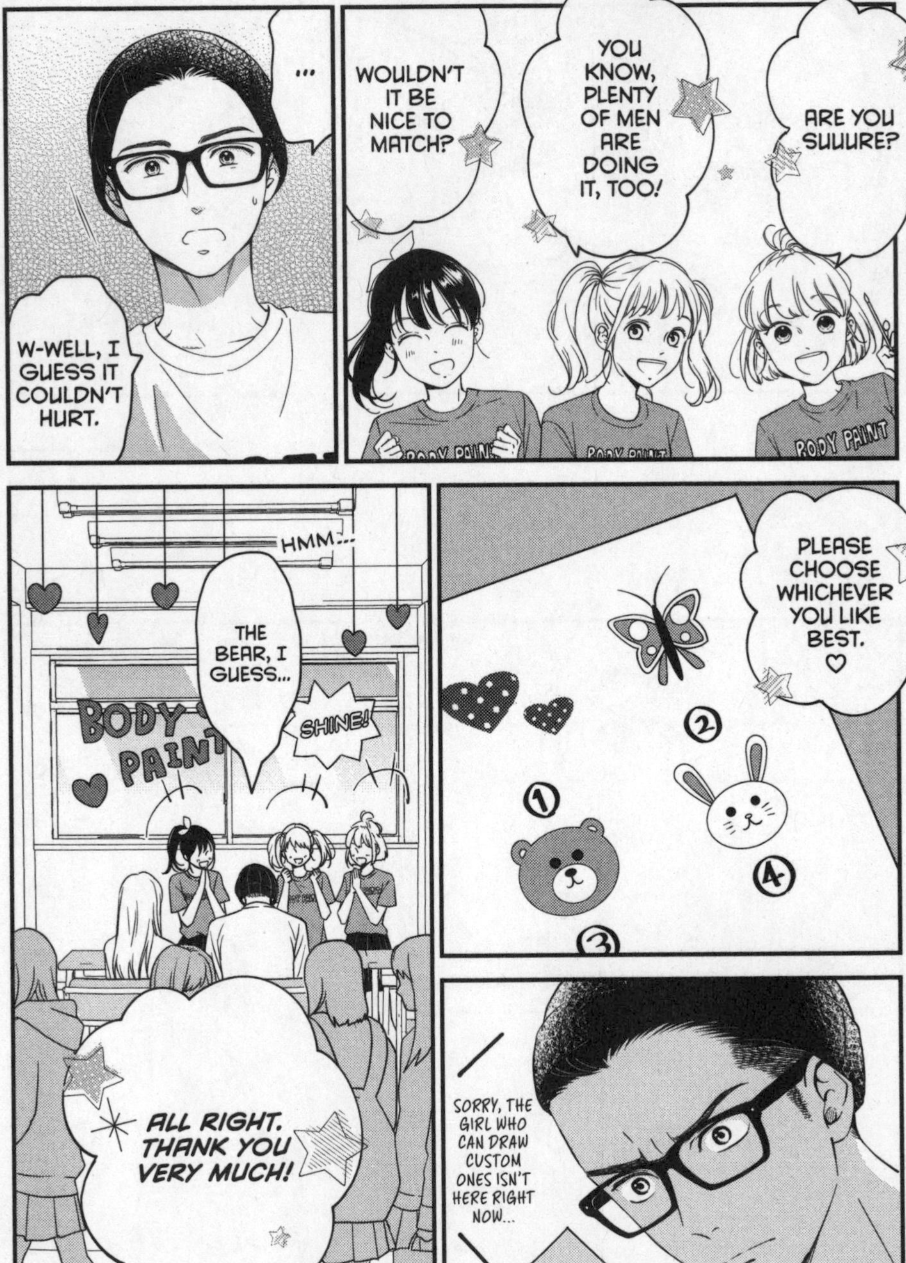

ARE YOU SUUURE?
YOU KNOW, PLENTY OF MEN ARE DOING IT, TOO!
WOULDN'T IT BE NICE TO MATCH?
BODY PAINT
...
W-WELL, I GUESS IT COULDN'T HURT.
PLEASE CHOOSE WHICHEVER YOU LIKE BEST. ♡
① ② ③ ④
SORRY, THE GIRL WHO CAN DRAW CUSTOM ONES ISN'T HERE RIGHT NOW...
HMM...
THE BEAR, I GUESS...
SHINE!
BODY PAINT
ALL RIGHT. THANK YOU VERY MUCH!

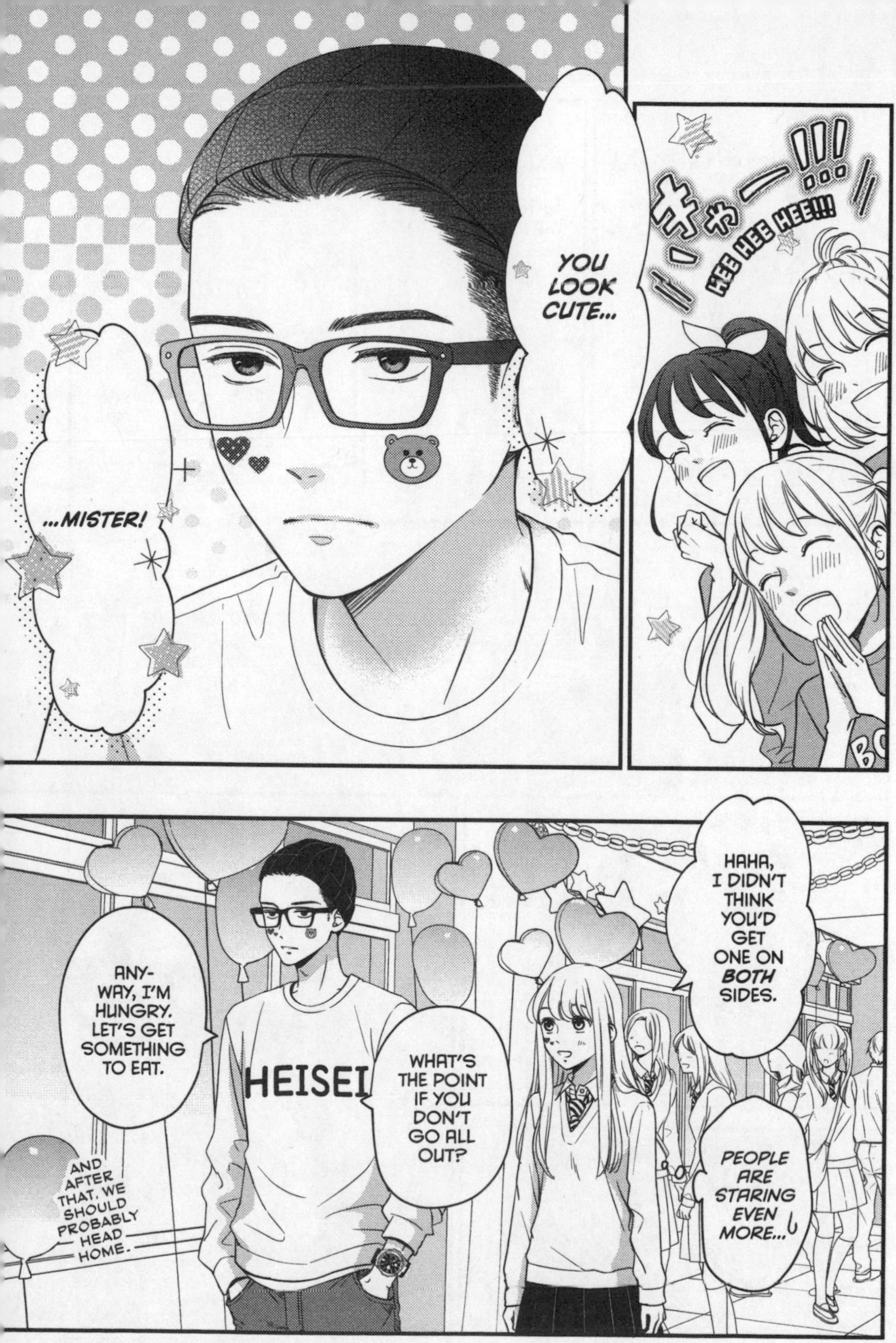

キャー!!!
HEE HEE HEE!!!
YOU LOOK CUTE...
...MISTER!
HAHA, I DIDN'T THINK YOU'D GET ONE ON *BOTH* SIDES.
PEOPLE ARE STARING EVEN MORE...
WHAT'S THE POINT IF YOU DON'T GO ALL OUT?
ANY-WAY, I'M HUNGRY. LET'S GET SOMETHING TO EAT.
AND AFTER THAT, WE SHOULD PROBABLY HEAD HOME.
HEISEI

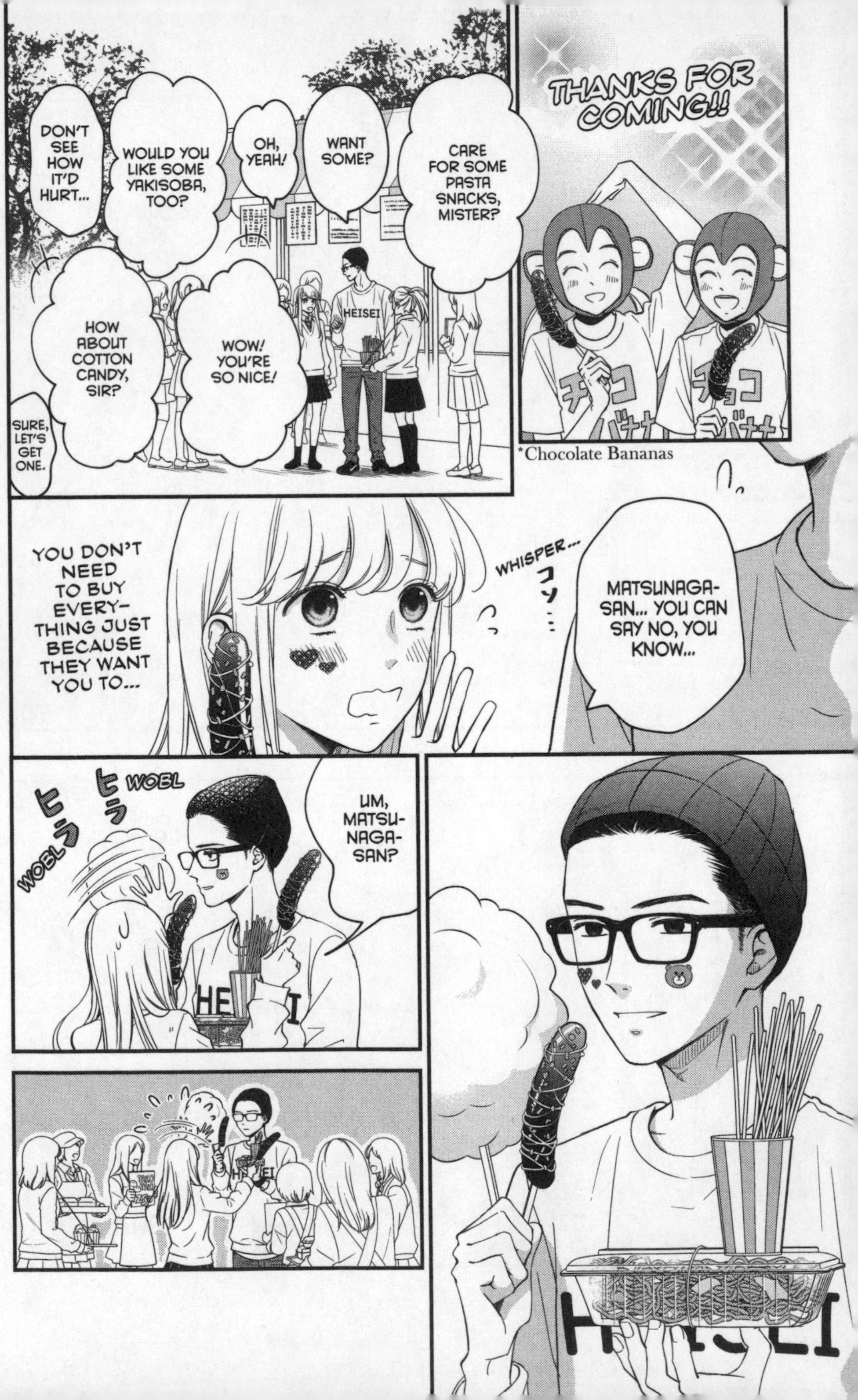
THANKS FOR COMING!!
CARE FOR SOME PASTA SNACKS, MISTER?
WANT SOME?
OH, YEAH!
WOULD YOU LIKE SOME YAKISOBA, TOO?
DON'T SEE HOW IT'D HURT...
HEISEI
WOW! YOU'RE SO NICE!
HOW ABOUT COTTON CANDY, SIR?
SURE, LET'S GET ONE.
MATSUNAGA-SAN... YOU CAN SAY NO, YOU KNOW...
WHISPER...
YOU DON'T NEED TO BUY EVERYTHING JUST BECAUSE THEY WANT YOU TO...
UM, MATSUNAGA-SAN?
WOBL
WOBL
*Chocolate Bananas

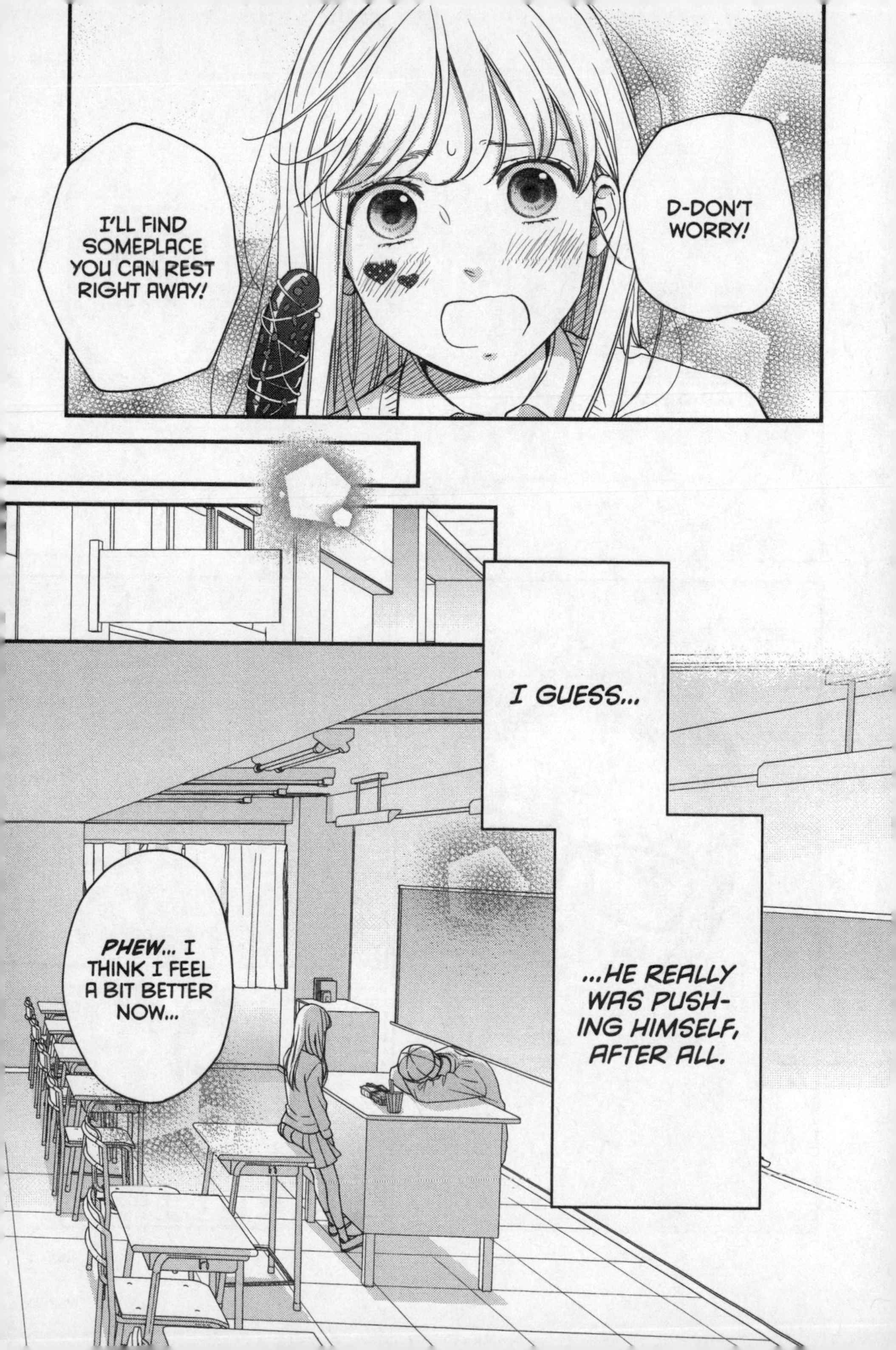
D-DON'T WORRY!
I'LL FIND SOMEPLACE YOU CAN REST RIGHT AWAY!
I GUESS...
...HE REALLY WAS PUSH-ING HIMSELF, AFTER ALL.
PHEW... I THINK I FEEL A BIT BETTER NOW...

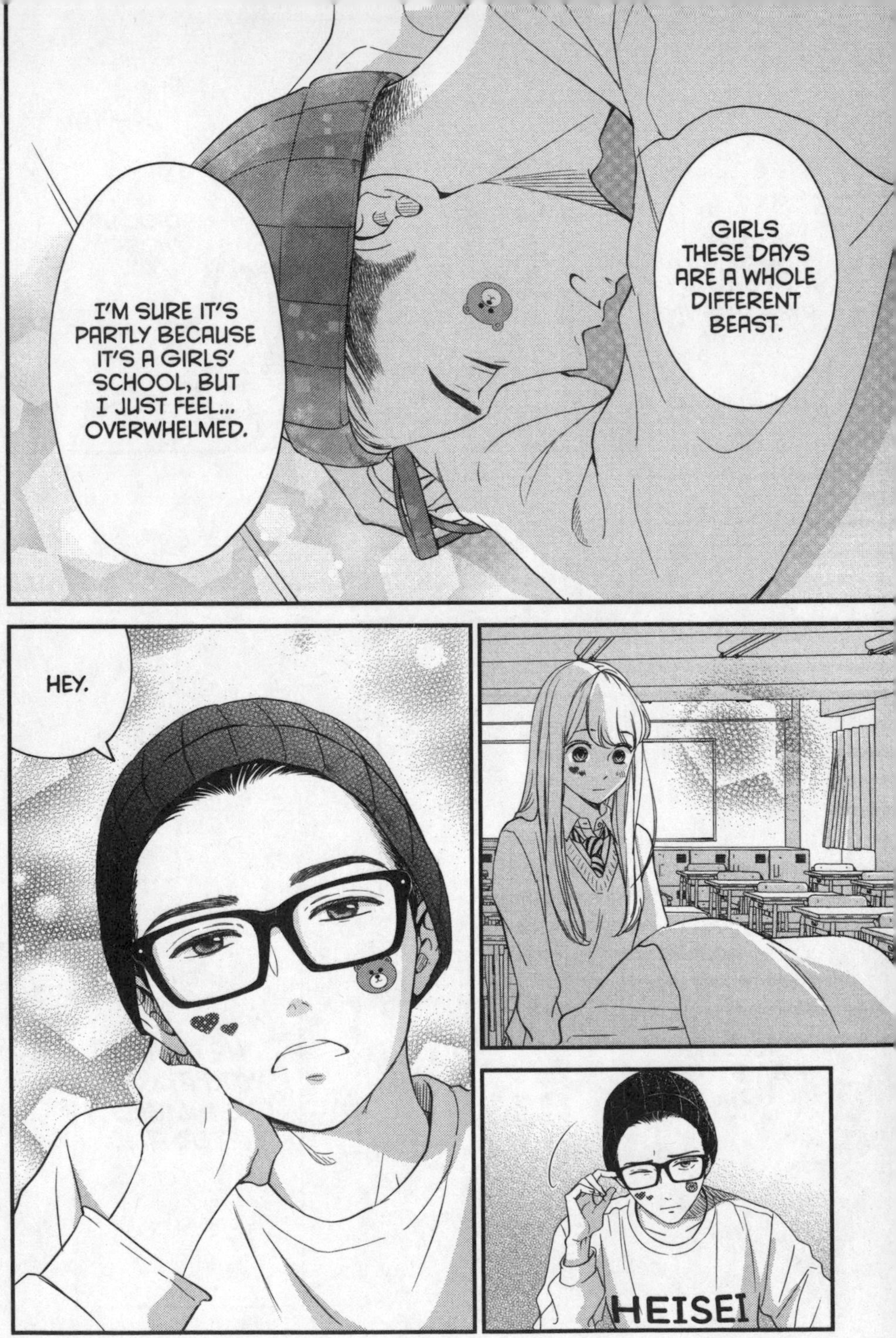
GIRLS THESE DAYS ARE A WHOLE DIFFERENT BEAST.
I'M SURE IT'S PARTLY BECAUSE IT'S A GIRLS' SCHOOL, BUT I JUST FEEL... OVERWHELMED.
HEISEI
HEY.

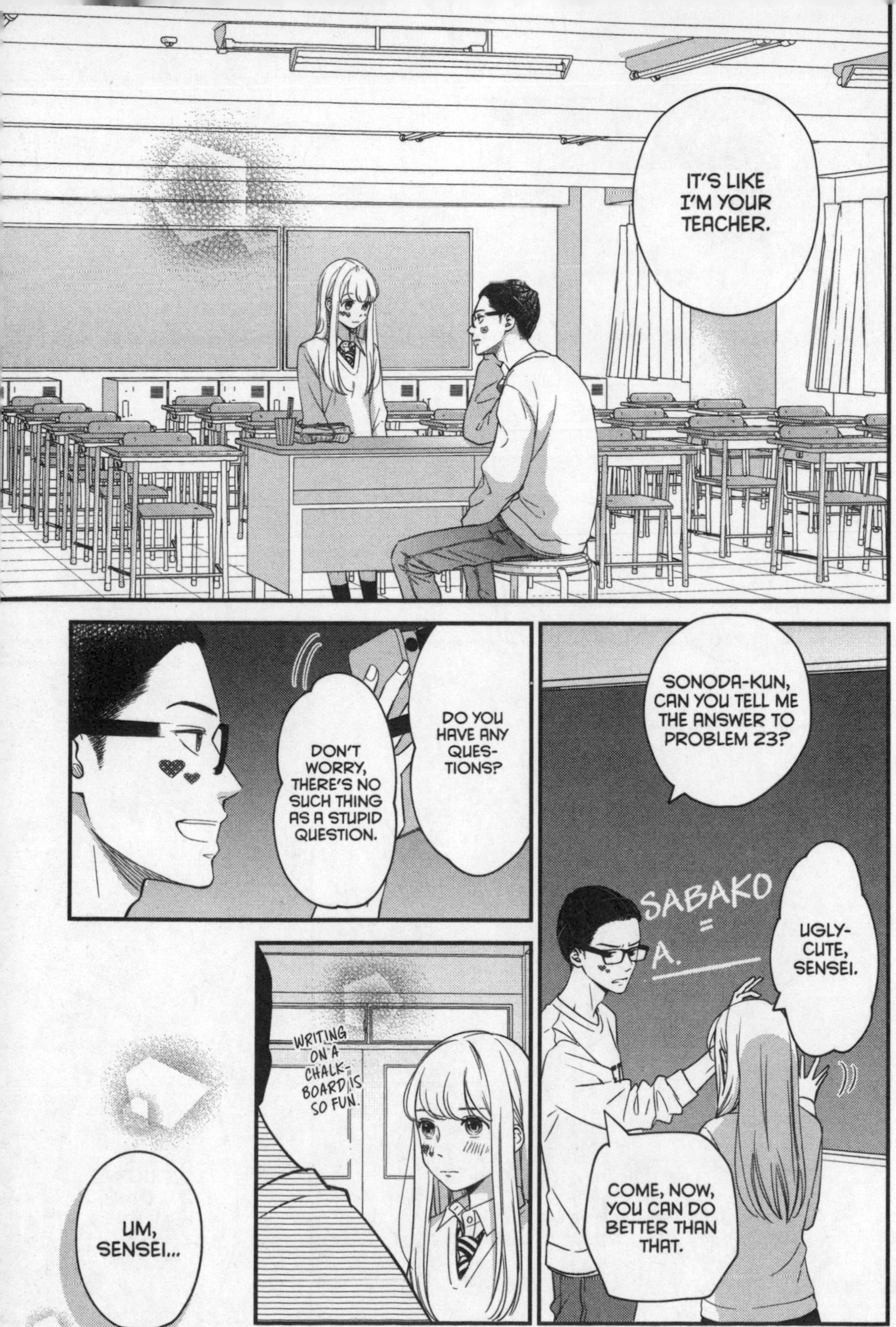
IT'S LIKE I'M YOUR TEACHER.
SONODA-KUN, CAN YOU TELL ME THE ANSWER TO PROBLEM 23?
SABAKO = A.
UGLY-CUTE, SENSEI.
COME, NOW, YOU CAN DO BETTER THAN THAT.
DO YOU HAVE ANY QUES-TIONS?
DON'T WORRY, THERE'S NO SUCH THING AS A STUPID QUESTION.
WRITING ON A CHALK-BOARD IS SO FUN.
UM, SENSEI...

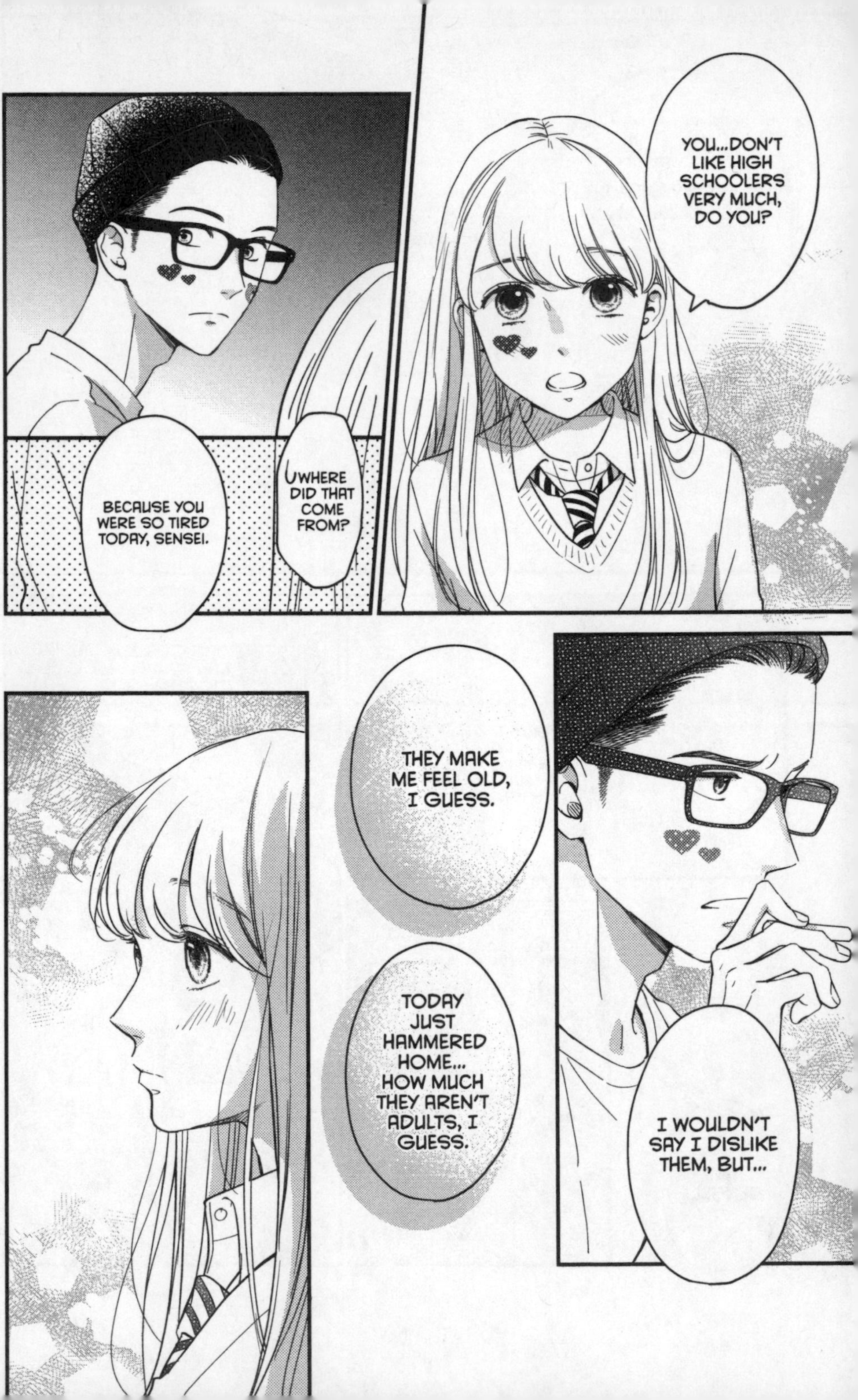
YOU...DON'T LIKE HIGH SCHOOLERS VERY MUCH, DO YOU?
WHERE DID THAT COME FROM?
BECAUSE YOU WERE SO TIRED TODAY, SENSEI.
I WOULDN'T SAY I DISLIKE THEM, BUT...
THEY MAKE ME FEEL OLD, I GUESS.
TODAY JUST HAMMERED HOME... HOW MUCH THEY AREN'T ADULTS, I GUESS.

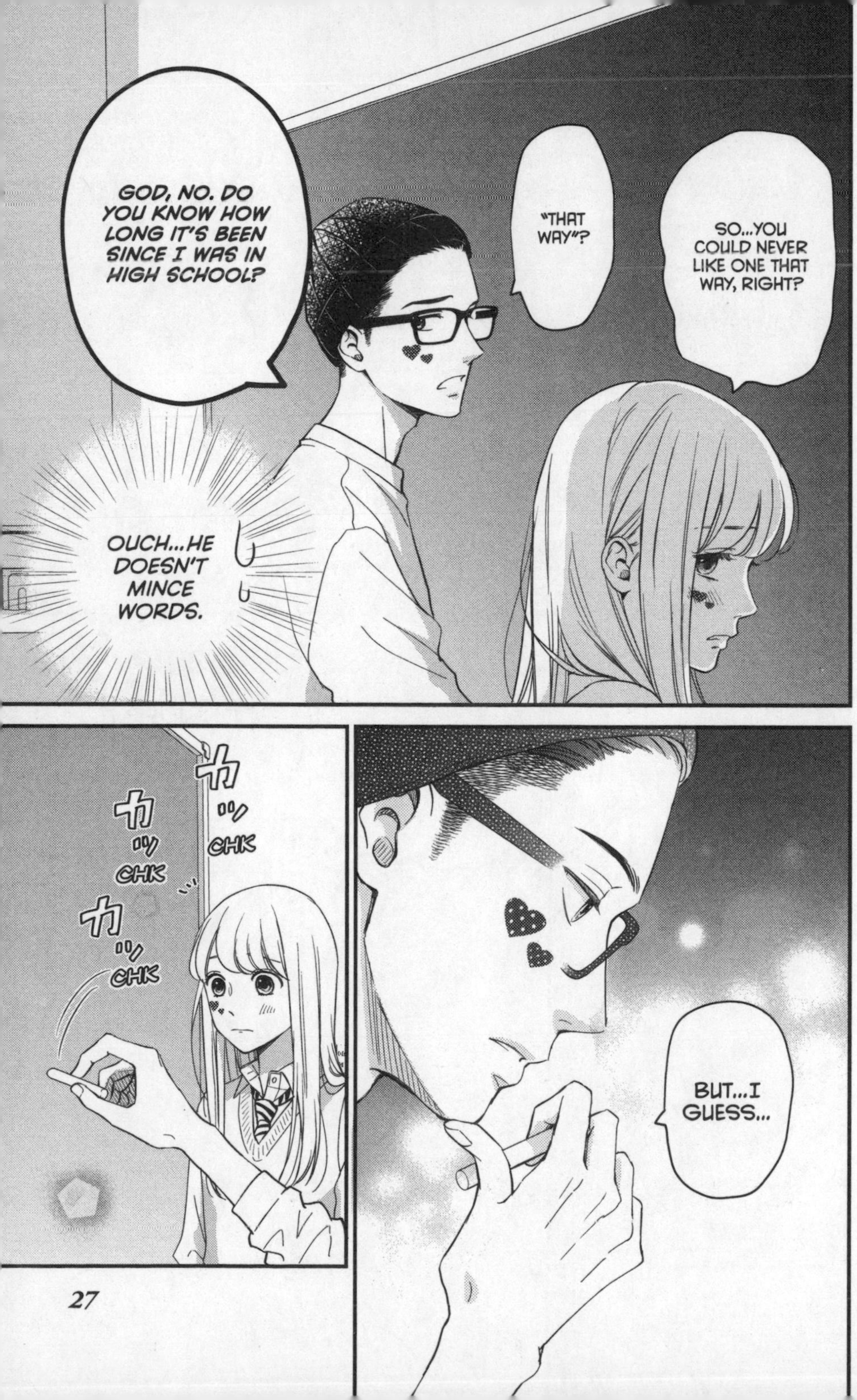
SO...YOU COULD NEVER LIKE ONE THAT WAY, RIGHT?
"THAT WAY"?
GOD, NO. DO YOU KNOW HOW LONG IT'S BEEN SINCE I WAS IN HIGH SCHOOL?
OUCH...HE DOESN'T MINCE WORDS.
BUT...I GUESS...
カッ CHK
カッ CHK
カッ CHK

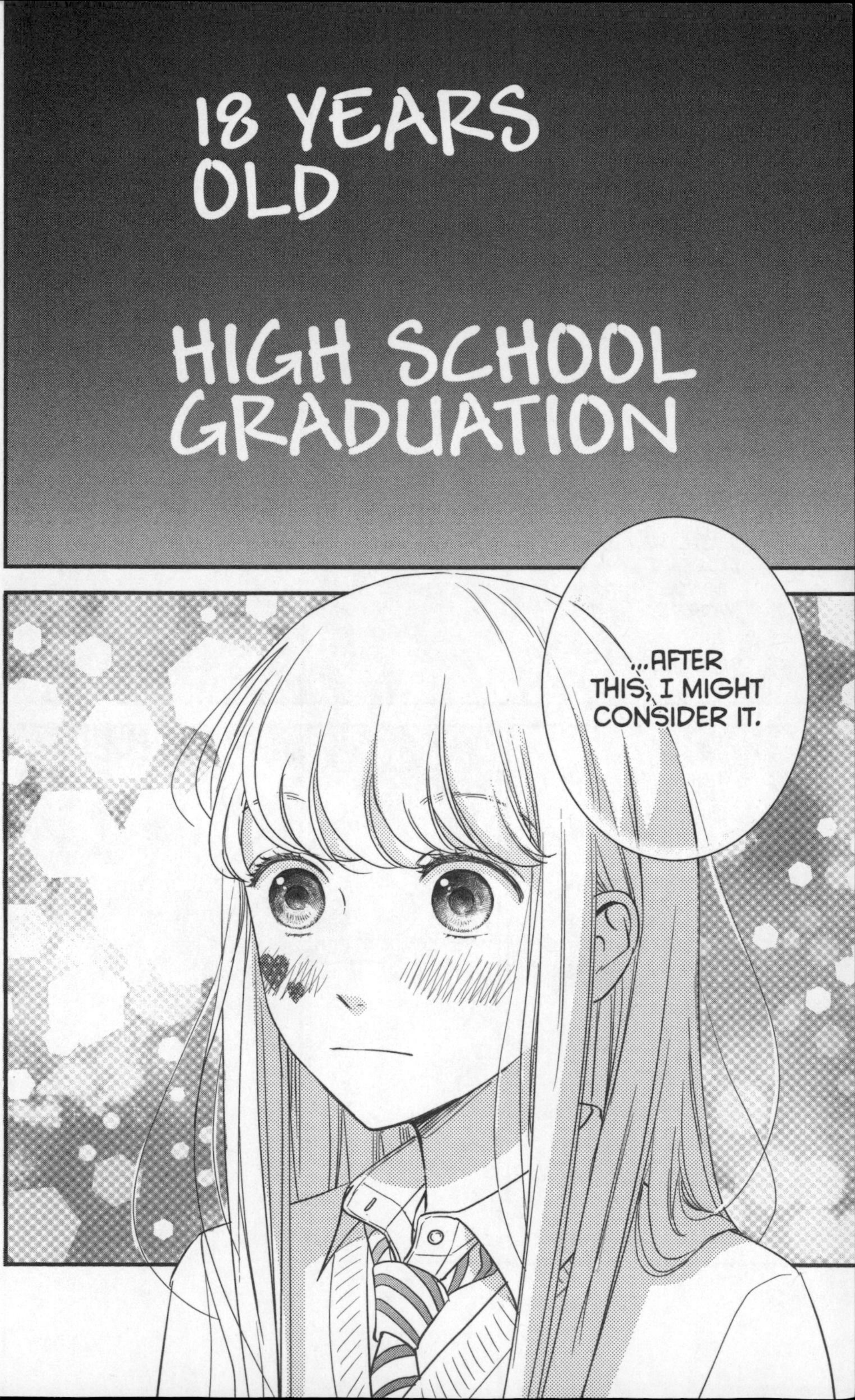
18 YEARS OLD
HIGH SCHOOL GRADUATION
...AFTER THIS, I MIGHT CONSIDER IT.

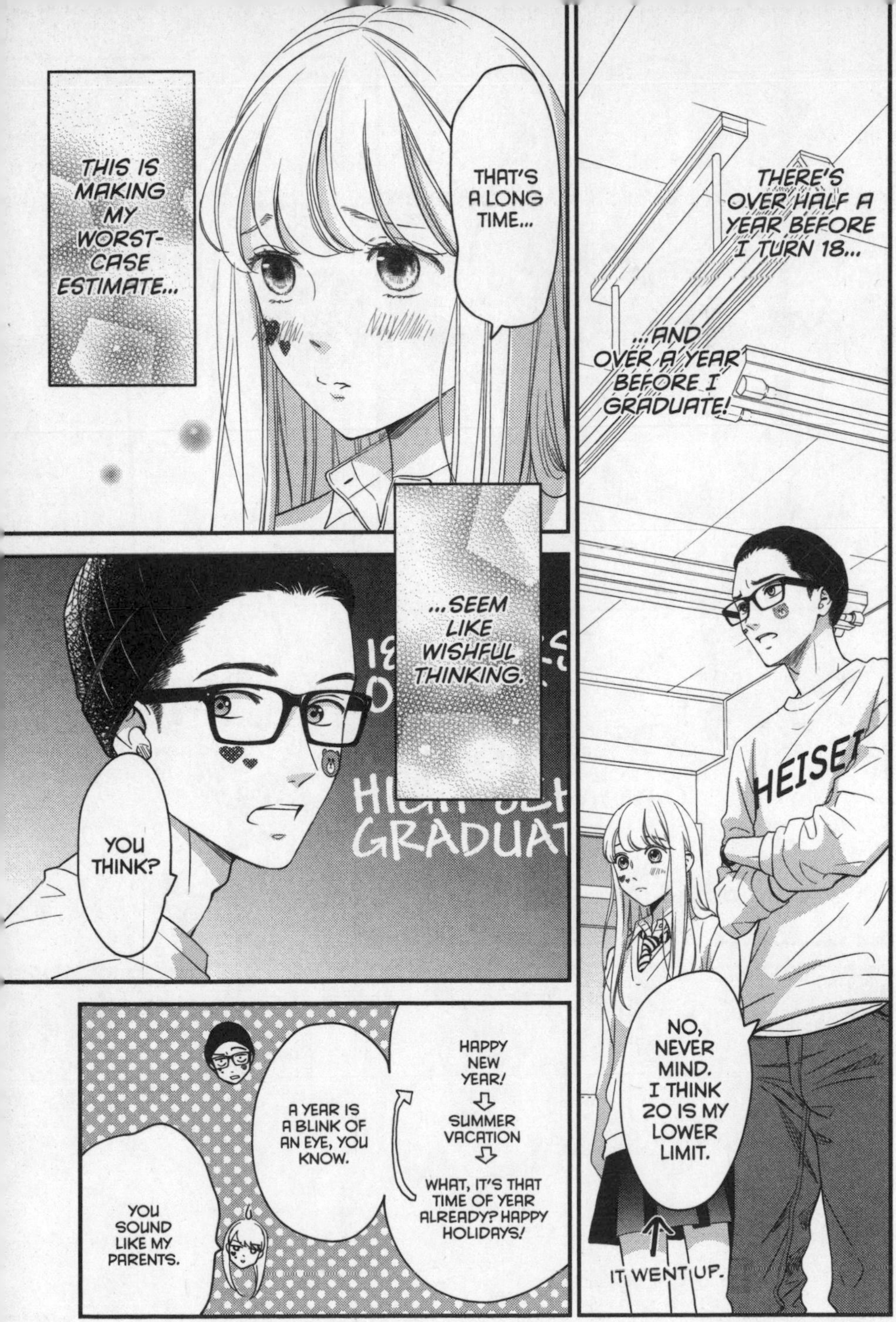
THERE'S OVER HALF A YEAR BEFORE I TURN 18...
...AND OVER A YEAR BEFORE I GRADUATE!
NO, NEVER MIND. I THINK 20 IS MY LOWER LIMIT.
IT WENT UP.
THAT'S A LONG TIME...
THIS IS MAKING MY WORST-CASE ESTIMATE...
...SEEM LIKE WISHFUL THINKING.
YOU THINK?
HAPPY NEW YEAR! ⇩ SUMMER VACATION ⇩ WHAT, IT'S THAT TIME OF YEAR ALREADY? HAPPY HOLIDAYS!
A YEAR IS A BLINK OF AN EYE, YOU KNOW.
YOU SOUND LIKE MY PARENTS.

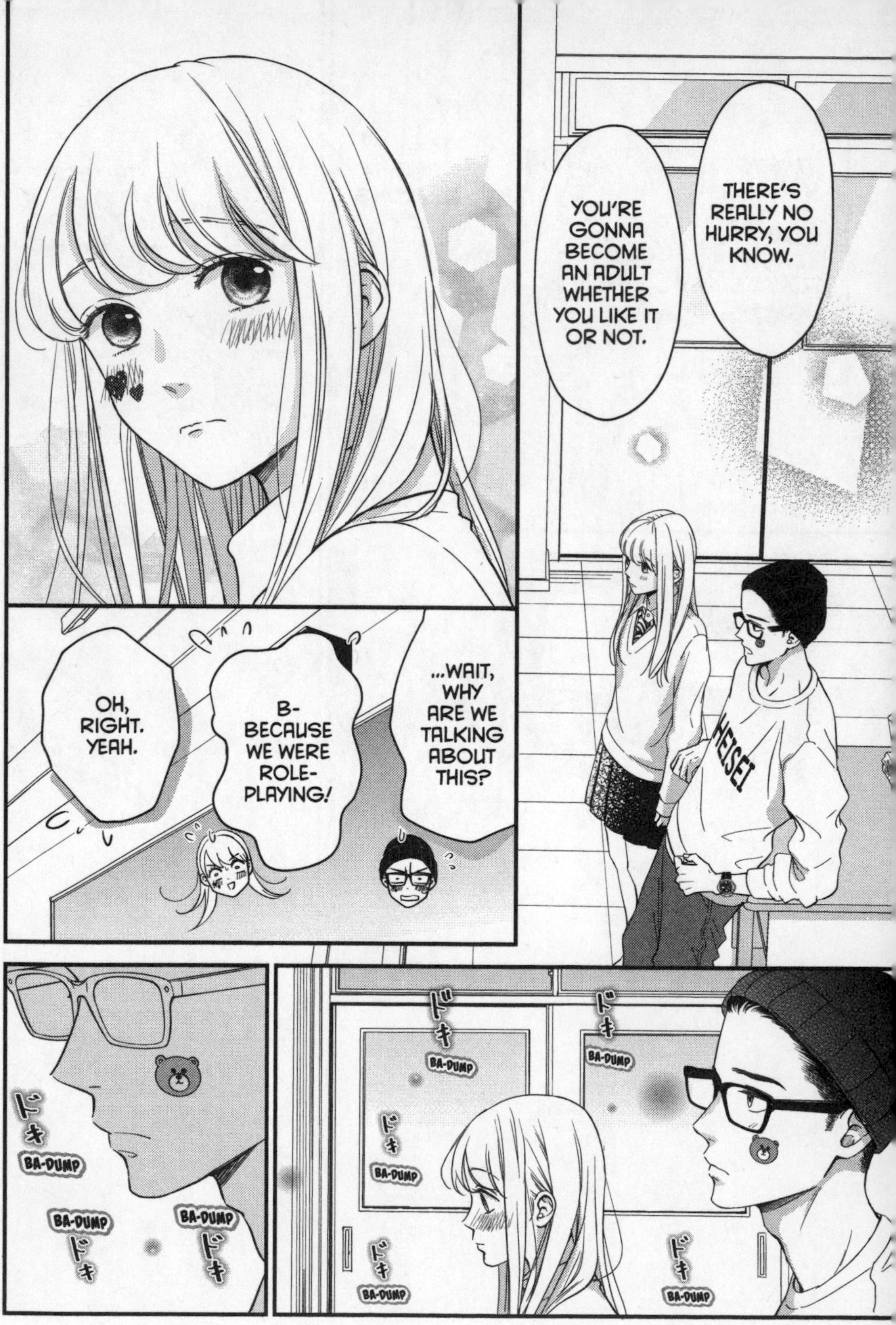
THERE'S REALLY NO HURRY, YOU KNOW.
YOU'RE GONNA BECOME AN ADULT WHETHER YOU LIKE IT OR NOT.
...WAIT, WHY ARE WE TALKING ABOUT THIS?
B- BECAUSE WE WERE ROLE-PLAYING!
OH, RIGHT. YEAH.
ドキ BA-DUMP
ドキ BA-DUMP
ドキ BA-DUMP
ドキ BA-DUMP
ドキ BA-DUMP
ドキ BA-DUMP
ドキ BA-DUMP
ドキ BA-DUMP

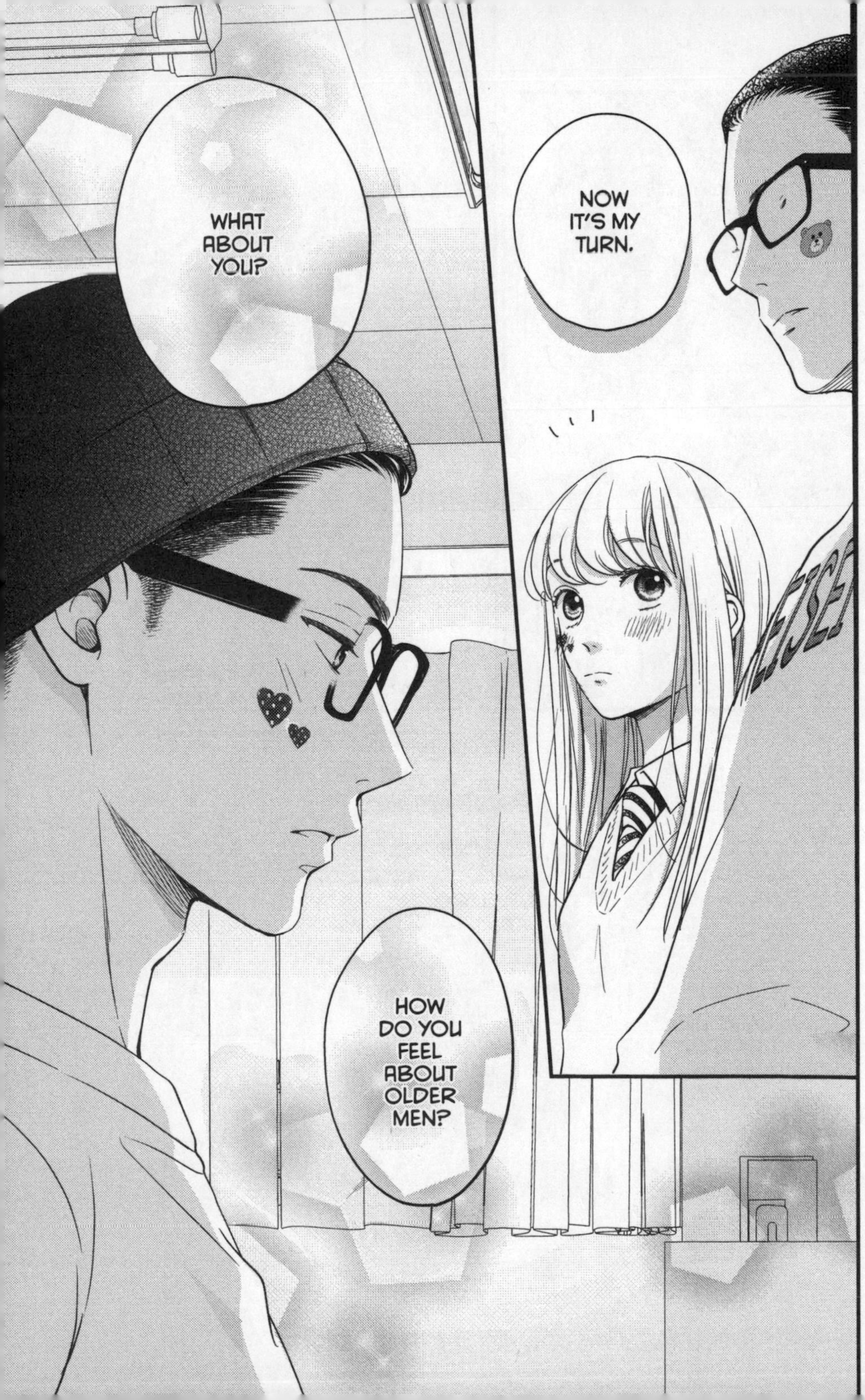
NOW IT'S MY TURN.
WHAT ABOUT YOU?
HOW DO YOU FEEL ABOUT OLDER MEN?

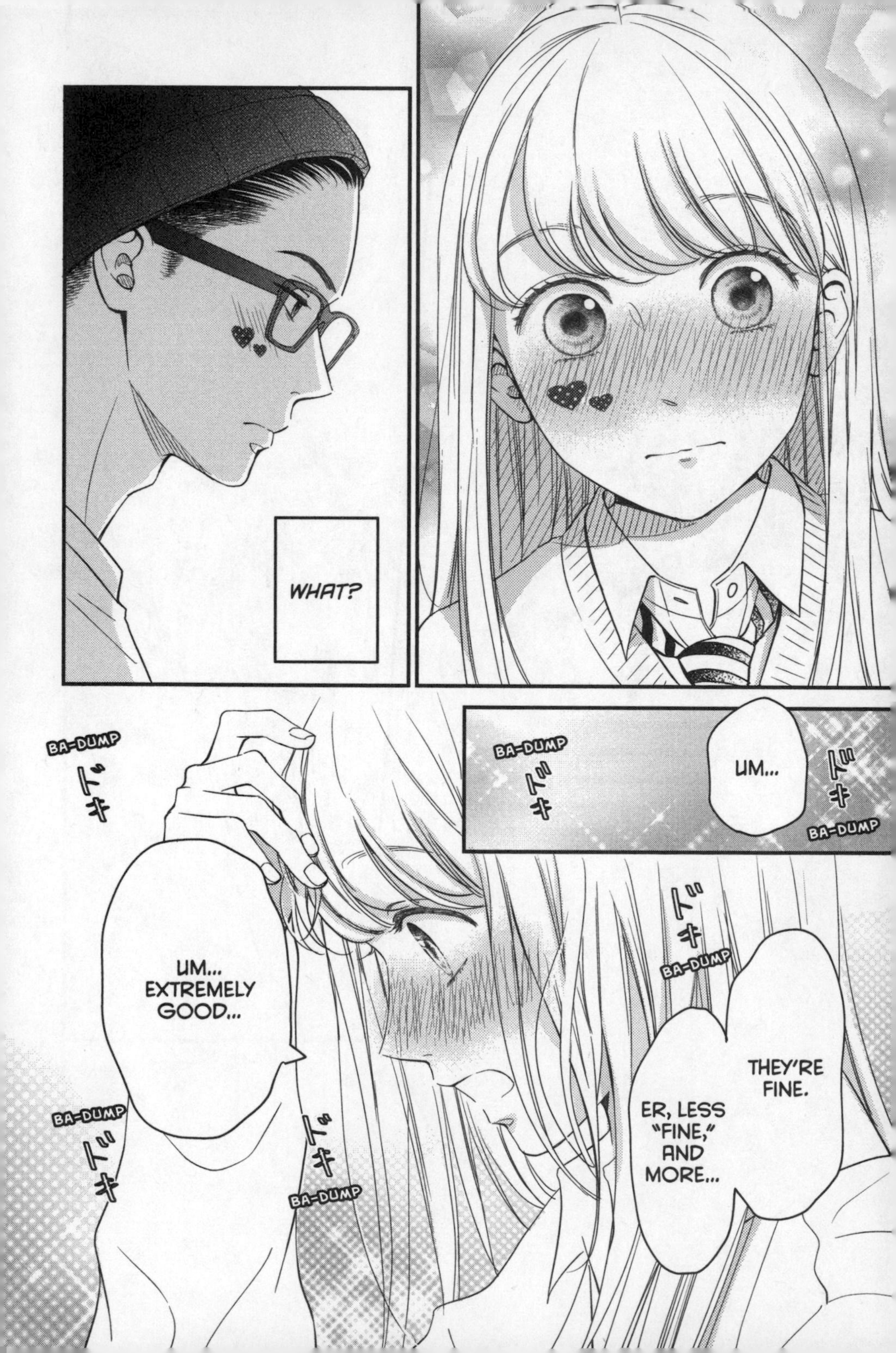
WHAT?
ドキ
BA-DUMP
UM...
BA-DUMP
ドキ
ドキ
BA-DUMP
THEY'RE FINE.
ER, LESS "FINE," AND MORE...
UM... EXTREMELY GOOD...
BA-DUMP
ドキ
ドキ
BA-DUMP
BA-DUMP
ドキ

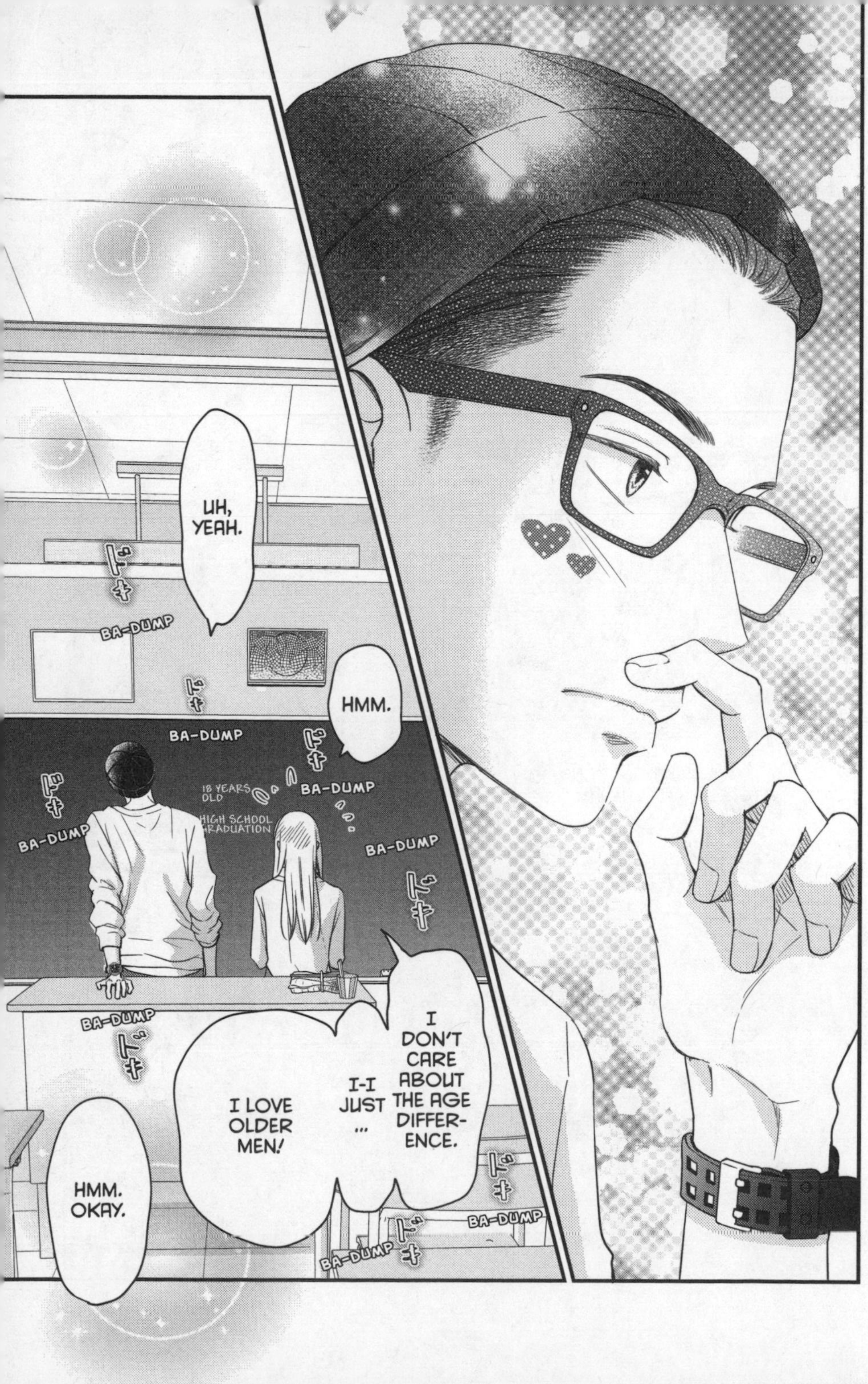
UH, YEAH.
BA-DUMP
HMM.
BA-DUMP
BA-DUMP
18 YEARS OLD
HIGH SCHOOL GRADUATION
BA-DUMP
BA-DUMP
I DON'T CARE ABOUT THE AGE DIFFERENCE.
I-I JUST ...
I LOVE OLDER MEN!
BA-DUMP
HMM. OKAY.
BA-DUMP
BA-DUMP

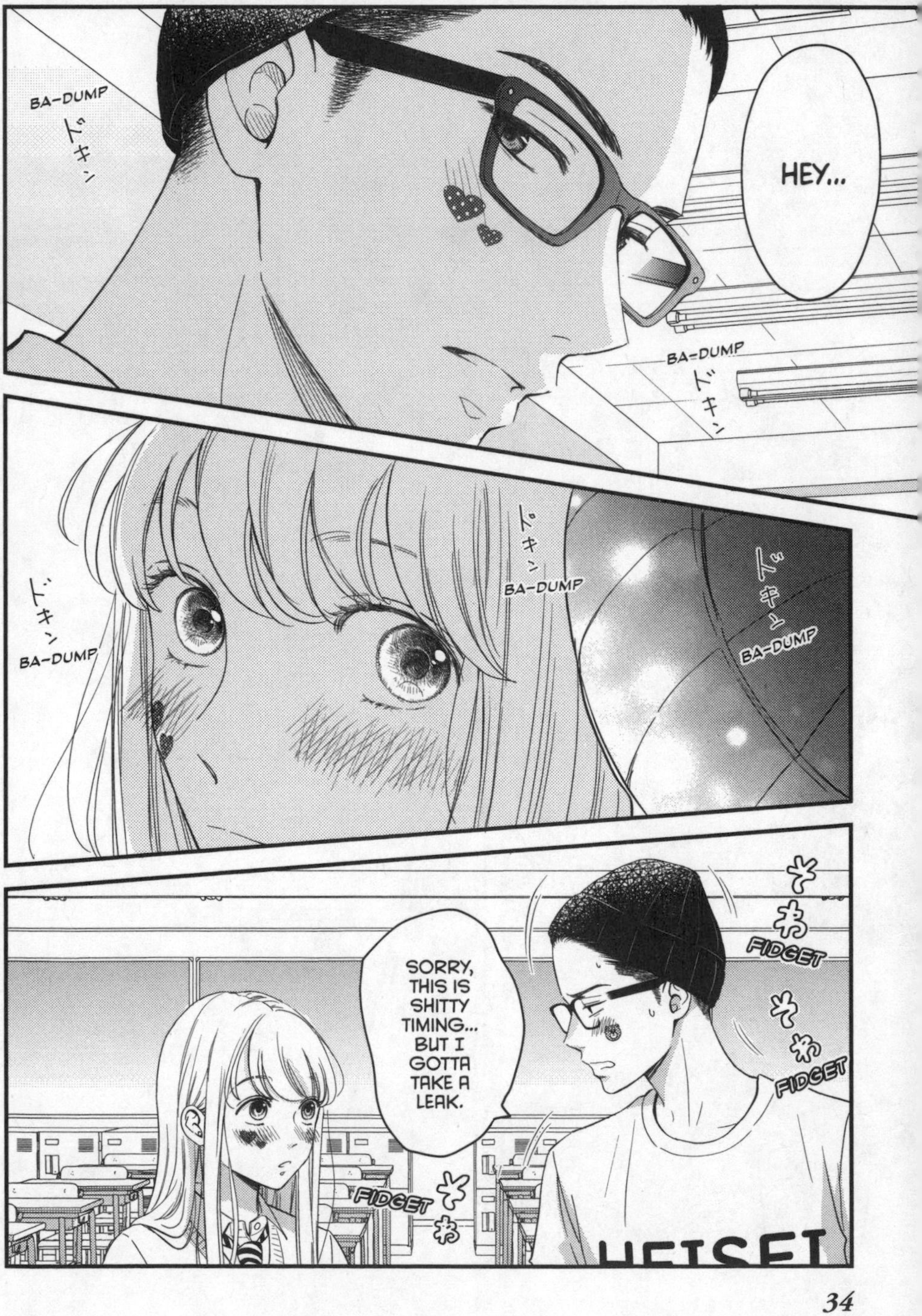
HEY...
ドキン
BA-DUMP
ドキン
BA-DUMP
ドキュ
BA-DUMP
ドキン
BA-DUMP
ドキン
BA-DUMP
ドキン
BA-DUMP
そわ
FIDGET
そわ
FIDGET
SORRY, THIS IS SHITTY TIMING... BUT I GOTTA TAKE A LEAK.
そわ
FIDGET

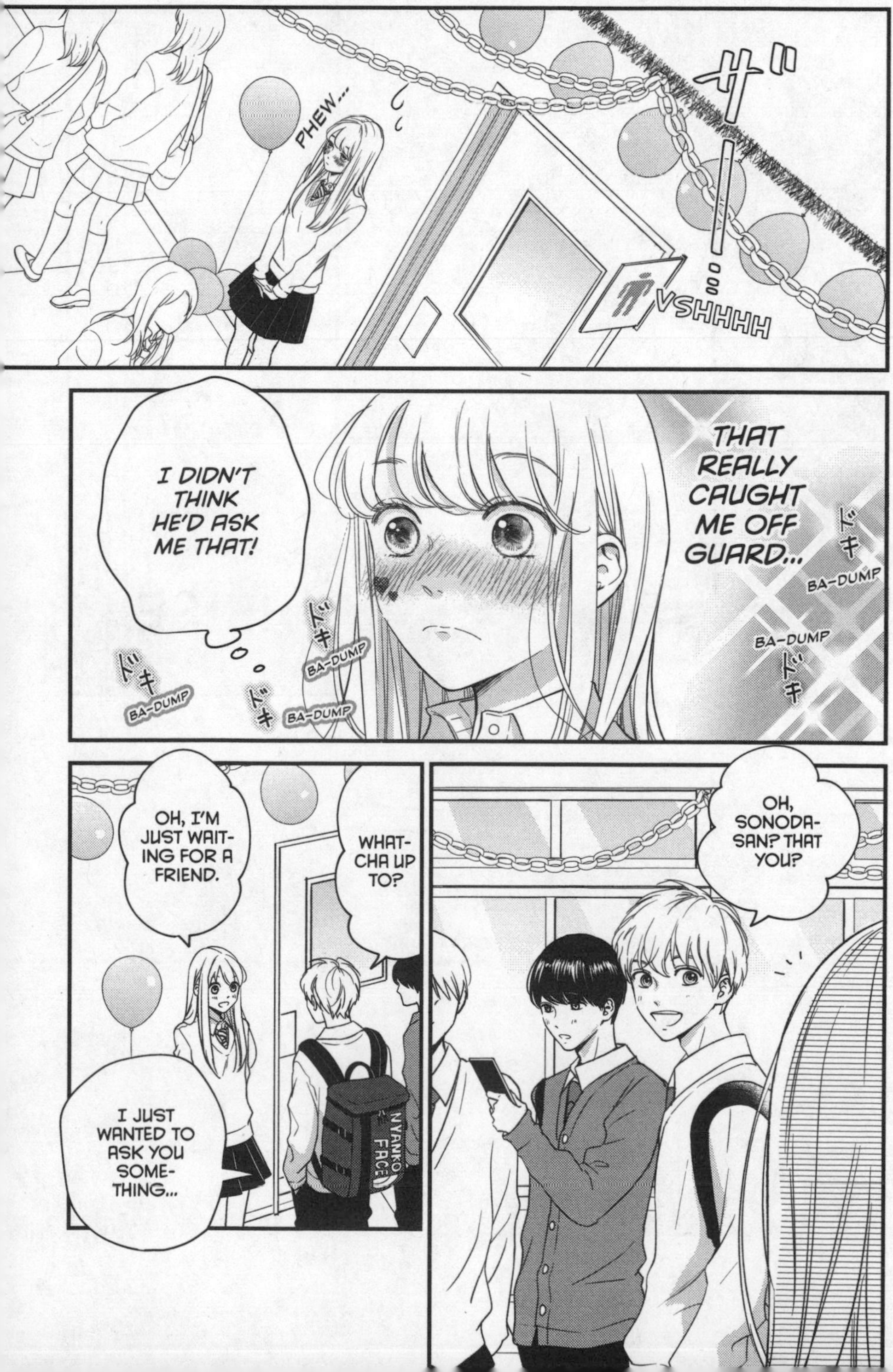
ザー
VSHHHH
PHEW...
THAT REALLY CAUGHT ME OFF GUARD...
ドキ
BA-DUMP
BA-DUMP
ドキ
I DIDN'T THINK HE'D ASK ME THAT!
ドキ
BA-DUMP
ドキ
BA-DUMP
ドキ
BA-DUMP
OH, SONODA-SAN? THAT YOU?
WHATCHA UP TO?
OH, I'M JUST WAITING FOR A FRIEND.
NYANKO FACE
I JUST WANTED TO ASK YOU SOMETHING...

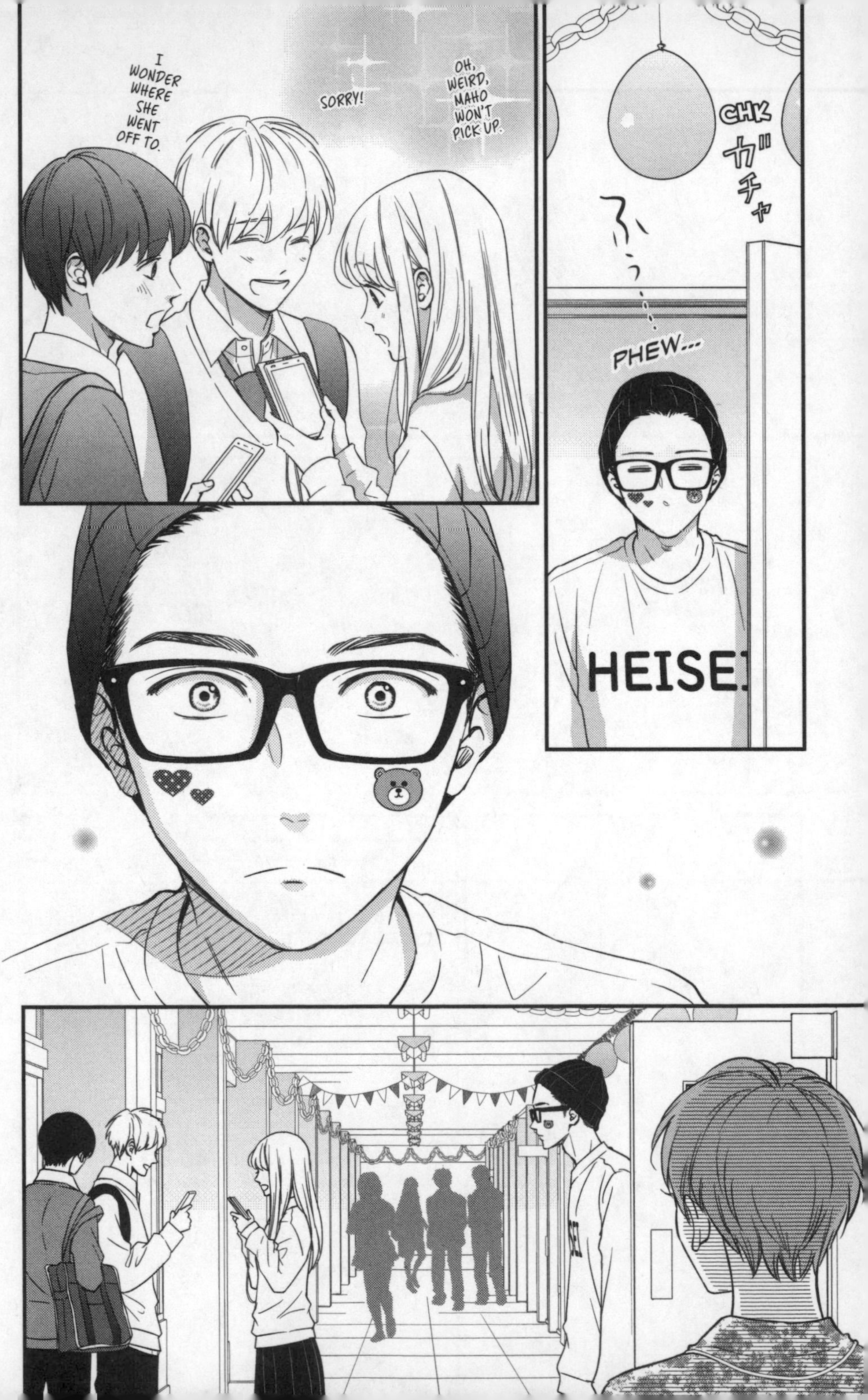
CHK
ガチャ
ふぅ…
PHEW...
HEISEI
OH, WEIRD, MAHO WON'T PICK UP.
SORRY!
I WONDER WHERE SHE WENT OFF TO.

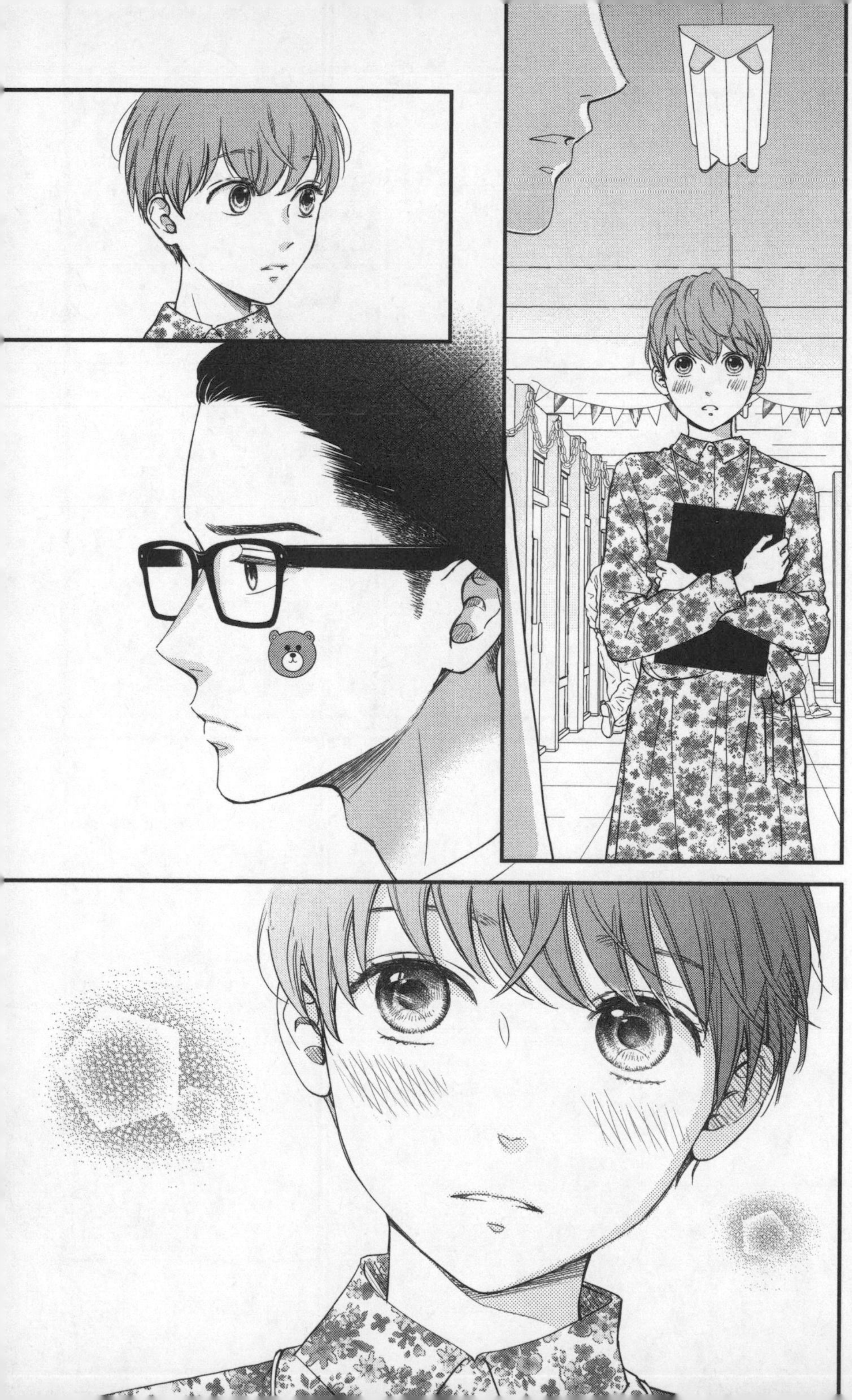

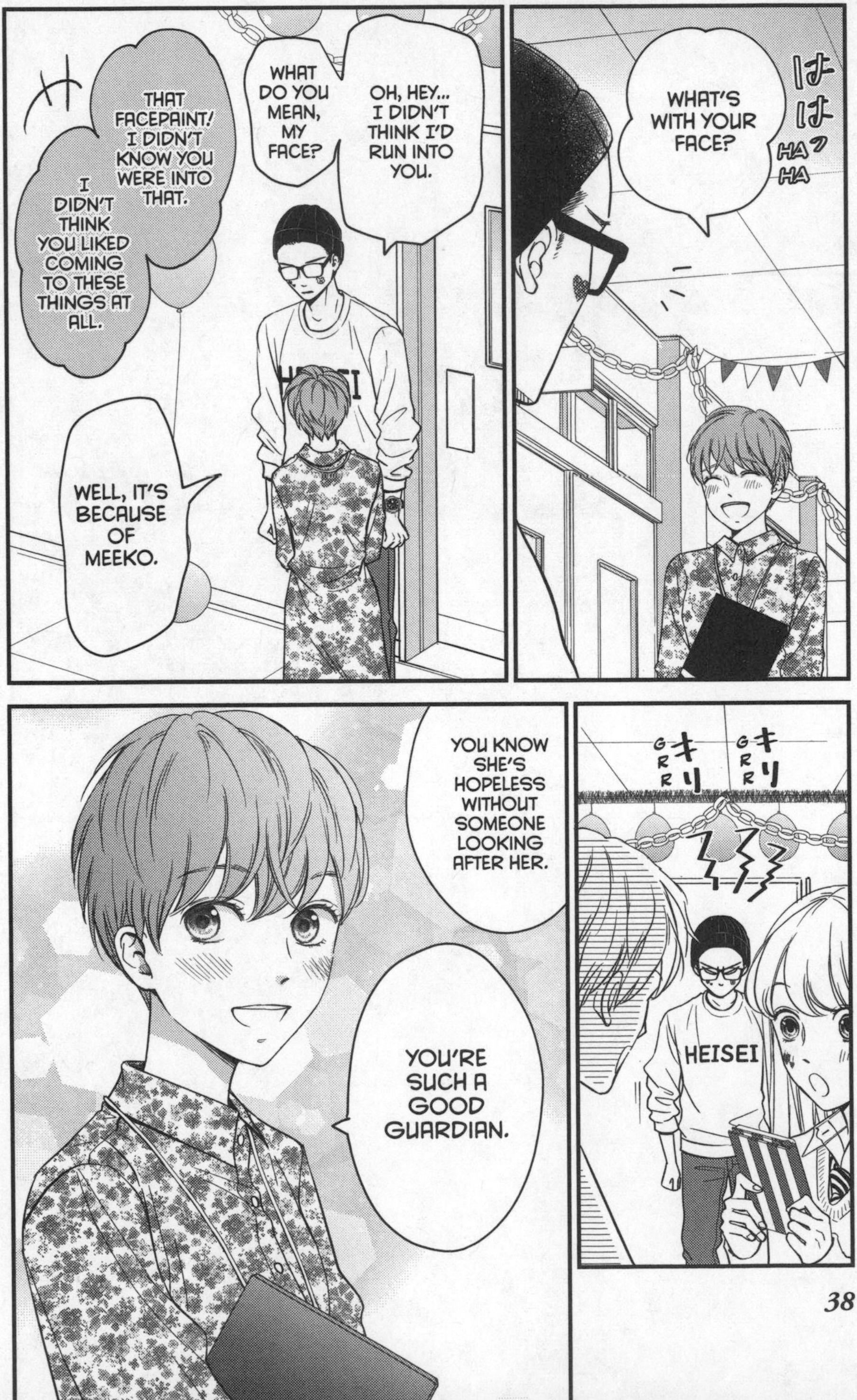
WHAT'S WITH YOUR FACE?
ははっ HA HA
OH, HEY... I DIDN'T THINK I'D RUN INTO YOU.
WHAT DO YOU MEAN, MY FACE?
THAT FACEPAINT! I DIDN'T KNOW YOU WERE INTO THAT.
I DIDN'T THINK YOU LIKED COMING TO THESE THINGS AT ALL.
WELL, IT'S BECAUSE OF MEEKO.
キリ GRR
キリ GRR
HEISEI
YOU KNOW SHE'S HOPELESS WITHOUT SOMEONE LOOKING AFTER HER.
YOU'RE SUCH A GOOD GUARDIAN.

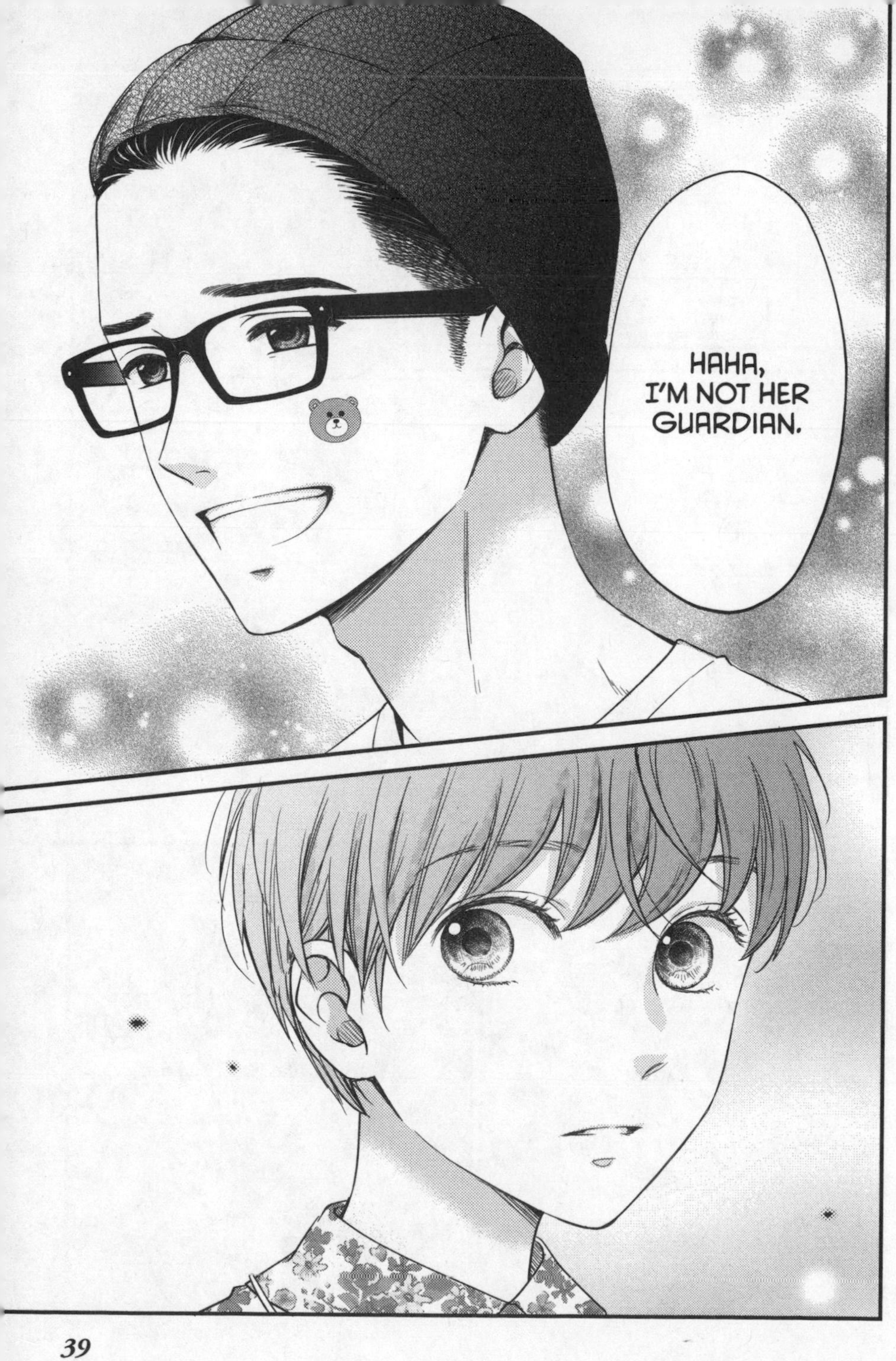
HAHA, I'M NOT HER GUARDIAN.

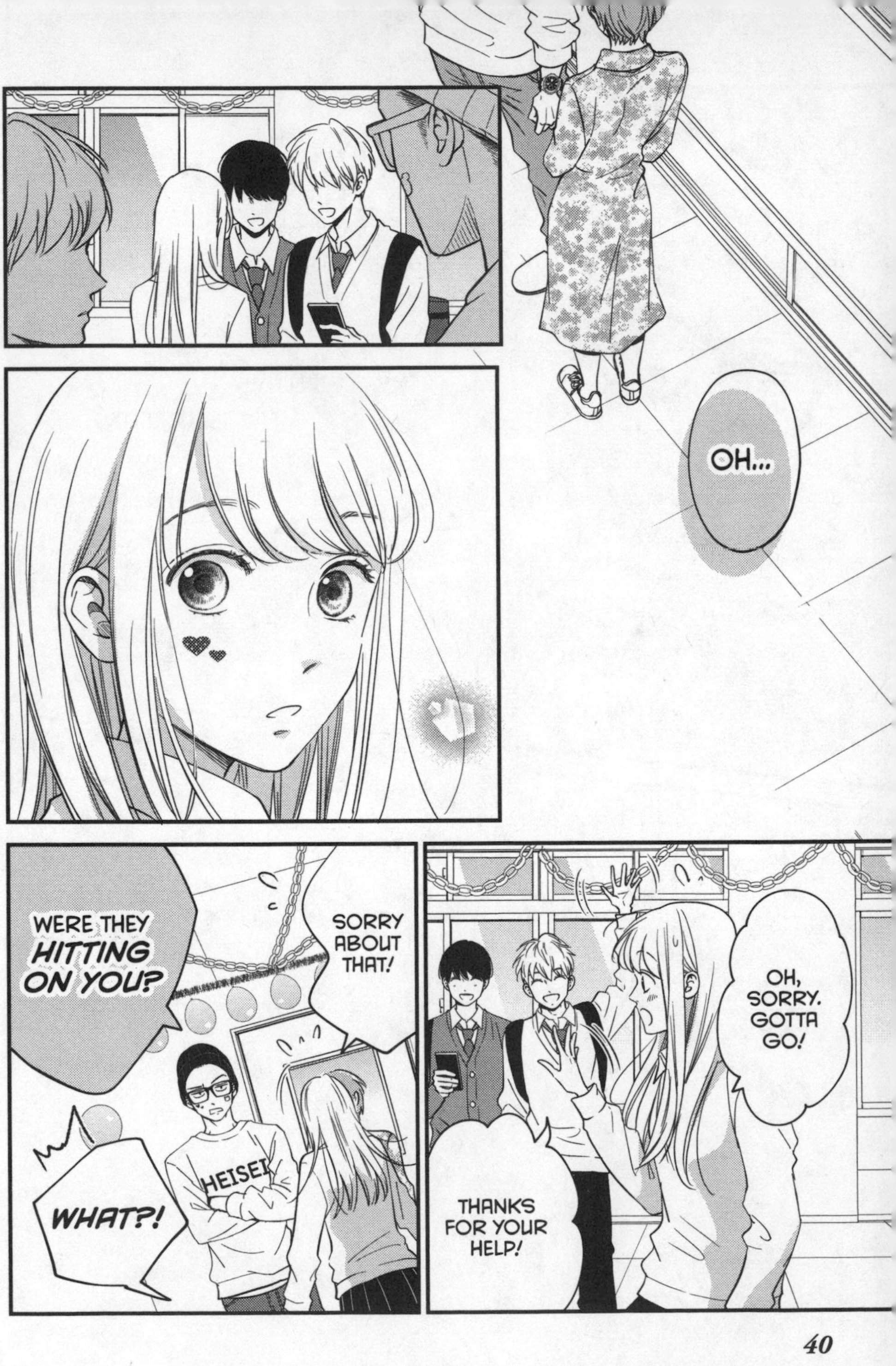
OH...
OH, SORRY. GOTTA GO!
THANKS FOR YOUR HELP!
SORRY ABOUT THAT!
WERE THEY HITTING ON YOU?
WHAT?!
HEISEI

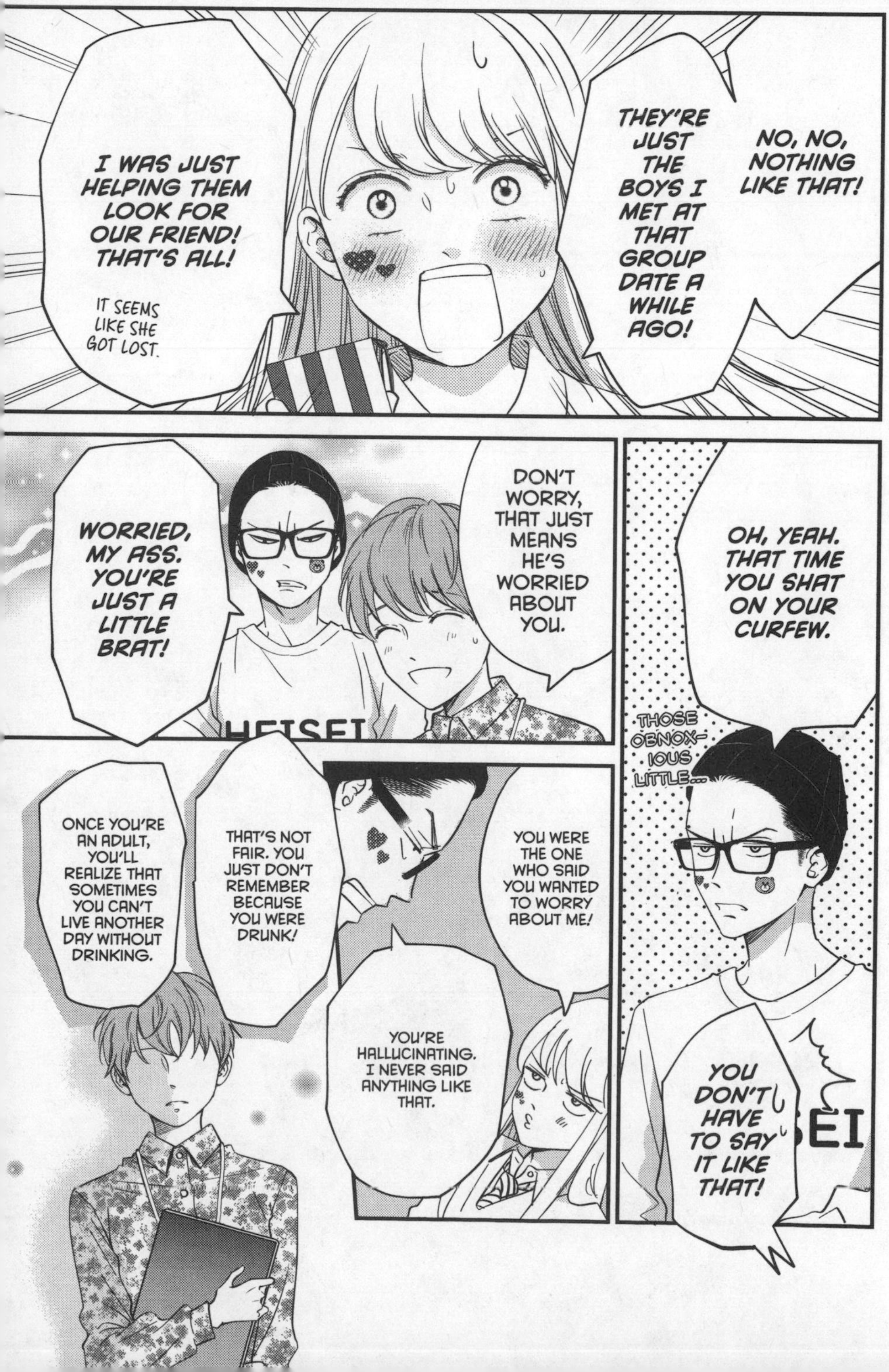
NO, NO, NOTHING LIKE THAT!
THEY'RE JUST THE BOYS I MET AT THAT GROUP DATE A WHILE AGO!
I WAS JUST HELPING THEM LOOK FOR OUR FRIEND! THAT'S ALL!
IT SEEMS LIKE SHE GOT LOST.
OH, YEAH. THAT TIME YOU SHAT ON YOUR CURFEW.
THOSE OBNOX-IOUS LITTLE...
YOU DON'T HAVE TO SAY IT LIKE THAT!
DON'T WORRY, THAT JUST MEANS HE'S WORRIED ABOUT YOU.
WORRIED, MY ASS. YOU'RE JUST A LITTLE BRAT!
YOU WERE THE ONE WHO SAID YOU WANTED TO WORRY ABOUT ME!
YOU'RE HALLUCINATING. I NEVER SAID ANYTHING LIKE THAT.
THAT'S NOT FAIR. YOU JUST DON'T REMEMBER BECAUSE YOU WERE DRUNK!
ONCE YOU'RE AN ADULT, YOU'LL REALIZE THAT SOMETIMES YOU CAN'T LIVE ANOTHER DAY WITHOUT DRINKING.

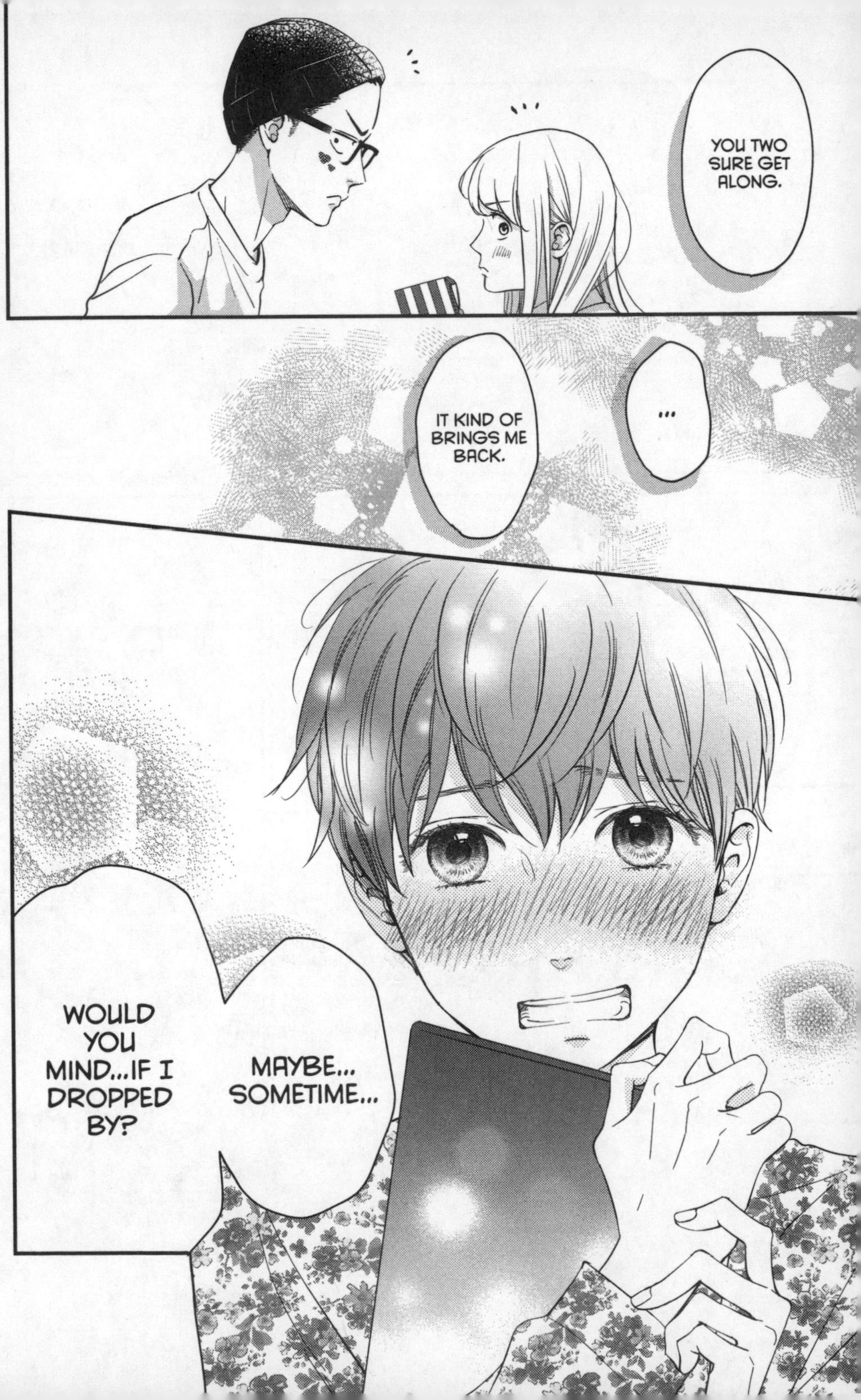
YOU TWO SURE GET ALONG.
...
IT KIND OF BRINGS ME BACK.
MAYBE... SOMETIME...
WOULD YOU MIND...IF I DROPPED BY?

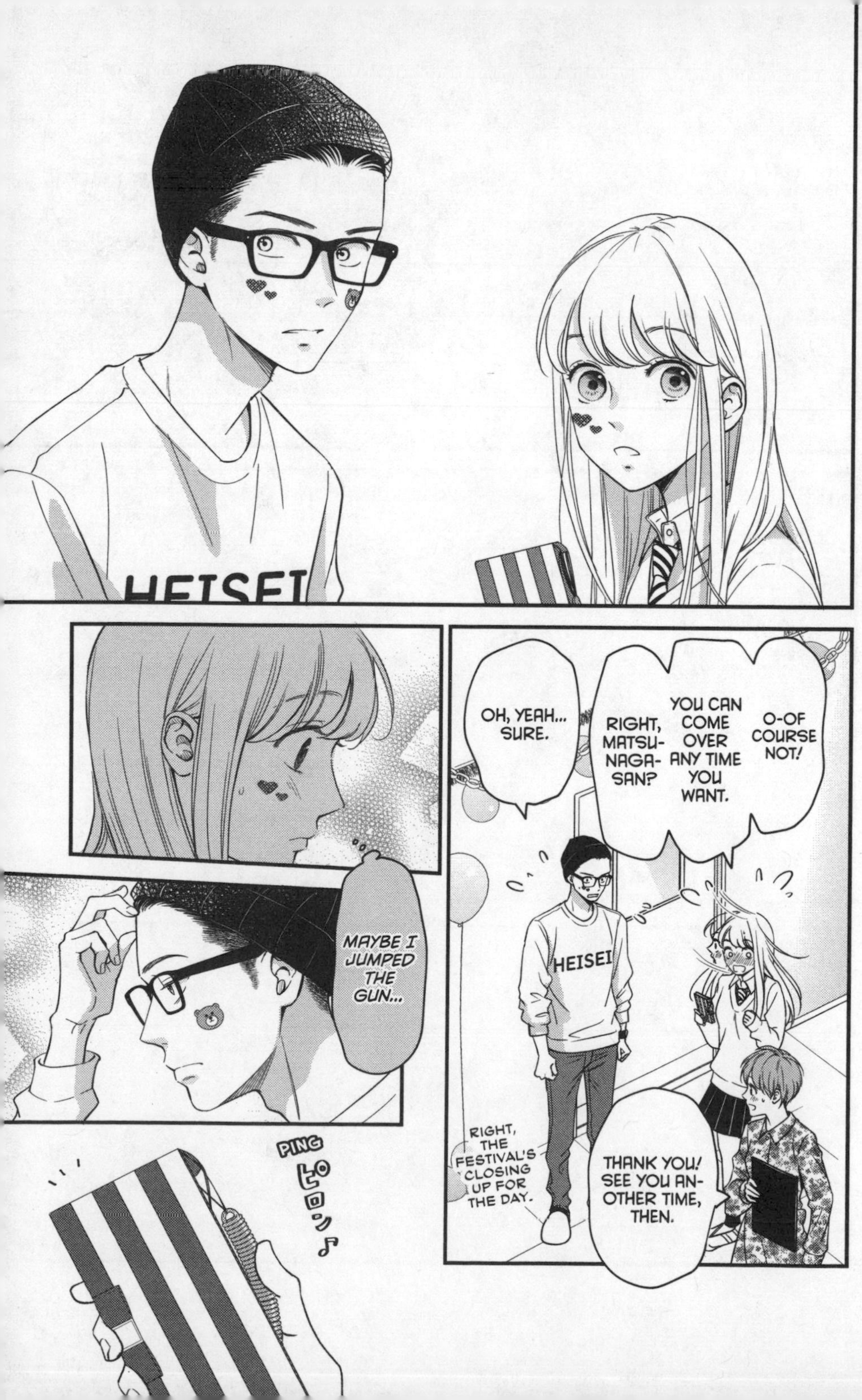
HEISEI
O-OF COURSE NOT!
RIGHT, MATSU-NAGA-SAN? YOU CAN COME OVER ANY TIME YOU WANT.
OH, YEAH... SURE.
HEISEI
THANK YOU! SEE YOU AN-OTHER TIME, THEN.
RIGHT, THE FESTIVAL'S CLOSING UP FOR THE DAY.
MAYBE I JUMPED THE GUN...
PING
ピロン♪

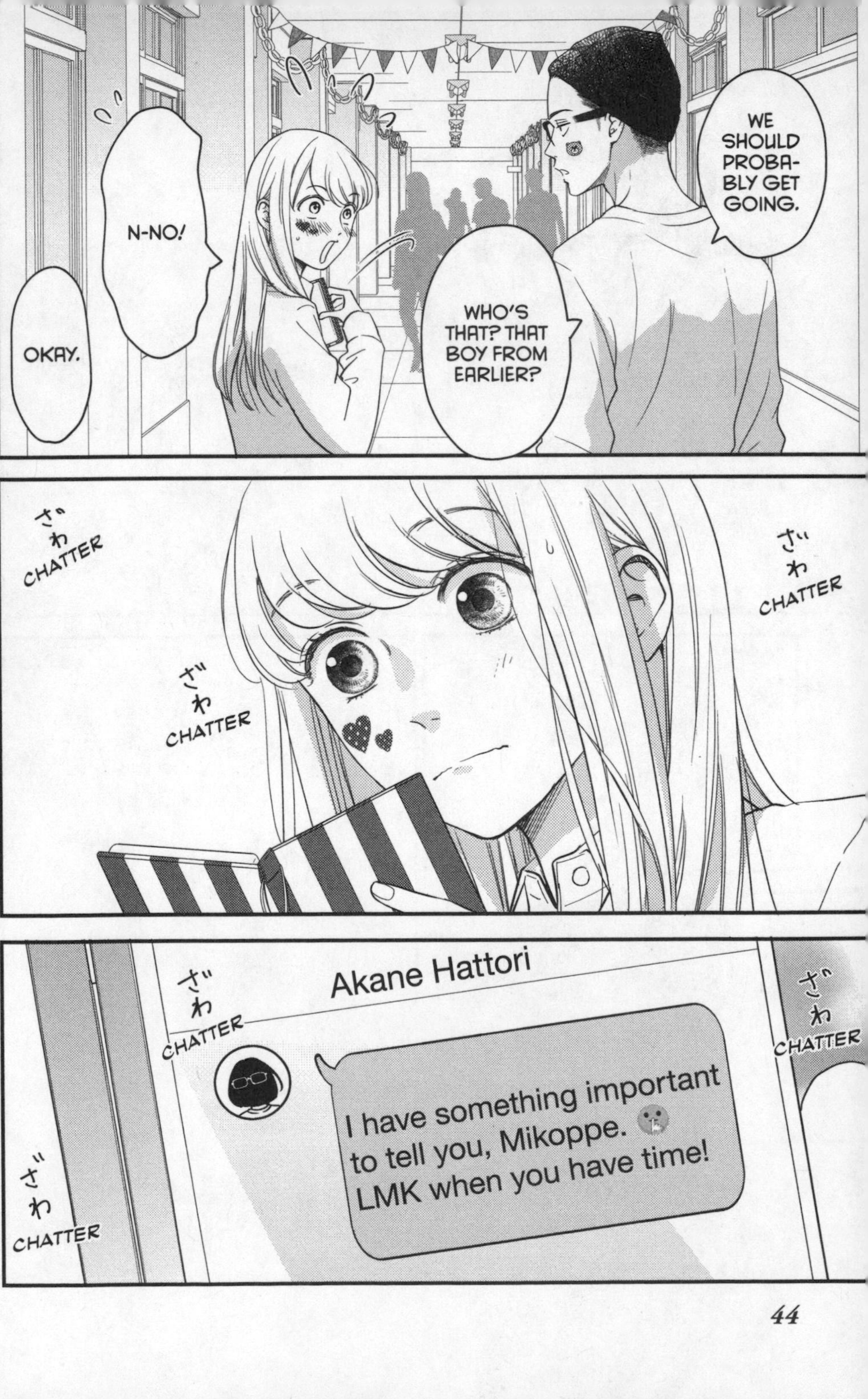
WE SHOULD PROBA-BLY GET GOING.
WHO'S THAT? THAT BOY FROM EARLIER?
N-NO!
OKAY.
ざわ CHATTER
ざわ CHATTER
ざわ CHATTER
ざわ CHATTER
Akane Hattori
I have something important to tell you, Mikoppe. LMK when you have time!
ざわ CHATTER
ざわ CHATTER

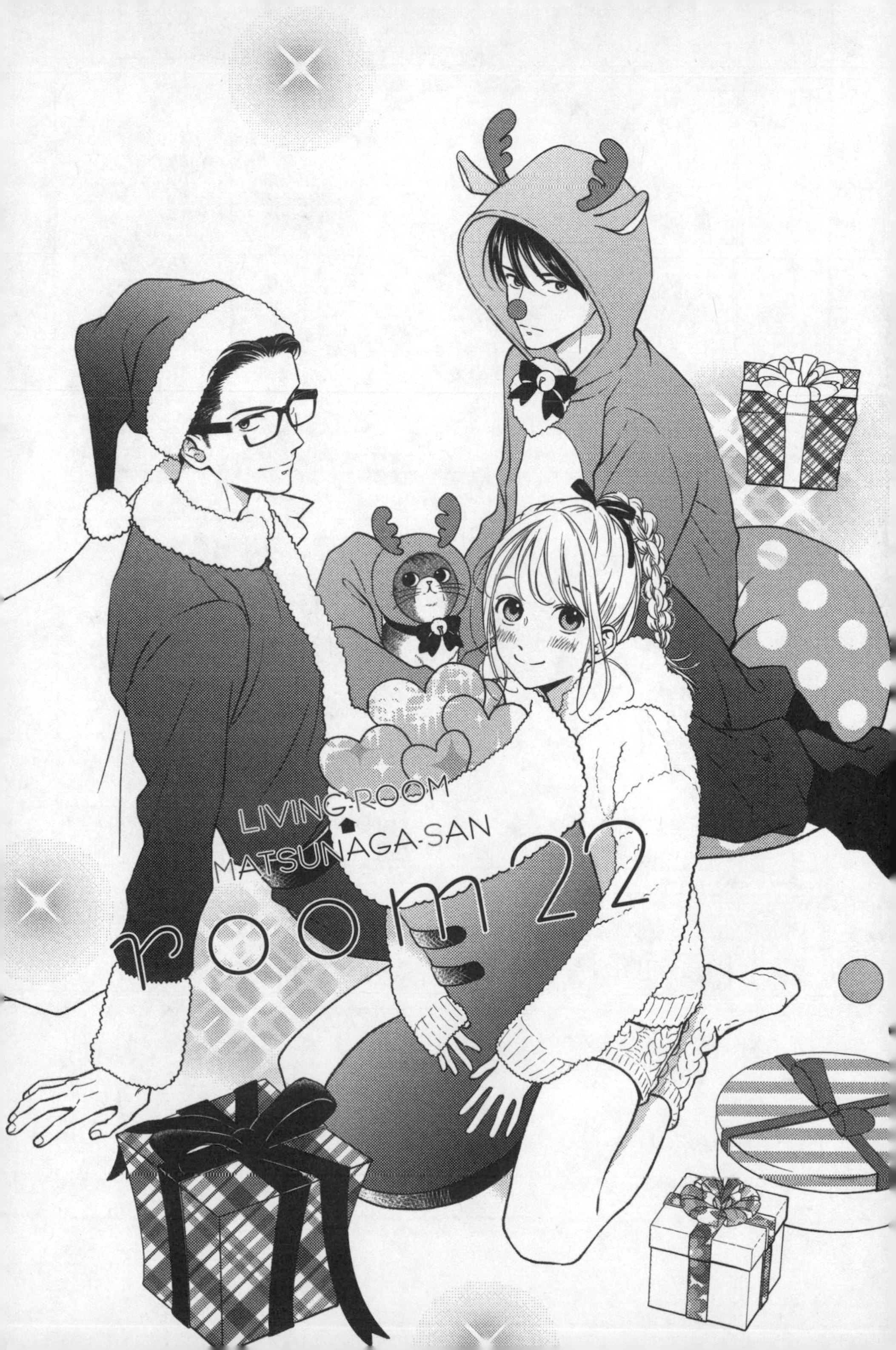
LIVING-ROOM MATSUNAGA-SAN
room 22

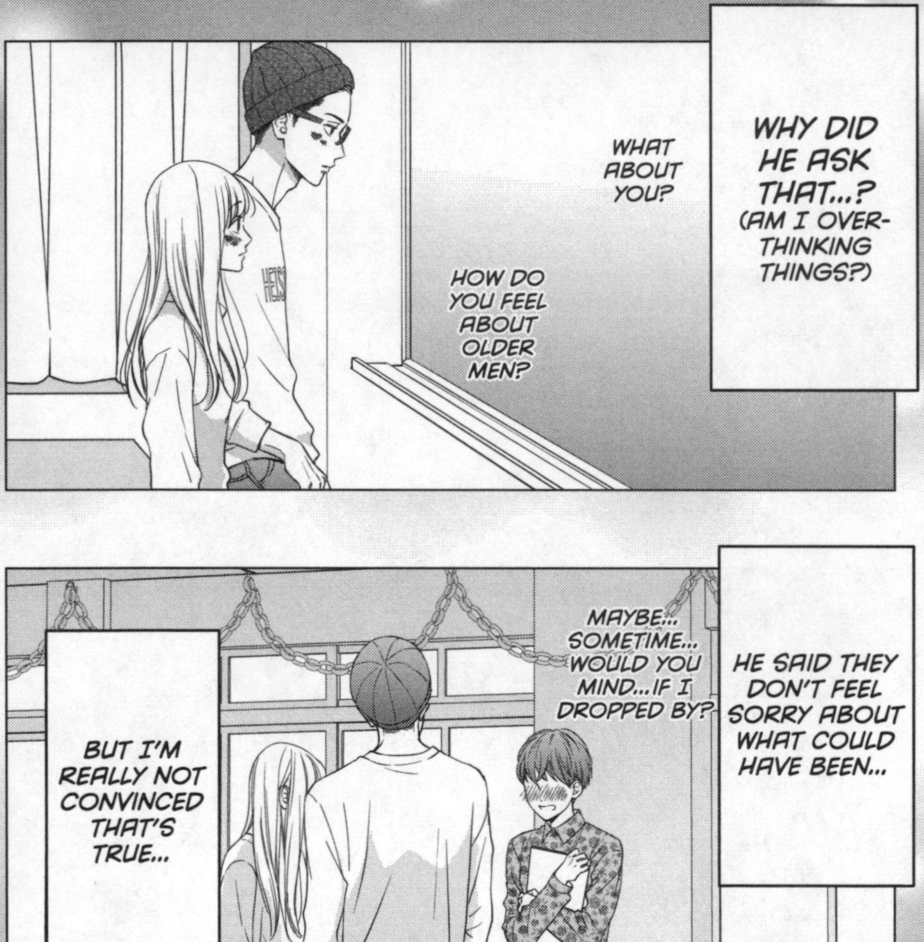
WHY DID HE ASK THAT...? (AM I OVER-THINKING THINGS?)
WHAT ABOUT YOU?
HOW DO YOU FEEL ABOUT OLDER MEN?
HE SAID THEY DON'T FEEL SORRY ABOUT WHAT COULD HAVE BEEN...
MAYBE... SOMETIME... WOULD YOU MIND...IF I DROPPED BY?
BUT I'M REALLY NOT CONVINCED THAT'S TRUE...

KEN-CHAN'S EASY-PEASY QUIZ

Q1: WHAT KIND OF HOT AM I? (SELF-PROCLAIMED)

1: WILD

2: GENTLE

3: ANDROGYNOUS

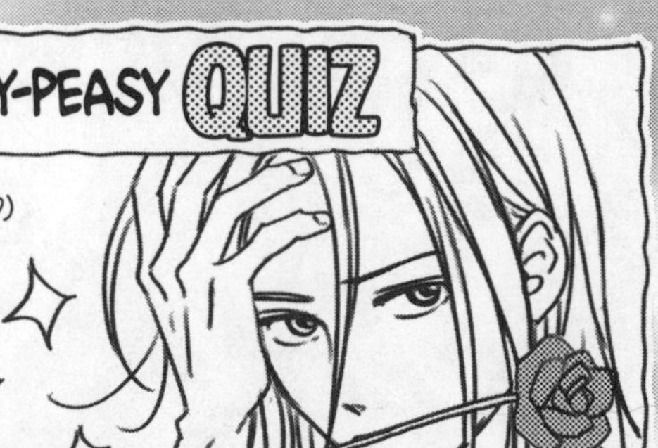

ANSWER: 3 ♡ (SEE VOLUME 2.) IF YOU GOT IT RIGHT, FEEL FREE TO DROP BY TONIGHT.

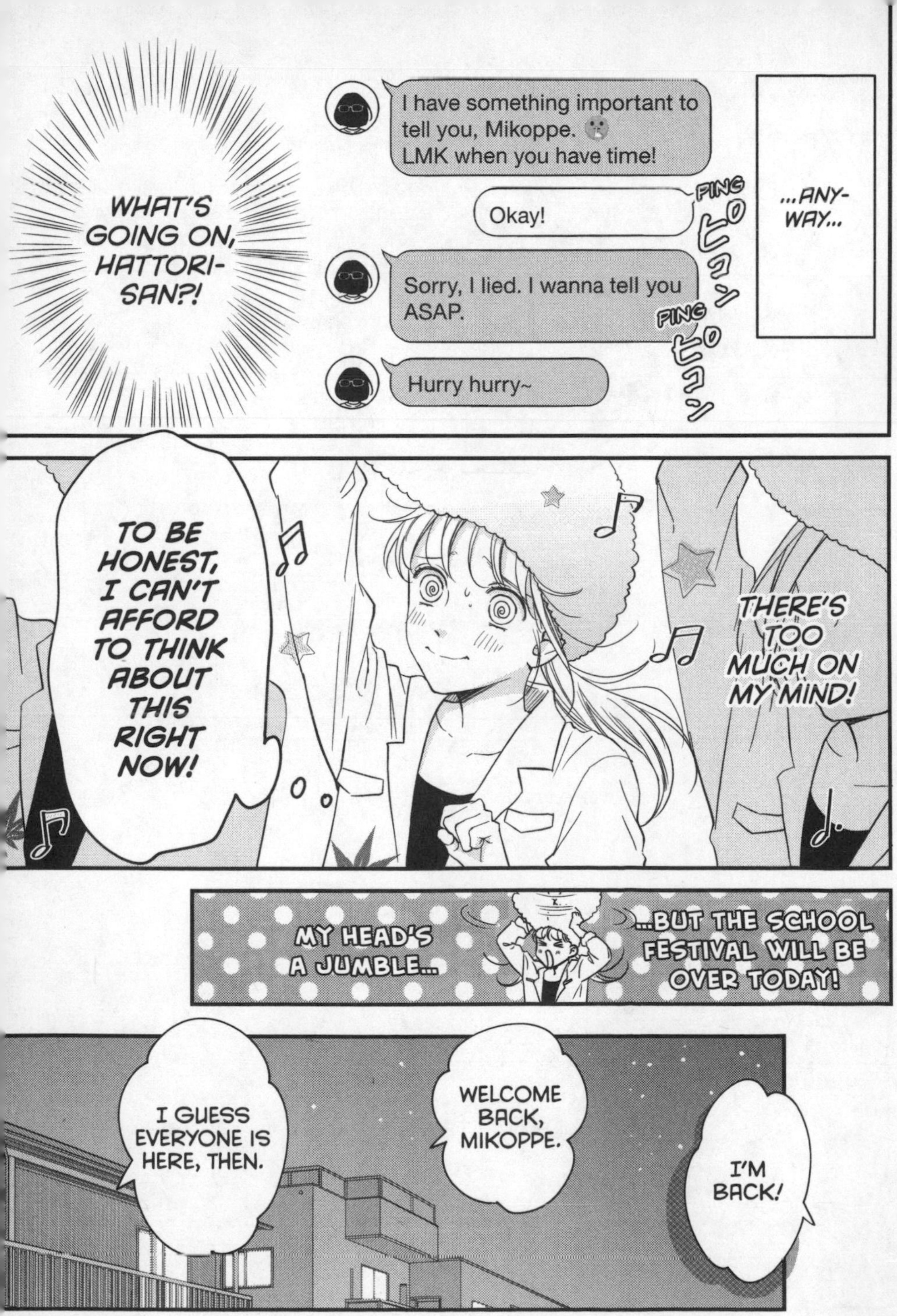
...ANY-WAY...
I have something important to tell you, Mikoppe. LMK when you have time!
Okay!
PING
ピコン
Sorry, I lied. I wanna tell you ASAP.
PING
ピコン
Hurry hurry~
WHAT'S GOING ON, HATTORI-SAN?!
THERE'S TOO MUCH ON MY MIND!
TO BE HONEST, I CAN'T AFFORD TO THINK ABOUT THIS RIGHT NOW!
...BUT THE SCHOOL FESTIVAL WILL BE OVER TODAY!
MY HEAD'S A JUMBLE...
I'M BACK!
WELCOME BACK, MIKOPPE.
I GUESS EVERYONE IS HERE, THEN.

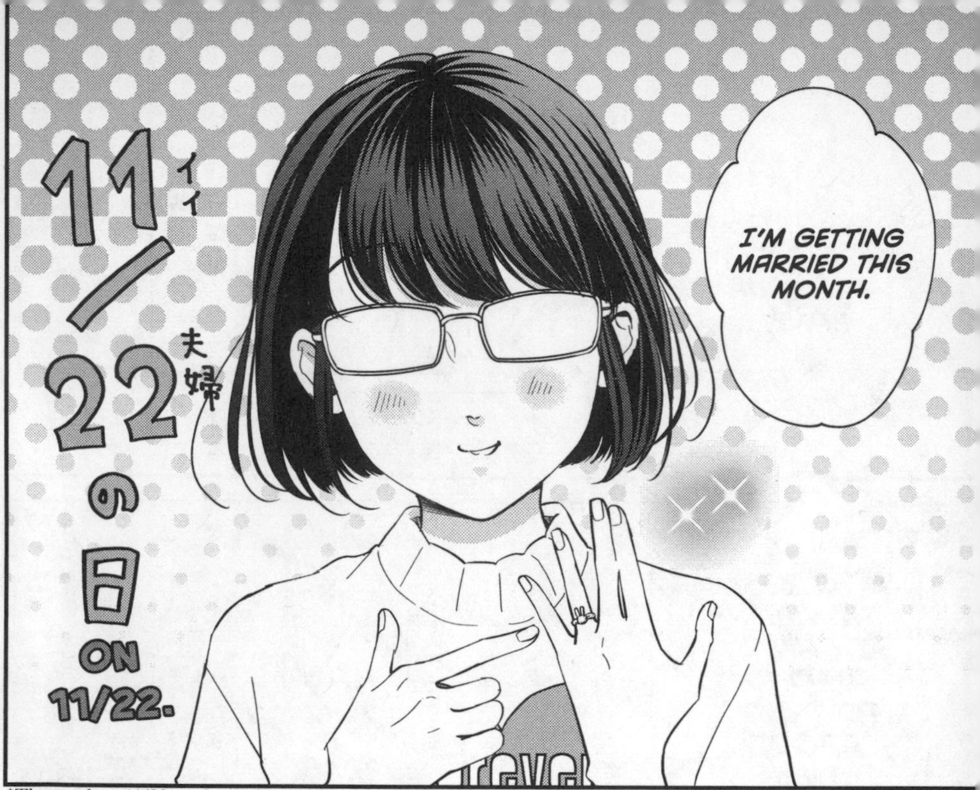
I'M GETTING MARRIED THIS MONTH.
11 イイ / 22 夫婦 の日
ON 11/22.

*The numbers 11/22 can be read as *ii fufu* in Japanese, meaning, "happy married couple."

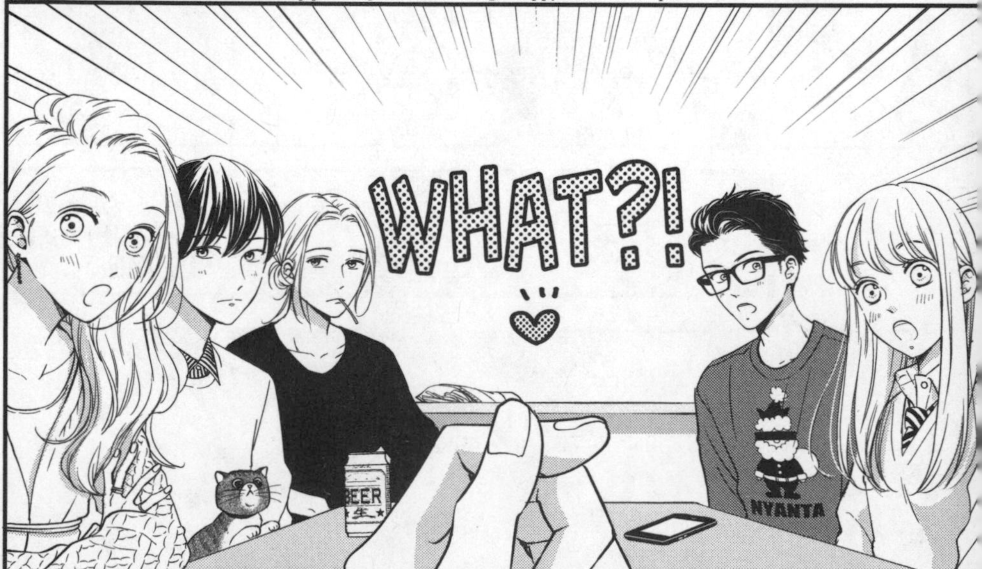
WHAT?!

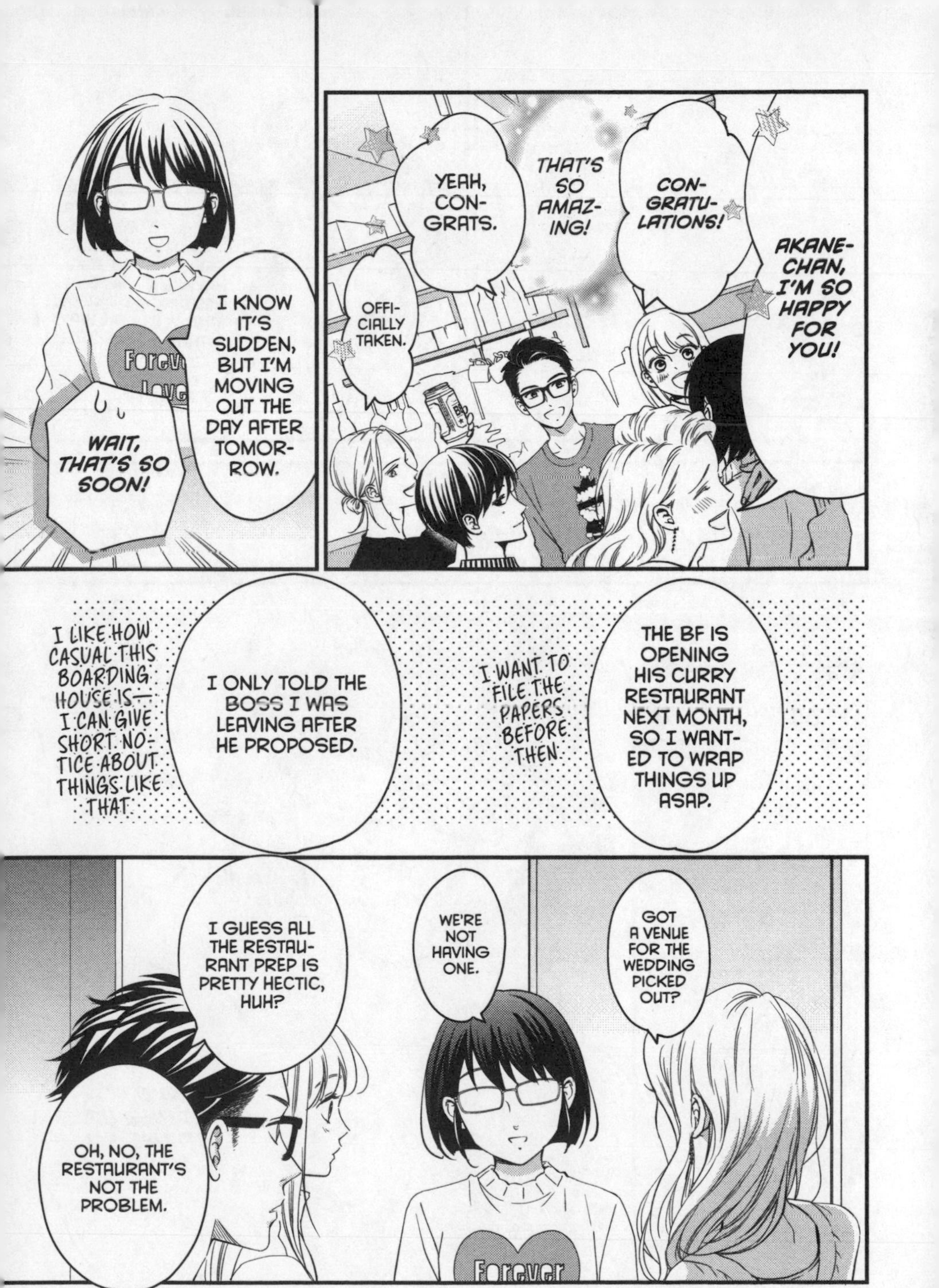
AKANE-CHAN, I'M SO HAPPY FOR YOU!
CONGRATULATIONS!
THAT'S SO AMAZING!
YEAH, CONGRATS.
OFFICIALLY TAKEN.
I KNOW IT'S SUDDEN, BUT I'M MOVING OUT THE DAY AFTER TOMORROW.
WAIT, THAT'S SO SOON!
THE BF IS OPENING HIS CURRY RESTAURANT NEXT MONTH, SO I WANTED TO WRAP THINGS UP ASAP.
I WANT TO FILE THE PAPERS BEFORE THEN.
I ONLY TOLD THE BOSS I WAS LEAVING AFTER HE PROPOSED.
I LIKE HOW CASUAL THIS BOARDING HOUSE IS— I CAN GIVE SHORT NOTICE ABOUT THINGS LIKE THAT.
GOT A VENUE FOR THE WEDDING PICKED OUT?
WE'RE NOT HAVING ONE.
I GUESS ALL THE RESTAURANT PREP IS PRETTY HECTIC, HUH?
OH, NO, THE RESTAURANT'S NOT THE PROBLEM.

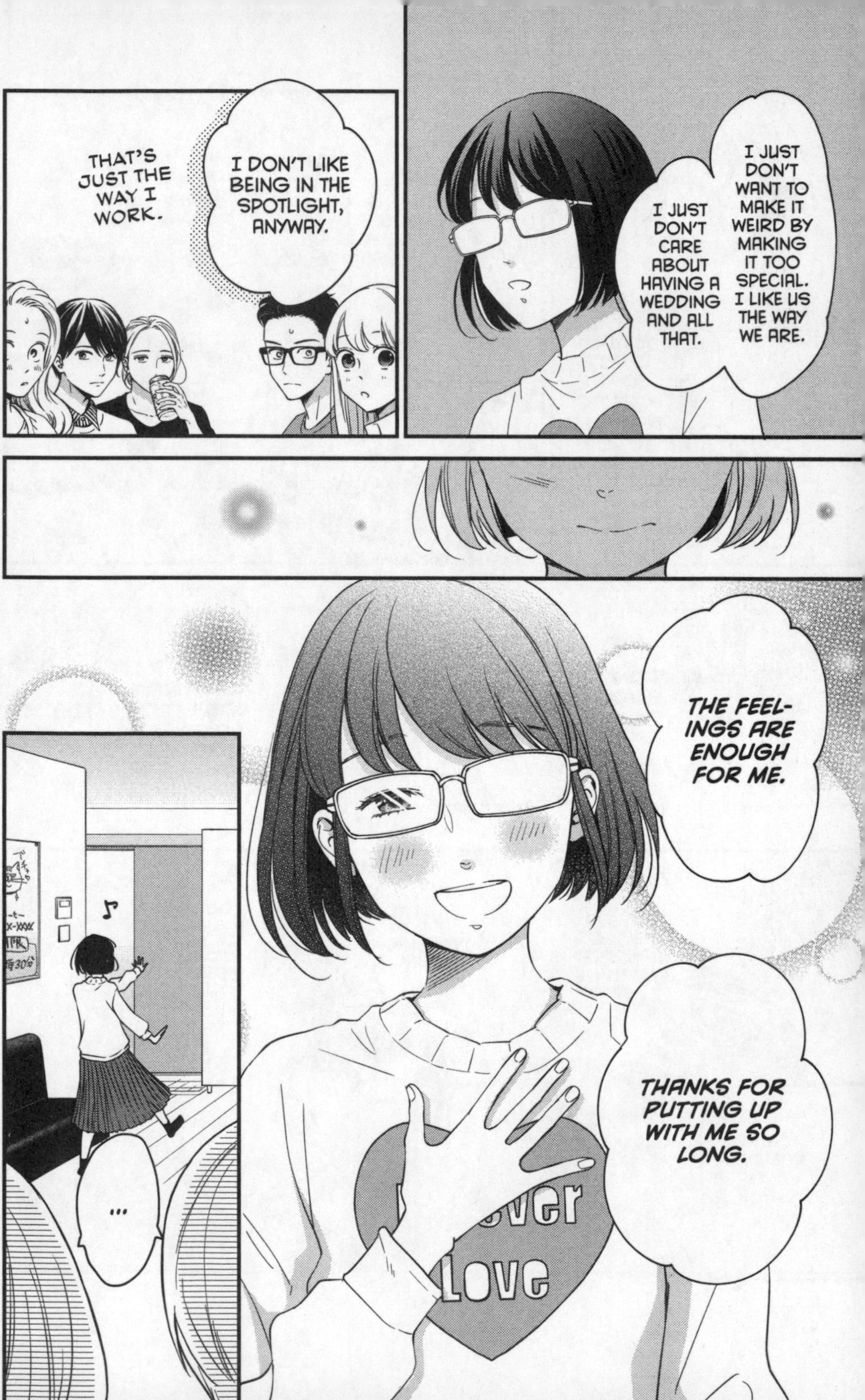

I JUST DON'T WANT TO MAKE IT WEIRD BY MAKING IT TOO SPECIAL. I LIKE US THE WAY WE ARE.
I JUST DON'T CARE ABOUT HAVING A WEDDING AND ALL THAT.
I DON'T LIKE BEING IN THE SPOTLIGHT, ANYWAY.
THAT'S JUST THE WAY I WORK.
THE FEELINGS ARE ENOUGH FOR ME.
THANKS FOR PUTTING UP WITH ME SO LONG.
...

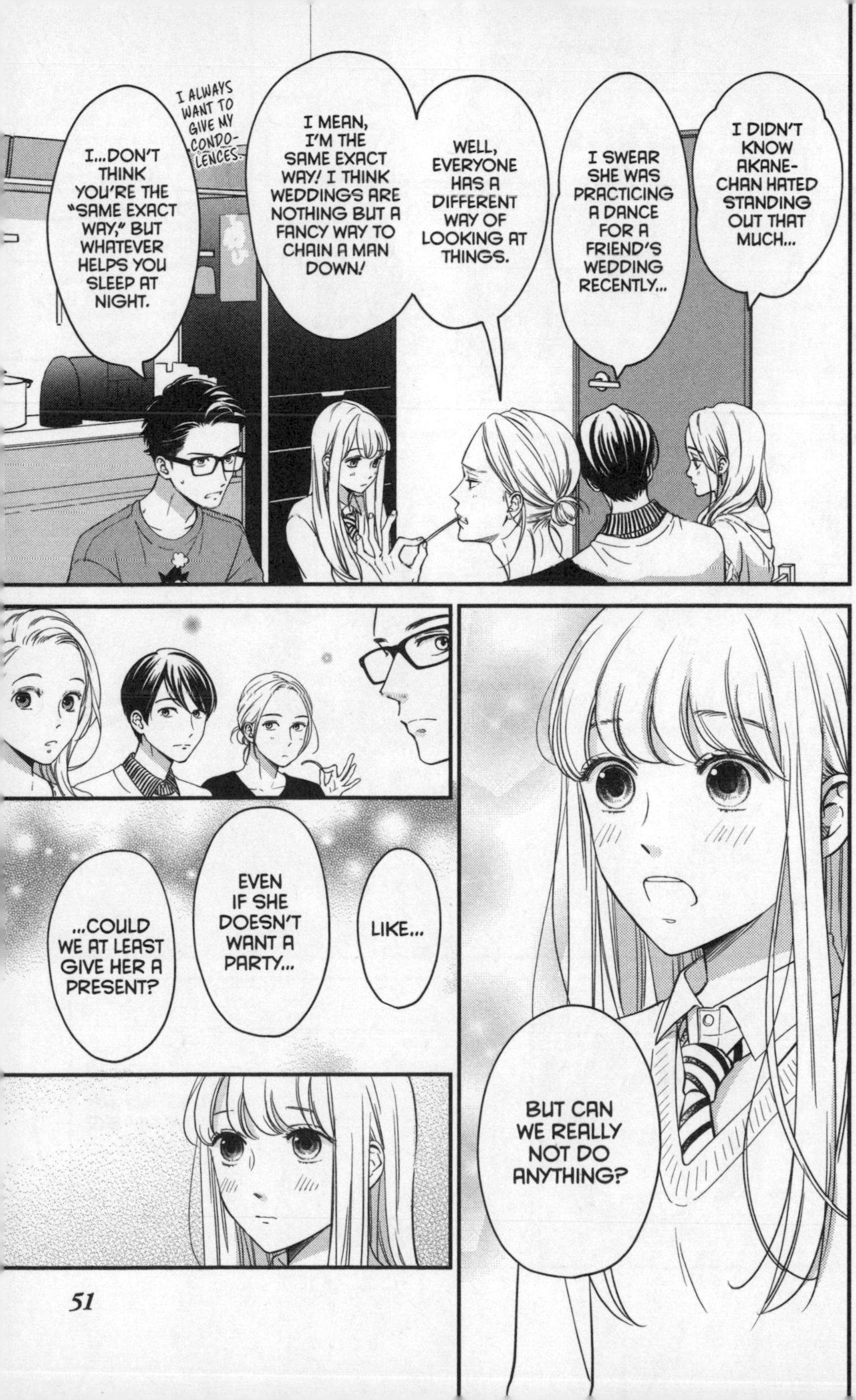
I DIDN'T KNOW AKANE-CHAN HATED STANDING OUT THAT MUCH...
I SWEAR SHE WAS PRACTICING A DANCE FOR A FRIEND'S WEDDING RECENTLY...
WELL, EVERYONE HAS A DIFFERENT WAY OF LOOKING AT THINGS.
I MEAN, I'M THE SAME EXACT WAY! I THINK WEDDINGS ARE NOTHING BUT A FANCY WAY TO CHAIN A MAN DOWN!
I ALWAYS WANT TO GIVE MY CONDO-LENCES.
I...DON'T THINK YOU'RE THE "SAME EXACT WAY," BUT WHATEVER HELPS YOU SLEEP AT NIGHT.
BUT CAN WE REALLY NOT DO ANYTHING?
LIKE...
EVEN IF SHE DOESN'T WANT A PARTY...
...COULD WE AT LEAST GIVE HER A PRESENT?

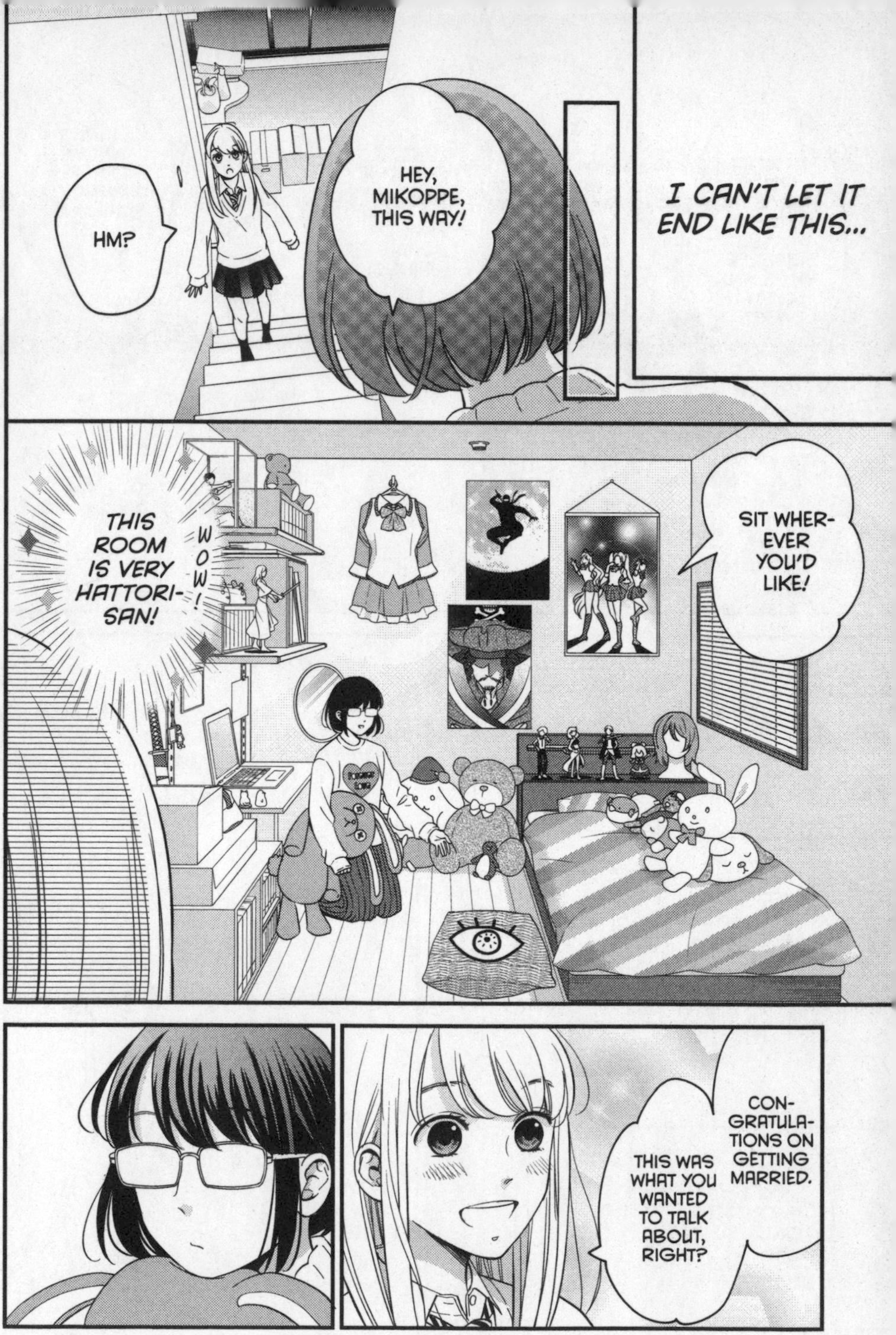
I CAN'T LET IT END LIKE THIS...
HEY, MIKOPPE, THIS WAY!
HM?
SIT WHEREVER YOU'D LIKE!
WOW!
THIS ROOM IS VERY HATTORI-SAN!
CONGRATULATIONS ON GETTING MARRIED.
THIS WAS WHAT YOU WANTED TO TALK ABOUT, RIGHT?

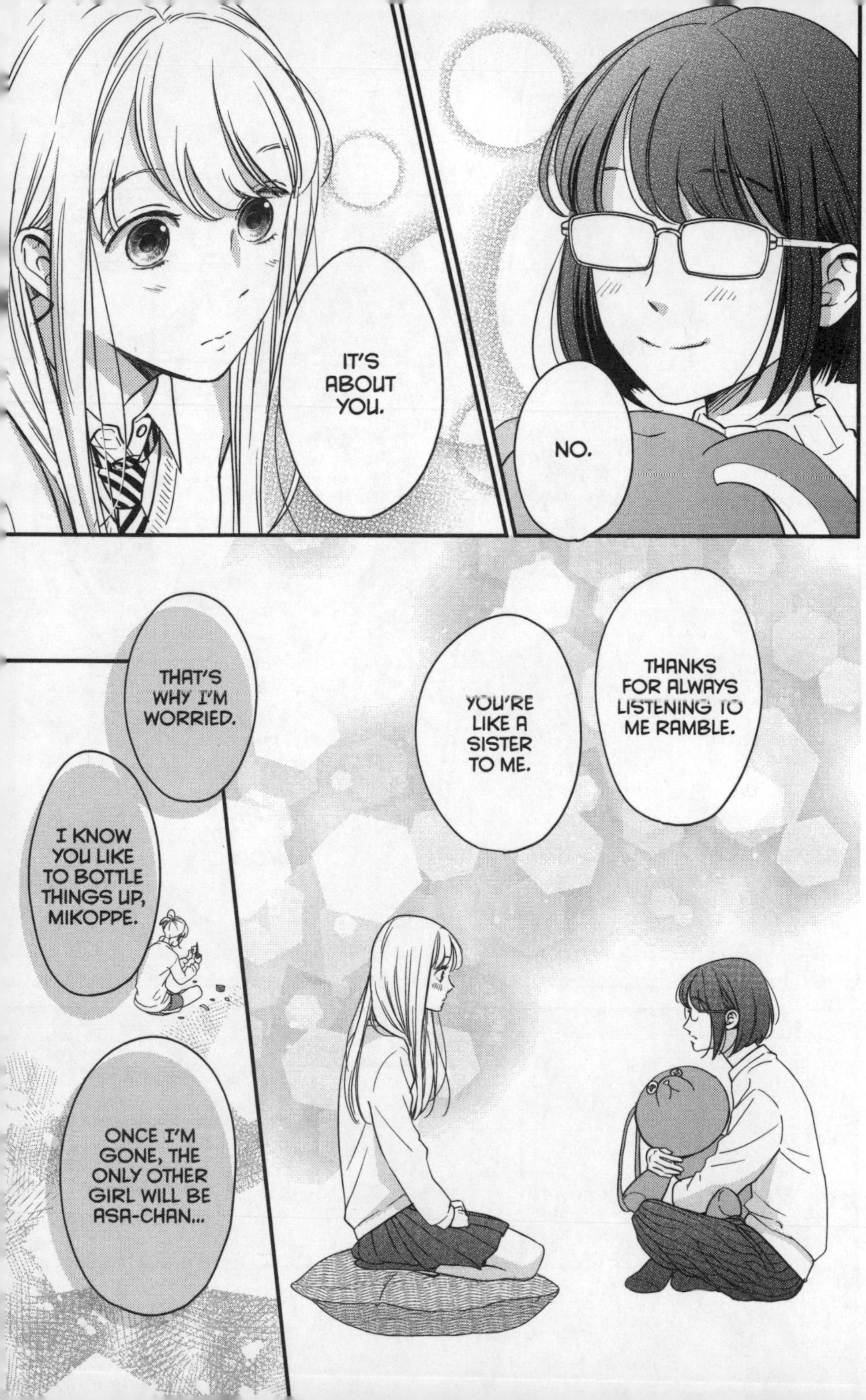
NO.
IT'S ABOUT YOU.
THANKS FOR ALWAYS LISTENING TO ME RAMBLE.
YOU'RE LIKE A SISTER TO ME.
THAT'S WHY I'M WORRIED.
I KNOW YOU LIKE TO BOTTLE THINGS UP, MIKOPPE.
ONCE I'M GONE, THE ONLY OTHER GIRL WILL BE ASA-CHAN...

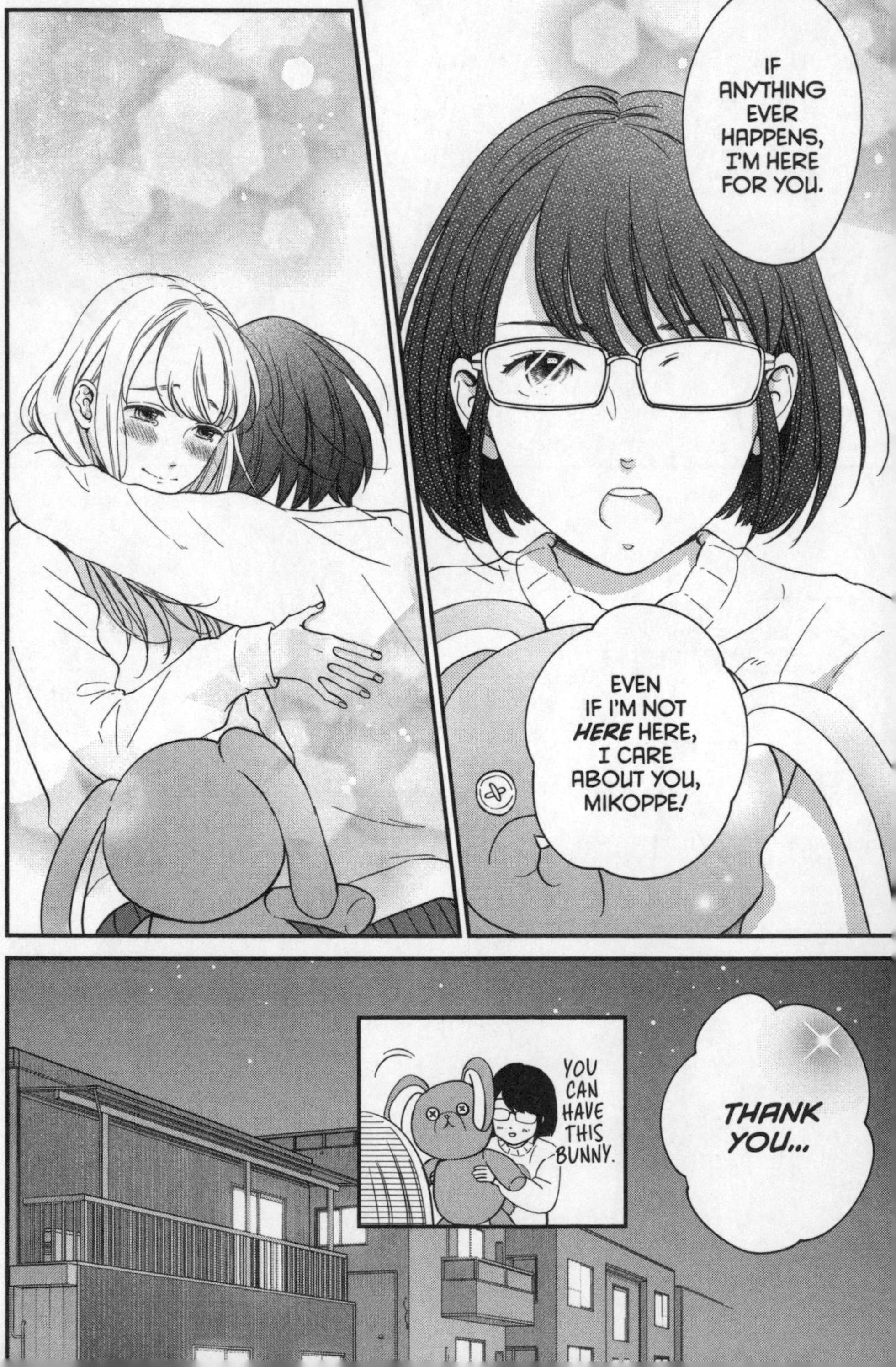
IF ANYTHING EVER HAPPENS, I'M HERE FOR YOU.
EVEN IF I'M NOT *HERE* HERE, I CARE ABOUT YOU, MIKOPPE!
THANK YOU...
YOU CAN HAVE THIS BUNNY.

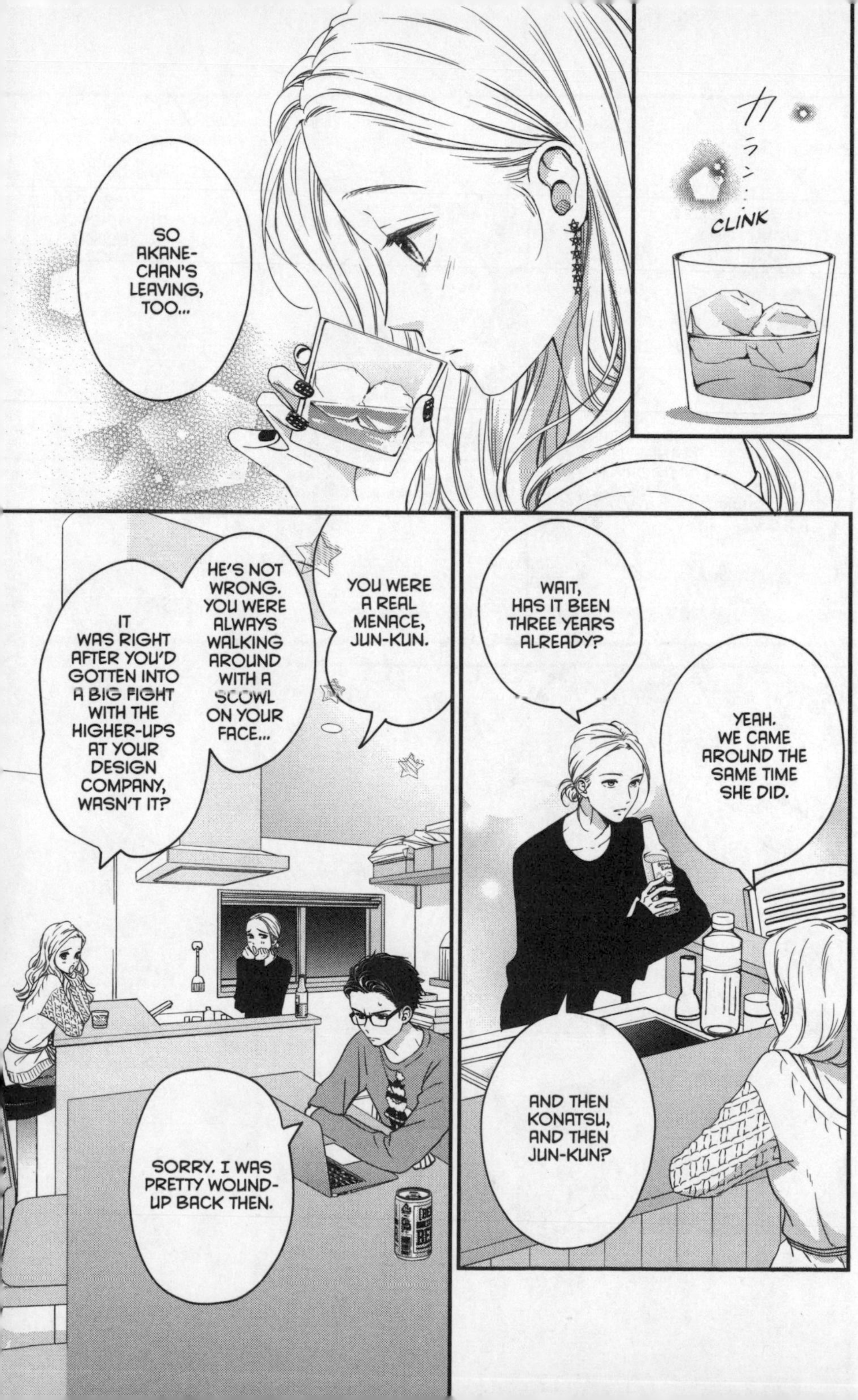
カラン…
CLINK
SO AKANE-CHAN'S LEAVING, TOO...
WAIT, HAS IT BEEN THREE YEARS ALREADY?
YEAH. WE CAME AROUND THE SAME TIME SHE DID.
AND THEN KONATSU, AND THEN JUN-KUN?
YOU WERE A REAL MENACE, JUN-KUN.
HE'S NOT WRONG. YOU WERE ALWAYS WALKING AROUND WITH A SCOWL ON YOUR FACE...
IT WAS RIGHT AFTER YOU'D GOTTEN INTO A BIG FIGHT WITH THE HIGHER-UPS AT YOUR DESIGN COMPANY, WASN'T IT?
SORRY. I WAS PRETTY WOUND-UP BACK THEN.

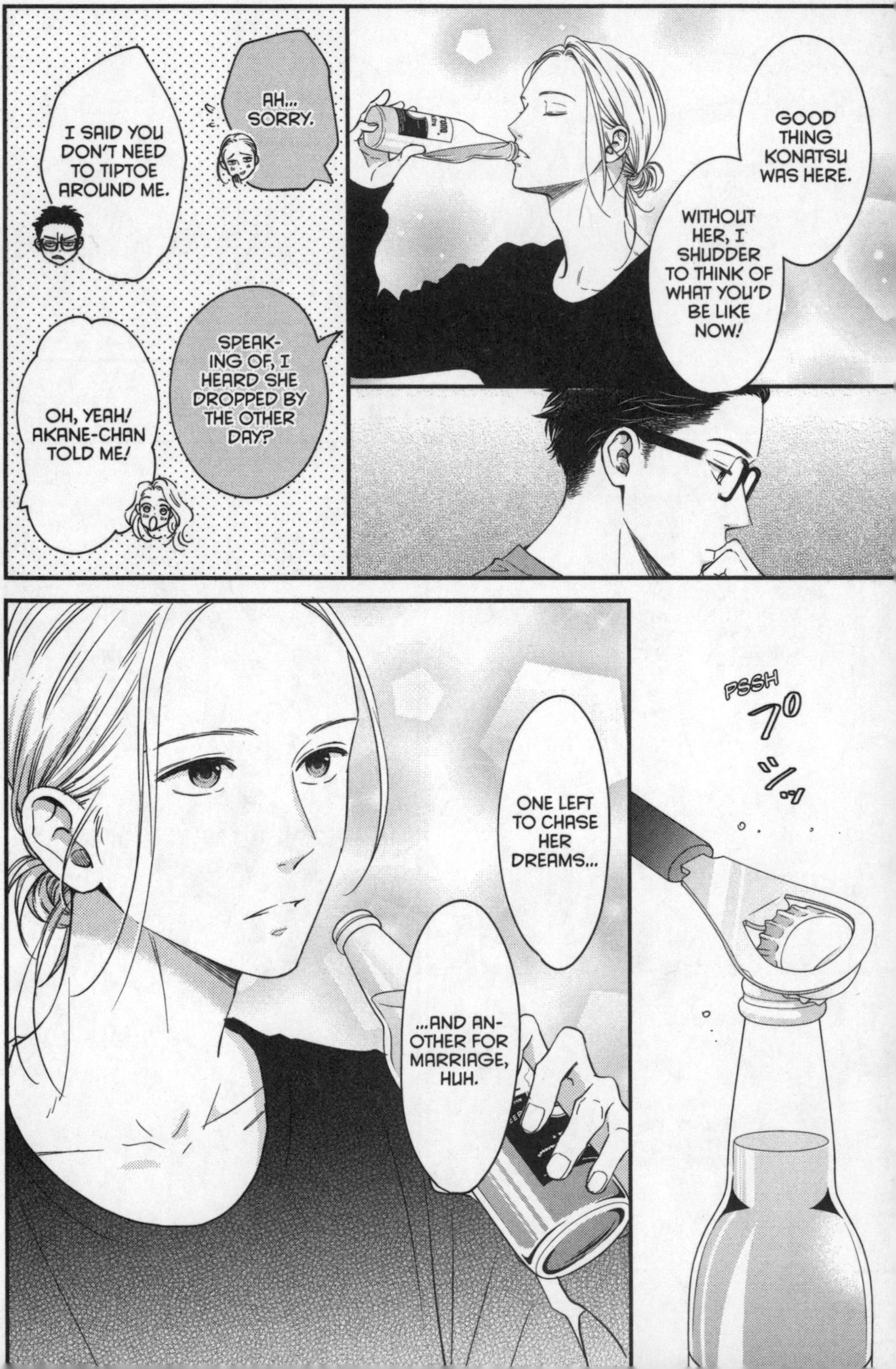
GOOD THING KONATSU WAS HERE.
WITHOUT HER, I SHUDDER TO THINK OF WHAT YOU'D BE LIKE NOW!
AH... SORRY.
I SAID YOU DON'T NEED TO TIPTOE AROUND ME.
SPEAKING OF, I HEARD SHE DROPPED BY THE OTHER DAY?
OH, YEAH! AKANE-CHAN TOLD ME!
PSSH
ONE LEFT TO CHASE HER DREAMS...
...AND ANOTHER FOR MARRIAGE, HUH.

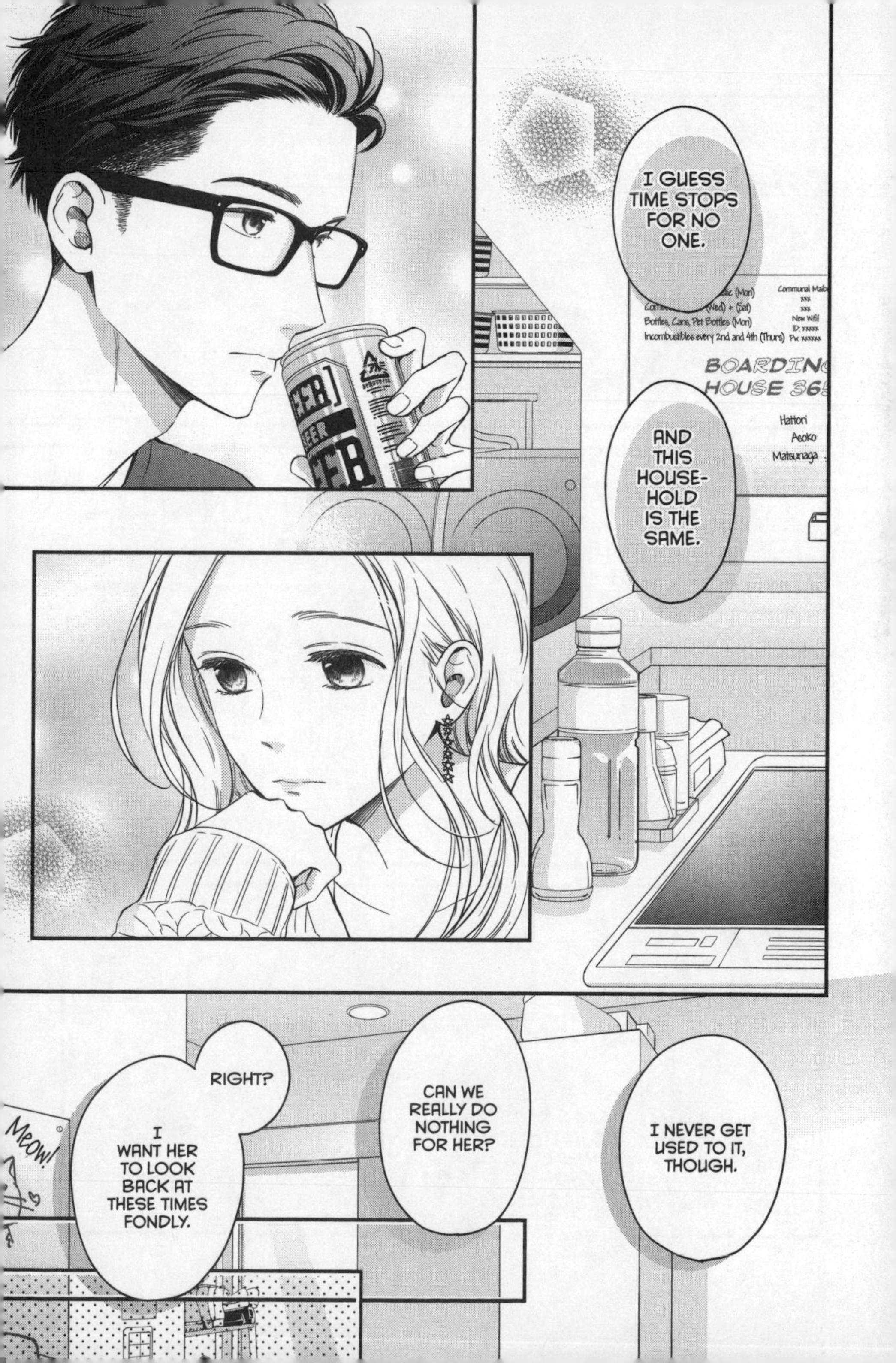
I GUESS TIME STOPS FOR NO ONE.
Bottles, Cans, Pet Bottles (Mon)
Incombustibles every 2nd and 4th (Thurs)
New Wifi!
Hattori
Asoko
Matsunaga
AND THIS HOUSE-HOLD IS THE SAME.
I NEVER GET USED TO IT, THOUGH.
CAN WE REALLY DO NOTHING FOR HER?
RIGHT?
I WANT HER TO LOOK BACK AT THESE TIMES FONDLY.
MEOW!

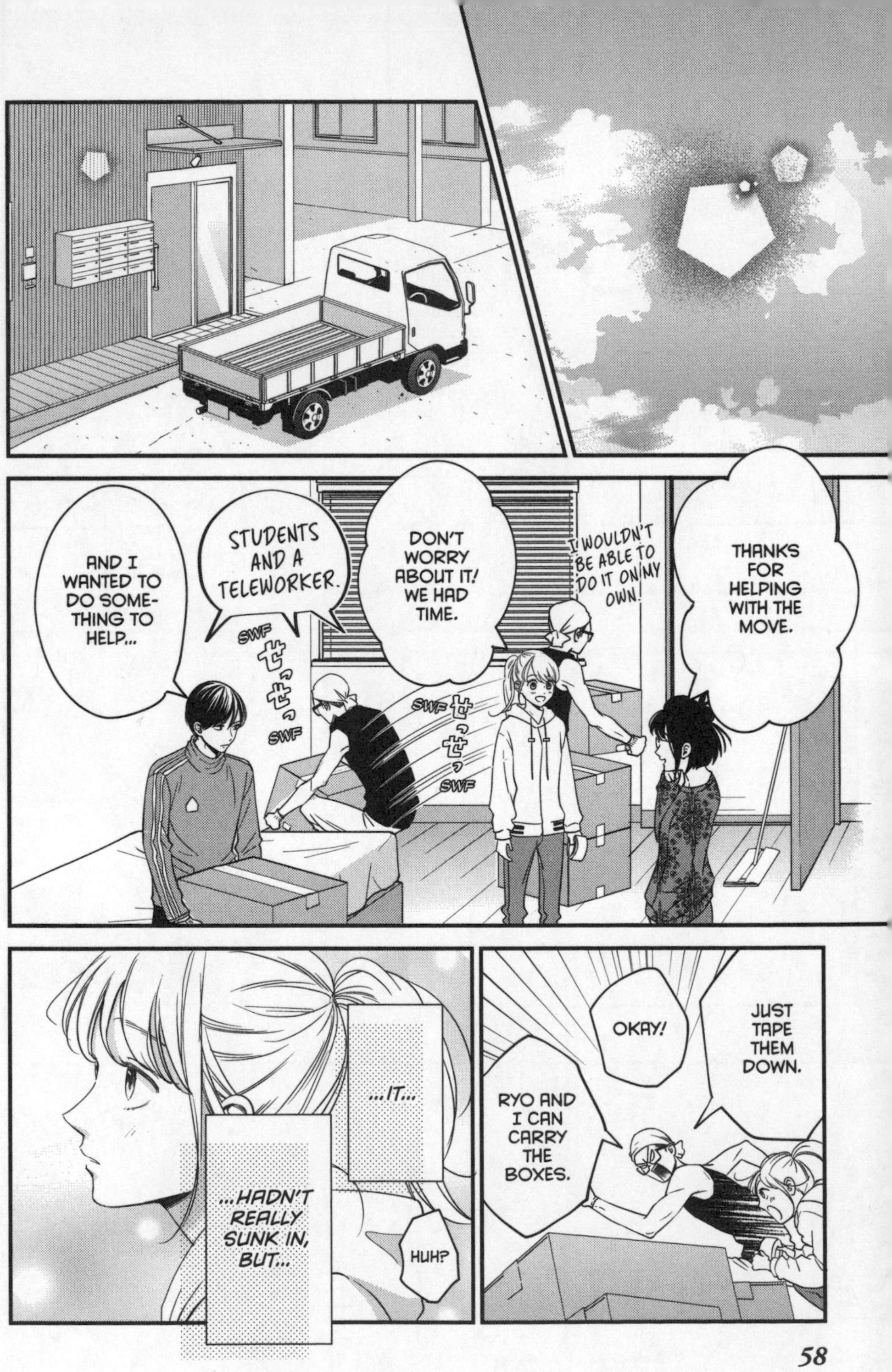
THANKS FOR HELPING WITH THE MOVE.
I WOULDN'T BE ABLE TO DO IT ON MY OWN!
DON'T WORRY ABOUT IT! WE HAD TIME.
SWF せっせっ SWF
SWF せっせっ SWF
STUDENTS AND A TELEWORKER.
AND I WANTED TO DO SOME-THING TO HELP...
JUST TAPE THEM DOWN.
OKAY!
RYO AND I CAN CARRY THE BOXES.
...IT...
HUH?
...HADN'T REALLY SUNK IN, BUT...

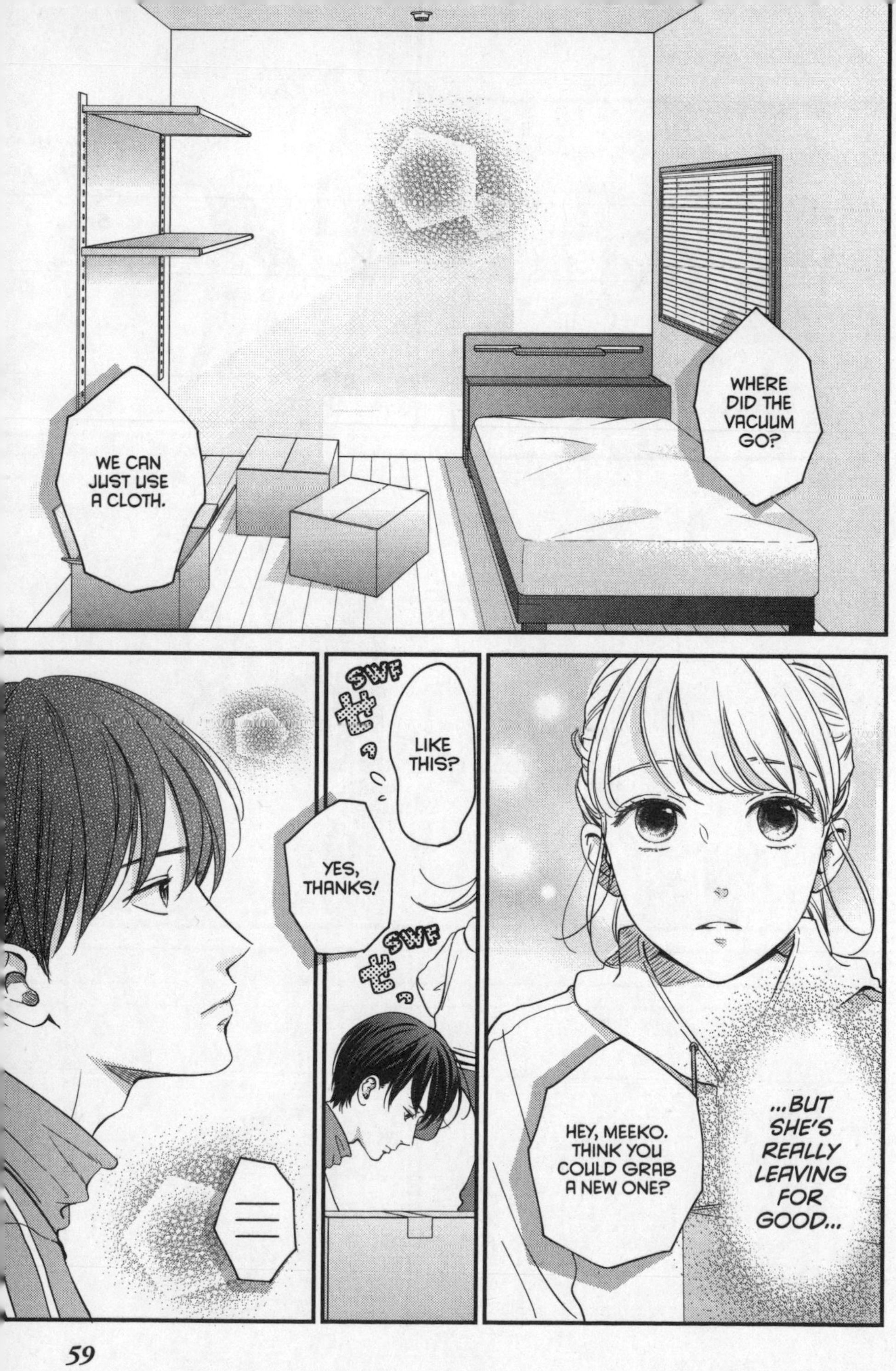
WHERE DID THE VACUUM GO?
WE CAN JUST USE A CLOTH.
...BUT SHE'S REALLY LEAVING FOR GOOD...
HEY, MEEKO. THINK YOU COULD GRAB A NEW ONE?
SWF
LIKE THIS?
YES, THANKS!
SWF
———

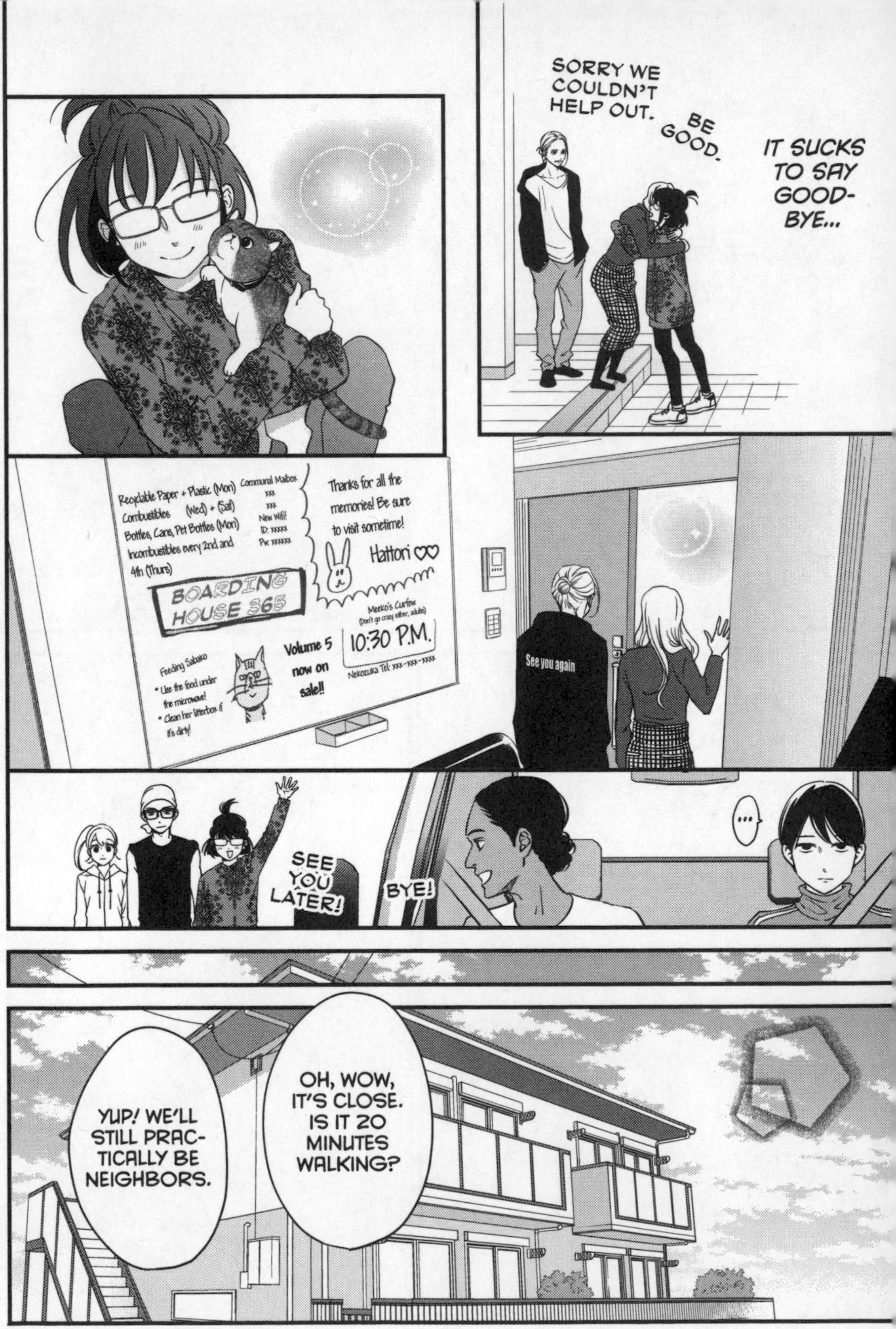
IT SUCKS TO SAY GOOD-BYE...
BE GOOD.
SORRY WE COULDN'T HELP OUT.
See you again
Recyclable Paper + Plastic (Mon)
Combustibles (Wed) + (Sat)
Bottles, Cans, Pet Bottles (Mon)
Incombustibles every 2nd and 4th (Thurs)
Communal Mailbox
xxx
xxx
New Wifi!
ID: xxxxx
Pw: xxxxxx
Thanks for all the memories! Be sure to visit sometime!
Hattori ♡♡
BOARDING HOUSE 365
Meeko's Curfew
(Don't go crazy either, adults)
10:30 P.M.
Nekozuka Tel: xxx-xxx-xxxx
Volume 5 now on sale!!
Feeding Sabako
• Use the food under the microwave!
• Clean her litterbox if it's dirty!
...
BYE!
SEE YOU LATER!
OH, WOW, IT'S CLOSE. IS IT 20 MINUTES WALKING?
YUP! WE'LL STILL PRAC-TICALLY BE NEIGHBORS.

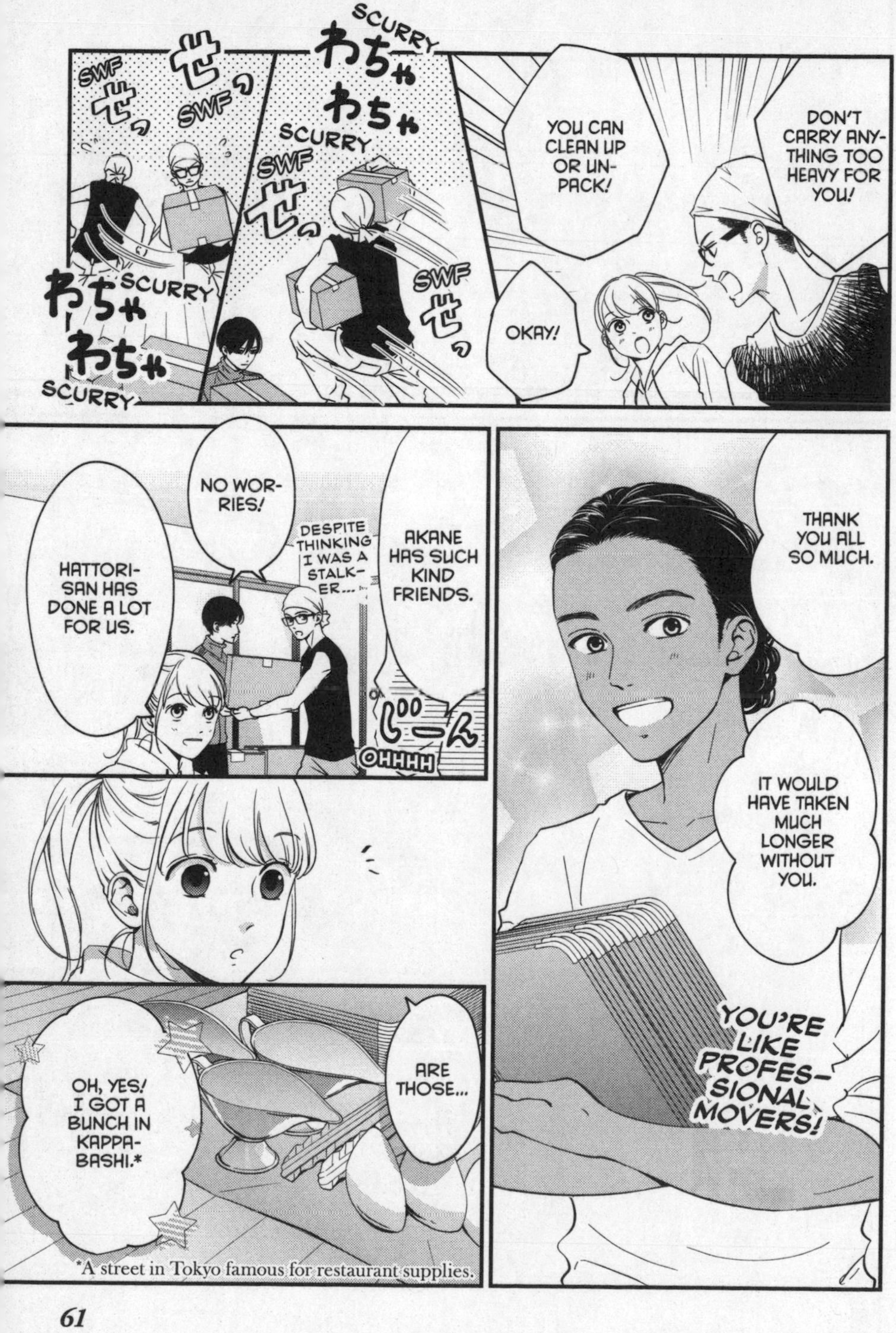
DON'T CARRY ANYTHING TOO HEAVY FOR YOU!
YOU CAN CLEAN UP OR UNPACK!
OKAY!
SCURRY わちゃ
わちゃ SCURRY
SWF ぜっ
SWF ぜっ
ぜ
SWF ぜっ
SWF
わちゃ SCURRY
わちゃ SCURRY
THANK YOU ALL SO MUCH.
IT WOULD HAVE TAKEN MUCH LONGER WITHOUT YOU.
YOU'RE LIKE PROFESSIONAL MOVERS!
AKANE HAS SUCH KIND FRIENDS.
DESPITE THINKING I WAS A STALKER...
NO WORRIES!
HATTORI-SAN HAS DONE A LOT FOR US.
じーん OHHHH
ARE THOSE...
OH, YES! I GOT A BUNCH IN KAPPABASHI.*
*A street in Tokyo famous for restaurant supplies.

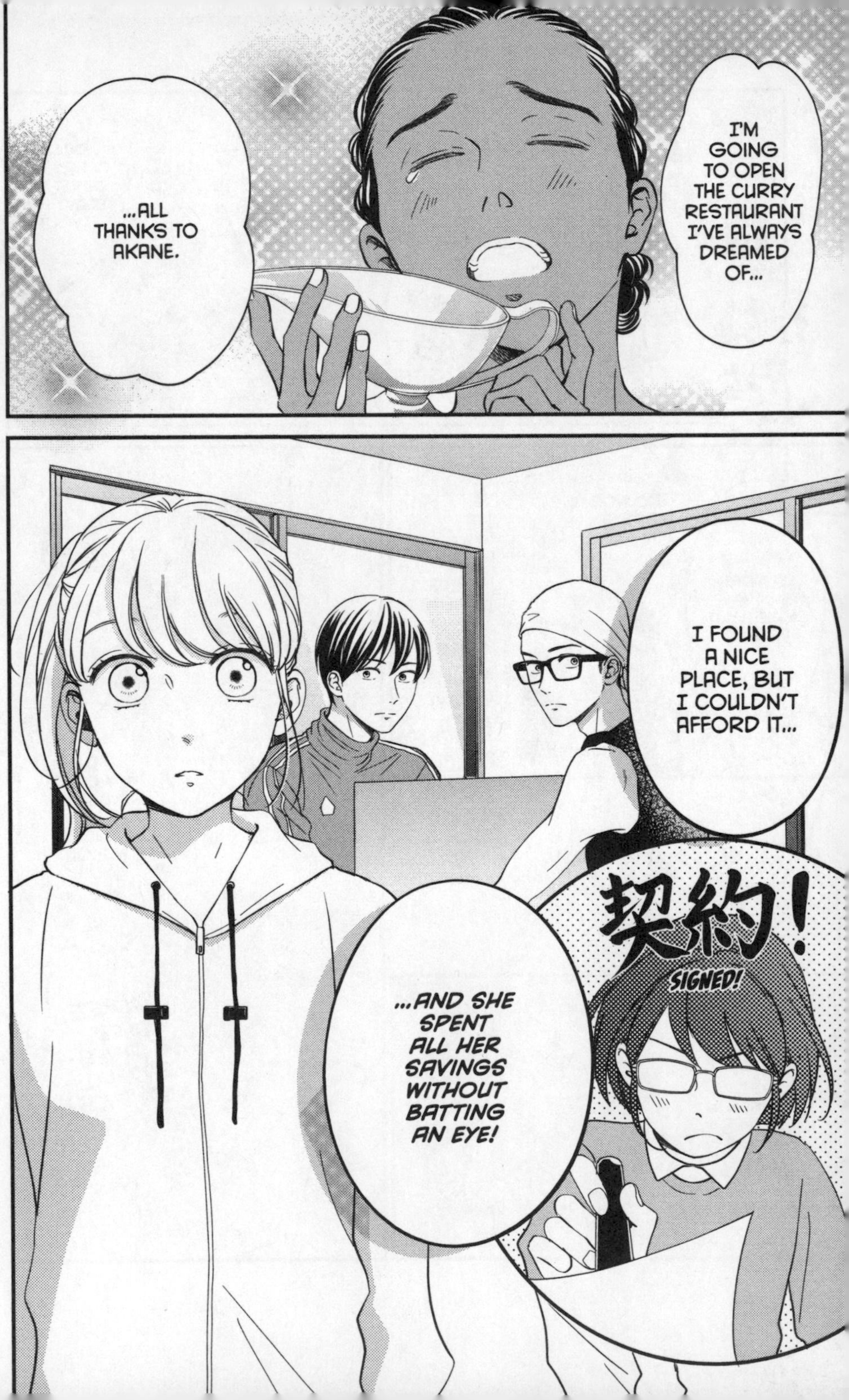
I'M GOING TO OPEN THE CURRY RESTAURANT I'VE ALWAYS DREAMED OF...
...ALL THANKS TO AKANE.
I FOUND A NICE PLACE, BUT I COULDN'T AFFORD IT...
契約!
SIGNED!
...AND SHE SPENT ALL HER SAVINGS WITHOUT BATTING AN EYE!

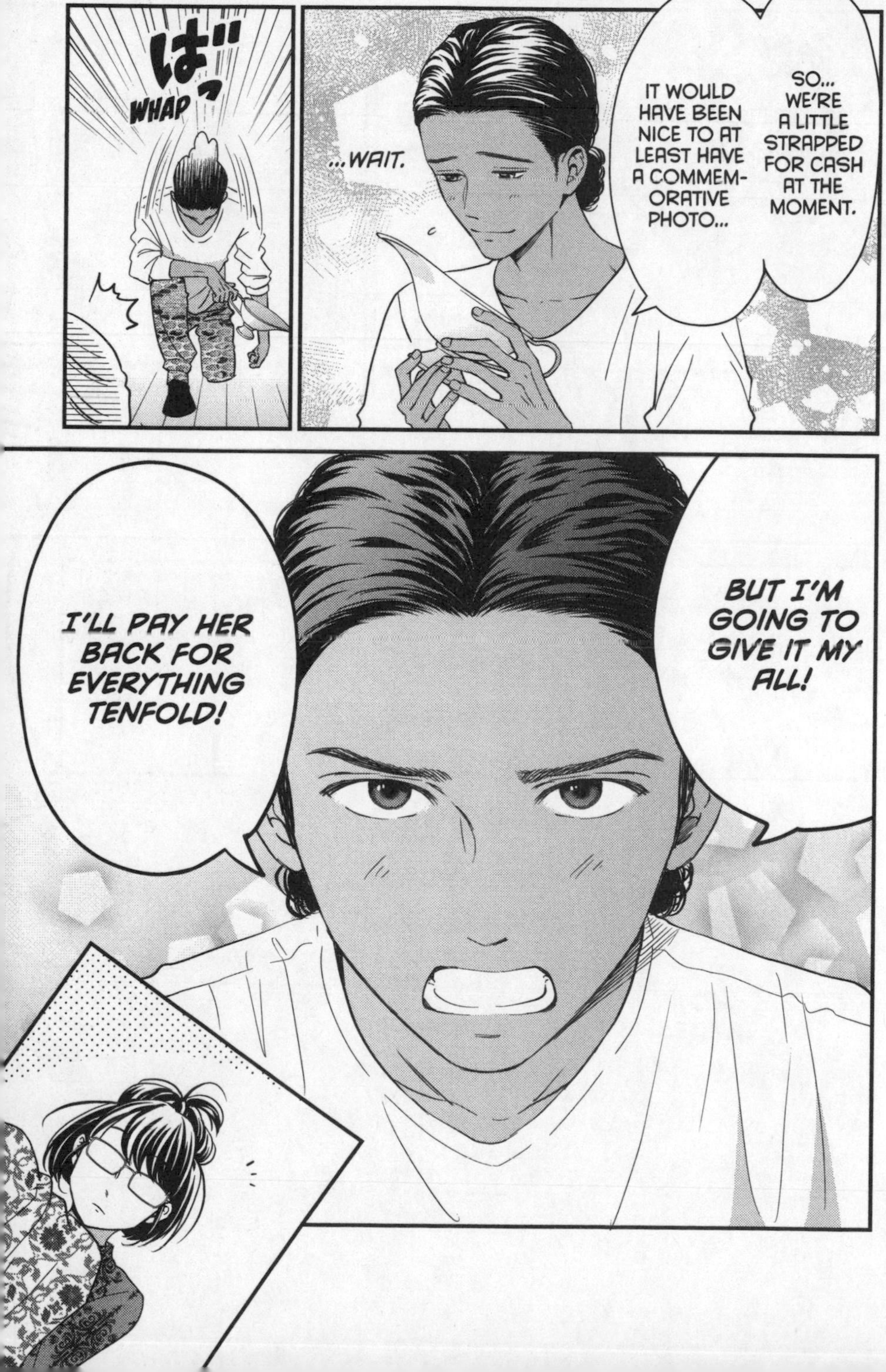
SO... WE'RE A LITTLE STRAPPED FOR CASH AT THE MOMENT.
IT WOULD HAVE BEEN NICE TO AT LEAST HAVE A COMMEM-ORATIVE PHOTO...
...WAIT.
ばっ
WHAP
BUT I'M GOING TO GIVE IT MY ALL!
I'LL PAY HER BACK FOR EVERYTHING TENFOLD!

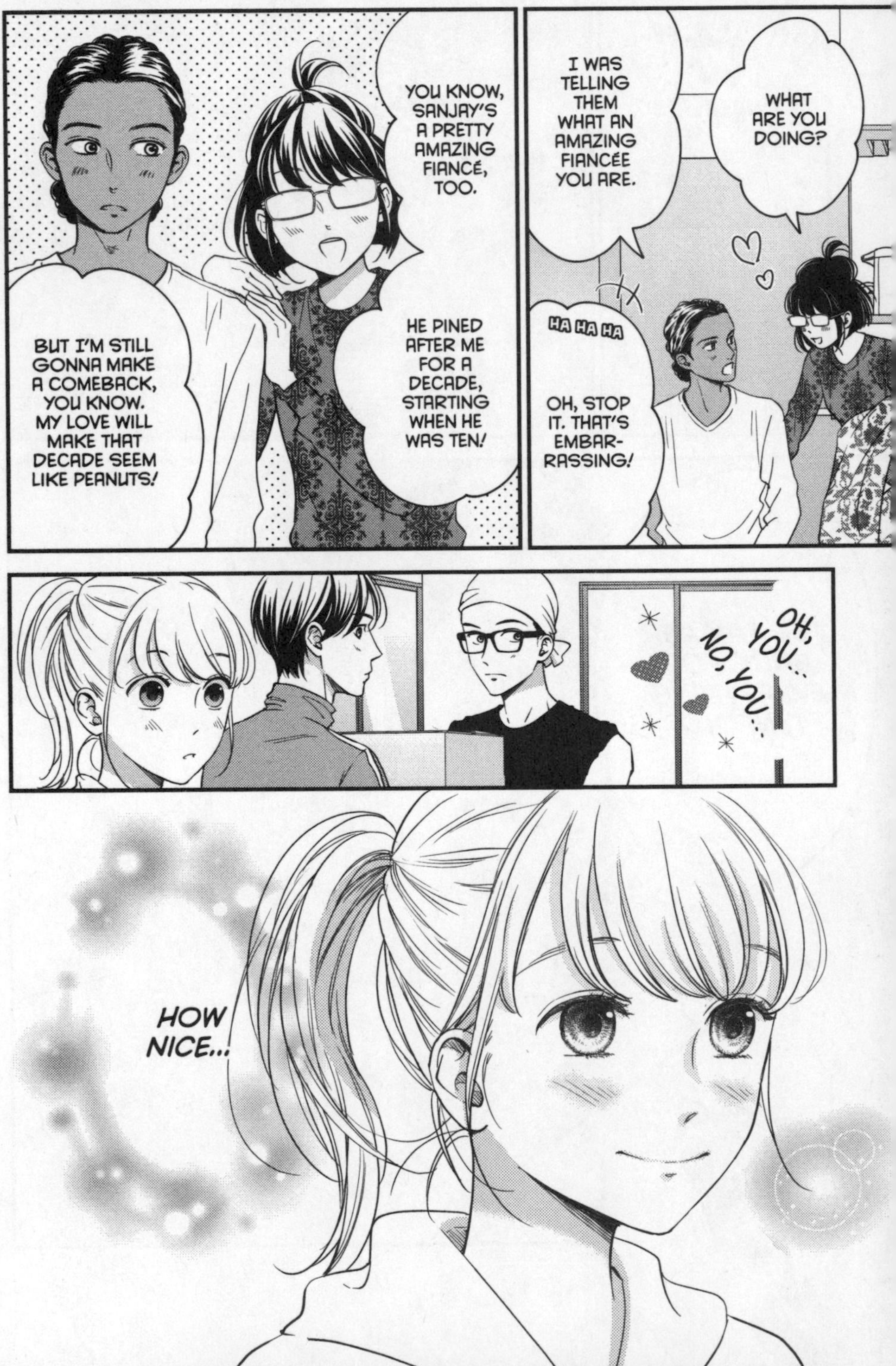
WHAT ARE YOU DOING?
I WAS TELLING THEM WHAT AN AMAZING FIANCÉE YOU ARE.
HA HA HA
OH, STOP IT. THAT'S EMBAR-RASSING!
YOU KNOW, SANJAY'S A PRETTY AMAZING FIANCÉ, TOO.
HE PINED AFTER ME FOR A DECADE, STARTING WHEN HE WAS TEN!
BUT I'M STILL GONNA MAKE A COMEBACK, YOU KNOW. MY LOVE WILL MAKE THAT DECADE SEEM LIKE PEANUTS!
OH, YOU...
NO, YOU...
HOW NICE...

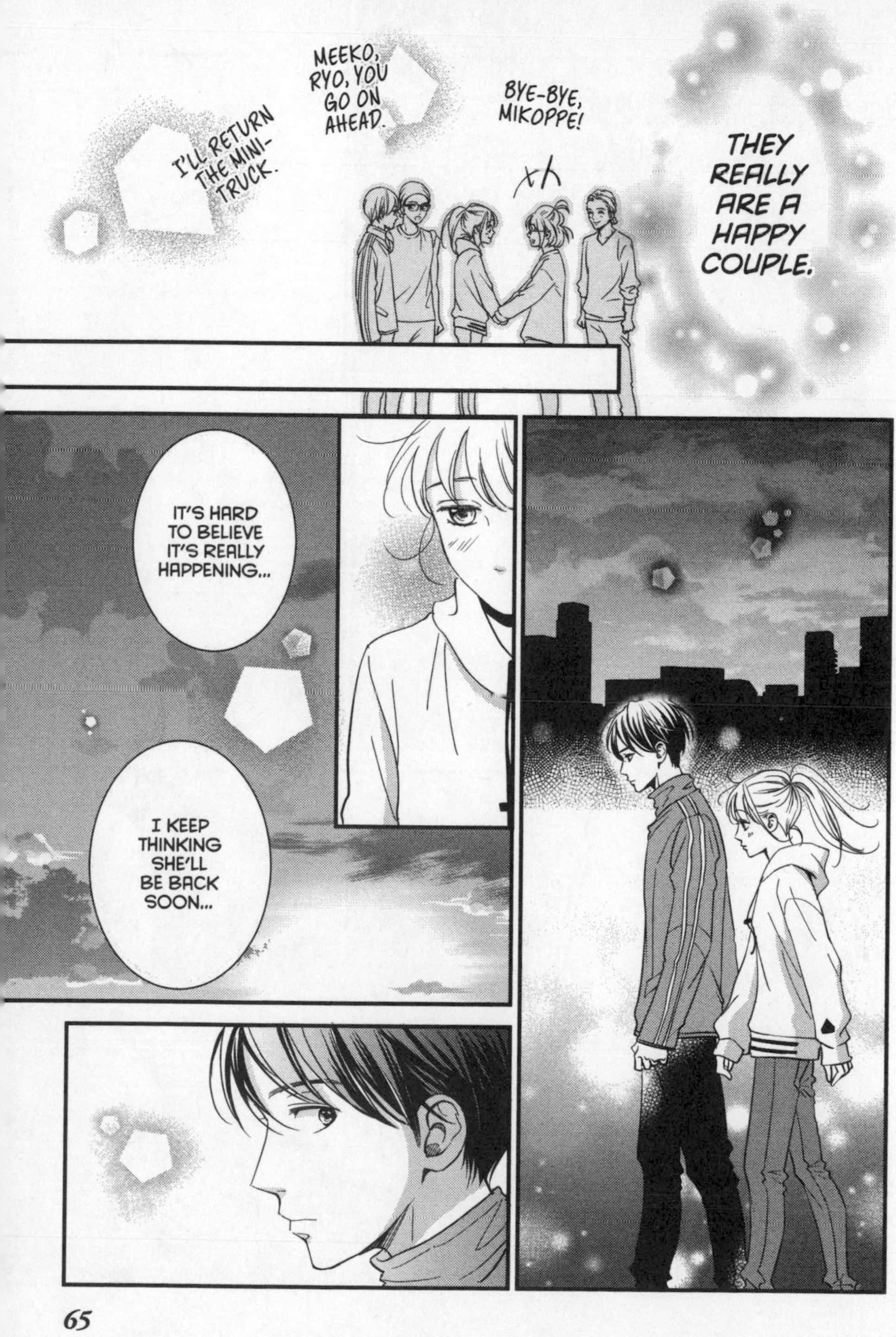
THEY REALLY ARE A HAPPY COUPLE.
BYE-BYE, MIKOPPE!
MEEKO, RYO, YOU GO ON AHEAD.
I'LL RETURN THE MINI-TRUCK.
IT'S HARD TO BELIEVE IT'S REALLY HAPPENING...
I KEEP THINKING SHE'LL BE BACK SOON...

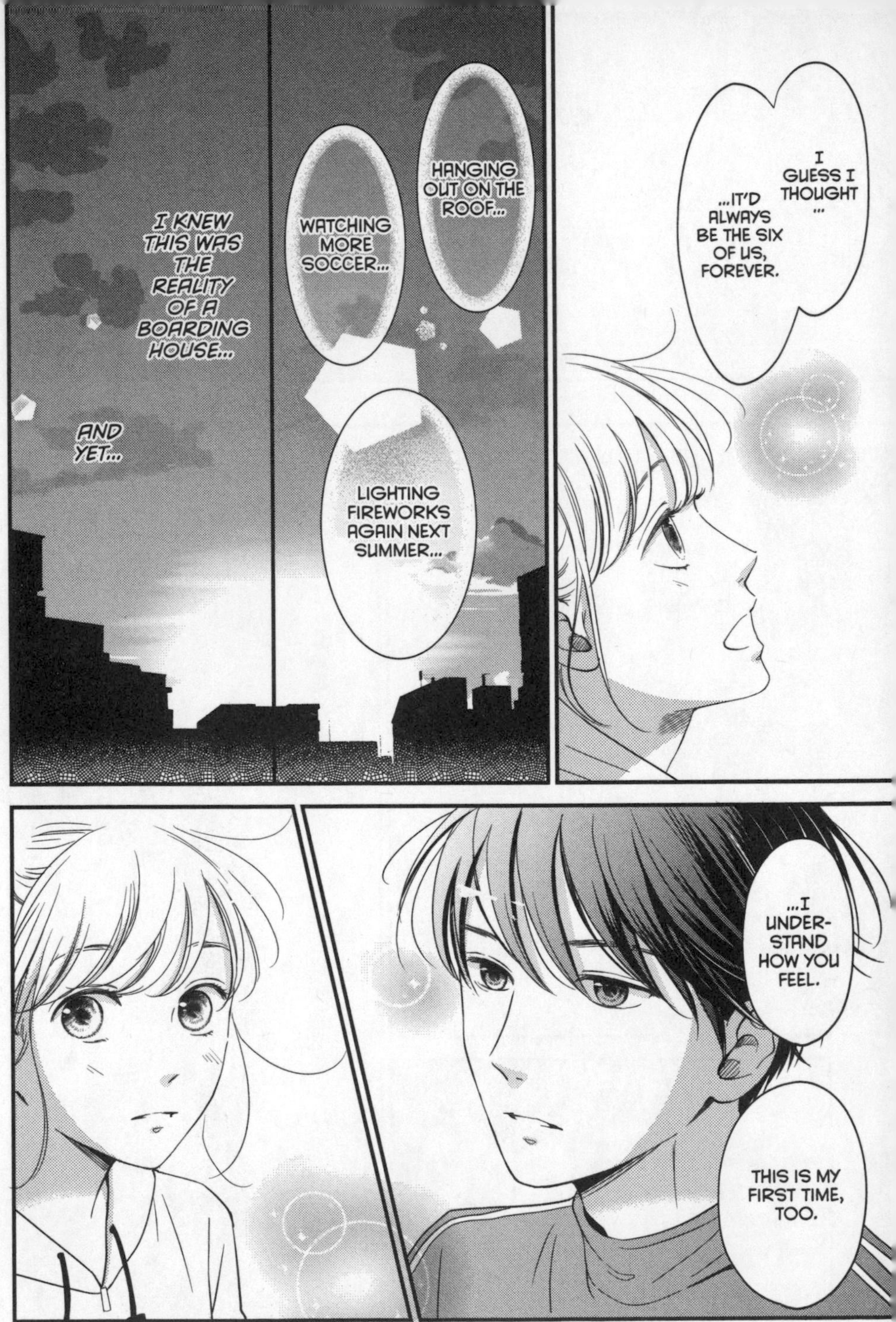
I GUESS I THOUGHT...
...IT'D ALWAYS BE THE SIX OF US, FOREVER.
HANGING OUT ON THE ROOF...
WATCHING MORE SOCCER...
LIGHTING FIREWORKS AGAIN NEXT SUMMER...
I KNEW THIS WAS THE REALITY OF A BOARDING HOUSE...
AND YET...
...I UNDER-STAND HOW YOU FEEL.
THIS IS MY FIRST TIME, TOO.

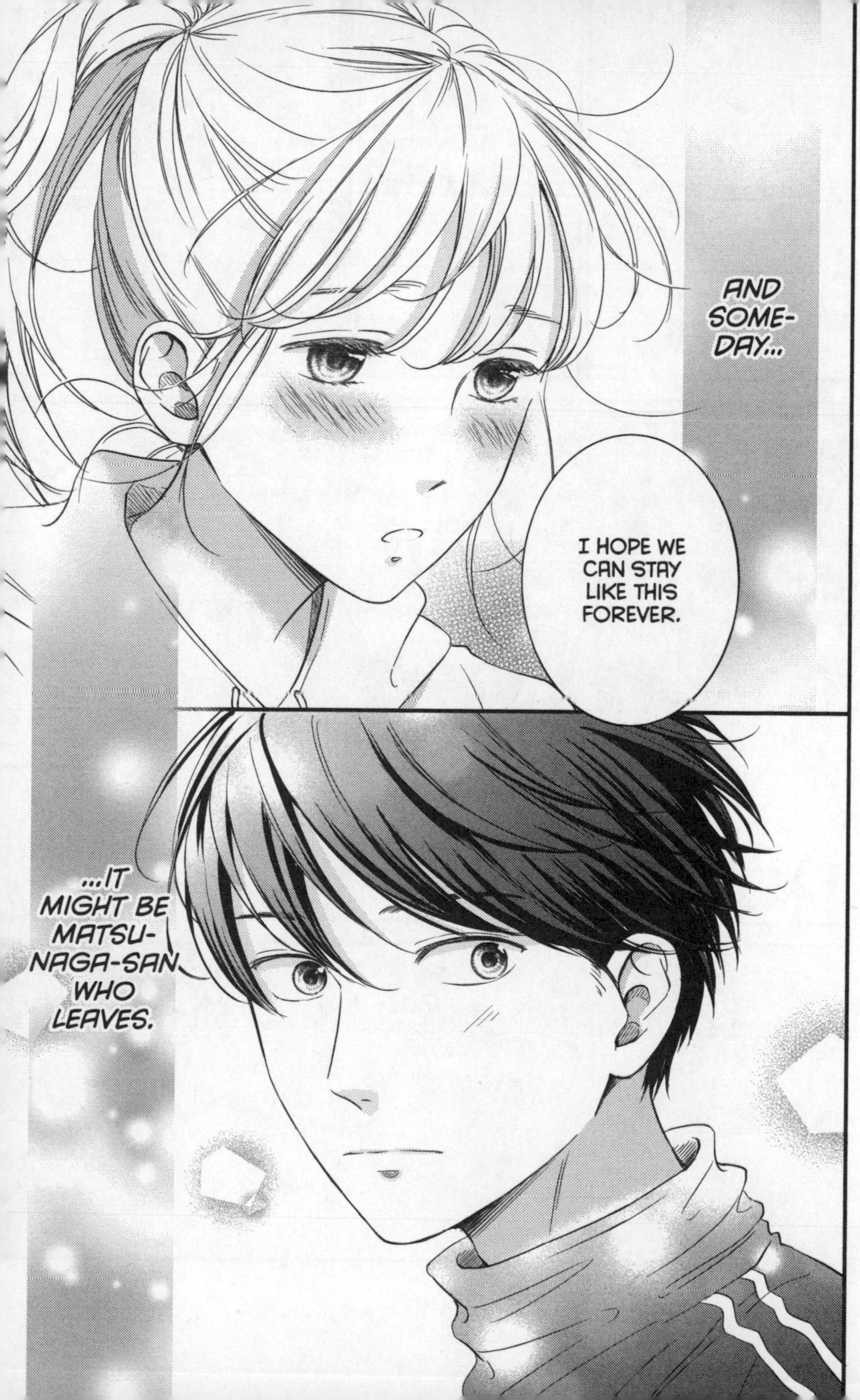
AND SOMEDAY...
I HOPE WE CAN STAY LIKE THIS FOREVER.
...IT MIGHT BE MATSUNAGA-SAN WHO LEAVES.

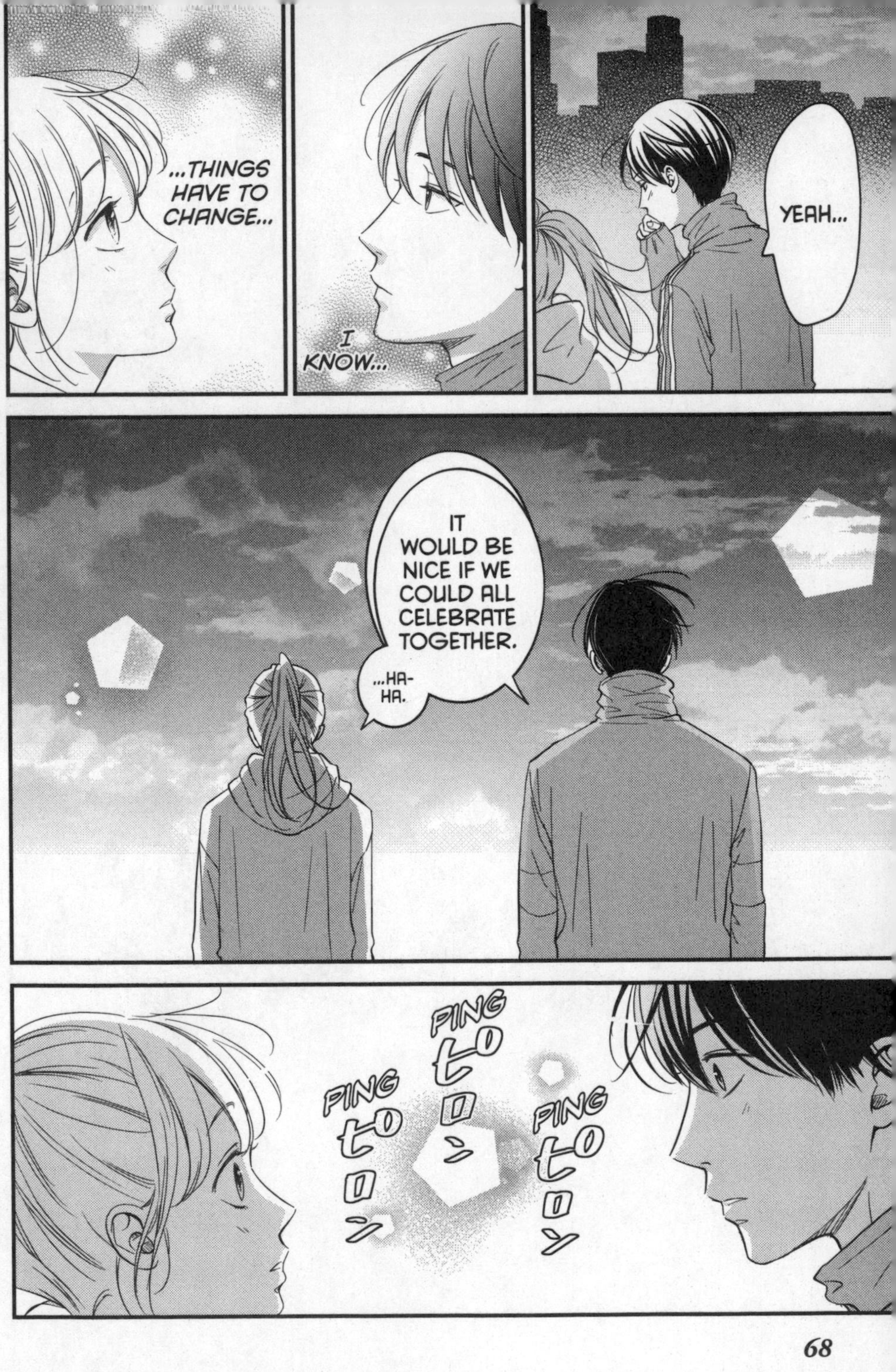
YEAH...
I KNOW...
...THINGS HAVE TO CHANGE...
IT WOULD BE NICE IF WE COULD ALL CELEBRATE TOGETHER.
...HA-HA.
PING ピロン
PING ピロン
PING ピロン

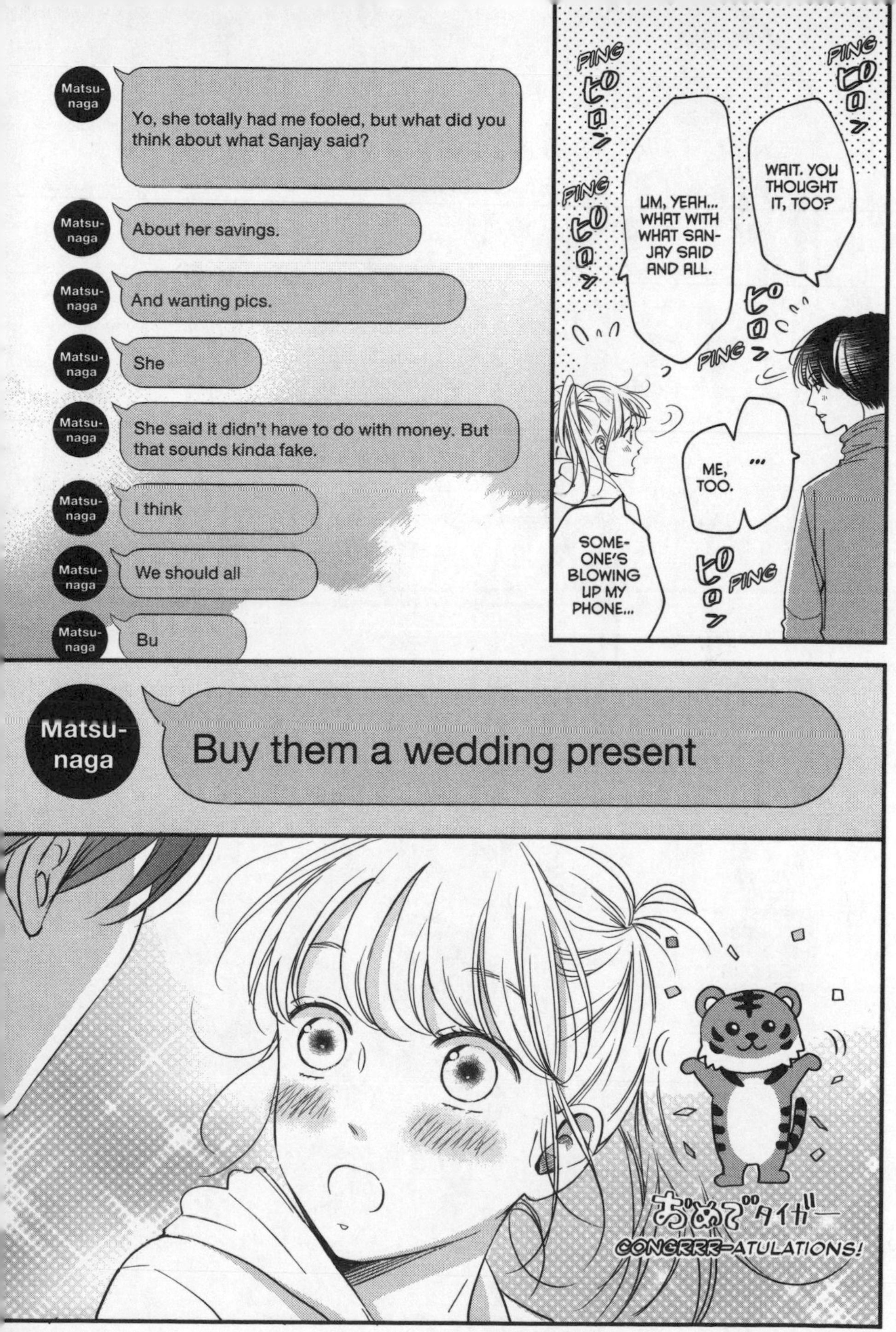
PING ピロン
WAIT. YOU THOUGHT IT, TOO?
PING ピロン
UM, YEAH... WHAT WITH WHAT SAN-JAY SAID AND ALL.
ピロン PING
ME, TOO. ...
ピロン PING
SOME-ONE'S BLOWING UP MY PHONE...
Matsu-naga
Yo, she totally had me fooled, but what did you think about what Sanjay said?
Matsu-naga
About her savings.
Matsu-naga
And wanting pics.
Matsu-naga
She
Matsu-naga
She said it didn't have to do with money. But that sounds kinda fake.
Matsu-naga
I think
Matsu-naga
We should all
Matsu-naga
Bu
Matsu-naga
Buy them a wedding present
おめでタイガー
CONGRRR-ATULATIONS!

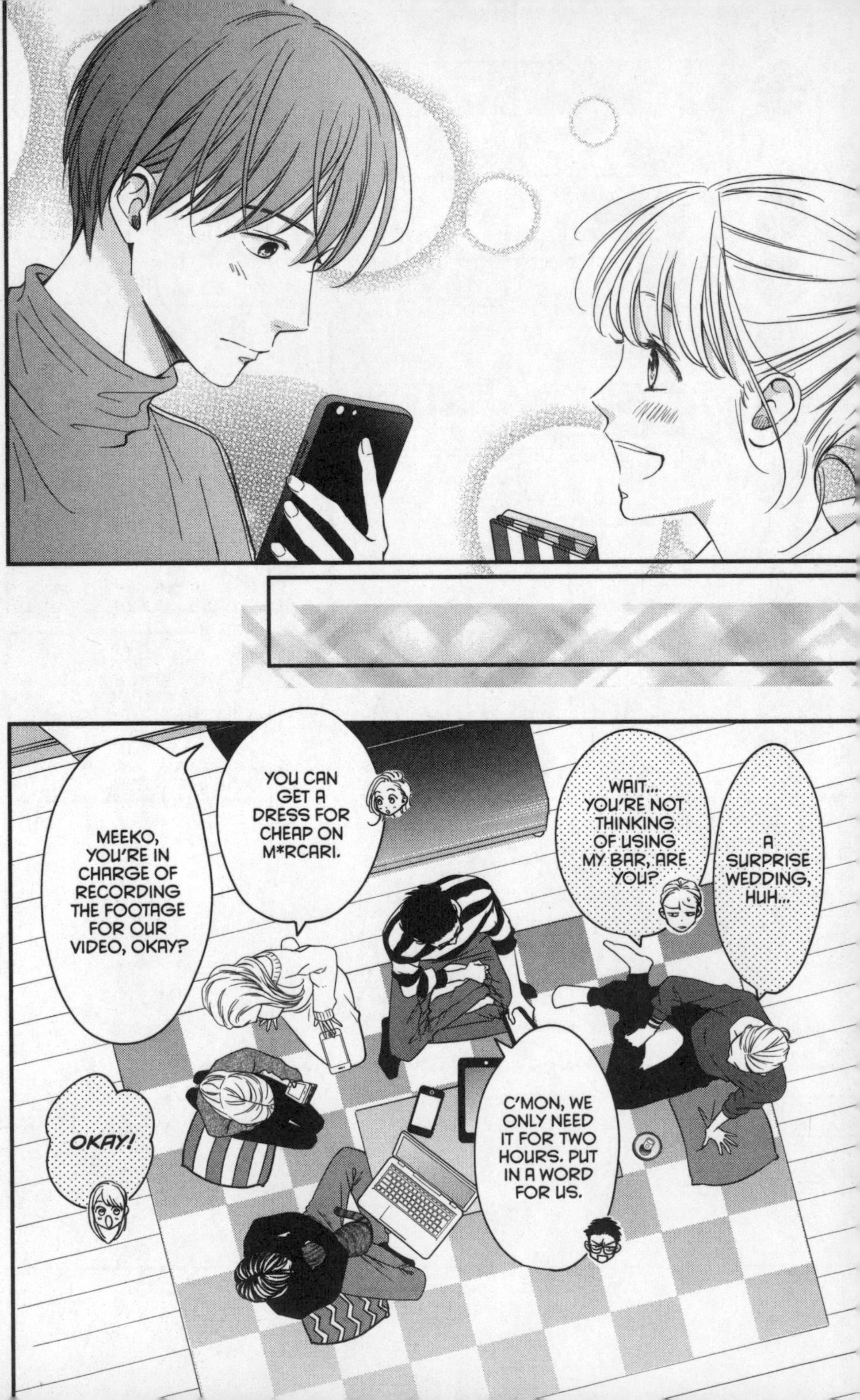
A SURPRISE WEDDING, HUH...
WAIT... YOU'RE NOT THINKING OF USING MY BAR, ARE YOU?
C'MON, WE ONLY NEED IT FOR TWO HOURS. PUT IN A WORD FOR US.
YOU CAN GET A DRESS FOR CHEAP ON M*RCARI.
MEEKO, YOU'RE IN CHARGE OF RECORDING THE FOOTAGE FOR OUR VIDEO, OKAY?
OKAY!

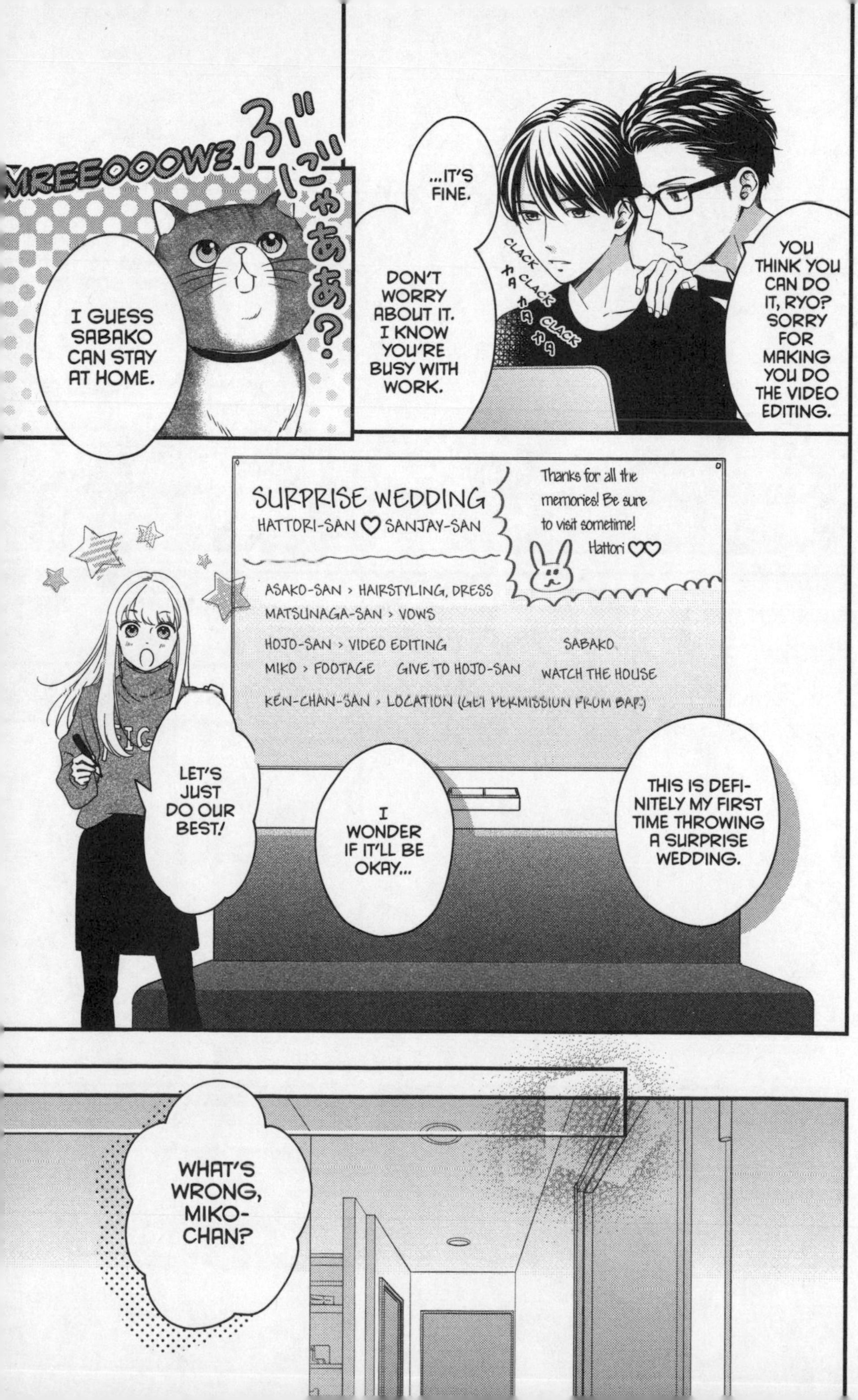
YOU THINK YOU CAN DO IT, RYO? SORRY FOR MAKING YOU DO THE VIDEO EDITING.
CLACK CLACK CLACK
...IT'S FINE.
DON'T WORRY ABOUT IT. I KNOW YOU'RE BUSY WITH WORK.
MREEEOOOW?
I GUESS SABAKO CAN STAY AT HOME.
SURPRISE WEDDING
HATTORI-SAN ♡ SANJAY-SAN
Thanks for all the memories! Be sure to visit sometime! Hattori ♡♡
ASAKO-SAN > HAIRSTYLING, DRESS
MATSUNAGA-SAN > VOWS
HOJO-SAN > VIDEO EDITING
MIKO > FOOTAGE GIVE TO HOJO-SAN
KEN-CHAN-SAN > LOCATION (GET PERMISSION FROM DAD)
SABAKO WATCH THE HOUSE
THIS IS DEFINITELY MY FIRST TIME THROWING A SURPRISE WEDDING.
I WONDER IF IT'LL BE OKAY...
LET'S JUST DO OUR BEST!
WHAT'S WRONG, MIKO-CHAN?

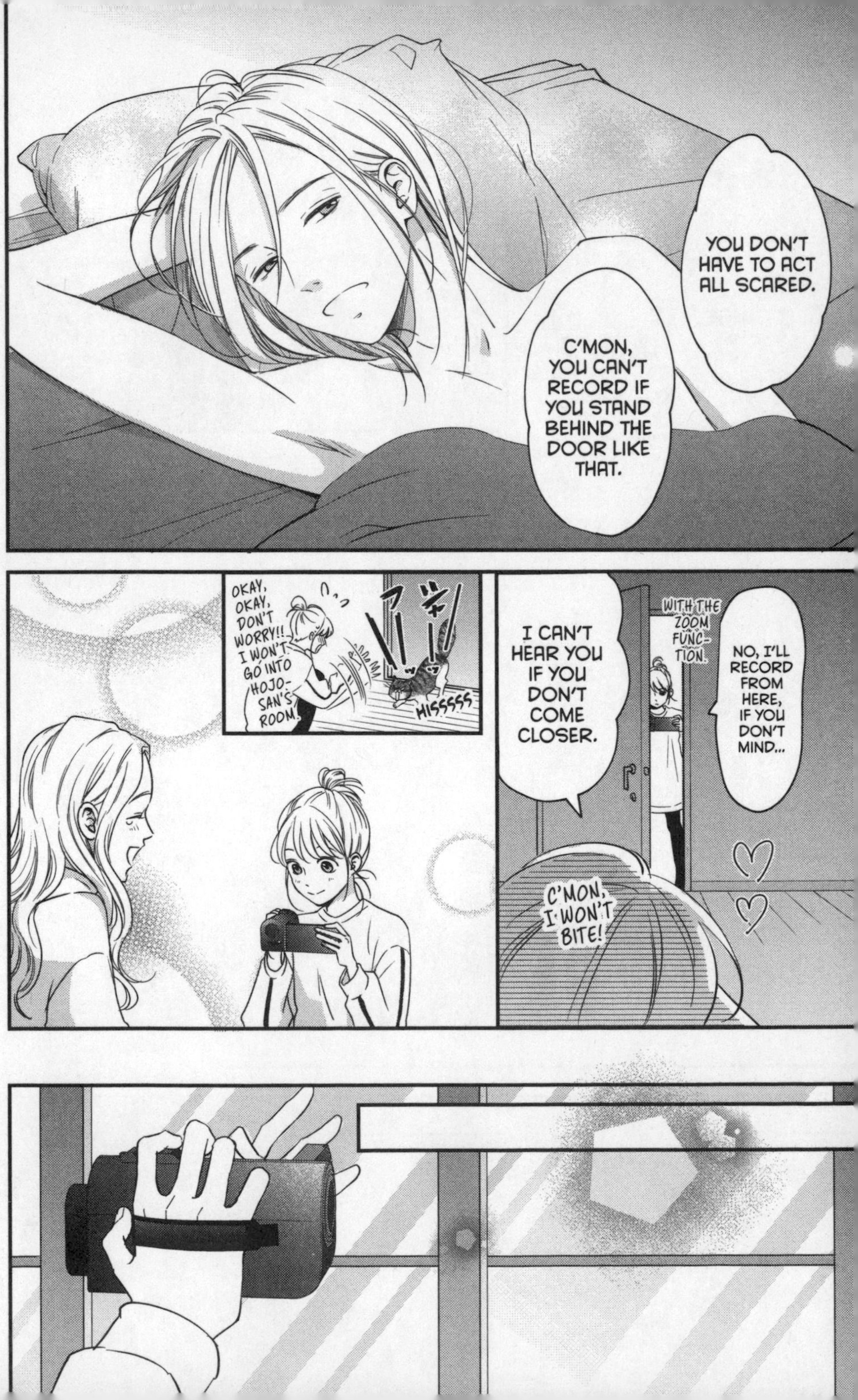
YOU DON'T HAVE TO ACT ALL SCARED.
C'MON, YOU CAN'T RECORD IF YOU STAND BEHIND THE DOOR LIKE THAT.
NO, I'LL RECORD FROM HERE, IF YOU DON'T MIND...
WITH THE ZOOM FUNCTION.
I CAN'T HEAR YOU IF YOU DON'T COME CLOSER.
C'MON, I WON'T BITE!
OKAY, OKAY, DON'T WORRY!! I WON'T GO INTO HOJO-SAN'S ROOM.
HISSSSS

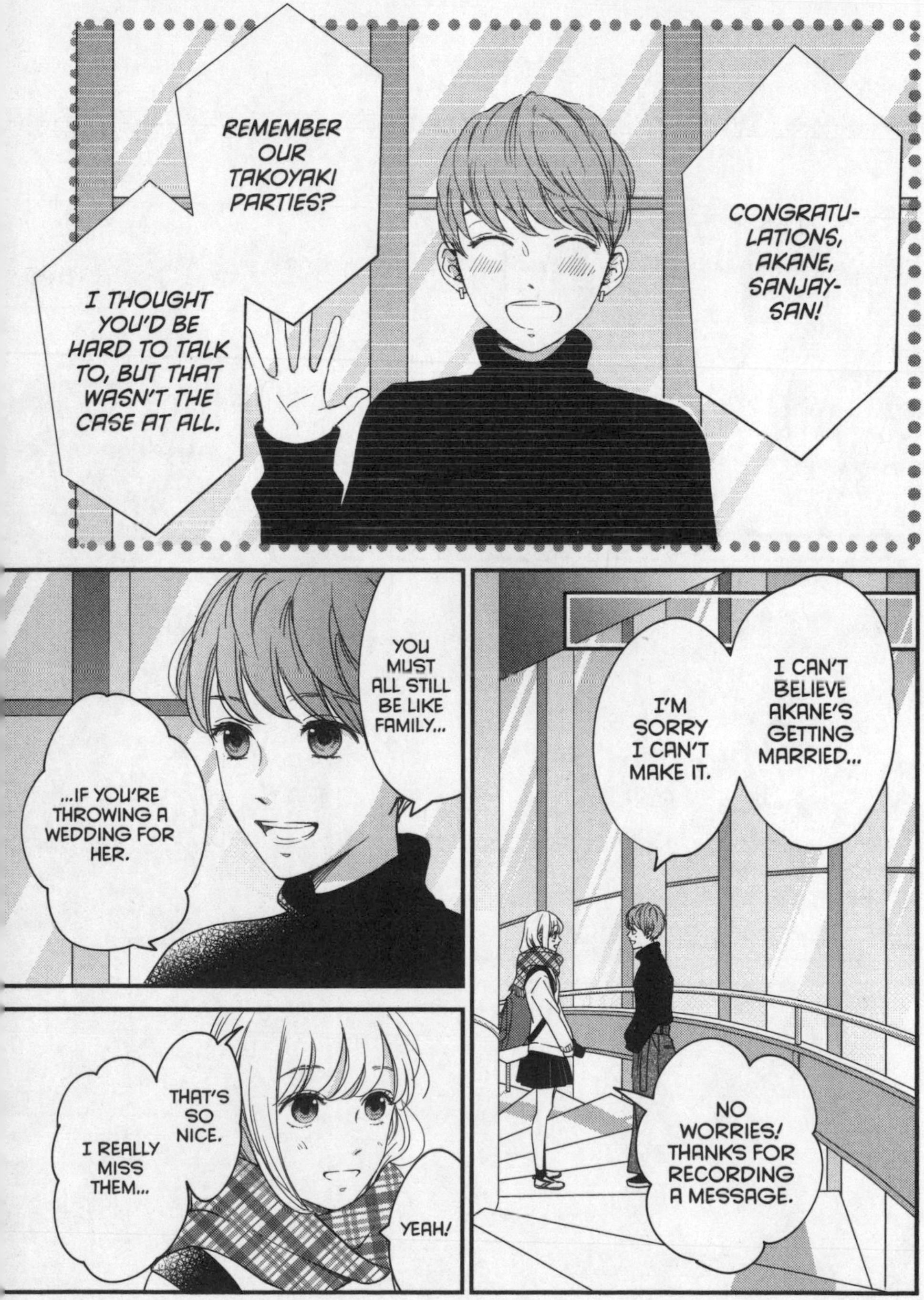
CONGRATULATIONS, AKANE, SANJAY-SAN!
REMEMBER OUR TAKOYAKI PARTIES?
I THOUGHT YOU'D BE HARD TO TALK TO, BUT THAT WASN'T THE CASE AT ALL.
I CAN'T BELIEVE AKANE'S GETTING MARRIED...
I'M SORRY I CAN'T MAKE IT.
NO WORRIES! THANKS FOR RECORDING A MESSAGE.
YOU MUST ALL STILL BE LIKE FAMILY...
...IF YOU'RE THROWING A WEDDING FOR HER.
THAT'S SO NICE.
I REALLY MISS THEM...
YEAH!

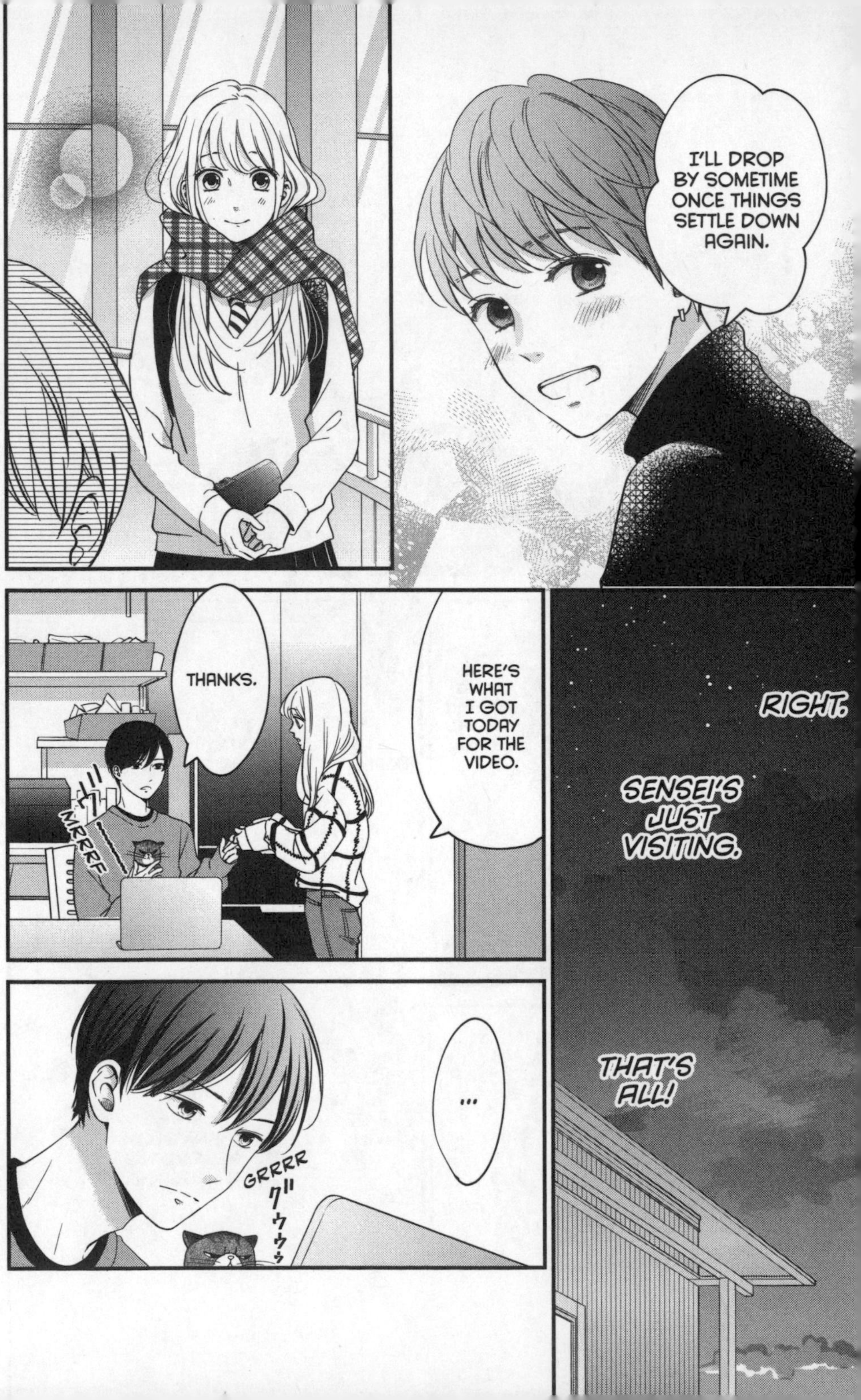
I'LL DROP BY SOMETIME ONCE THINGS SETTLE DOWN AGAIN.
RIGHT.
SENSEI'S JUST VISITING.
THAT'S ALL!
HERE'S WHAT I GOT TODAY FOR THE VIDEO.
THANKS.
MRRRF
...
GRRRR

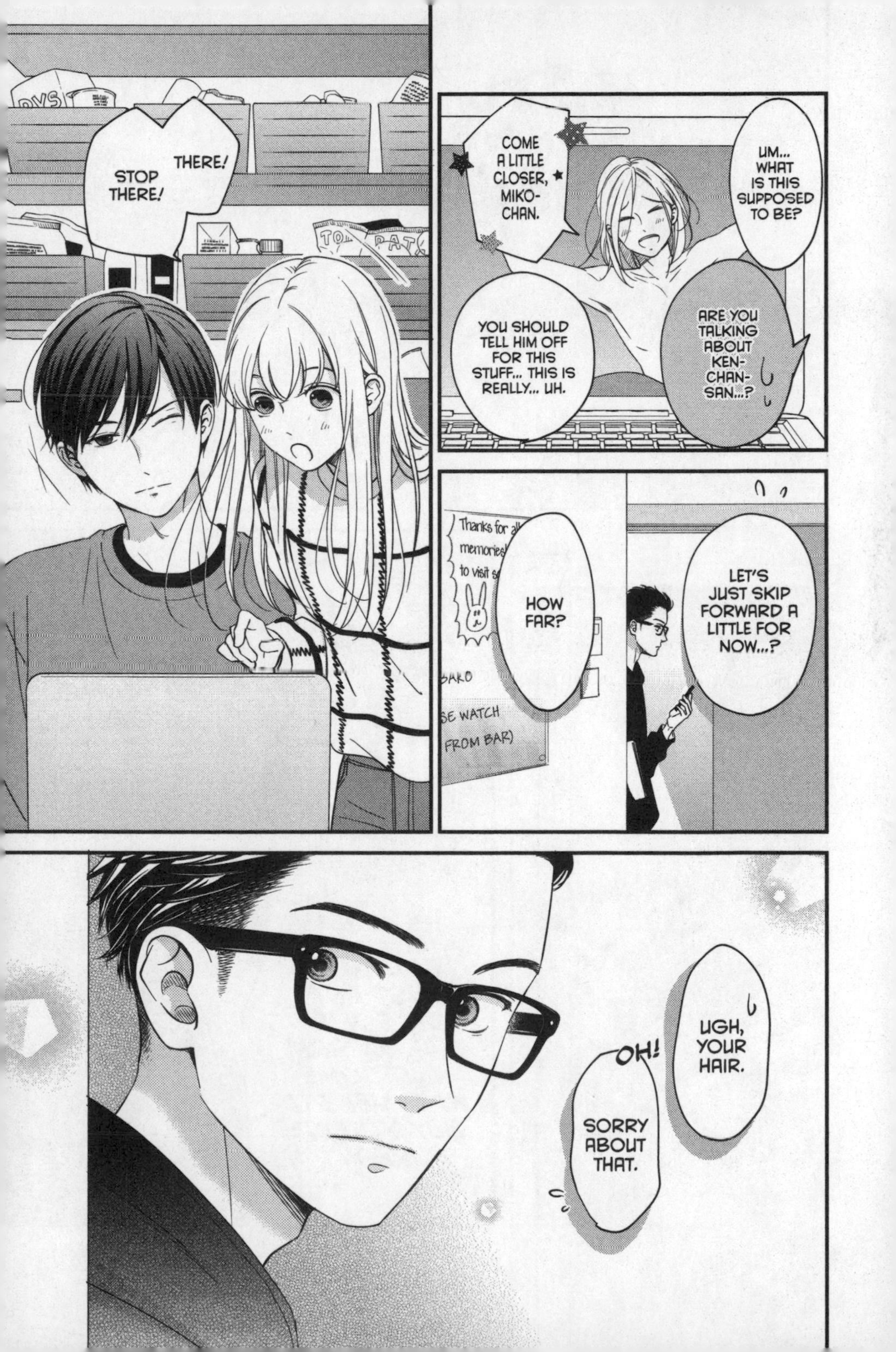
UM... WHAT IS THIS SUPPOSED TO BE?
COME A LITTLE CLOSER, MIKO-CHAN.
ARE YOU TALKING ABOUT KEN-CHAN-SAN...?
YOU SHOULD TELL HIM OFF FOR THIS STUFF... THIS IS REALLY... UH.
LET'S JUST SKIP FORWARD A LITTLE FOR NOW...?
HOW FAR?
THERE!
STOP THERE!
UGH, YOUR HAIR.
OH!
SORRY ABOUT THAT.

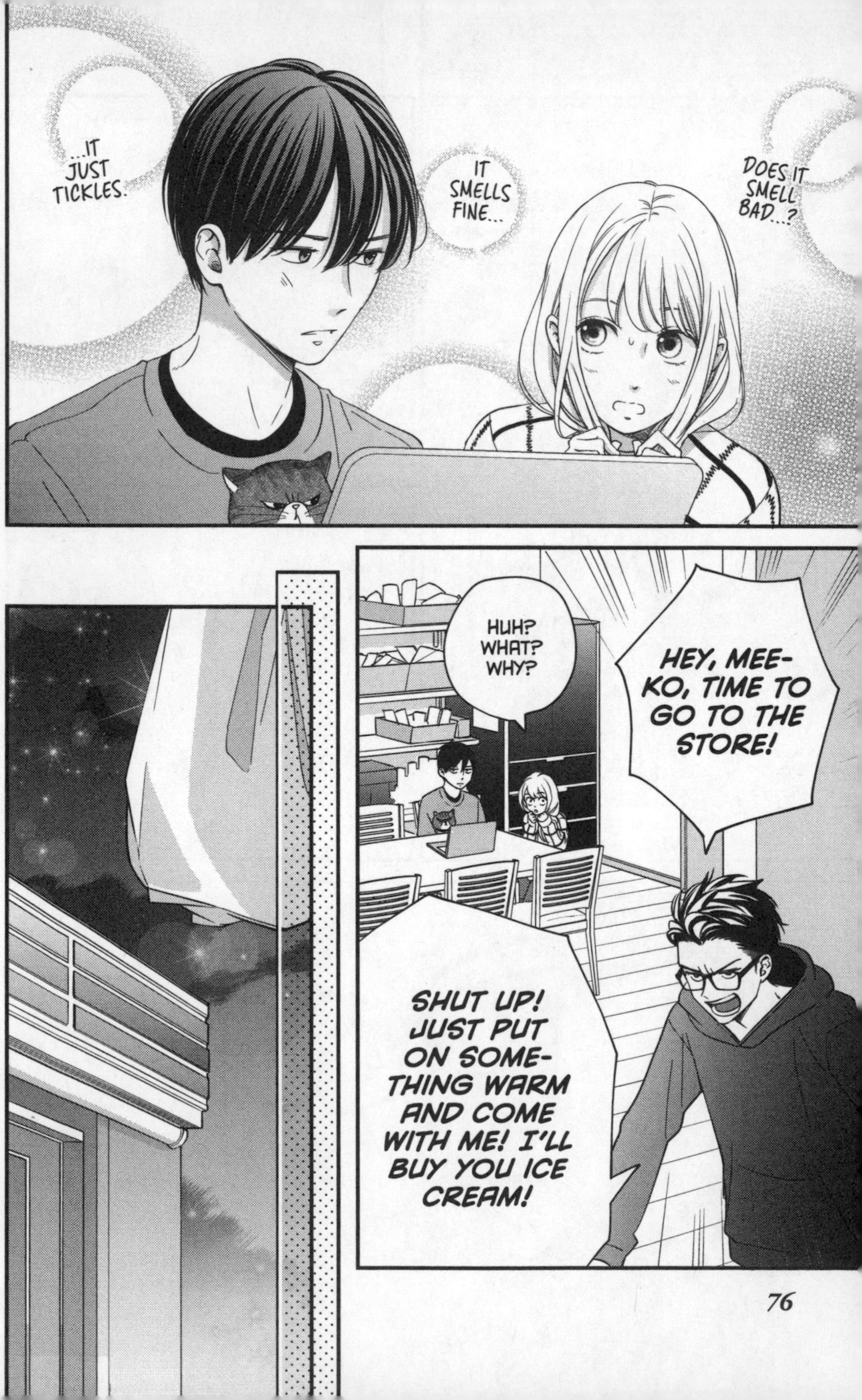
DOES IT SMELL BAD...?
IT SMELLS FINE...
...IT JUST TICKLES.
HEY, MEE-KO, TIME TO GO TO THE STORE!
HUH? WHAT? WHY?
SHUT UP! JUST PUT ON SOME-THING WARM AND COME WITH ME! I'LL BUY YOU ICE CREAM!

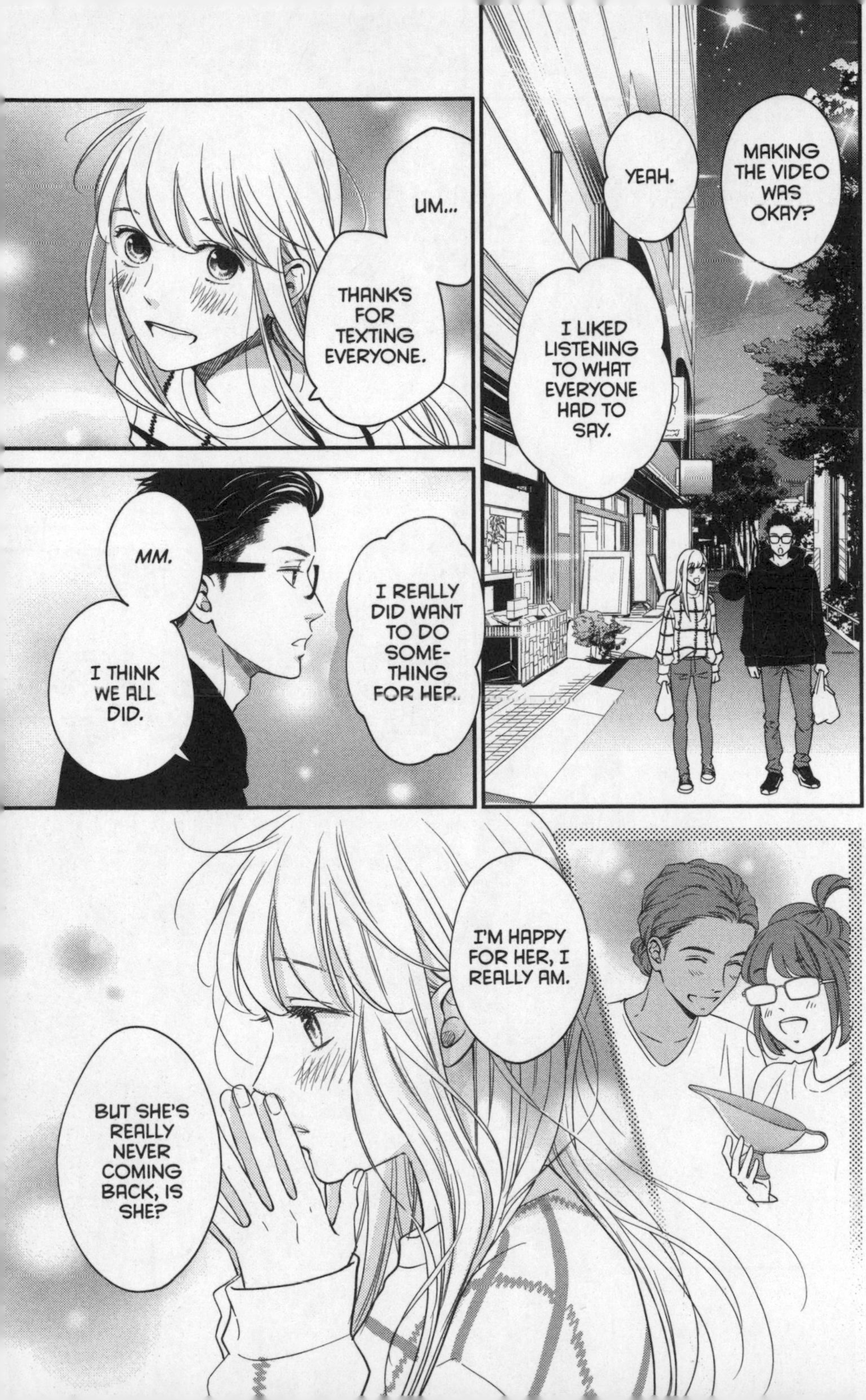
MAKING THE VIDEO WAS OKAY?
YEAH.
I LIKED LISTENING TO WHAT EVERYONE HAD TO SAY.
UM...
THANKS FOR TEXTING EVERYONE.
I REALLY DID WANT TO DO SOME-THING FOR HER..
MM.
I THINK WE ALL DID.
I'M HAPPY FOR HER, I REALLY AM.
BUT SHE'S REALLY NEVER COMING BACK, IS SHE?

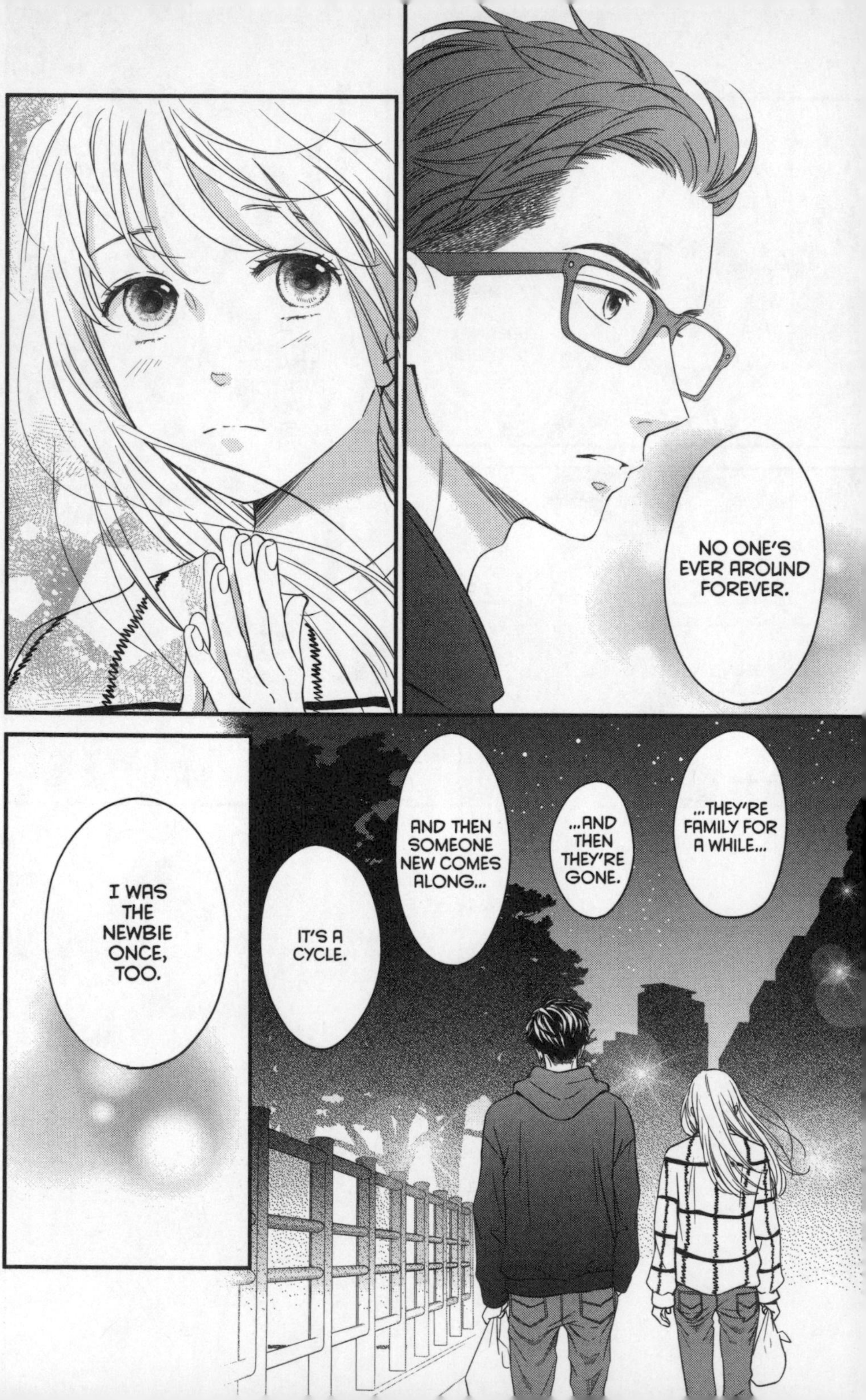
NO ONE'S EVER AROUND FOREVER.
...THEY'RE FAMILY FOR A WHILE...
...AND THEN THEY'RE GONE.
AND THEN SOMEONE NEW COMES ALONG...
IT'S A CYCLE.
I WAS THE NEWBIE ONCE, TOO.

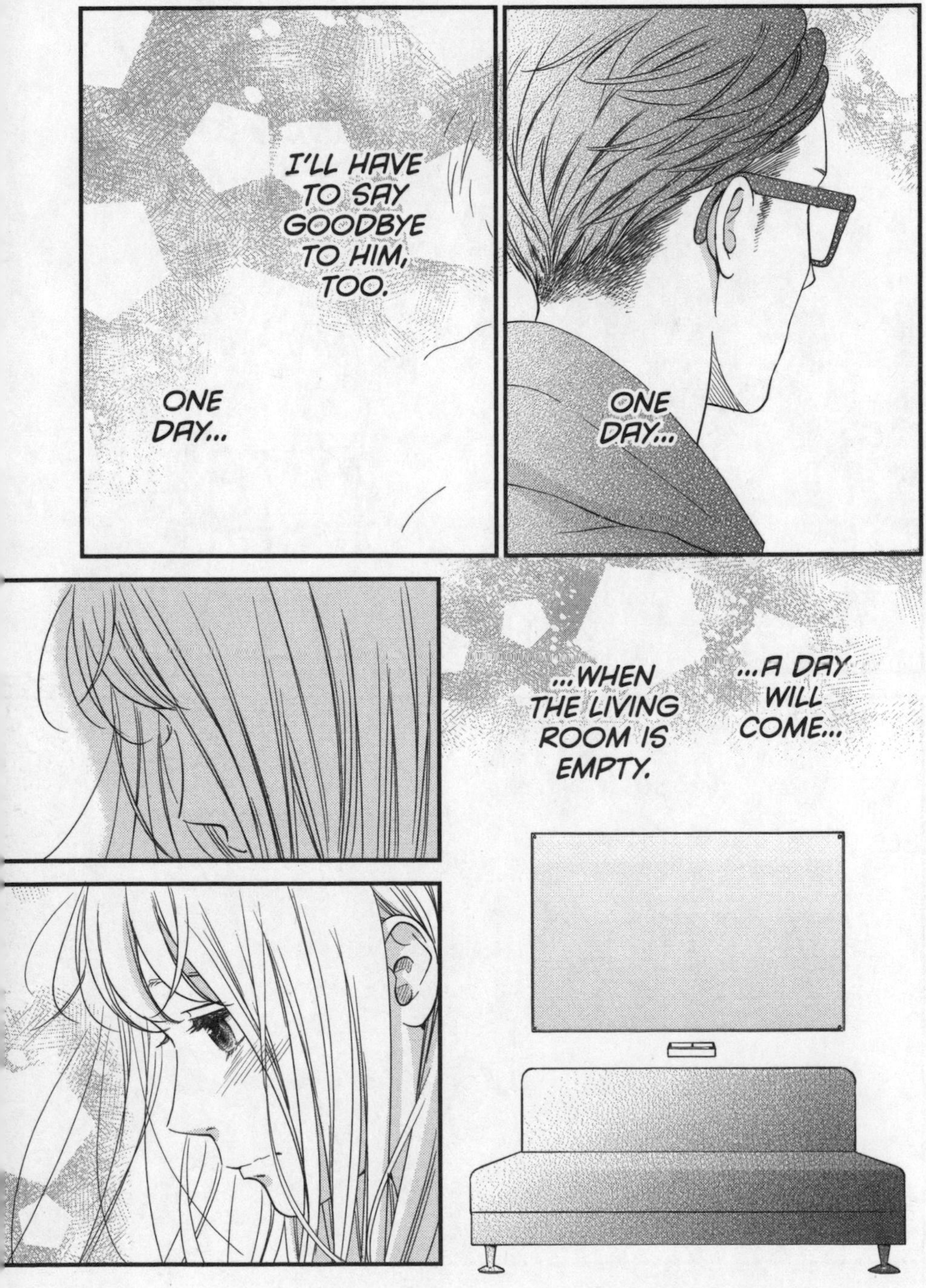
ONE DAY...
I'LL HAVE TO SAY GOODBYE TO HIM, TOO.
ONE DAY...
...A DAY WILL COME...
...WHEN THE LIVING ROOM IS EMPTY.

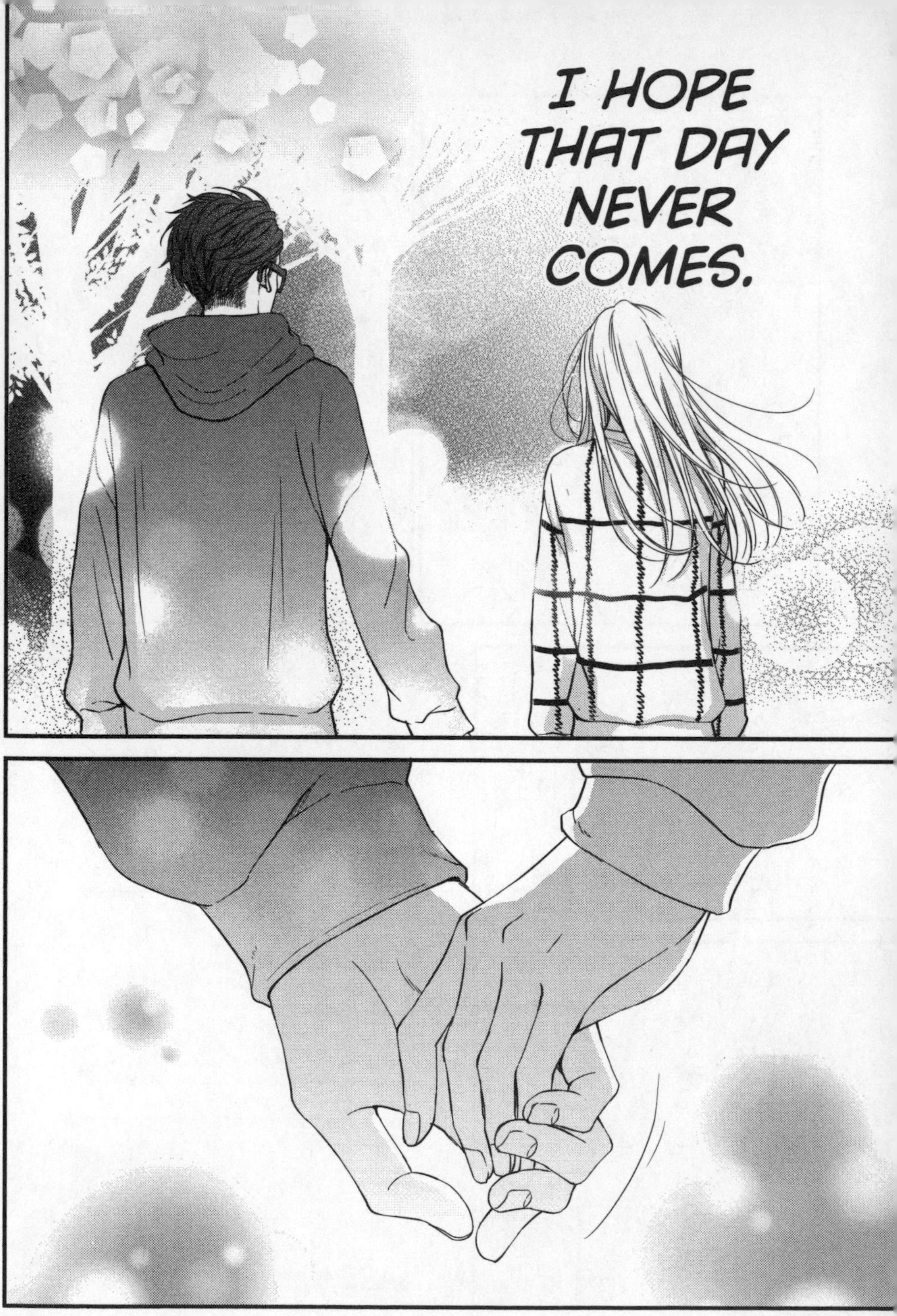
I HOPE THAT DAY NEVER COMES.

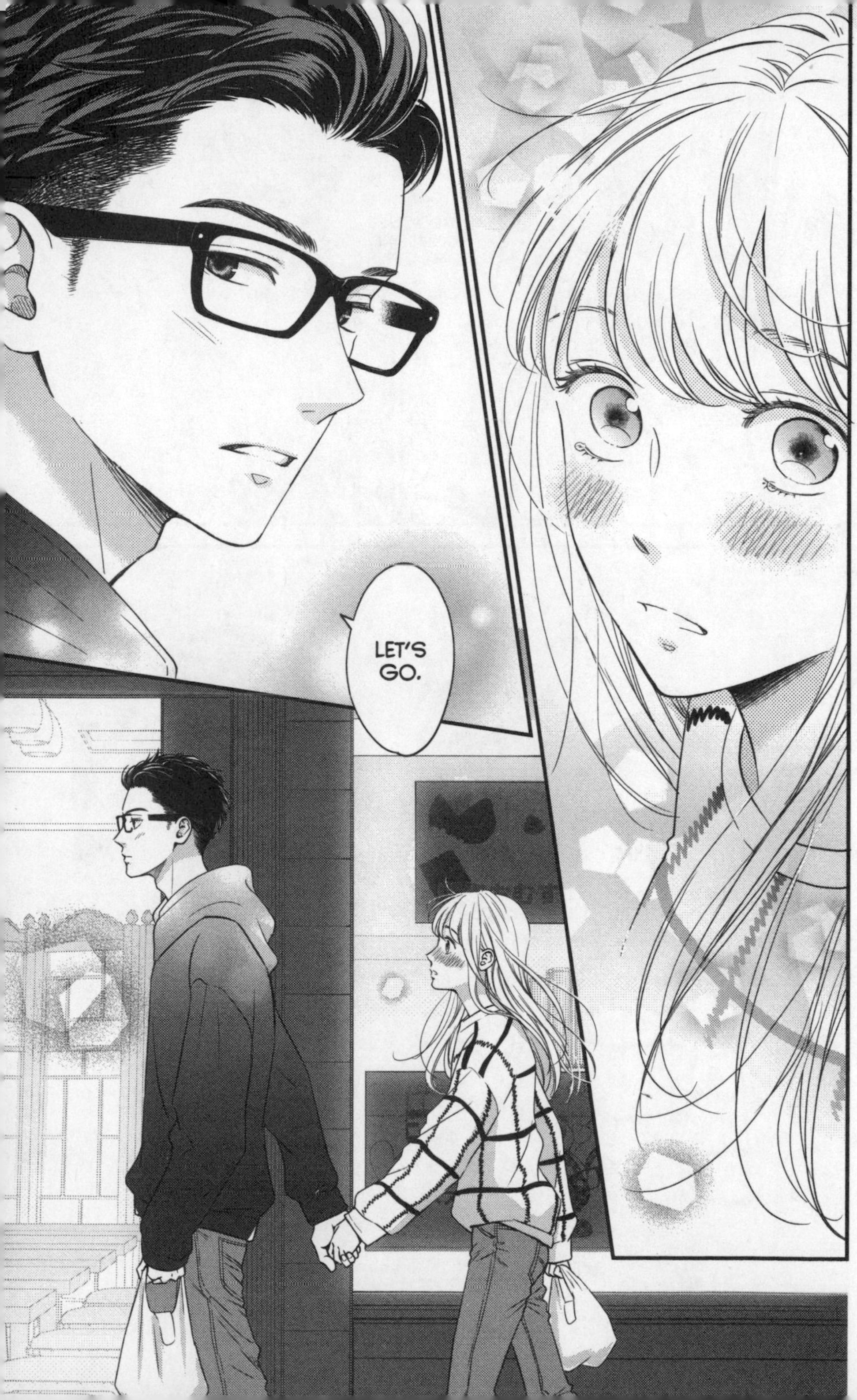
LET'S GO.

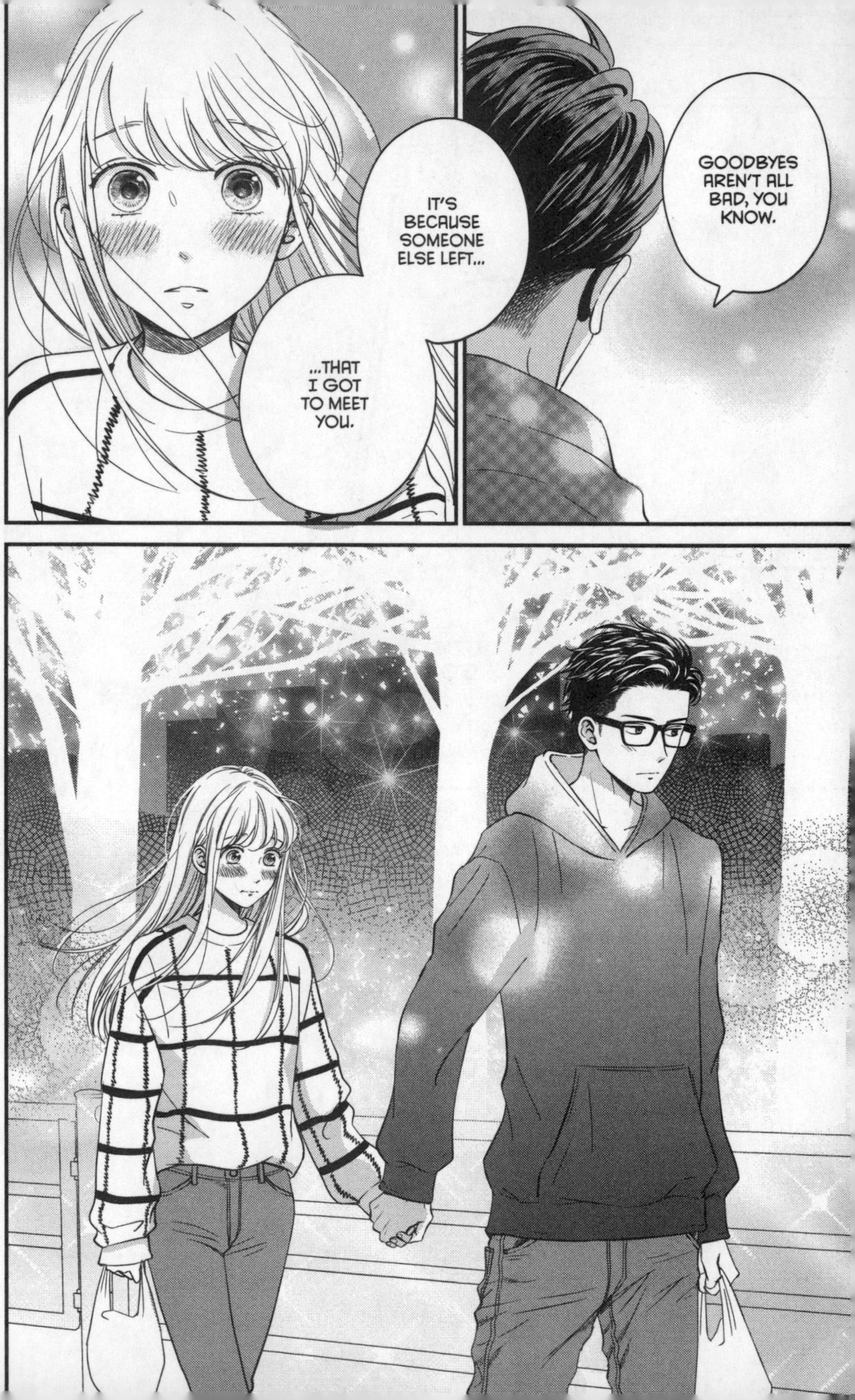
GOODBYES AREN'T ALL BAD, YOU KNOW.
IT'S BECAUSE SOMEONE ELSE LEFT...
...THAT I GOT TO MEET YOU.

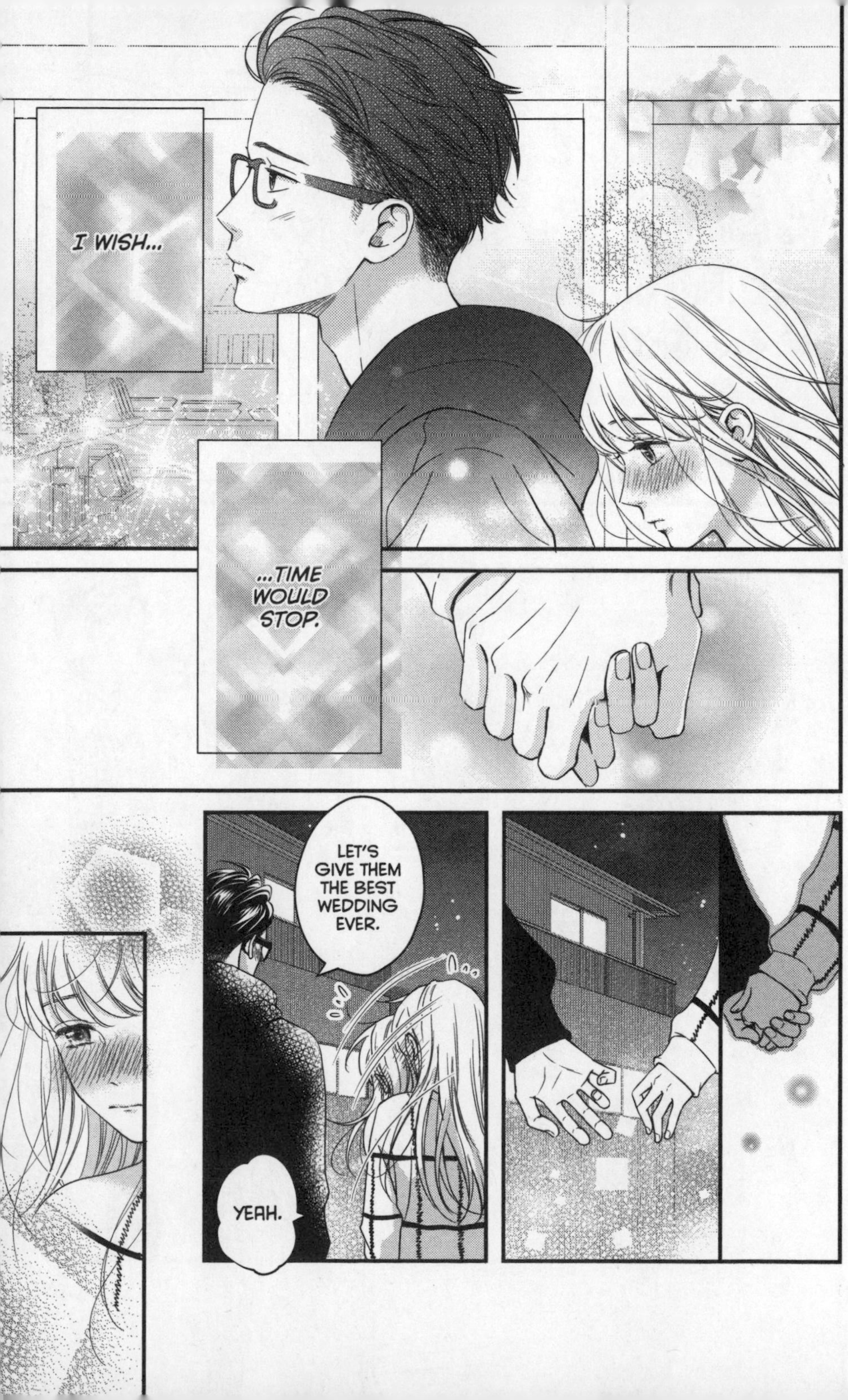
I WISH...
...TIME WOULD STOP.
LET'S GIVE THEM THE BEST WEDDING EVER.
YEAH.

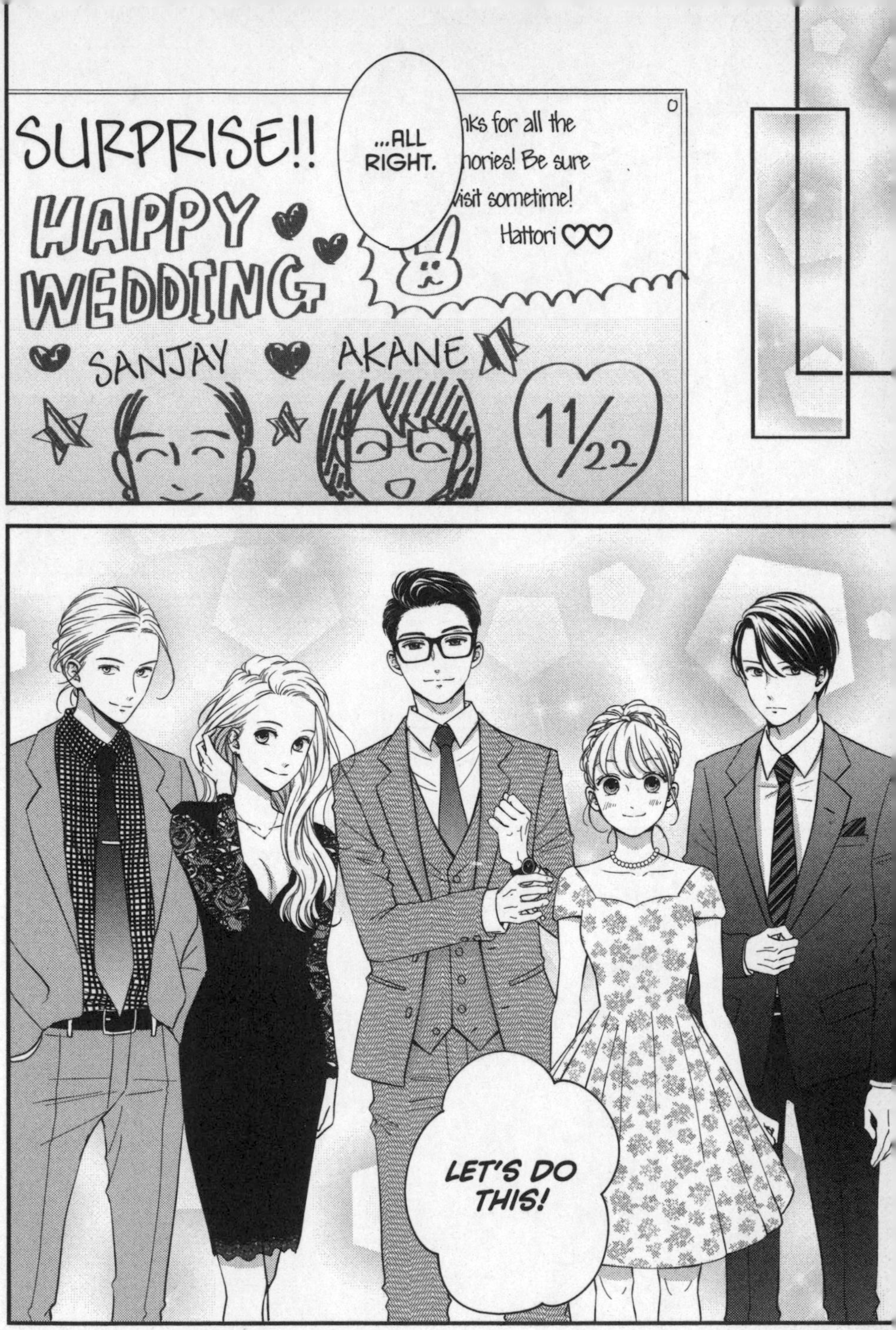
nks for all the
mories! Be sure
visit sometime!
Hattori
...ALL RIGHT.
SURPRISE!!
HAPPY WEDDING
SANJAY
AKANE
11/22
LET'S DO THIS!

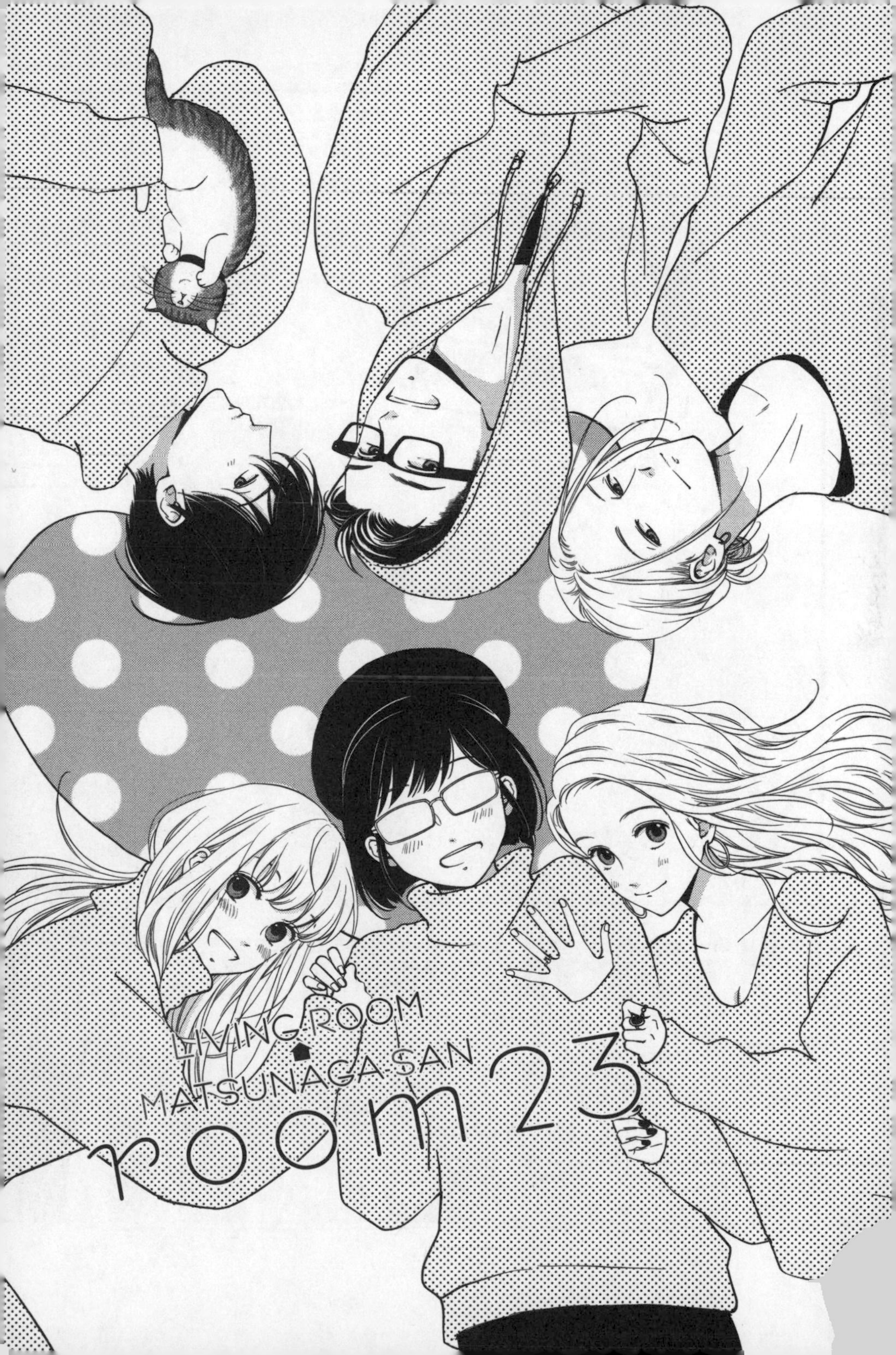
LIVING-ROOM
MATSUNAGA-SAN
room 23

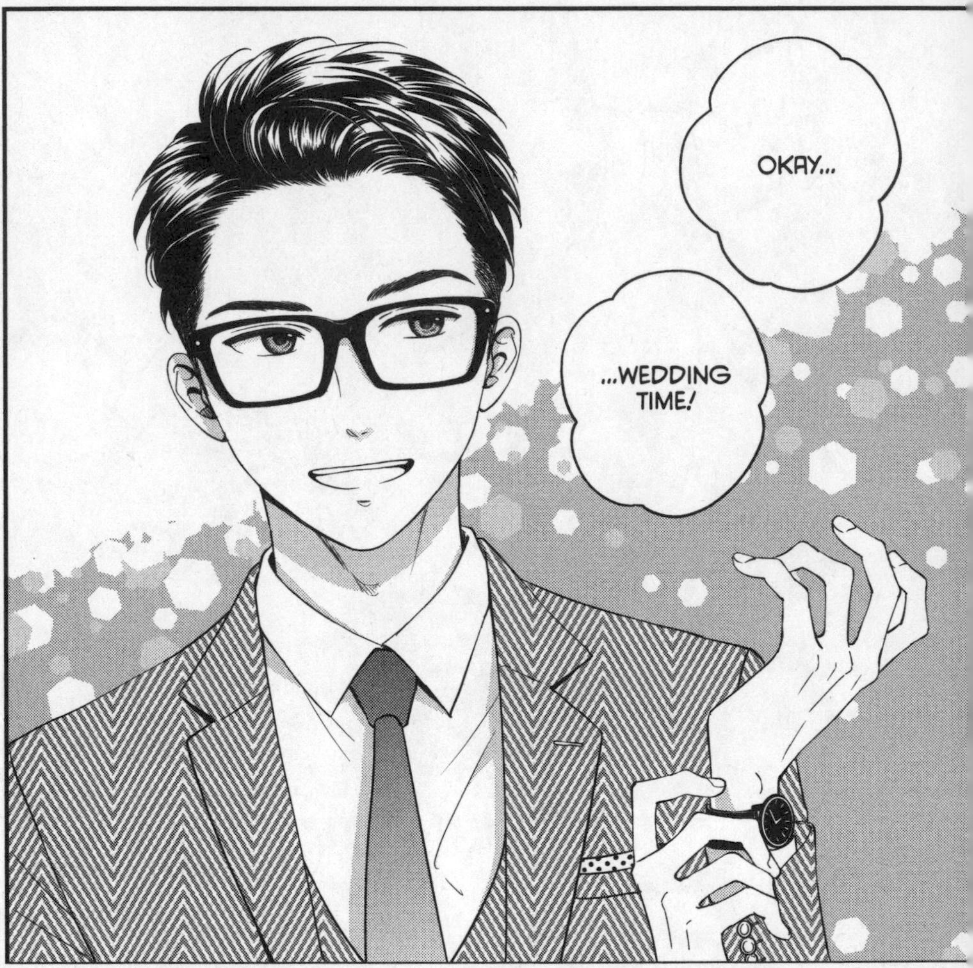
OKAY...
...WEDDING TIME!

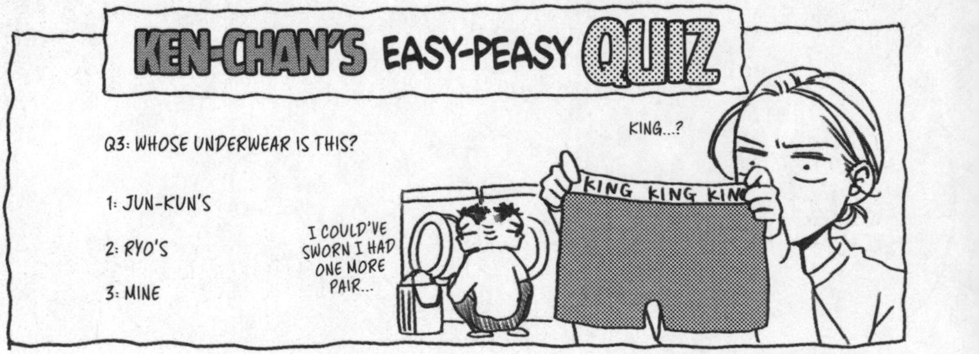
KEN-CHAN'S EASY-PEASY QUIZ
Q3: WHOSE UNDERWEAR IS THIS?
1: JUN-KUN'S
2: RYO'S
3: MINE
KING...?
KING KING KIN
I COULD'VE SWORN I HAD ONE MORE PAIR...

ANSWER: THEY'RE JUN-KUN'S ♥

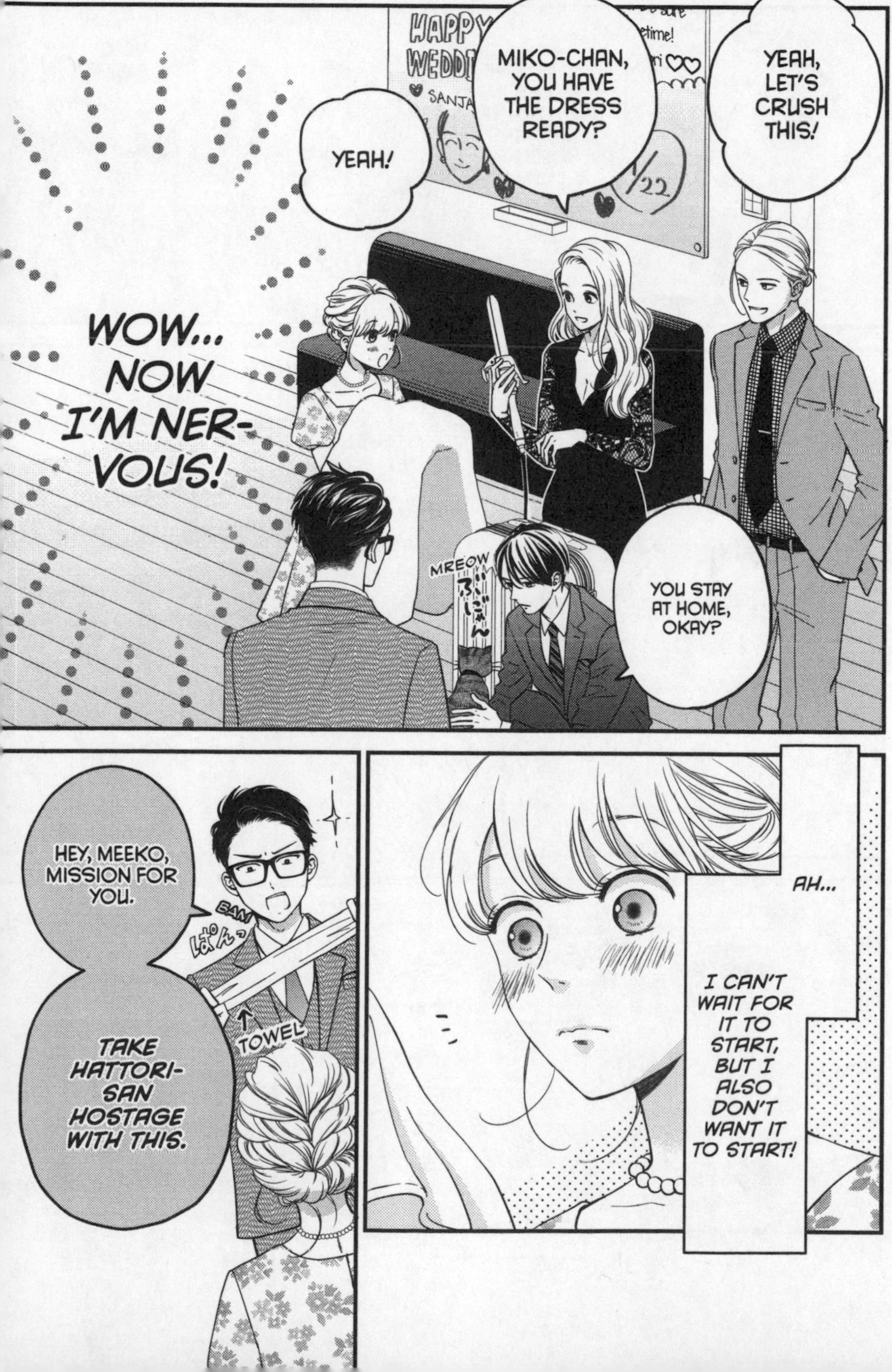
YEAH, LET'S CRUSH THIS!
MIKO-CHAN, YOU HAVE THE DRESS READY?
HAPPY
YEAH!
WOW... NOW I'M NER-VOUS!
MREOW
YOU STAY AT HOME, OKAY?
AH...
I CAN'T WAIT FOR IT TO START, BUT I ALSO DON'T WANT IT TO START!
HEY, MEEKO, MISSION FOR YOU.
BAM
TOWEL
TAKE HATTORI-SAN HOSTAGE WITH THIS.

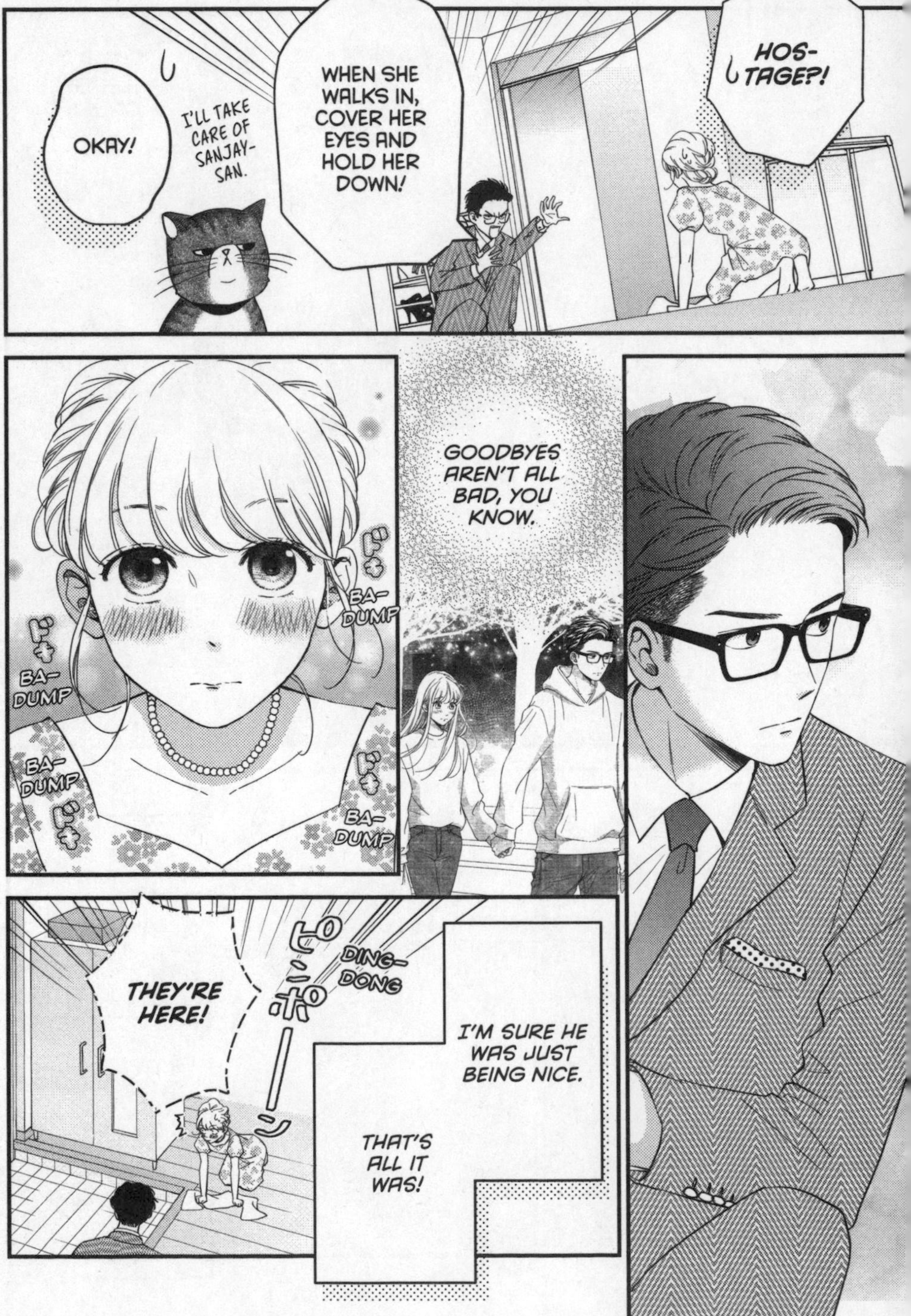
HOS-TAGE?!
WHEN SHE WALKS IN, COVER HER EYES AND HOLD HER DOWN!
I'LL TAKE CARE OF SANJAY-SAN.
OKAY!
GOODBYES AREN'T ALL BAD, YOU KNOW.
ドキ
BA-DUMP
ドキ
BA-DUMP
ドキ
BA-DUMP
ドキ
BA-DUMP
I'M SURE HE WAS JUST BEING NICE.
THAT'S ALL IT WAS!
ピンポーン
DING-DONG
THEY'RE HERE!

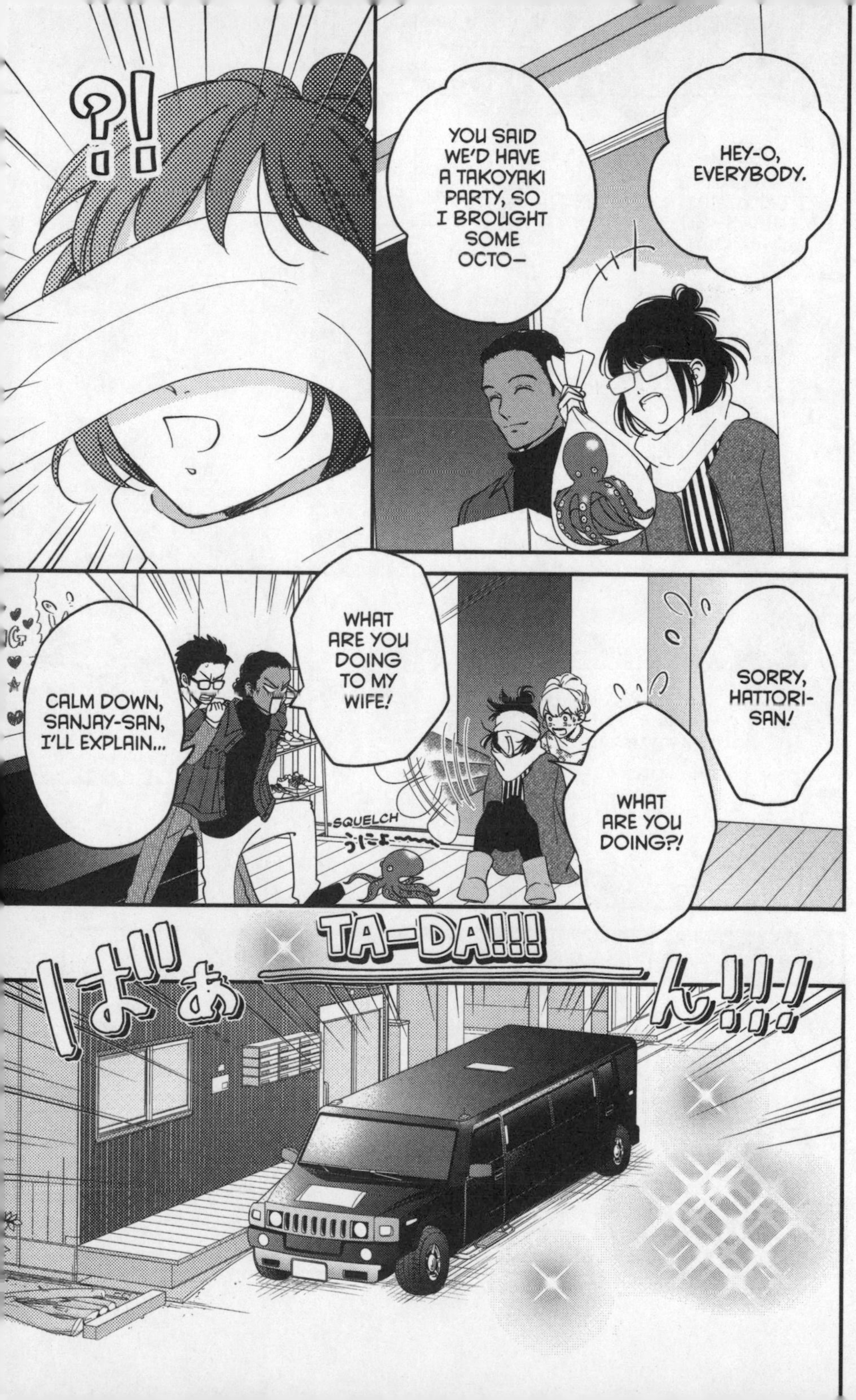
HEY-O, EVERYBODY.
YOU SAID WE'D HAVE A TAKOYAKI PARTY, SO I BROUGHT SOME OCTO—
?!
SORRY, HATTORI-SAN!
WHAT ARE YOU DOING?!
WHAT ARE YOU DOING TO MY WIFE!
CALM DOWN, SANJAY-SAN, I'LL EXPLAIN...
SQUELCH
うにょ〜〜
TA-DA!!!
ばぁん!!!!

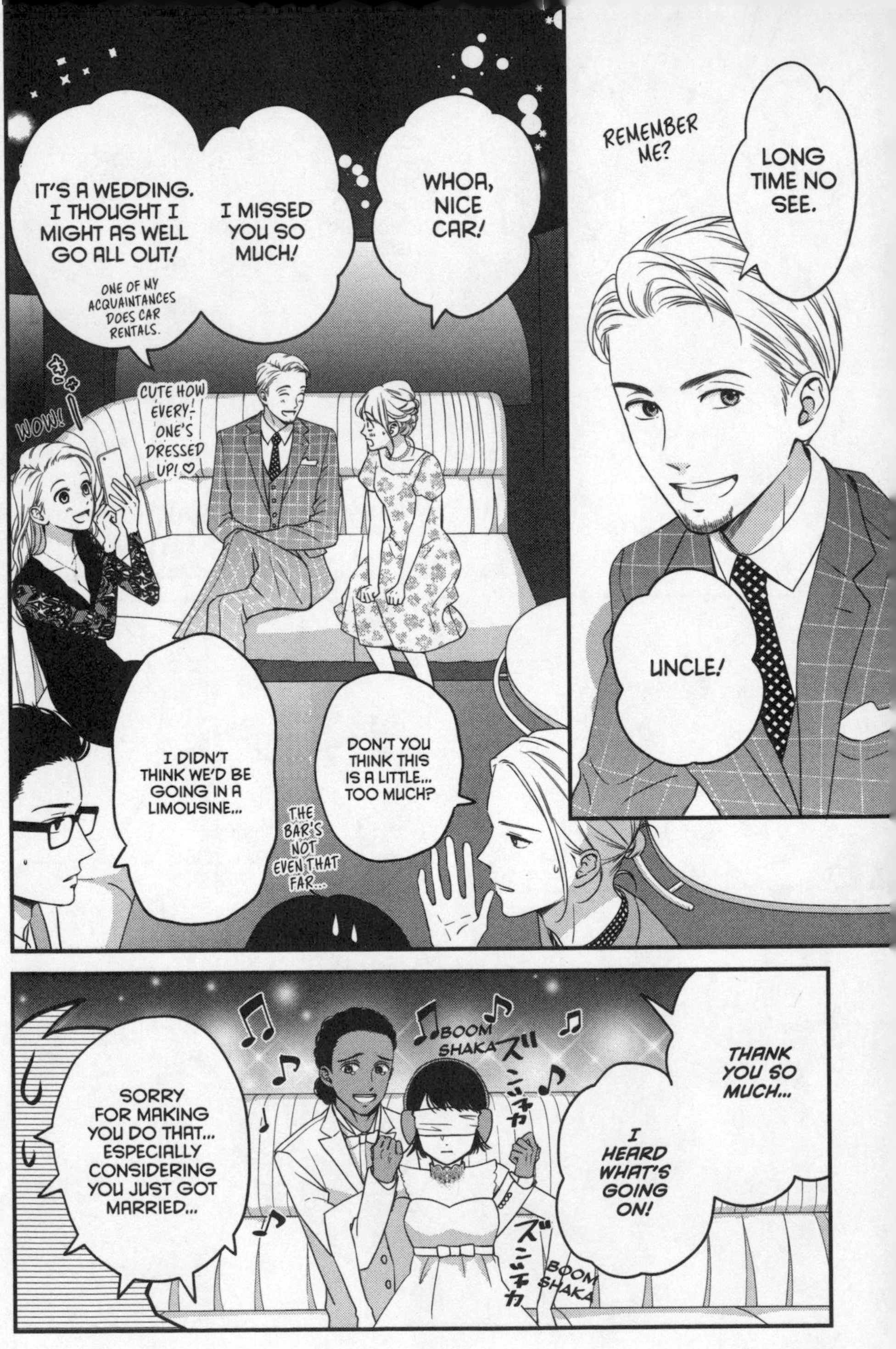
LONG TIME NO SEE.
REMEMBER ME?
UNCLE!
WHOA, NICE CAR!
I MISSED YOU SO MUCH!
IT'S A WEDDING. I THOUGHT I MIGHT AS WELL GO ALL OUT!
ONE OF MY ACQUAINTANCES DOES CAR RENTALS.
CUTE HOW EVERYONE'S DRESSED UP! ♡
WOW!
DON'T YOU THINK THIS IS A LITTLE... TOO MUCH?
THE BAR'S NOT EVEN THAT FAR...
I DIDN'T THINK WE'D BE GOING IN A LIMOUSINE...
THANK YOU SO MUCH...
I HEARD WHAT'S GOING ON!
BOOM SHAKA
BOOM SHAKA
SORRY FOR MAKING YOU DO THAT... ESPECIALLY CONSIDERING YOU JUST GOT MARRIED...

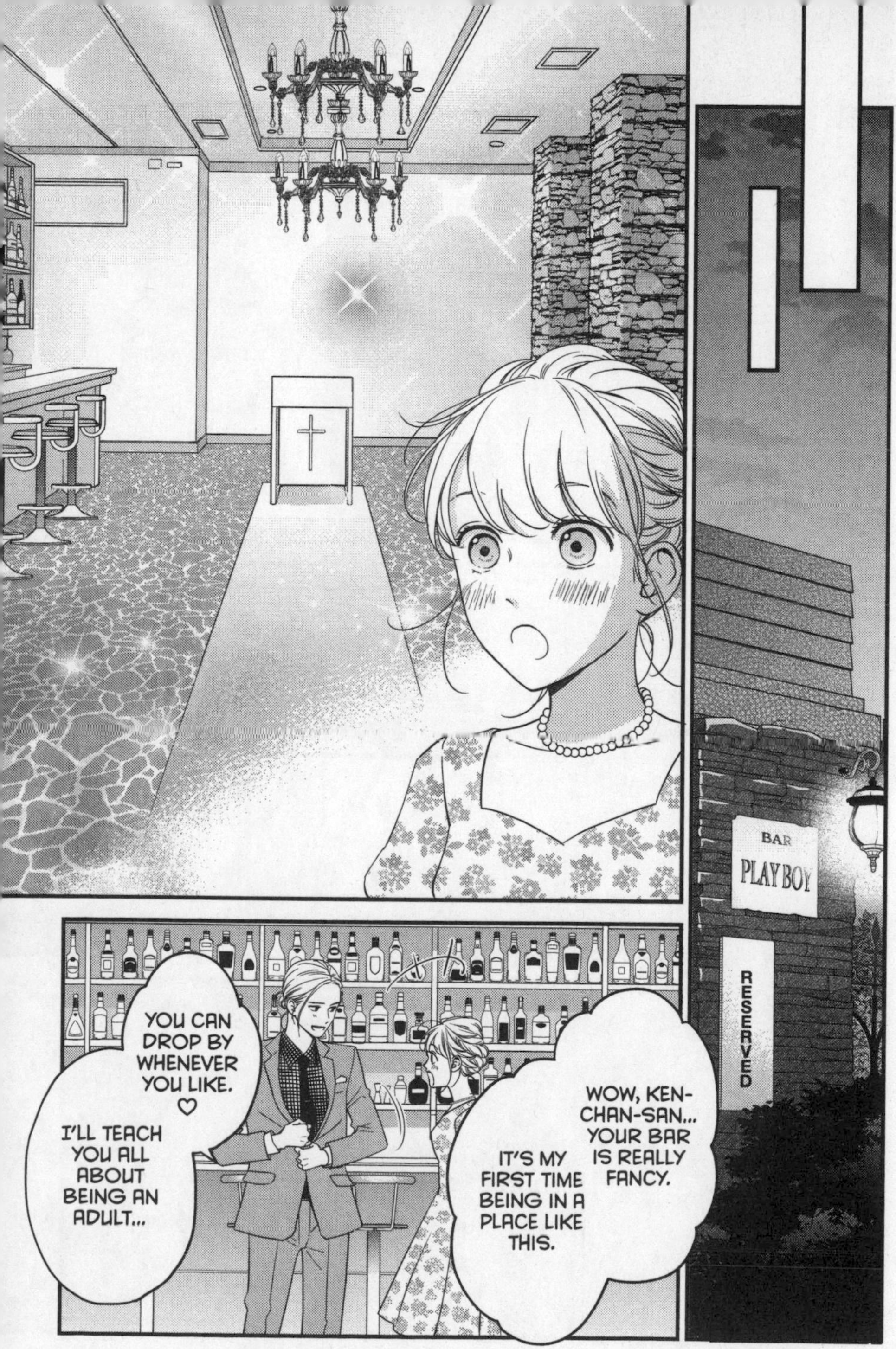
BAR
PLAYBOY
RESERVED
WOW, KEN-CHAN-SAN... YOUR BAR IS REALLY FANCY.
IT'S MY FIRST TIME BEING IN A PLACE LIKE THIS.
YOU CAN DROP BY WHENEVER YOU LIKE. ♡
I'LL TEACH YOU ALL ABOUT BEING AN ADULT...

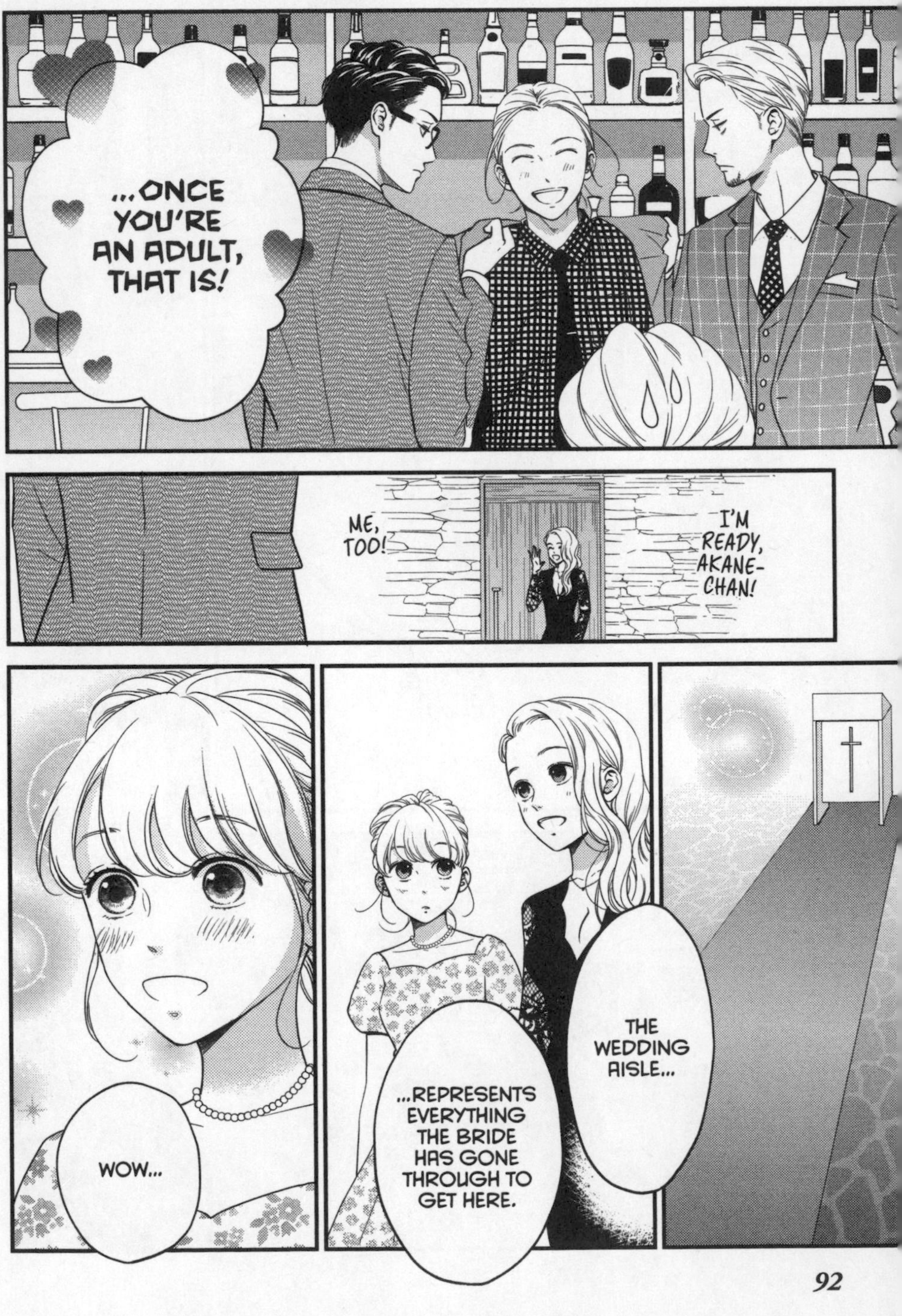
...ONCE YOU'RE AN ADULT, THAT IS!
I'M READY, AKANE-CHAN!
ME, TOO!
THE WEDDING AISLE...
...REPRESENTS EVERYTHING THE BRIDE HAS GONE THROUGH TO GET HERE.
WOW...

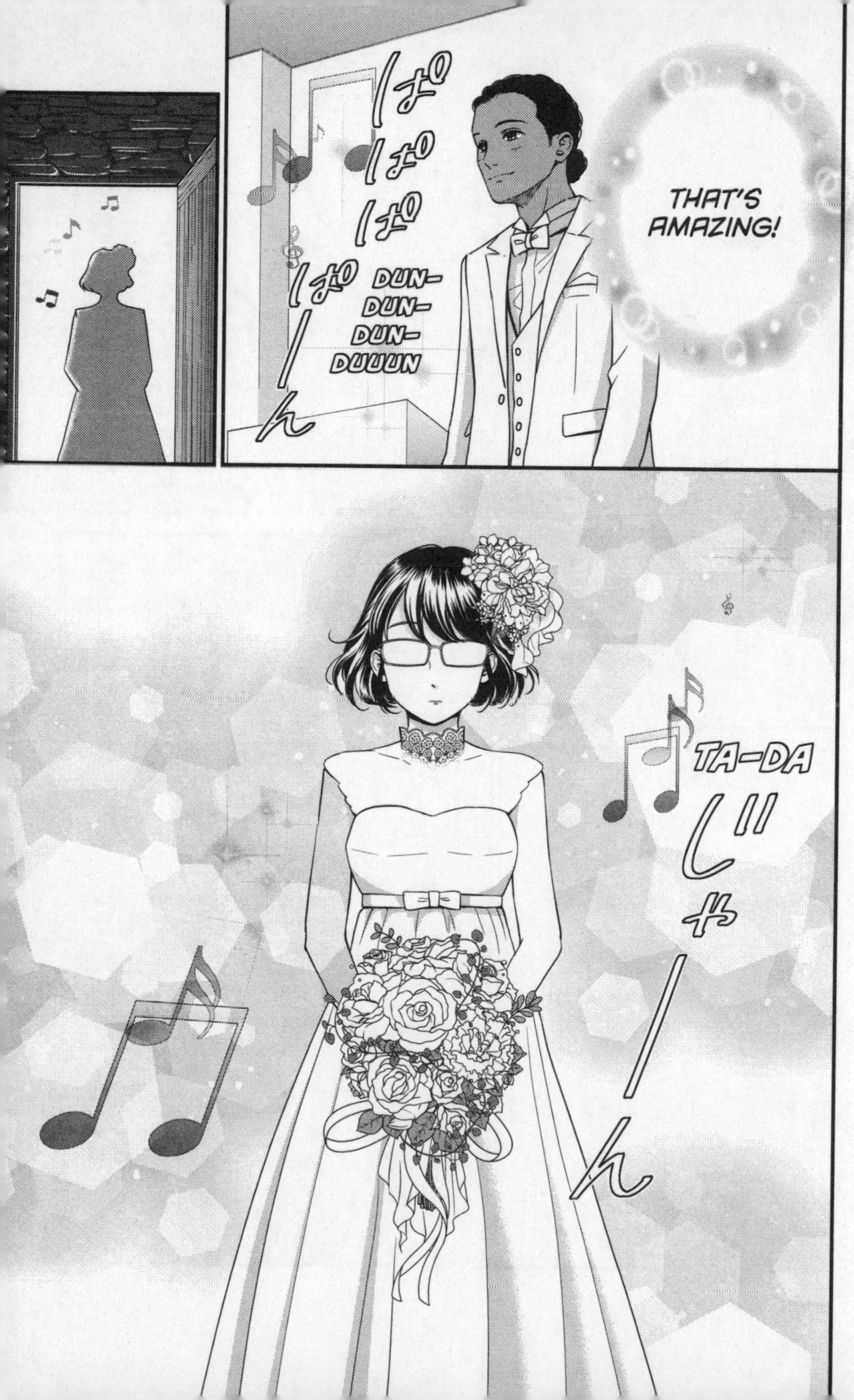
THAT'S AMAZING!
ぱぱぱぱーん
DUN-DUN-DUN-DUUUN
TA-DA
じゃーん

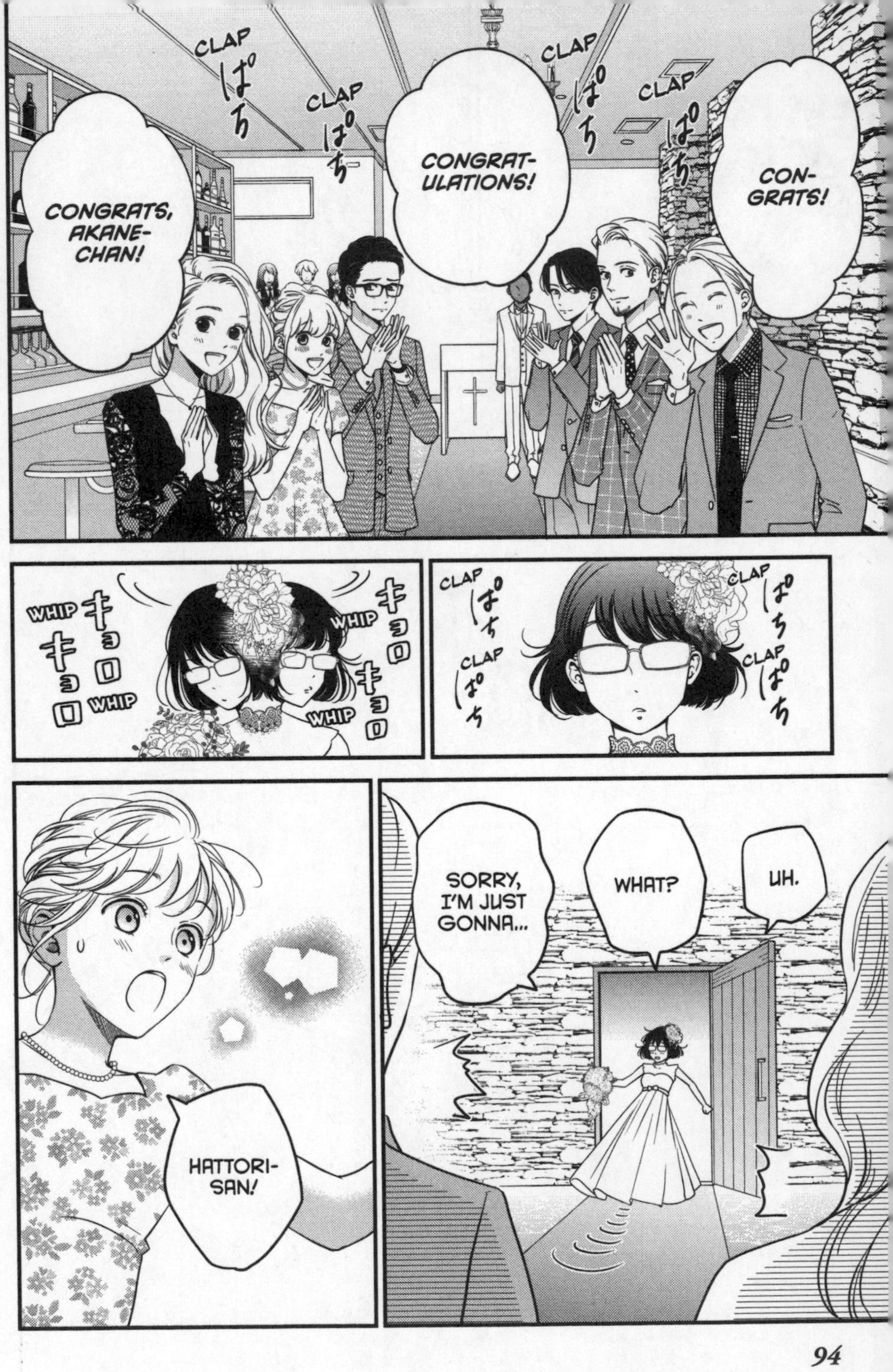
CON-GRATS!
CLAP ぱち
CLAP ぱち
CONGRAT-ULATIONS!
CLAP ぱち
CLAP ぱち
CLAP ぱち
CONGRATS, AKANE-CHAN!
CLAP ぱち
CLAP ぱち
CLAP ぱち
CLAP ぱち
キョロキョロ
WHIP
WHIP
キョロキョロ
WHIP
WHIP
UH.
WHAT?
SORRY, I'M JUST GONNA...
HATTORI-SAN!

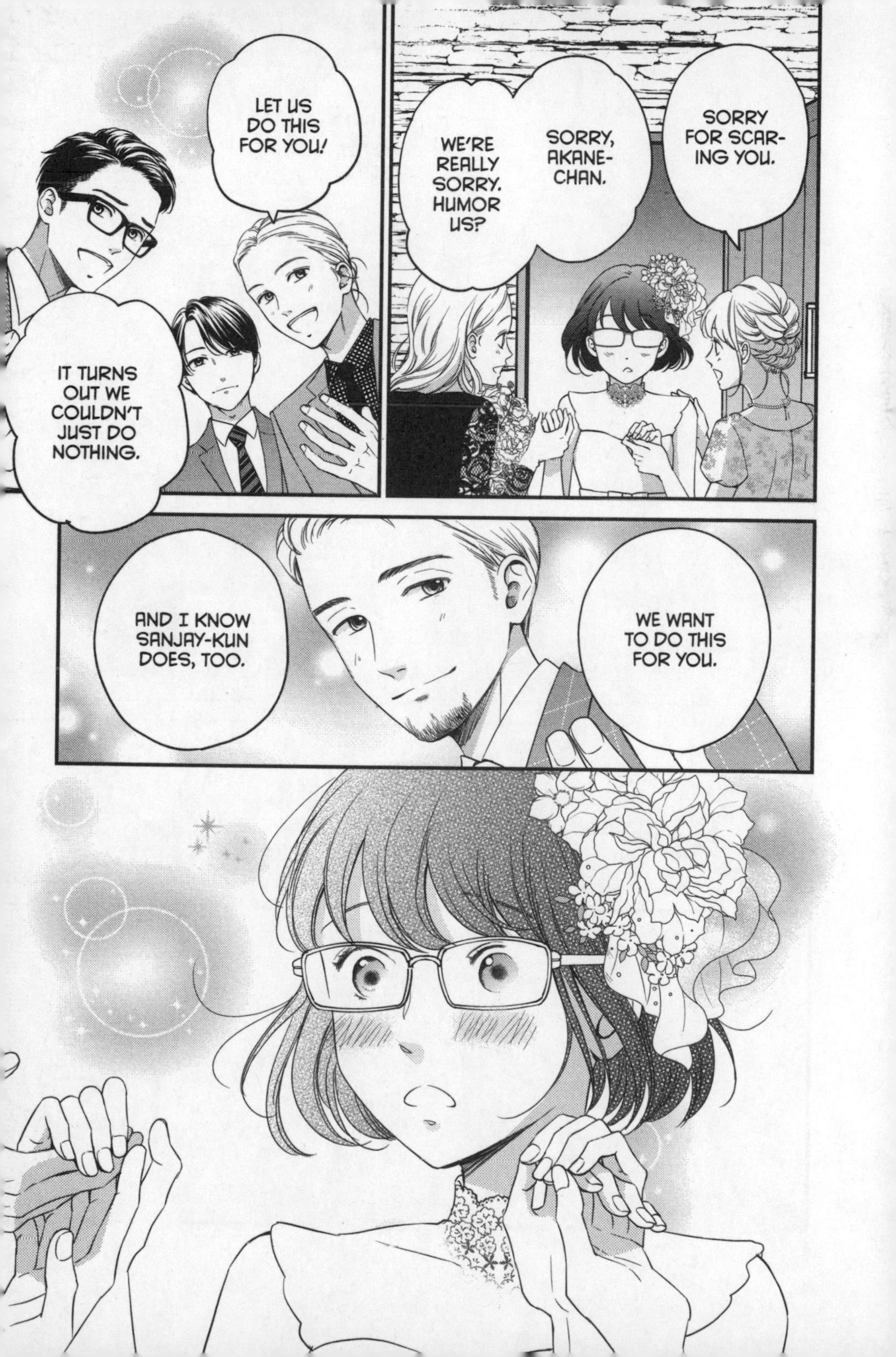
SORRY FOR SCAR-ING YOU.
SORRY, AKANE-CHAN.
WE'RE REALLY SORRY. HUMOR US?
LET US DO THIS FOR YOU!
IT TURNS OUT WE COULDN'T JUST DO NOTHING.
WE WANT TO DO THIS FOR YOU.
AND I KNOW SANJAY-KUN DOES, TOO.

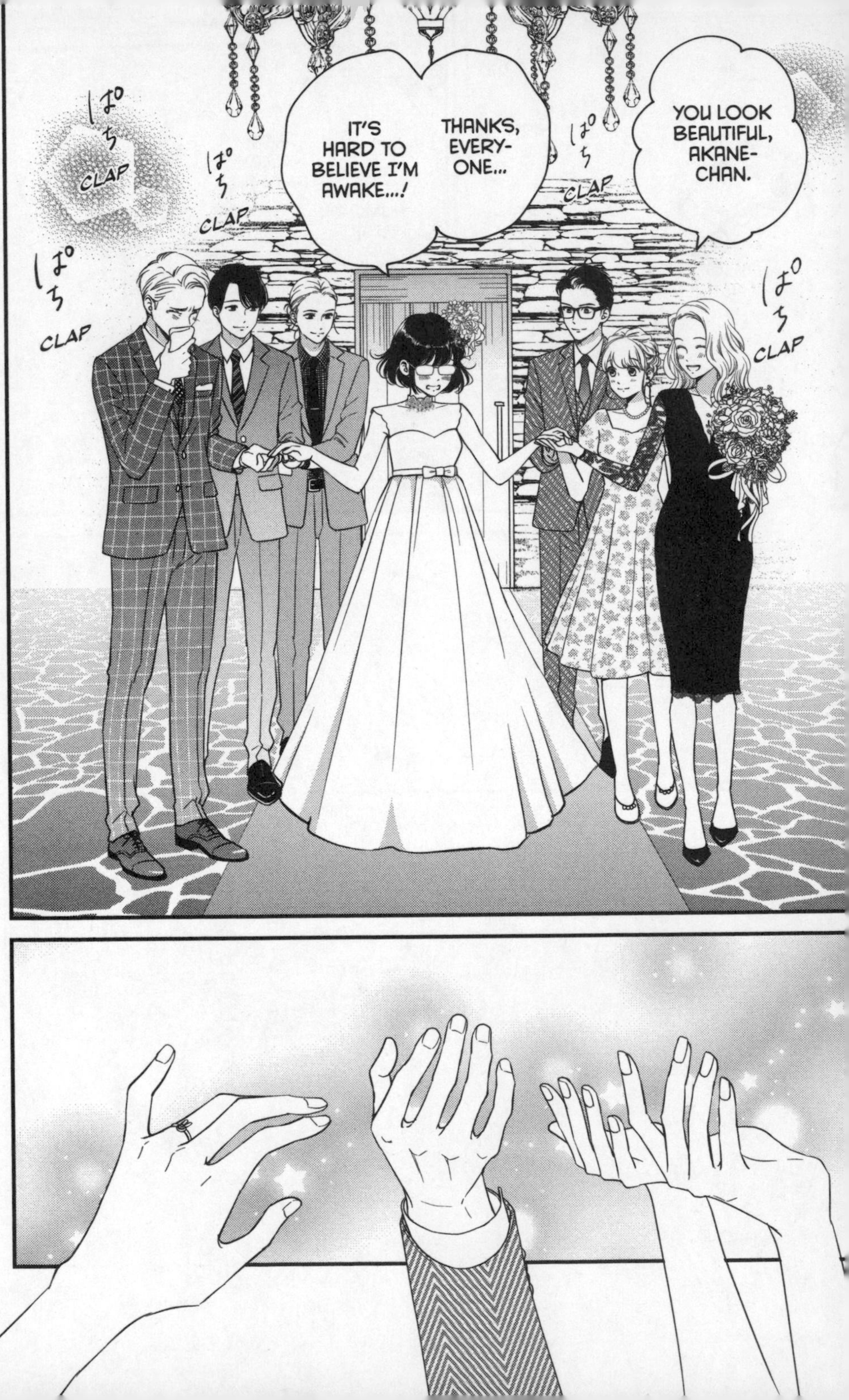
YOU LOOK BEAUTIFUL, AKANE-CHAN.
ぱち CLAP
THANKS, EVERY-ONE...
IT'S HARD TO BELIEVE I'M AWAKE...!
ぱち CLAP
ぱち CLAP
ぱち CLAP
ぱち CLAP

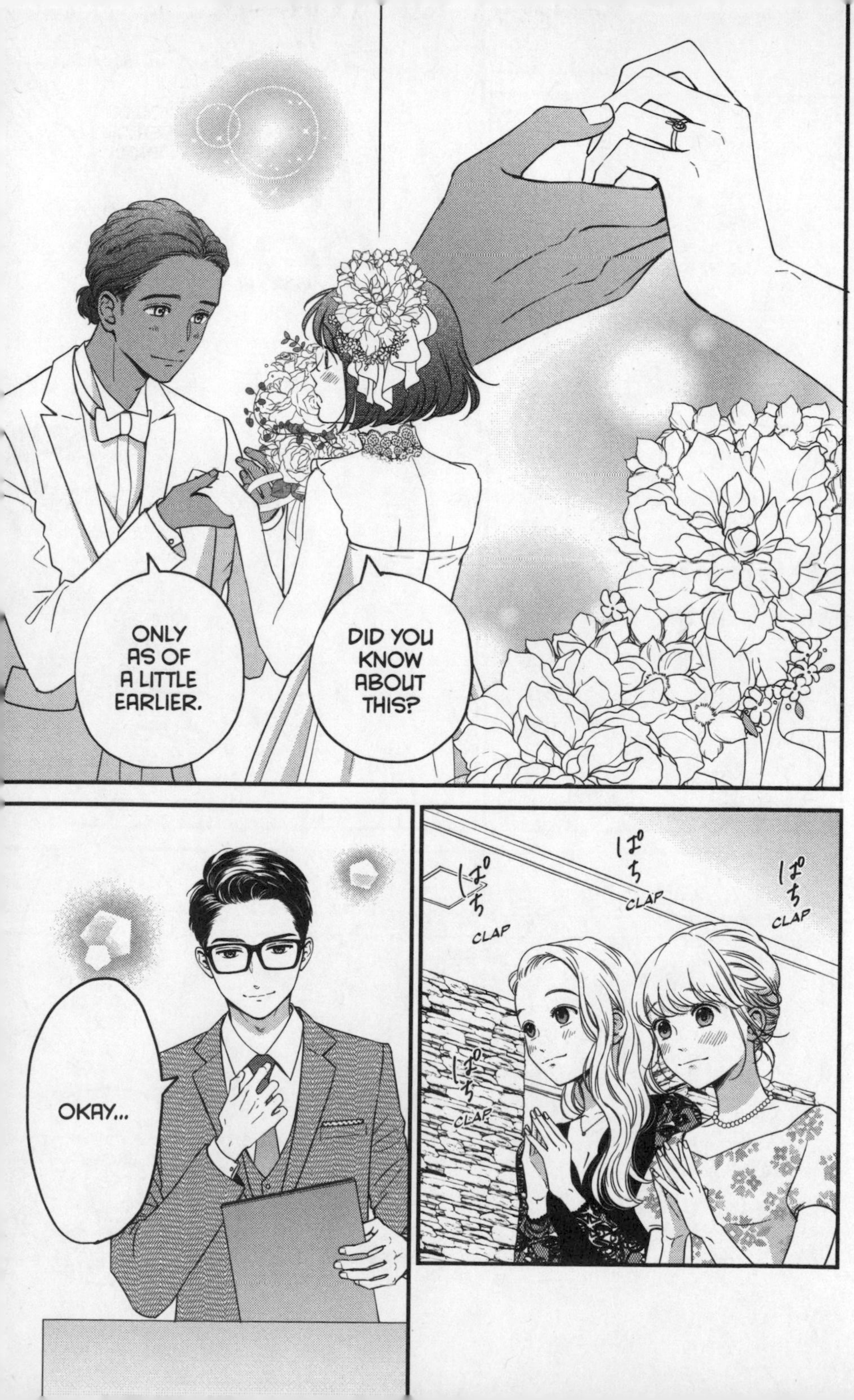
DID YOU KNOW ABOUT THIS?
ONLY AS OF A LITTLE EARLIER.
ぱち
CLAP
ぱち
CLAP
ぱち
CLAP
ぱち
CLAP
OKAY...

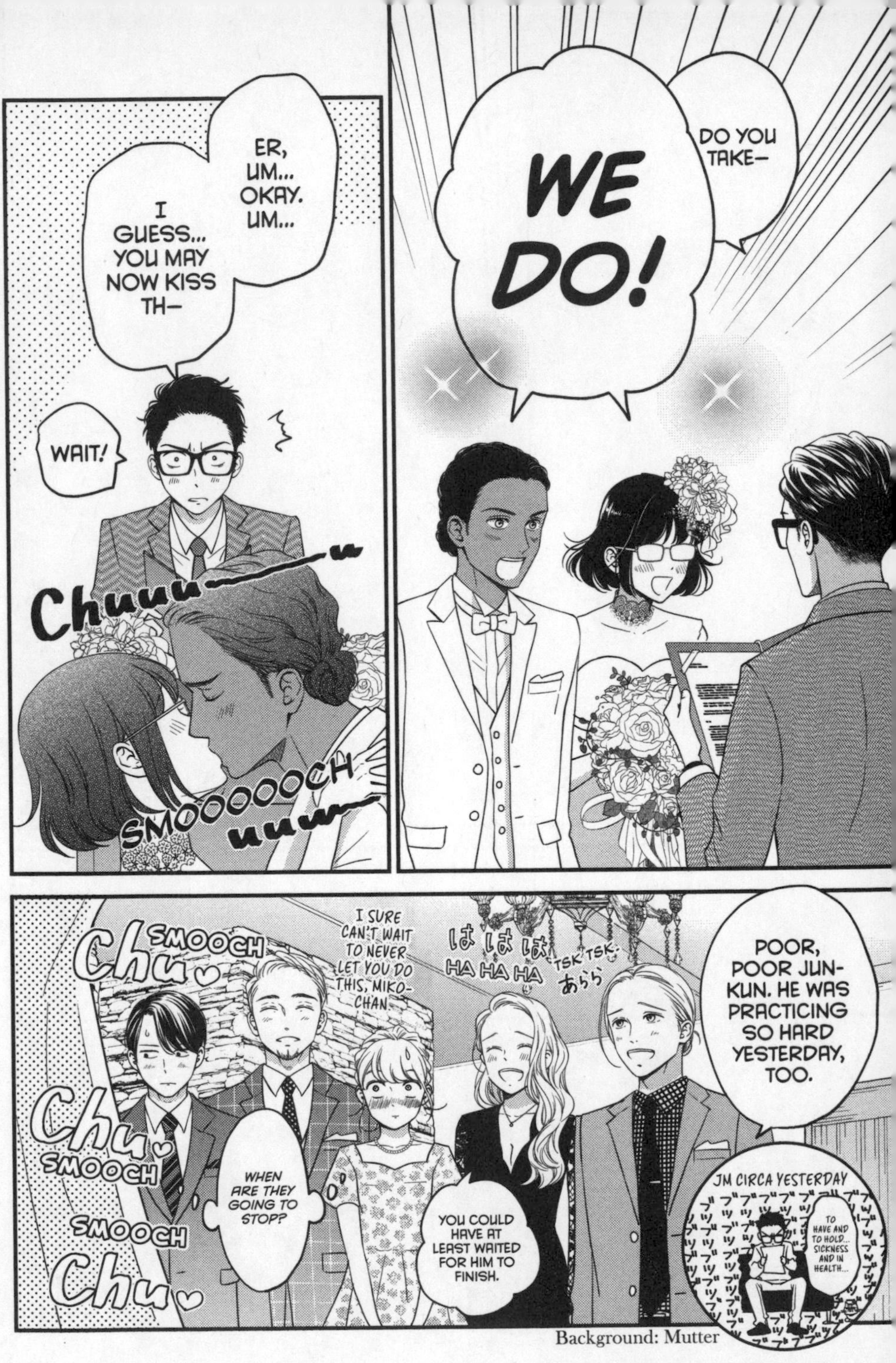
DO YOU TAKE—
WE DO!
ER, UM... OKAY. UM...
I GUESS... YOU MAY NOW KISS TH—
WAIT!
Chuuu—u
SMOOOOOCH uuu—
POOR, POOR JUN-KUN. HE WAS PRACTICING SO HARD YESTERDAY, TOO.
JM CIRCA YESTERDAY
TO HAVE AND TO HOLD... SICKNESS AND IN HEALTH...
TSK TSK. あらら
ははは HA HA HA
I SURE CAN'T WAIT TO NEVER LET YOU DO THIS, MIKO-CHAN.
YOU COULD HAVE AT LEAST WAITED FOR HIM TO FINISH.
WHEN ARE THEY GOING TO STOP?
Chu SMOOCH Chu♡
Chu♡ SMOOCH
SMOOCH Chu♡

Background: Mutter

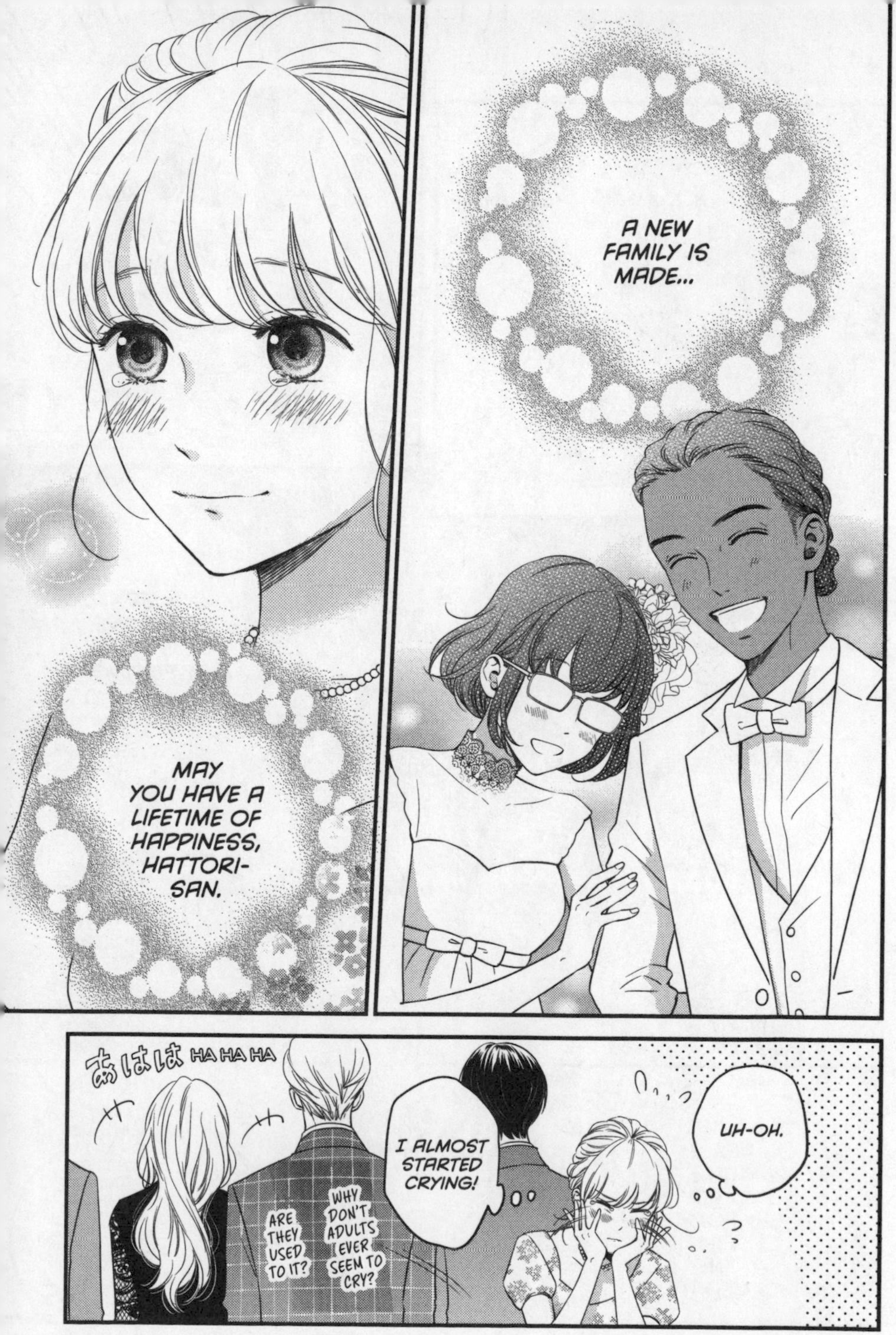
A NEW FAMILY IS MADE...
MAY YOU HAVE A LIFETIME OF HAPPINESS, HATTORI-SAN.
UH-OH.
I ALMOST STARTED CRYING!
WHY DON'T ADULTS EVER SEEM TO CRY?
ARE THEY USED TO IT?
あはは HA HA HA

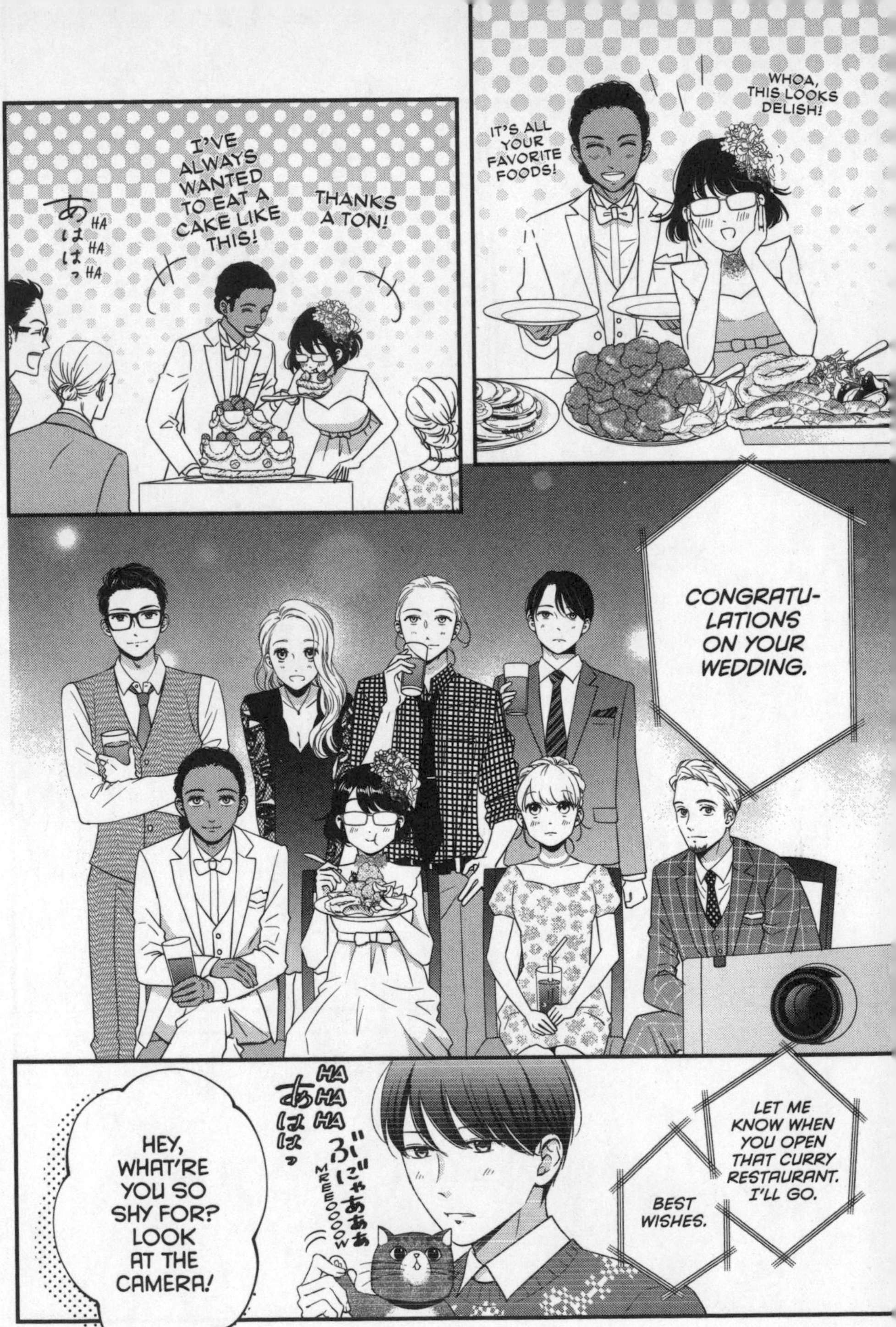
WHOA, THIS LOOKS DELISH!
IT'S ALL YOUR FAVORITE FOODS!
THANKS A TON!
I'VE ALWAYS WANTED TO EAT A CAKE LIKE THIS!
あははっ
HA HA HA
CONGRATU-LATIONS ON YOUR WEDDING.
LET ME KNOW WHEN YOU OPEN THAT CURRY RESTAURANT. I'LL GO.
BEST WISHES.
HA HA HA
あははっ
ぶにゃあああ
MREEOOOOW
HEY, WHAT'RE YOU SO SHY FOR? LOOK AT THE CAMERA!

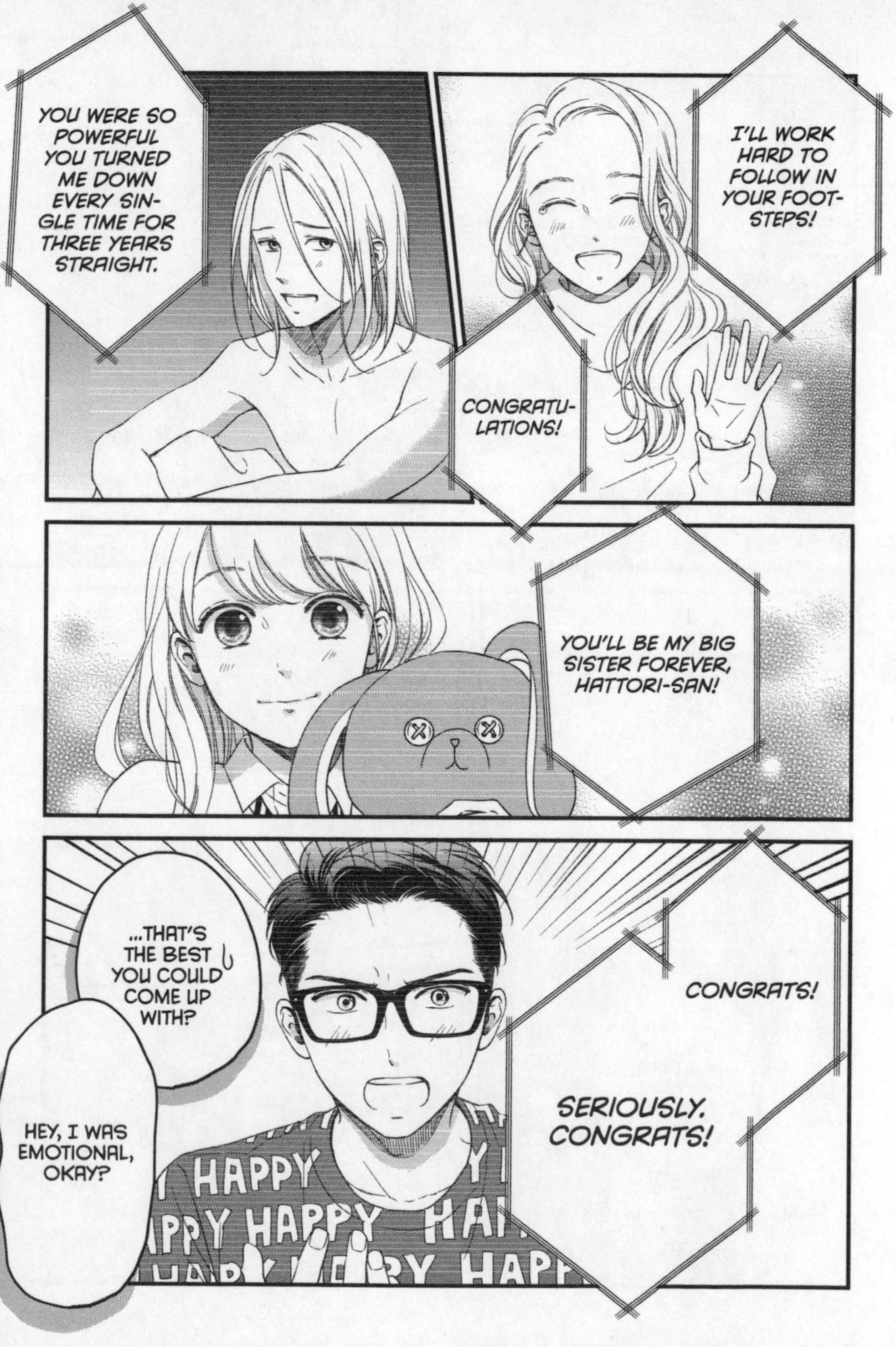
I'LL WORK HARD TO FOLLOW IN YOUR FOOT-STEPS!
CONGRATU-LATIONS!
YOU WERE SO POWERFUL YOU TURNED ME DOWN EVERY SIN-GLE TIME FOR THREE YEARS STRAIGHT.
YOU'LL BE MY BIG SISTER FOREVER, HATTORI-SAN!
CONGRATS!
SERIOUSLY. CONGRATS!
...THAT'S THE BEST YOU COULD COME UP WITH?
HEY, I WAS EMOTIONAL, OKAY?

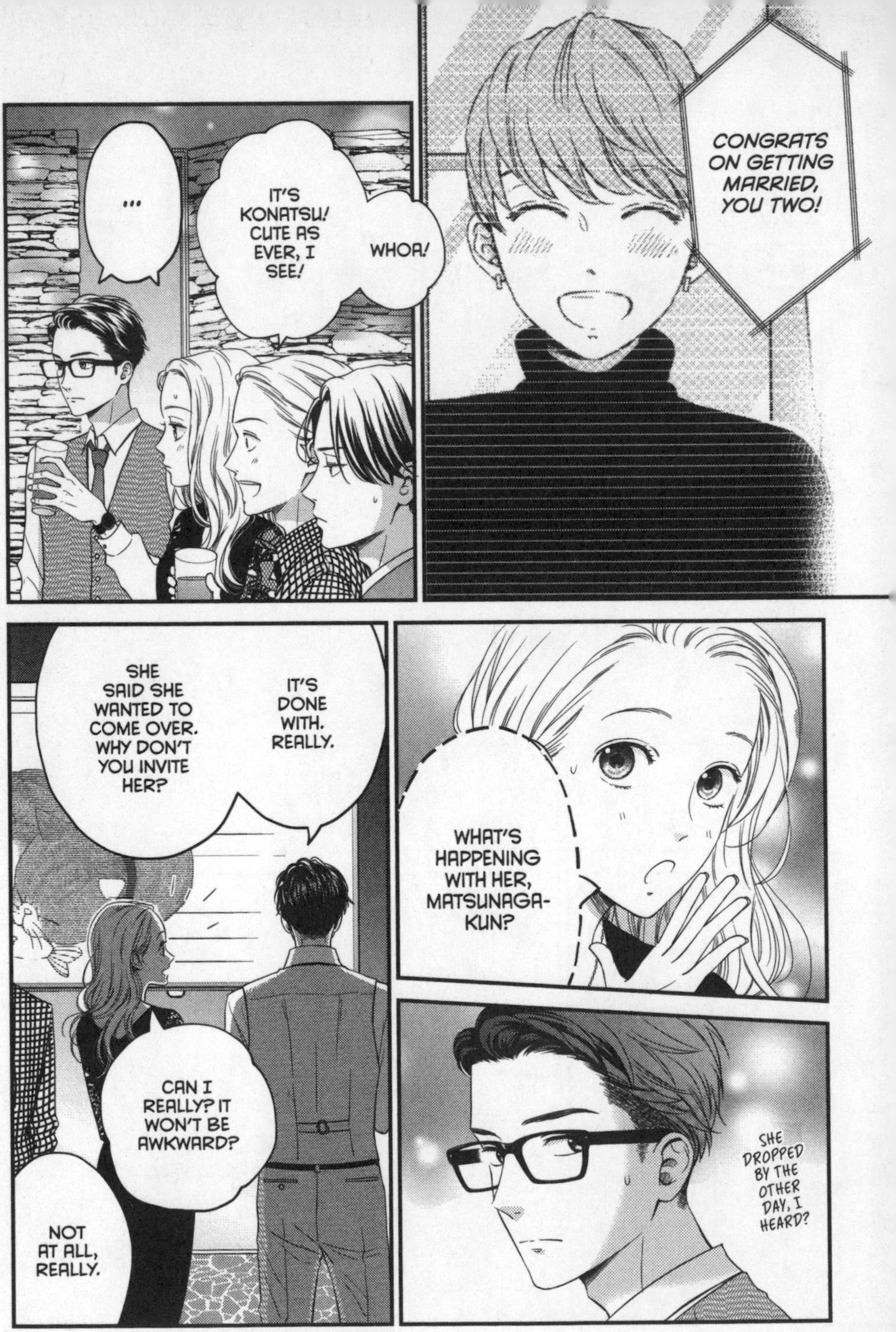
CONGRATS ON GETTING MARRIED, YOU TWO!
WHOA!
IT'S KONATSU! CUTE AS EVER, I SEE!
...
WHAT'S HAPPENING WITH HER, MATSUNAGA-KUN?
SHE DROPPED BY THE OTHER DAY, I HEARD?
IT'S DONE WITH. REALLY.
SHE SAID SHE WANTED TO COME OVER. WHY DON'T YOU INVITE HER?
CAN I REALLY? IT WON'T BE AWKWARD?
NOT AT ALL, REALLY.

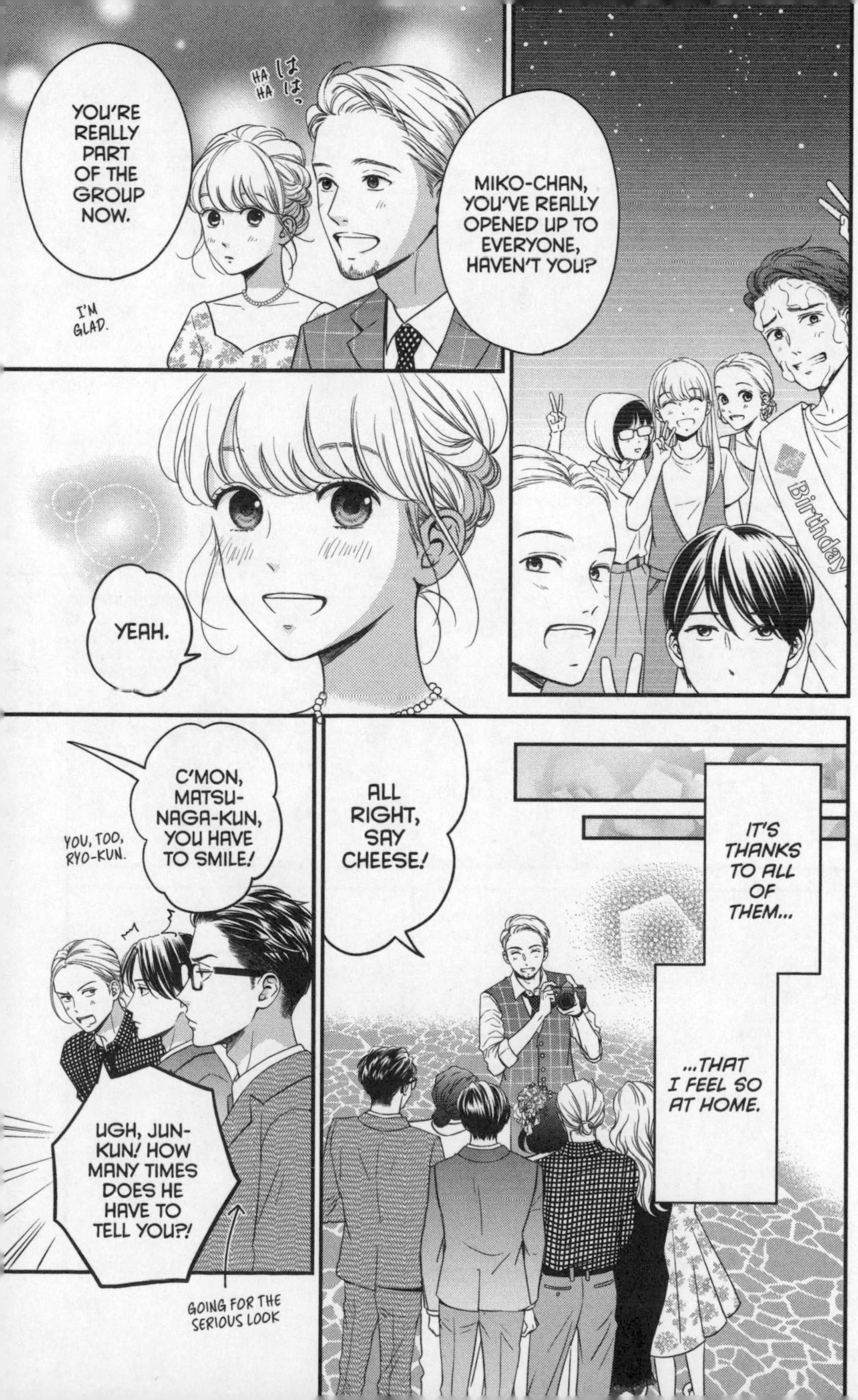
MIKO-CHAN, YOU'VE REALLY OPENED UP TO EVERYONE, HAVEN'T YOU?
HA HA ははっ
YOU'RE REALLY PART OF THE GROUP NOW.
I'M GLAD.
YEAH.
ALL RIGHT, SAY CHEESE!
IT'S THANKS TO ALL OF THEM...
...THAT I FEEL SO AT HOME.
C'MON, MATSU-NAGA-KUN, YOU HAVE TO SMILE!
YOU, TOO, RYO-KUN.
UGH, JUN-KUN! HOW MANY TIMES DOES HE HAVE TO TELL YOU?!
GOING FOR THE SERIOUS LOOK

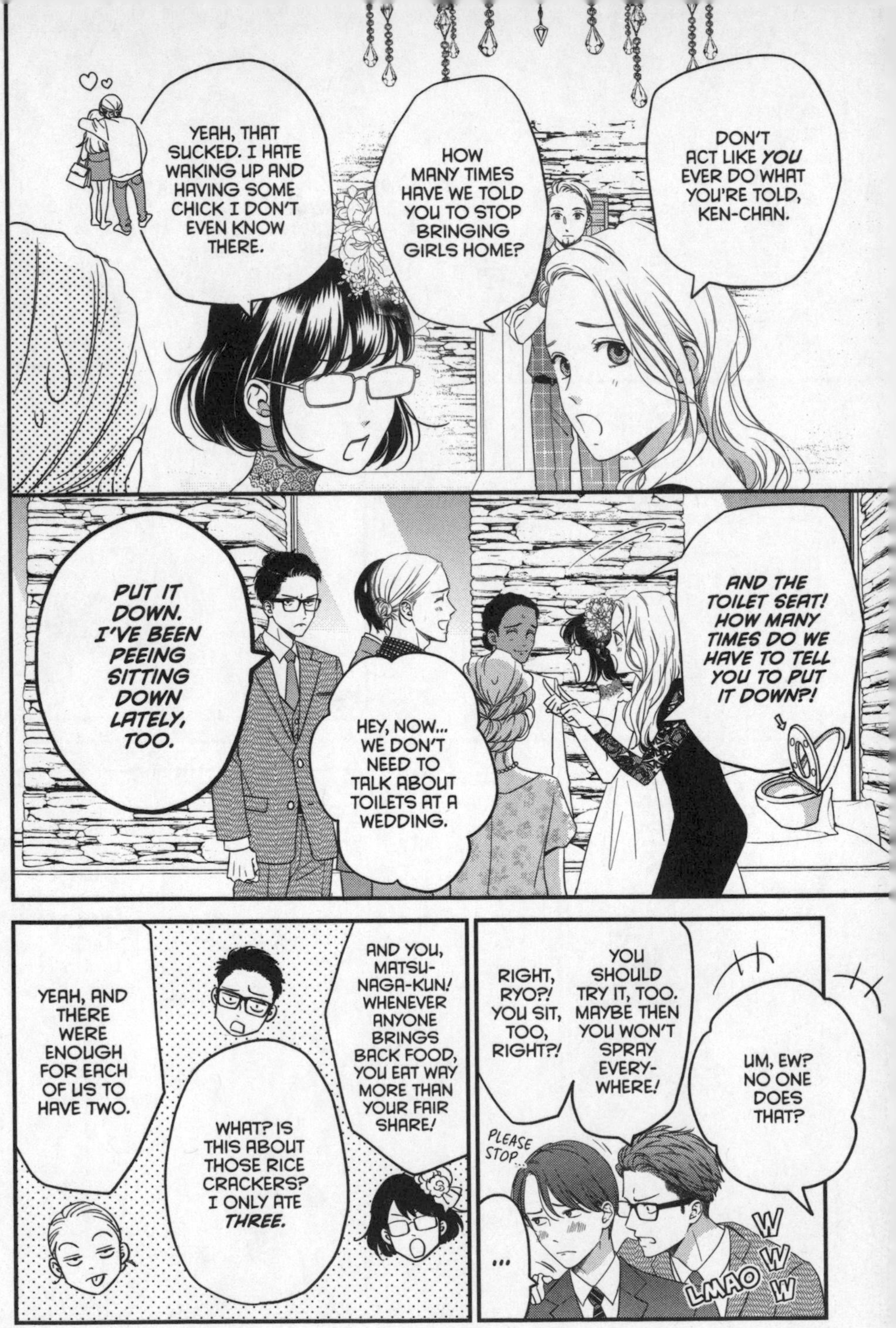
DON'T ACT LIKE *YOU* EVER DO WHAT YOU'RE TOLD, KEN-CHAN.
HOW MANY TIMES HAVE WE TOLD YOU TO STOP BRINGING GIRLS HOME?
YEAH, THAT SUCKED. I HATE WAKING UP AND HAVING SOME CHICK I DON'T EVEN KNOW THERE.
AND THE TOILET SEAT! HOW MANY TIMES DO WE HAVE TO TELL YOU TO PUT IT DOWN?!
PUT IT DOWN. I'VE BEEN PEEING SITTING DOWN LATELY, TOO.
HEY, NOW... WE DON'T NEED TO TALK ABOUT TOILETS AT A WEDDING.
YOU SHOULD TRY IT, TOO. MAYBE THEN YOU WON'T SPRAY EVERY-WHERE!
UM, EW? NO ONE DOES THAT?
RIGHT, RYO?! YOU SIT, TOO, RIGHT?!
PLEASE STOP...
...
LMAO WWWW
AND YOU, MATSU-NAGA-KUN! WHENEVER ANYONE BRINGS BACK FOOD, YOU EAT WAY MORE THAN YOUR FAIR SHARE!
WHAT? IS THIS ABOUT THOSE RICE CRACKERS? I ONLY ATE *THREE.*
YEAH, AND THERE WERE ENOUGH FOR EACH OF US TO HAVE TWO.

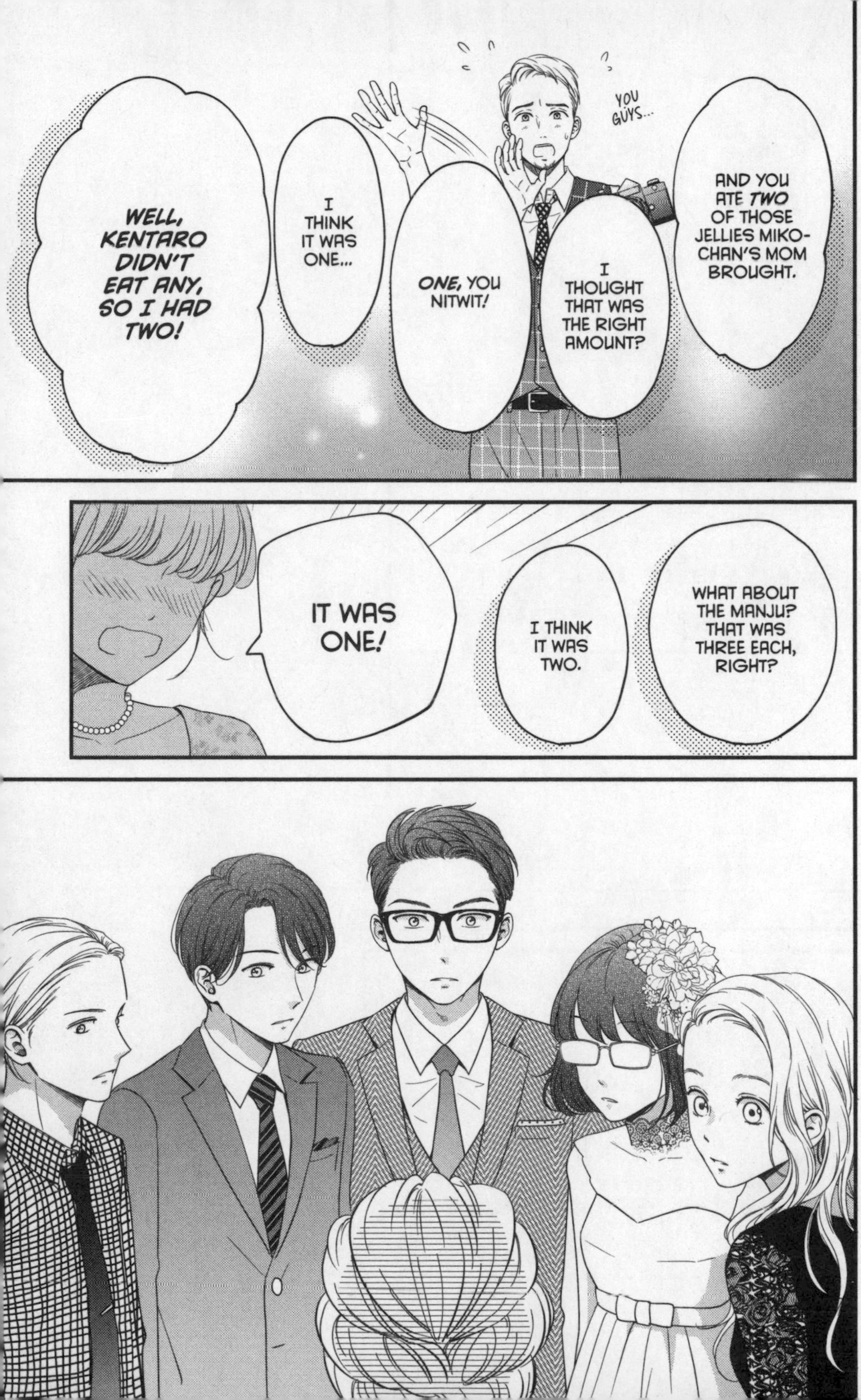
AND YOU ATE *TWO* OF THOSE JELLIES MIKO-CHAN'S MOM BROUGHT.
YOU GUYS...
I THOUGHT THAT WAS THE RIGHT AMOUNT?
ONE, YOU NITWIT!
I THINK IT WAS ONE...
WELL, KENTARO DIDN'T EAT ANY, SO I HAD TWO!
WHAT ABOUT THE MANJU? THAT WAS THREE EACH, RIGHT?
I THINK IT WAS TWO.
IT WAS ONE!

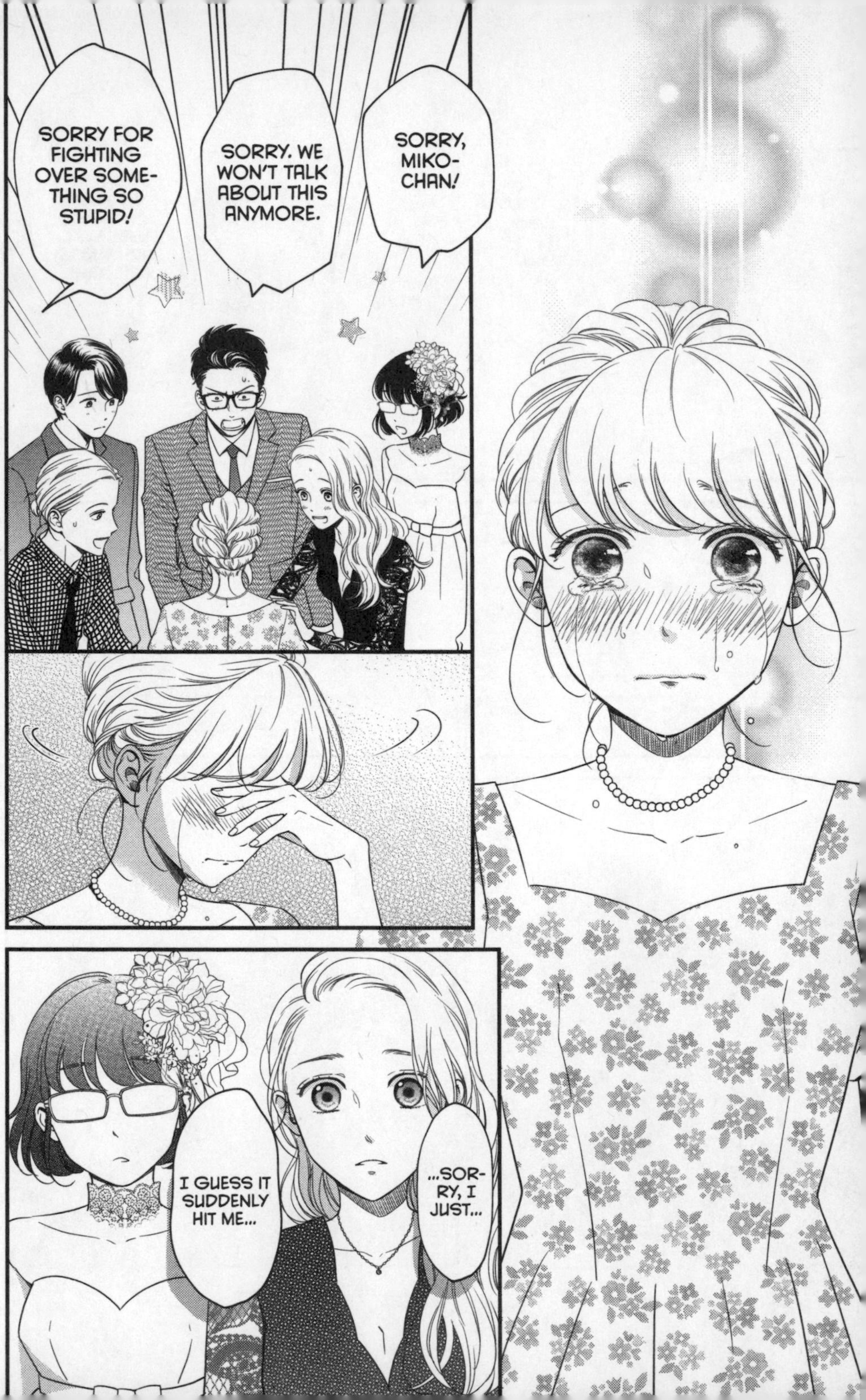
SORRY, MIKO-CHAN!
SORRY. WE WON'T TALK ABOUT THIS ANYMORE.
SORRY FOR FIGHTING OVER SOME-THING SO STUPID!
...SOR-RY, I JUST...
I GUESS IT SUDDENLY HIT ME...

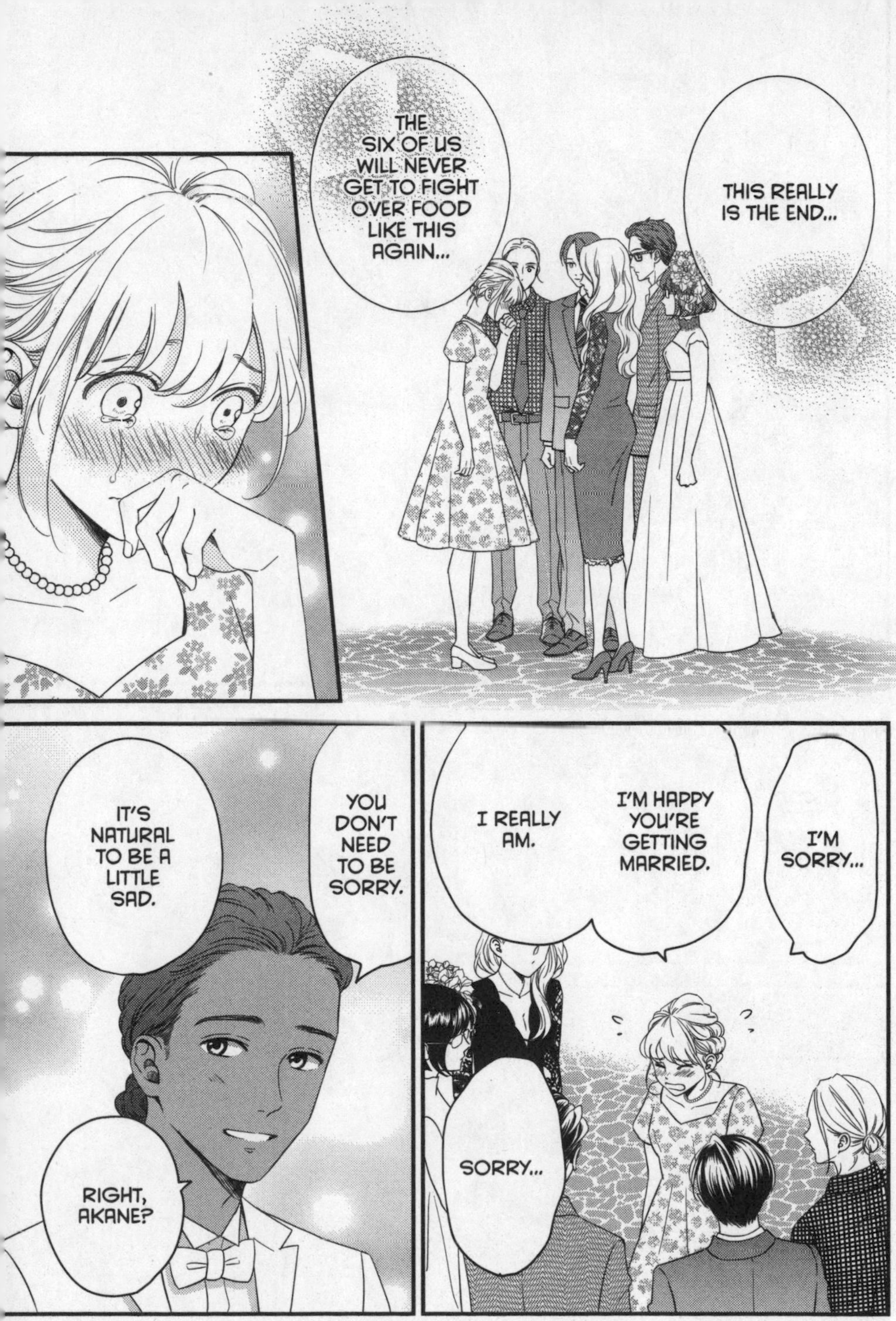
THIS REALLY IS THE END...
THE SIX OF US WILL NEVER GET TO FIGHT OVER FOOD LIKE THIS AGAIN...
I'M SORRY...
I'M HAPPY YOU'RE GETTING MARRIED.
I REALLY AM.
SORRY...
YOU DON'T NEED TO BE SORRY.
IT'S NATURAL TO BE A LITTLE SAD.
RIGHT, AKANE?

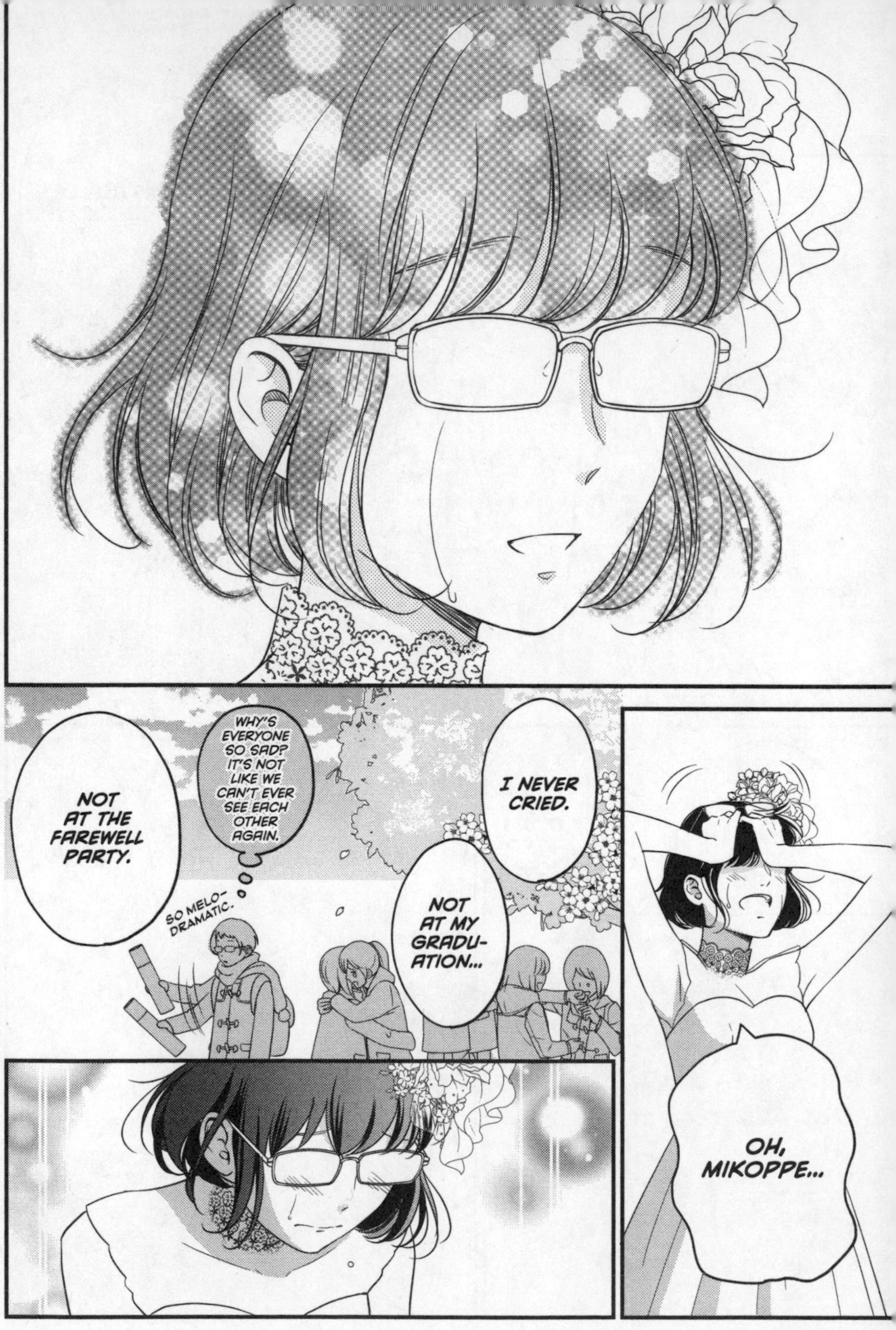
OH, MIKOPPE...
I NEVER CRIED.
NOT AT MY GRADUATION...
NOT AT THE FAREWELL PARTY.
WHY'S EVERYONE SO SAD? IT'S NOT LIKE WE CAN'T EVER SEE EACH OTHER AGAIN.
SO MELODRAMATIC.

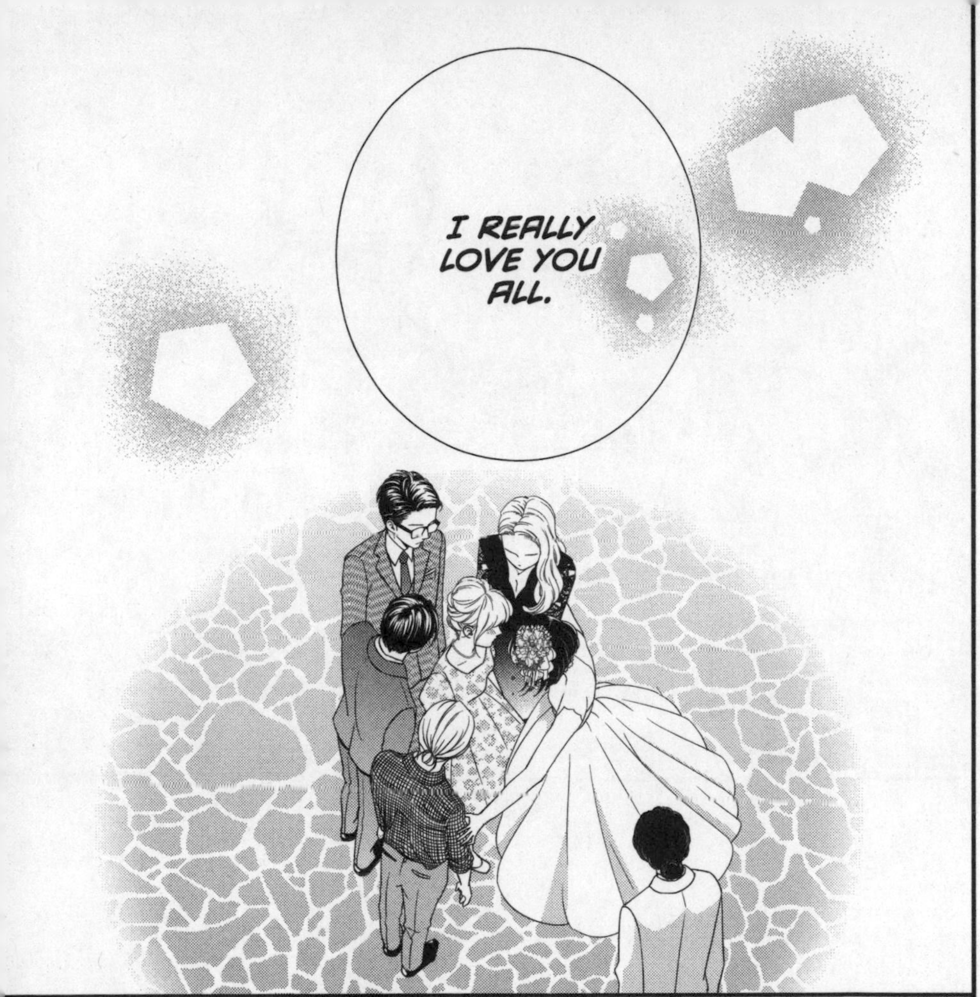
I REALLY LOVE YOU ALL.
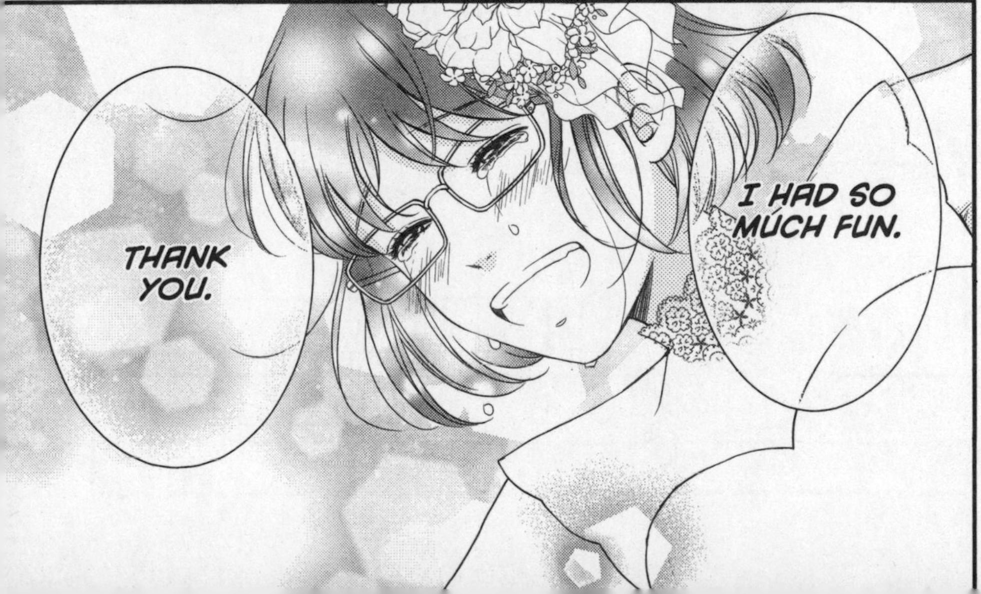
I HAD SO MUCH FUN.
THANK YOU.

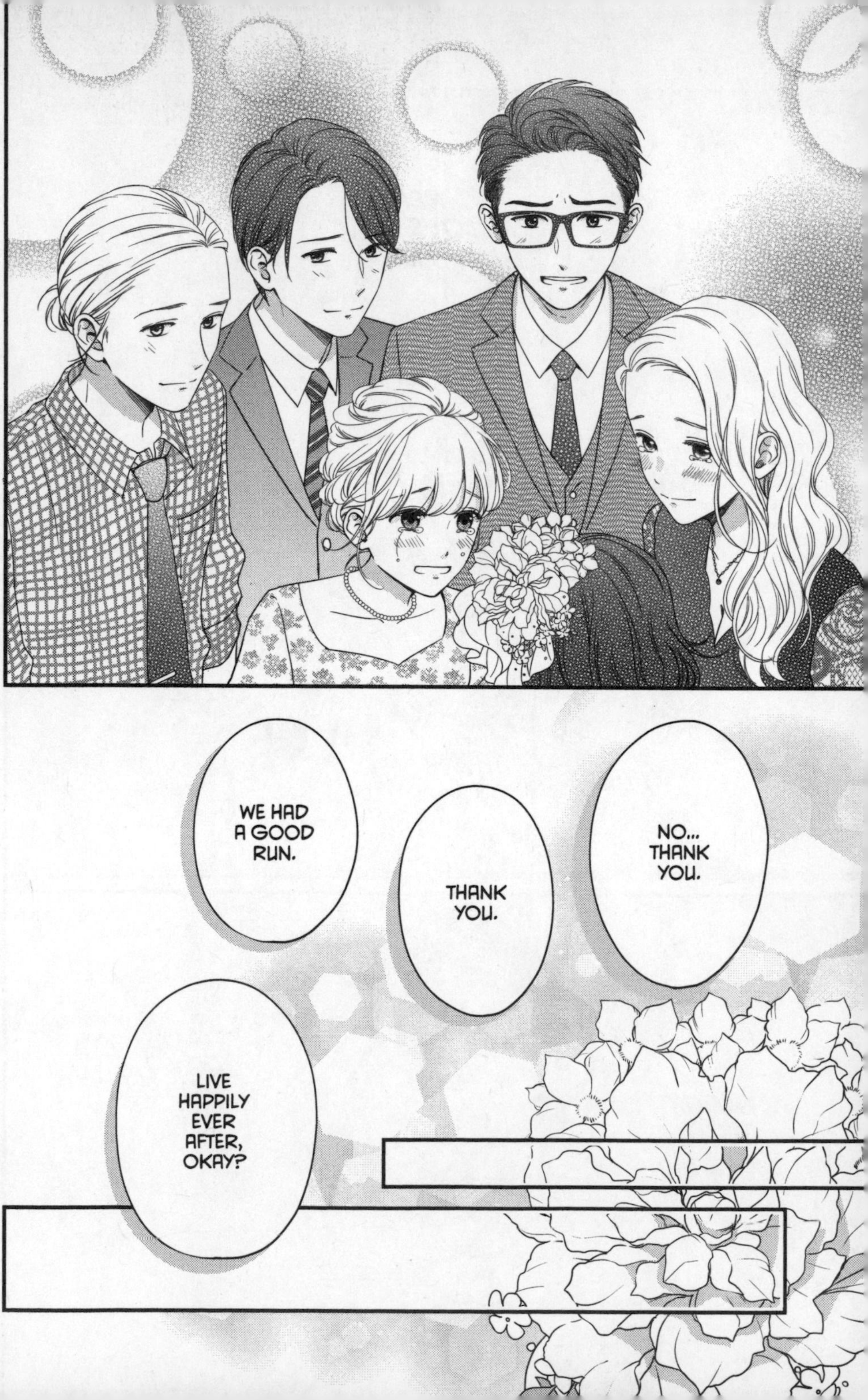
NO... THANK YOU.
THANK YOU.
WE HAD A GOOD RUN.
LIVE HAPPILY EVER AFTER, OKAY?

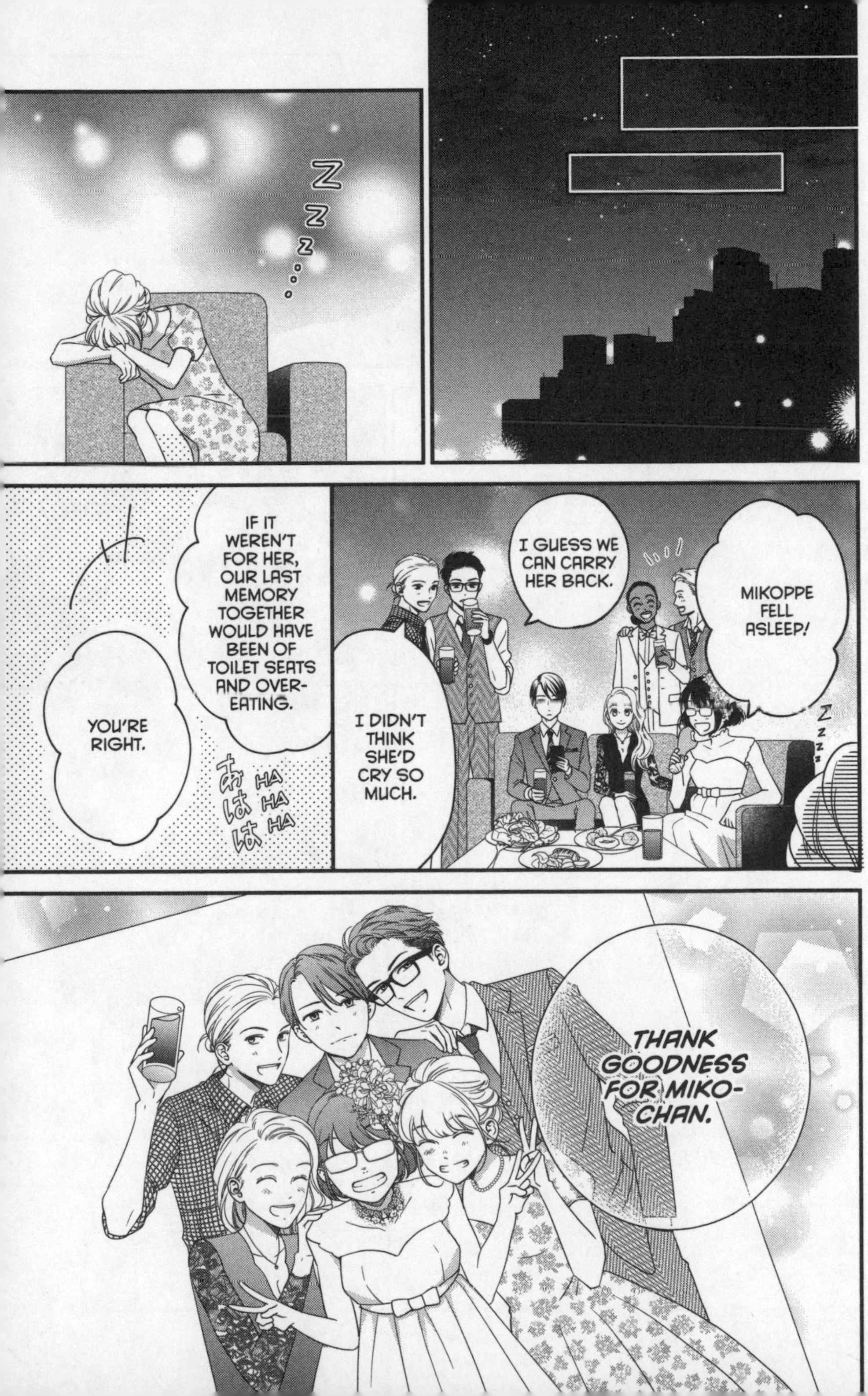
Z
Z
z
MIKOPPE FELL ASLEEP!
I GUESS WE CAN CARRY HER BACK.
I DIDN'T THINK SHE'D CRY SO MUCH.
IF IT WEREN'T FOR HER, OUR LAST MEMORY TOGETHER WOULD HAVE BEEN OF TOILET SEATS AND OVER-EATING.
YOU'RE RIGHT.
あはは HA HA HA
THANK GOODNESS FOR MIKO-CHAN.

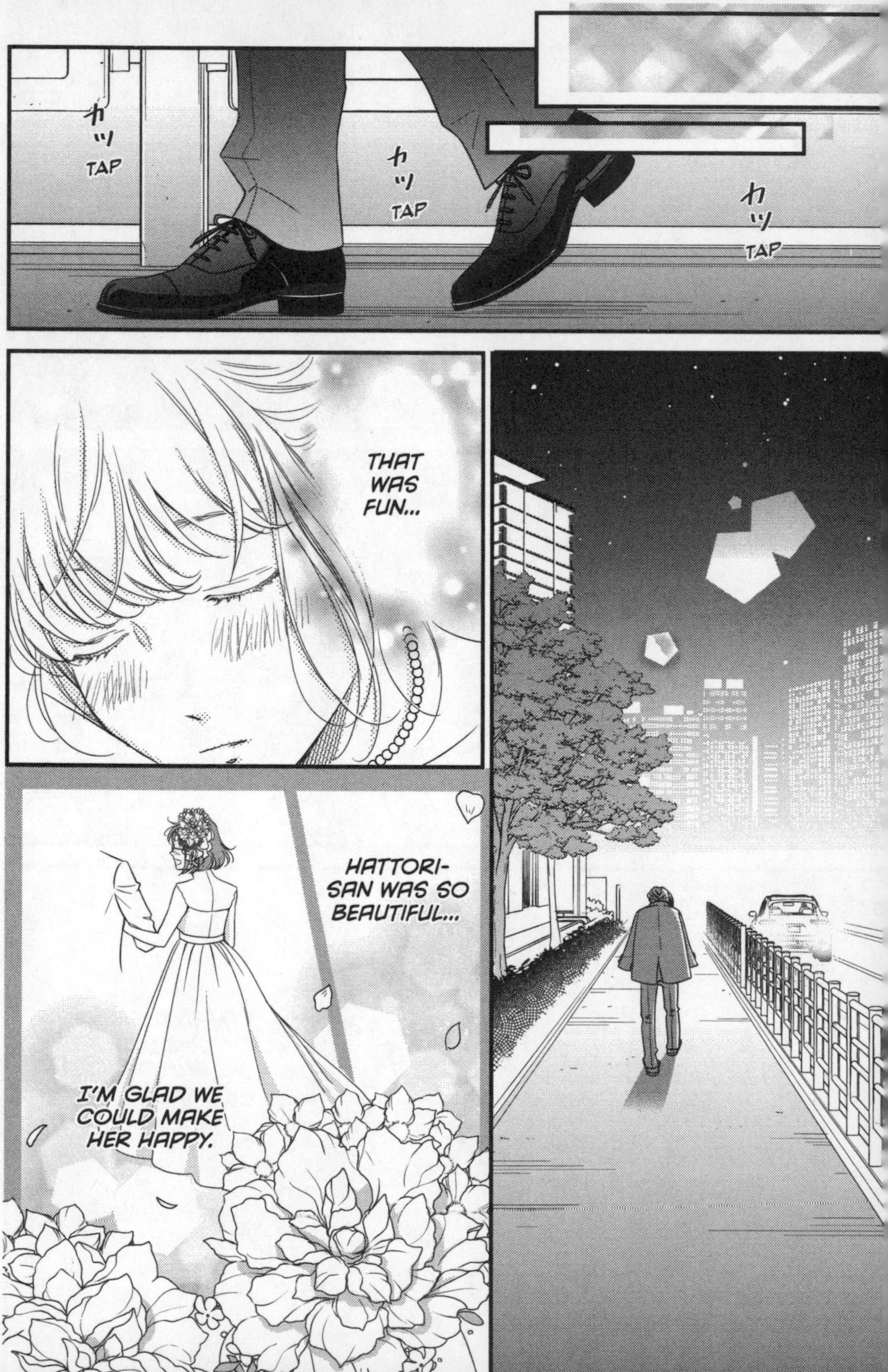

カッ TAP
カッ TAP
カッ TAP
THAT WAS FUN...
HATTORI-SAN WAS SO BEAUTIFUL...
I'M GLAD WE COULD MAKE HER HAPPY.

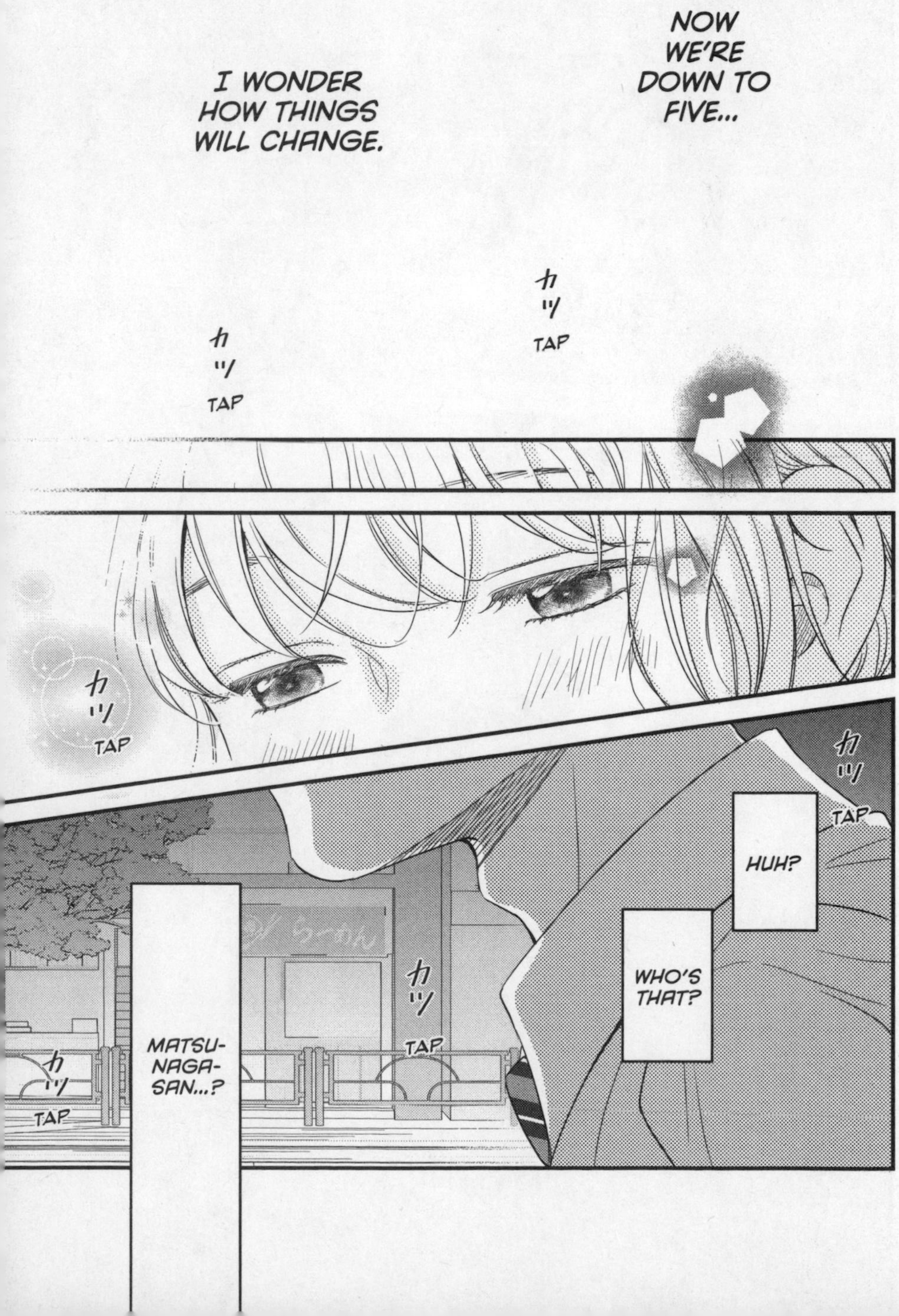
NOW WE'RE DOWN TO FIVE...
I WONDER HOW THINGS WILL CHANGE.
カツ TAP
カツ TAP
カツ TAP
カツ TAP
HUH?
WHO'S THAT?
カツ TAP
MATSU-NAGA-SAN...?
カツ TAP

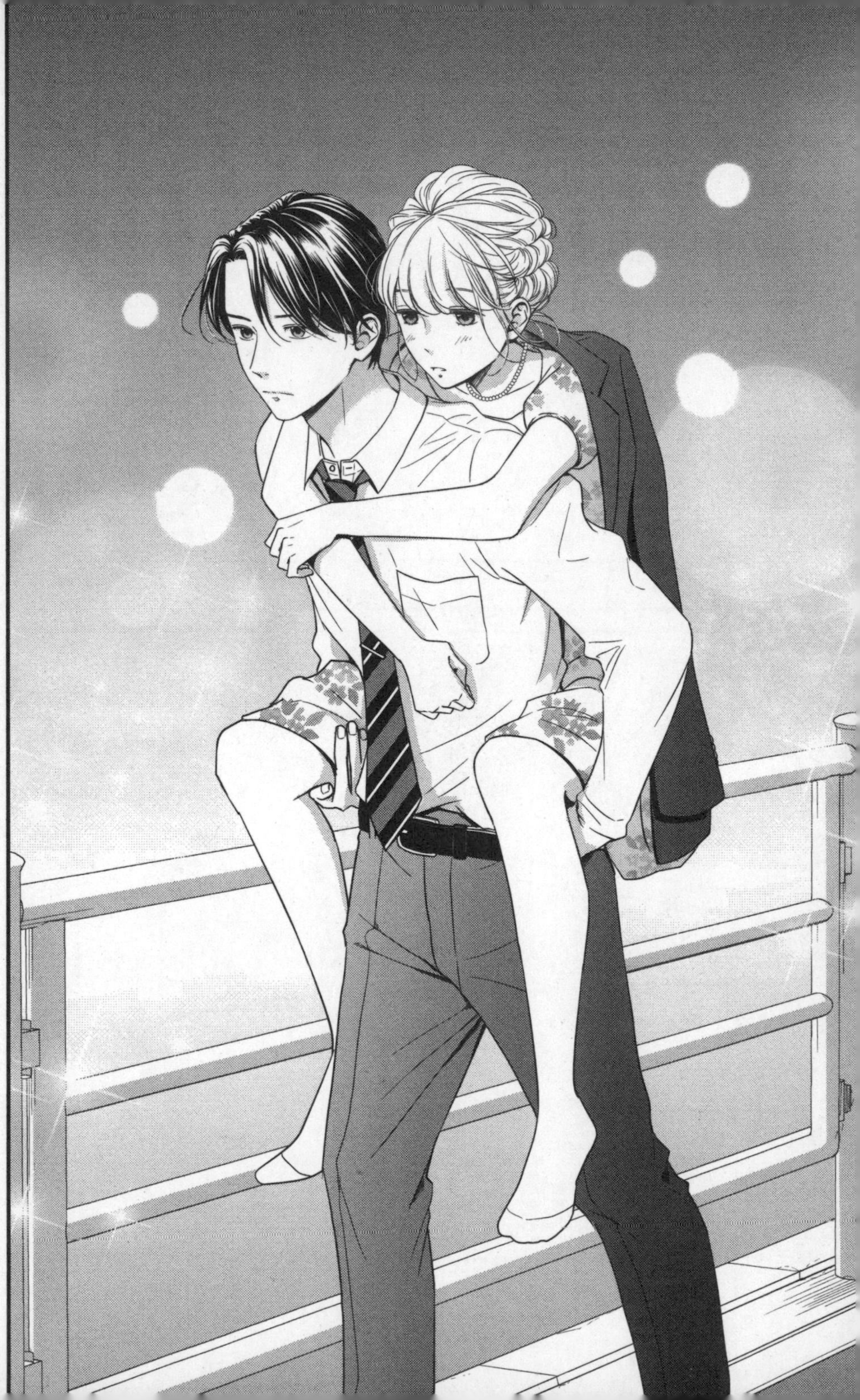

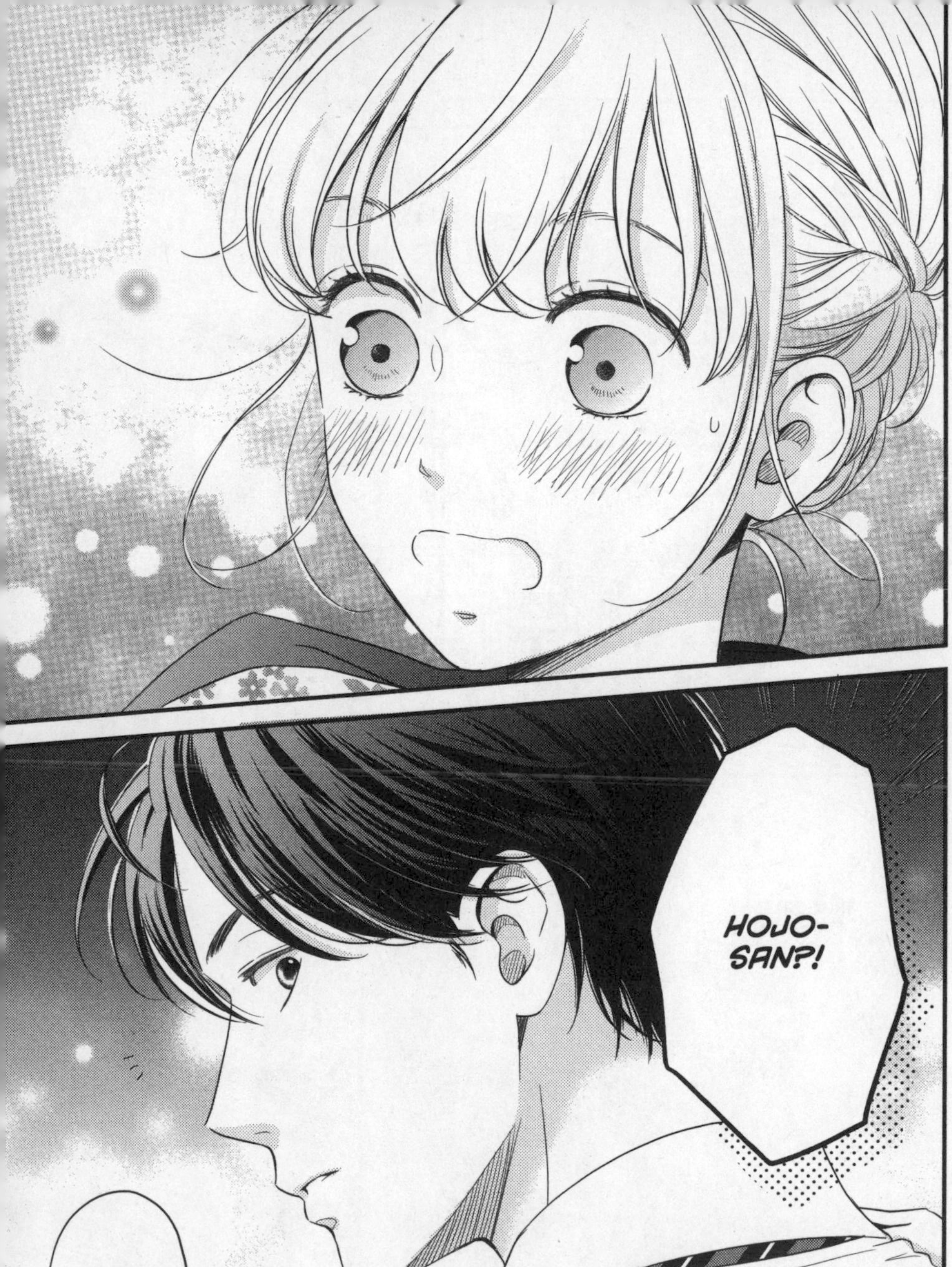
HOJO-SAN?!
YOU'RE UP?

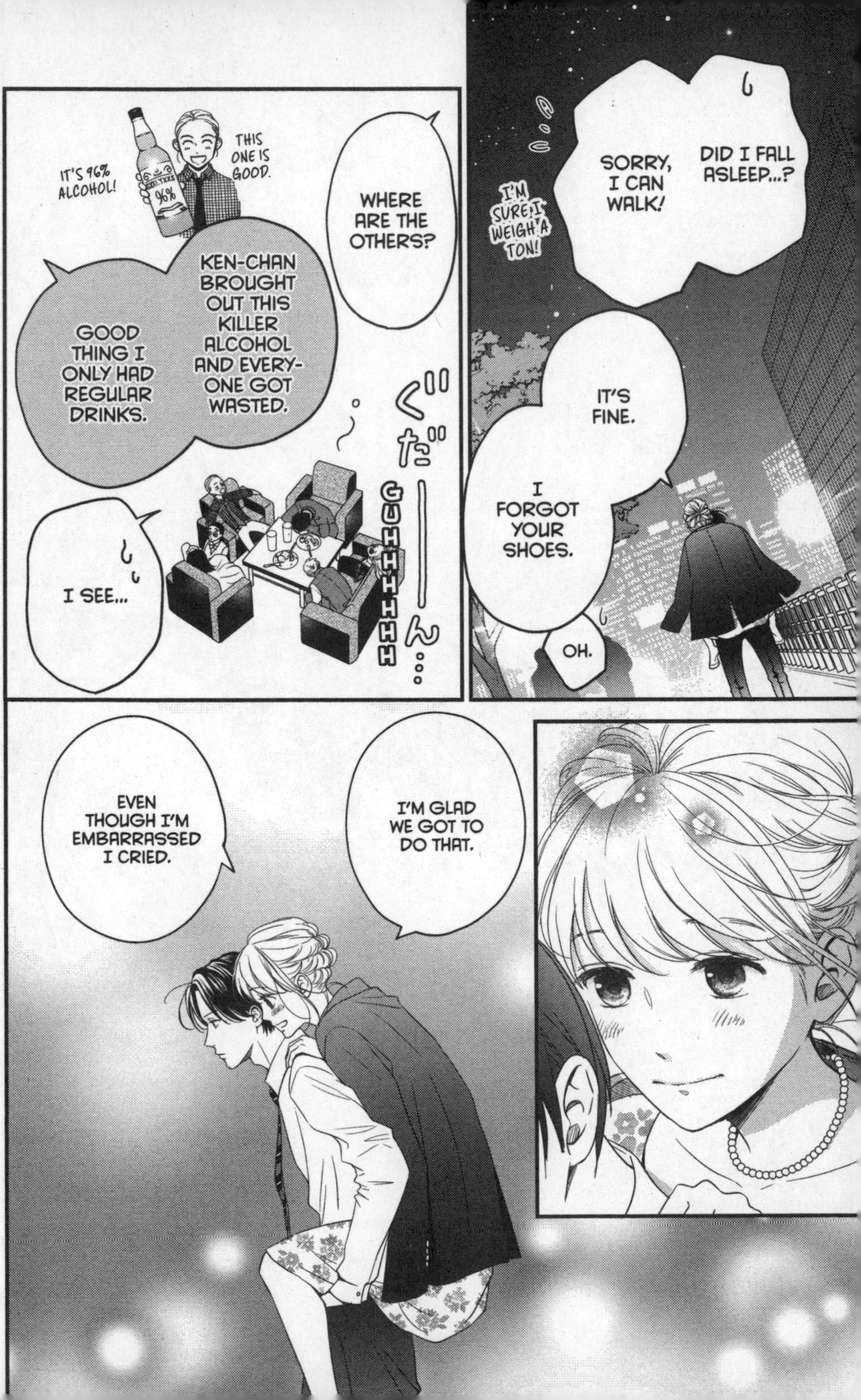
DID I FALL ASLEEP...?
SORRY, I CAN WALK!
I'M SURE I WEIGH A TON!
IT'S FINE.
I FORGOT YOUR SHOES.
OH.
WHERE ARE THE OTHERS?
THIS ONE IS GOOD.
IT'S 96% ALCOHOL!
96%
KEN-CHAN BROUGHT OUT THIS KILLER ALCOHOL AND EVERY-ONE GOT WASTED.
GOOD THING I ONLY HAD REGULAR DRINKS.
ぐたーん…
GUHHHHHH
I SEE...
I'M GLAD WE GOT TO DO THAT.
EVEN THOUGH I'M EMBARRASSED I CRIED.

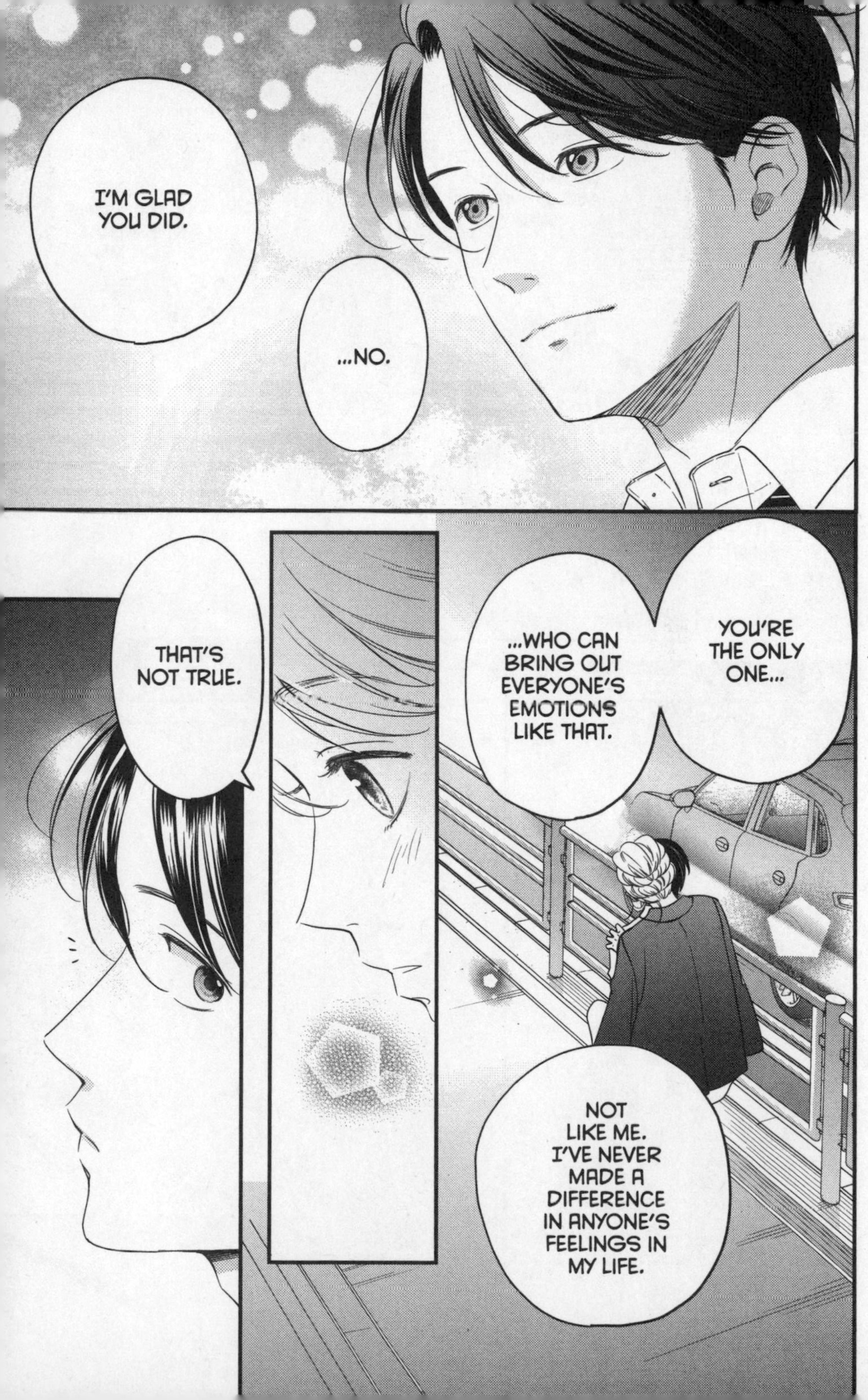
...NO.
I'M GLAD YOU DID.
YOU'RE THE ONLY ONE...
...WHO CAN BRING OUT EVERYONE'S EMOTIONS LIKE THAT.
NOT LIKE ME. I'VE NEVER MADE A DIFFERENCE IN ANYONE'S FEELINGS IN MY LIFE.
THAT'S NOT TRUE.

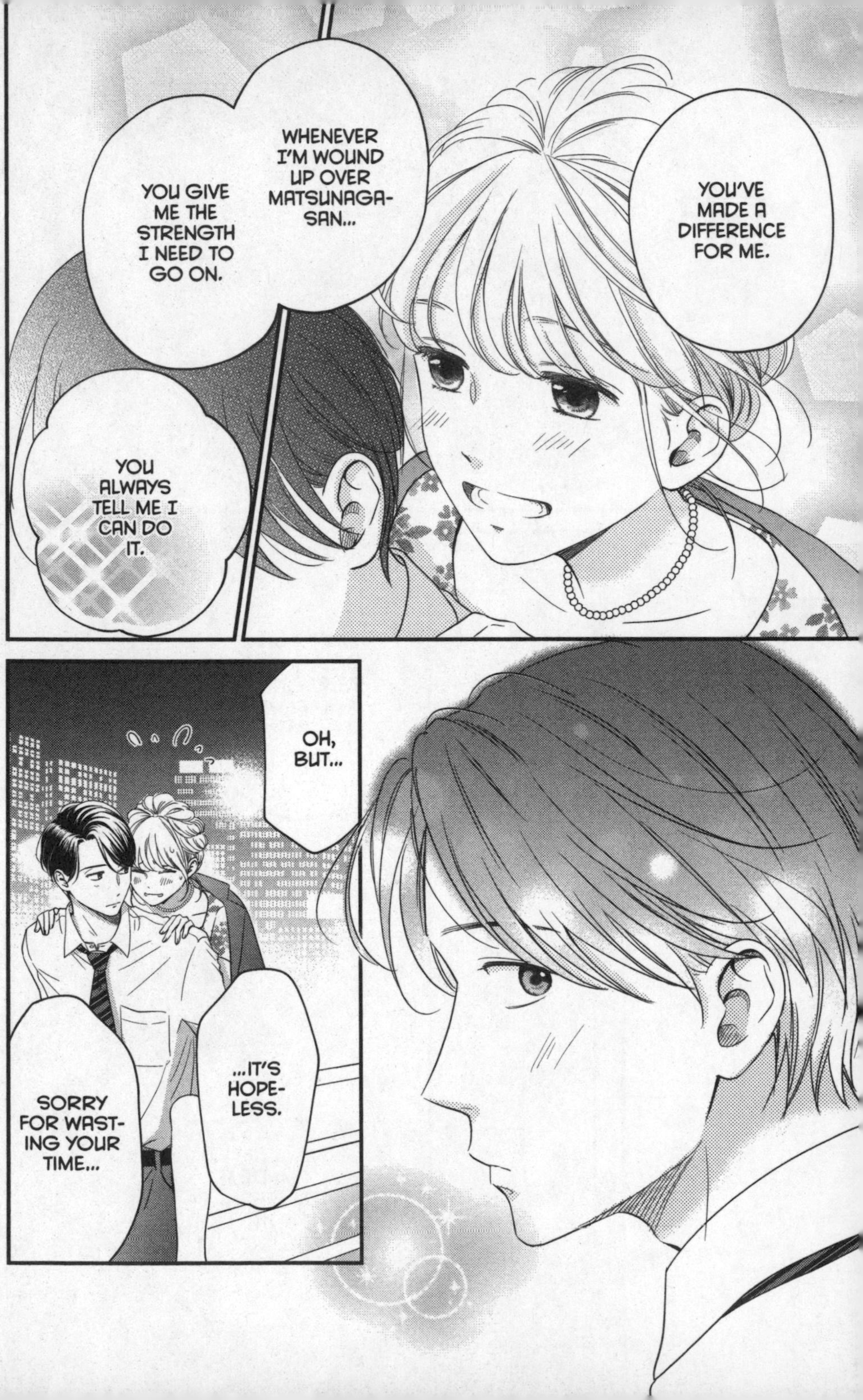
YOU'VE MADE A DIFFERENCE FOR ME.
WHENEVER I'M WOUND UP OVER MATSUNAGA-SAN...
YOU GIVE ME THE STRENGTH I NEED TO GO ON.
YOU ALWAYS TELL ME I CAN DO IT.
OH, BUT...
...IT'S HOPE-LESS.
SORRY FOR WAST-ING YOUR TIME...

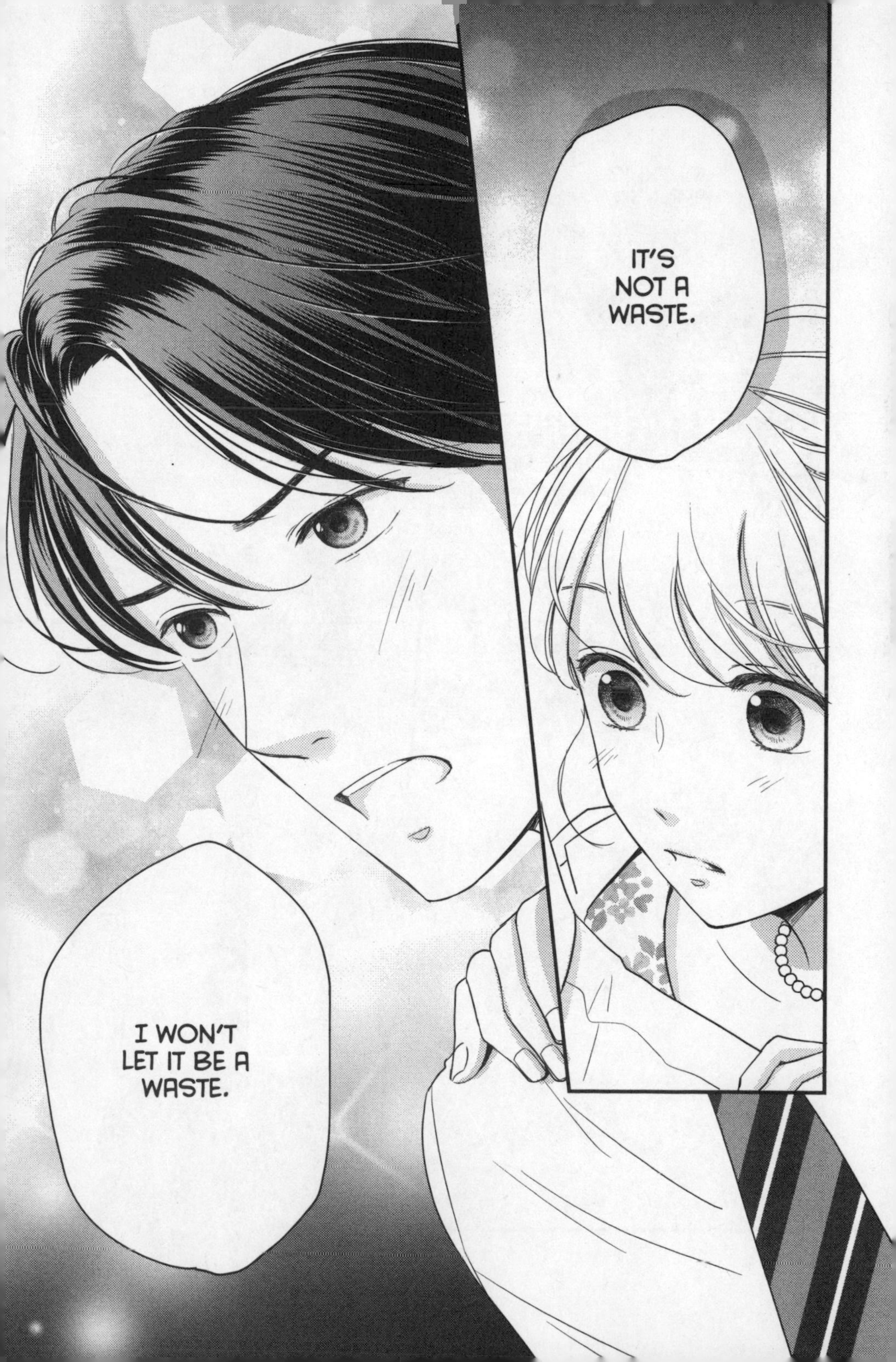
IT'S NOT A WASTE.
I WON'T LET IT BE A WASTE.

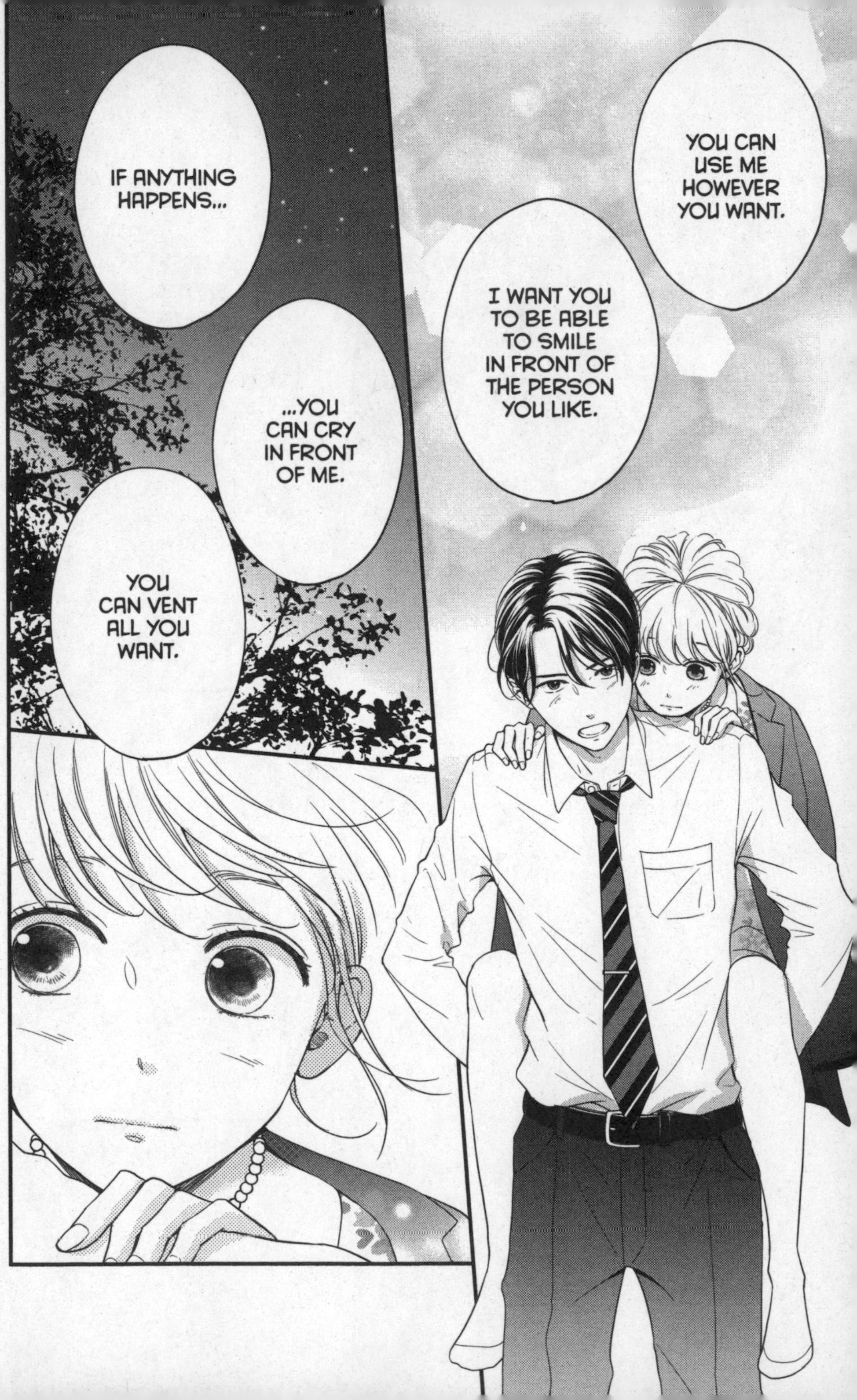
YOU CAN USE ME HOWEVER YOU WANT.
I WANT YOU TO BE ABLE TO SMILE IN FRONT OF THE PERSON YOU LIKE.
IF ANYTHING HAPPENS...
...YOU CAN CRY IN FRONT OF ME.
YOU CAN VENT ALL YOU WANT.

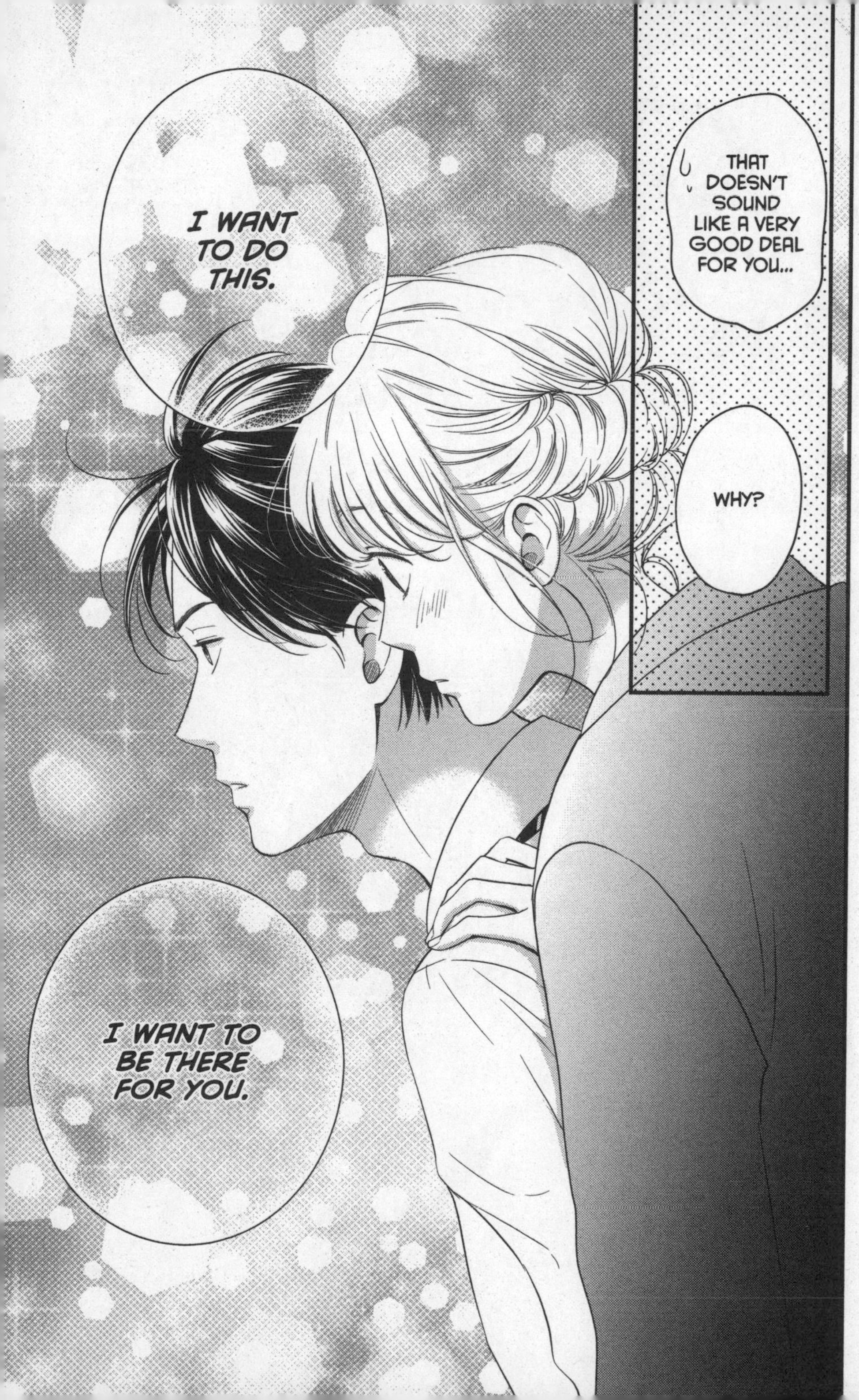
THAT DOESN'T SOUND LIKE A VERY GOOD DEAL FOR YOU...
WHY?
I WANT TO DO THIS.
I WANT TO BE THERE FOR YOU.

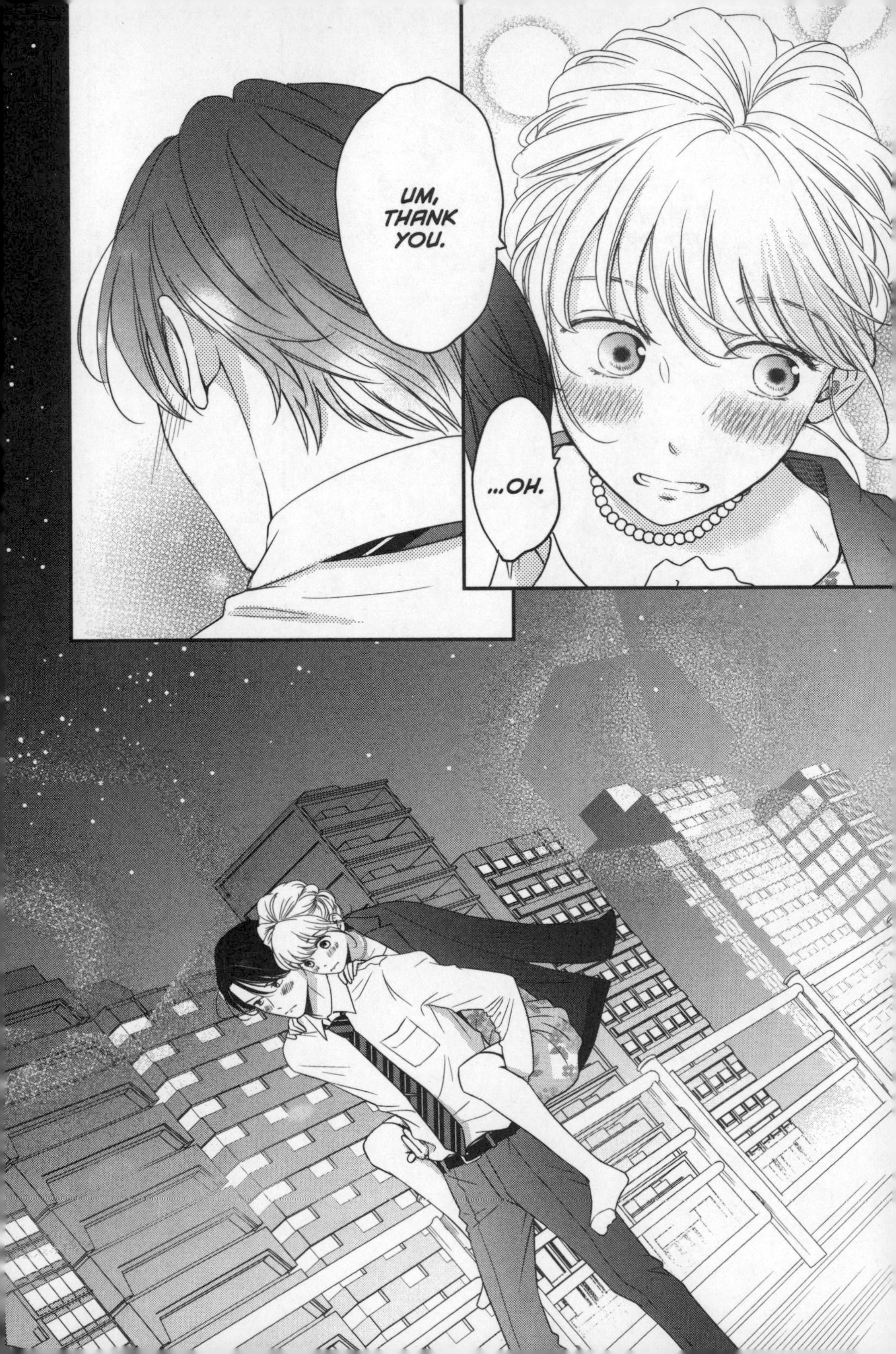
UM, THANK YOU.
...OH.

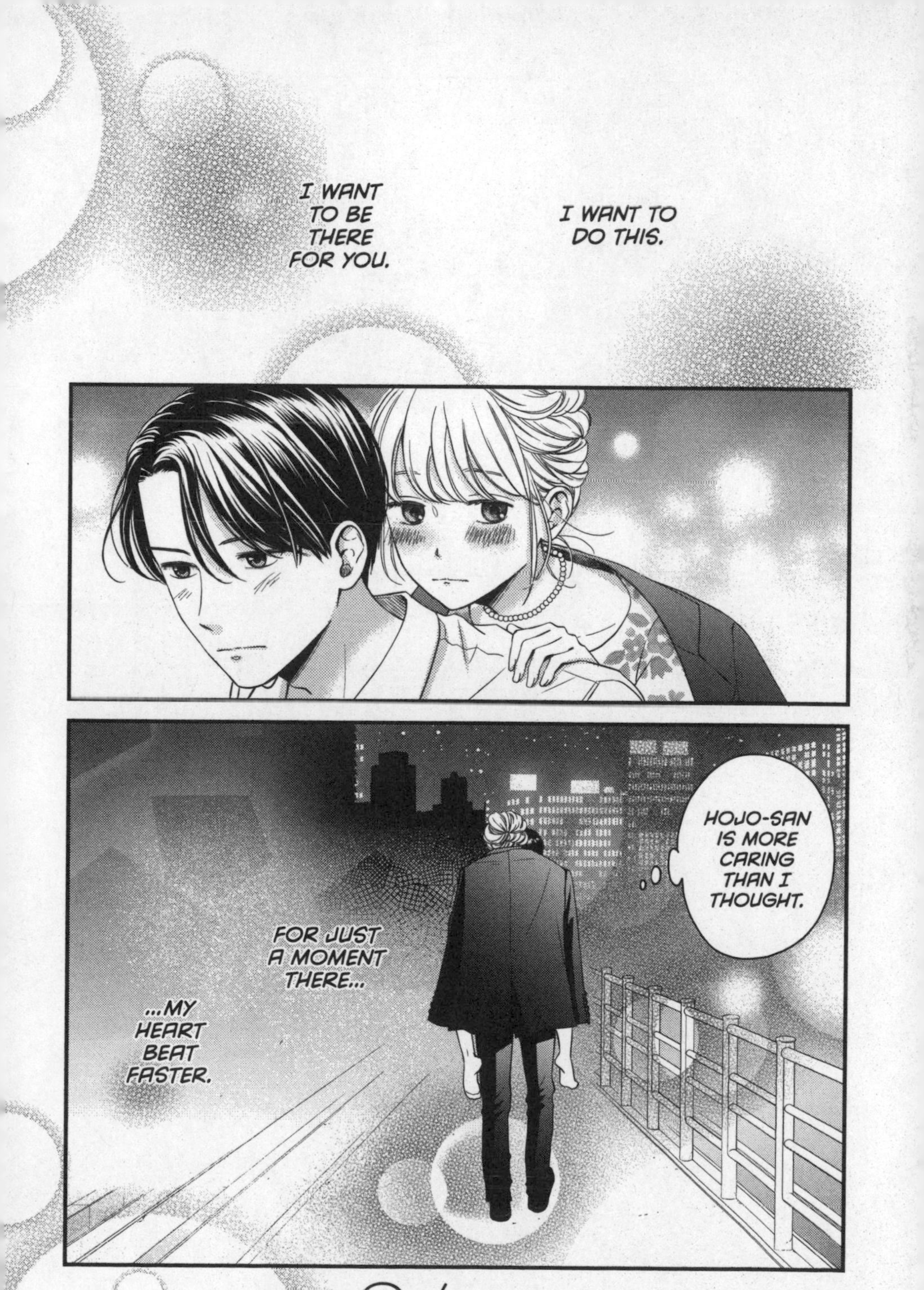
I WANT TO DO THIS.
I WANT TO BE THERE FOR YOU.
HOJO-SAN IS MORE CARING THAN I THOUGHT.
FOR JUST A MOMENT THERE...
...MY HEART BEAT FASTER.

room24

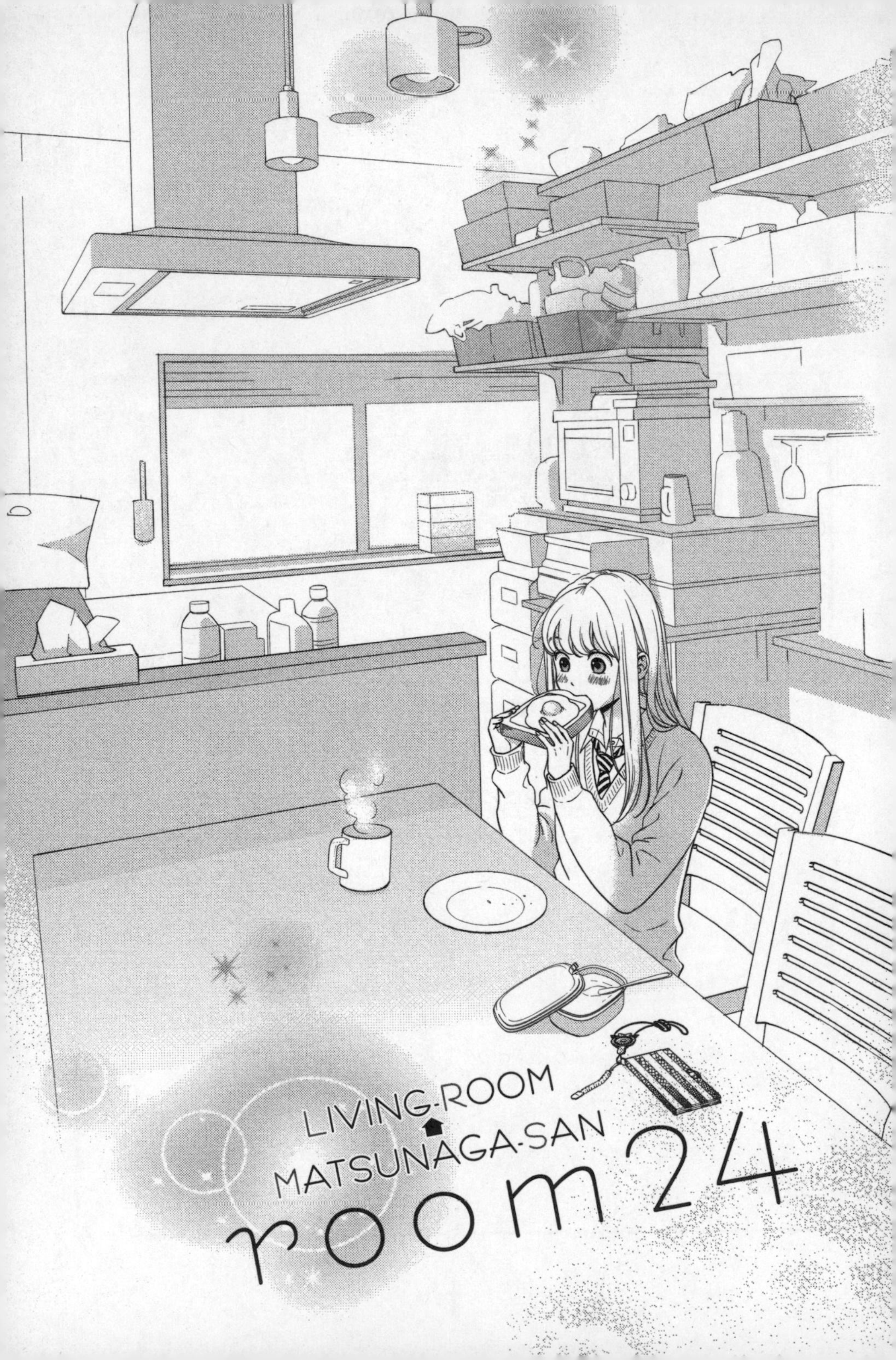
LIVING-ROOM
MATSUNAGA-SAN
room 24

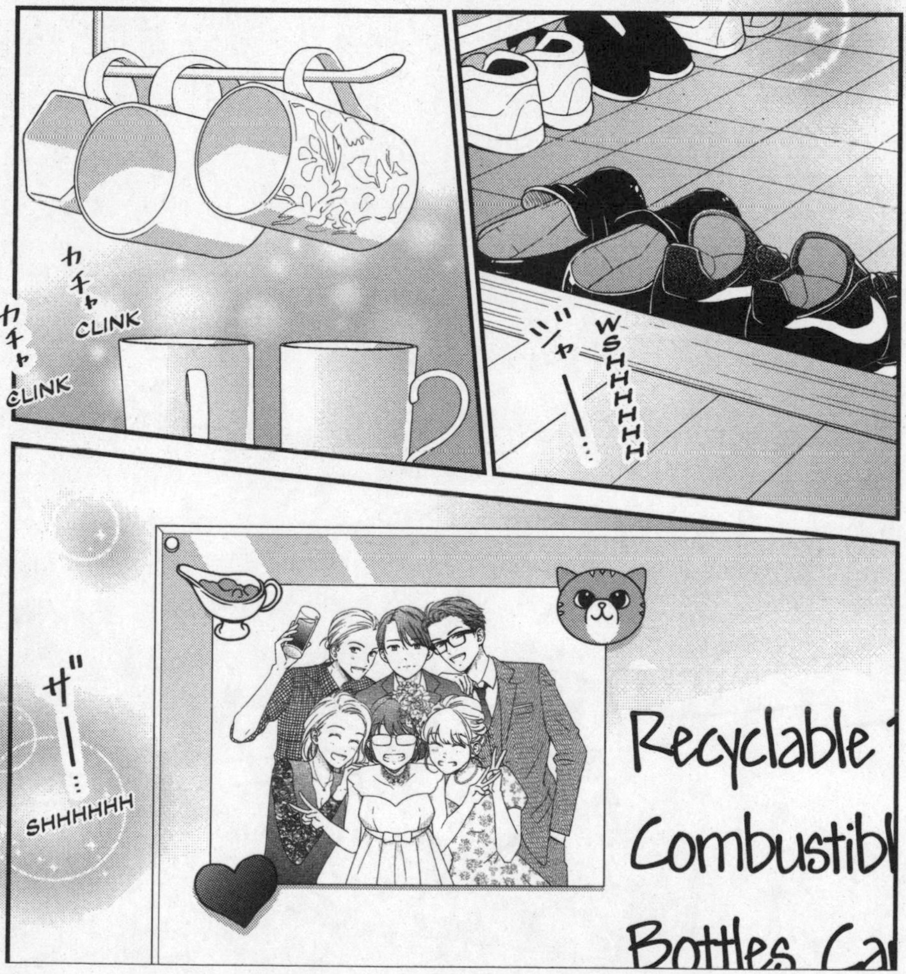
シャー…
WSHHHHHH
カチャ
CLINK
カチャ
CLINK
ザー…
SHHHHHH
Recyclable
Combustibl
Bottles Ca

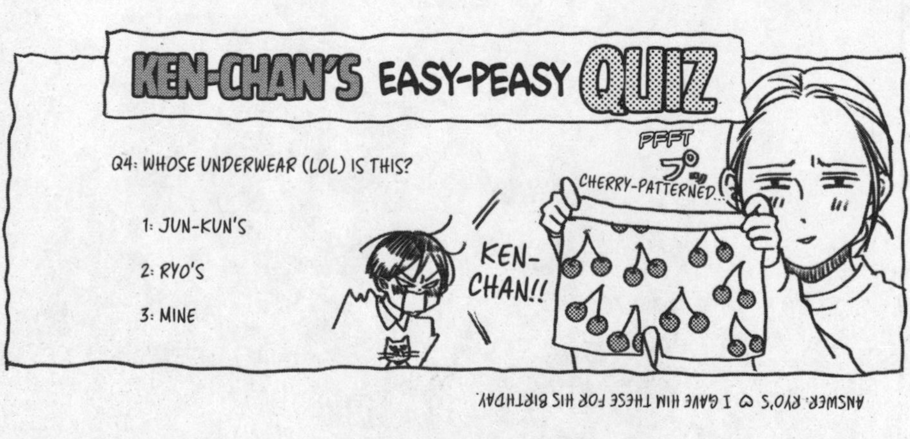
KEN-CHAN'S EASY-PEASY QUIZ
Q4: WHOSE UNDERWEAR (LOL) IS THIS?
1: JUN-KUN'S
2: RYO'S
3: MINE
PFFT
プッ
CHERRY-PATTERNED...
KEN-CHAN!!

ANSWER: RYO'S ♡ I GAVE HIM THESE FOR HIS BIRTHDAY.

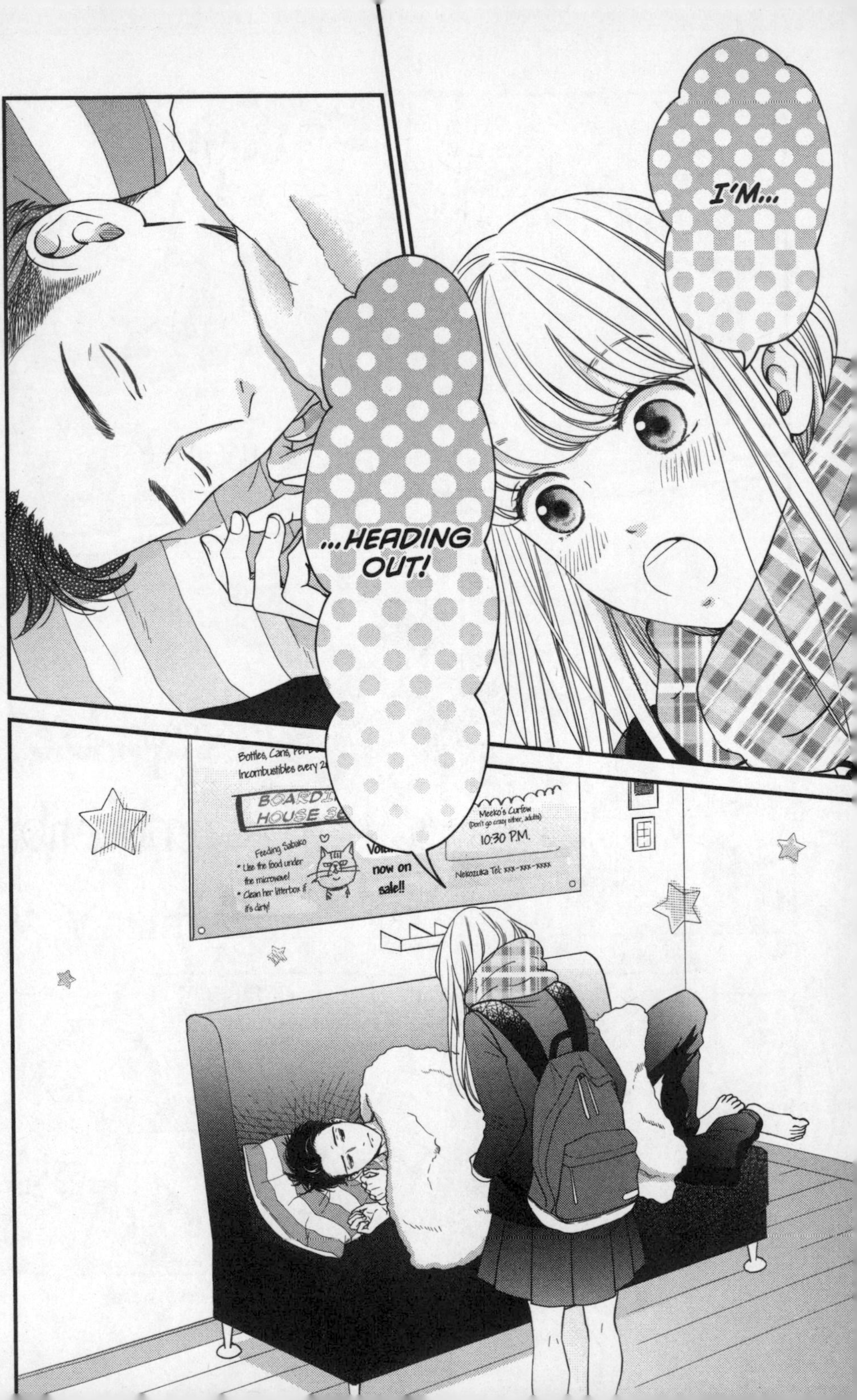
I'M...
...HEADING OUT!
Bottles, Cans, Pet Bo
Incombustibles every 2
BOARDI
HOUSE 3
Meeko's Curfew
(Don't go crazy either, adults)
10:30 P.M.
Nekozuka Tel: xxx-xxx-xxxx
Feeding Sabako
* Use the food under the microwave!
* Clean her litterbox if it's dirty!
now on sale!!

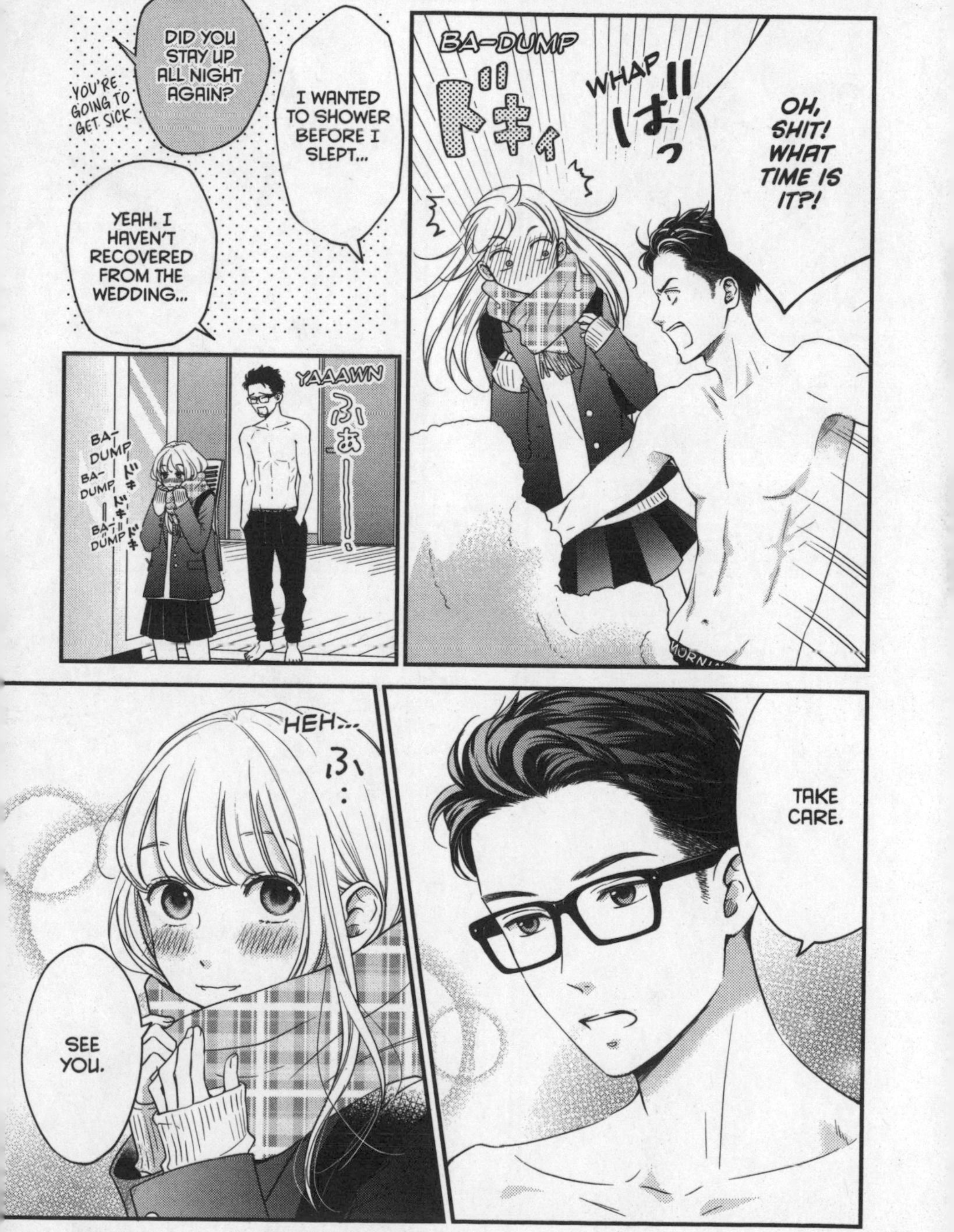
BA-DUMP
ドキィ
WHAP
ばっ
OH, SHIT! WHAT TIME IS IT?!
DID YOU STAY UP ALL NIGHT AGAIN?
YOU'RE GOING TO GET SICK.
I WANTED TO SHOWER BEFORE I SLEPT...
YEAH. I HAVEN'T RECOVERED FROM THE WEDDING...
YAAAWN
ふぁーー
BA-DUMP BA-DUMP BA-DUMP
ドキドキドキ
TAKE CARE.
HEH...
ふ
SEE YOU.

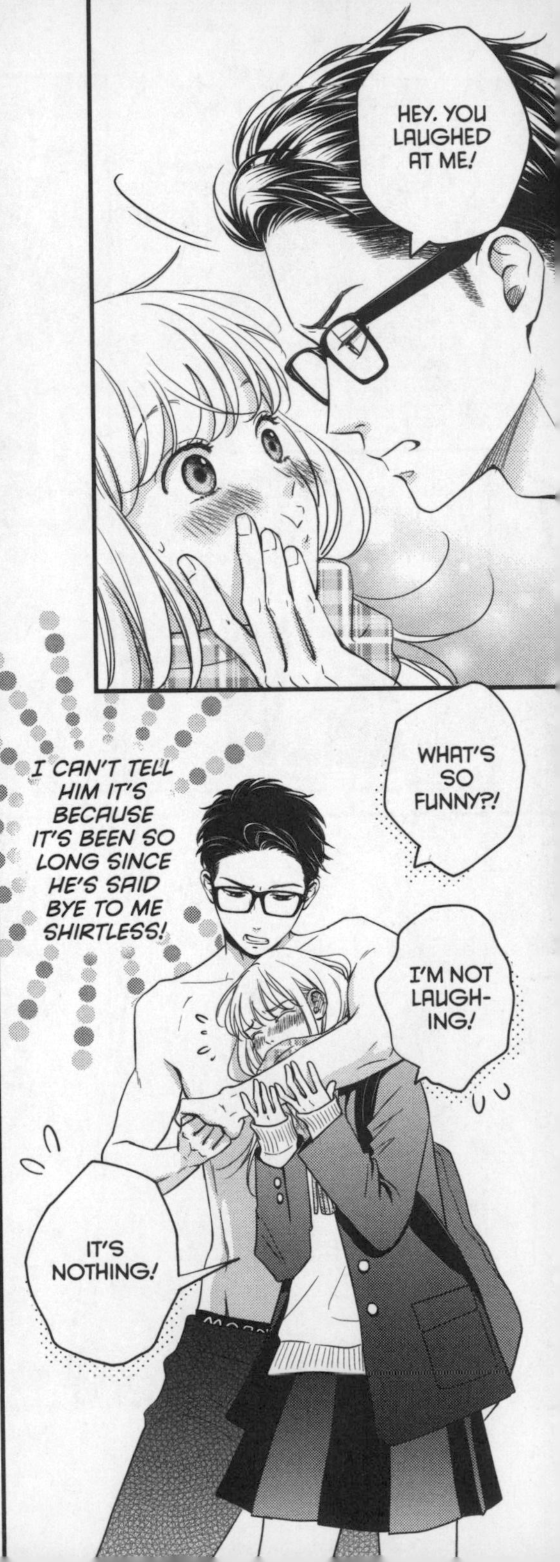
HEY. YOU LAUGHED AT ME!
WHAT'S SO FUNNY?!
I'M NOT LAUGHING!
I CAN'T TELL HIM IT'S BECAUSE IT'S BEEN SO LONG SINCE HE'S SAID BYE TO ME SHIRTLESS!
IT'S NOTHING!

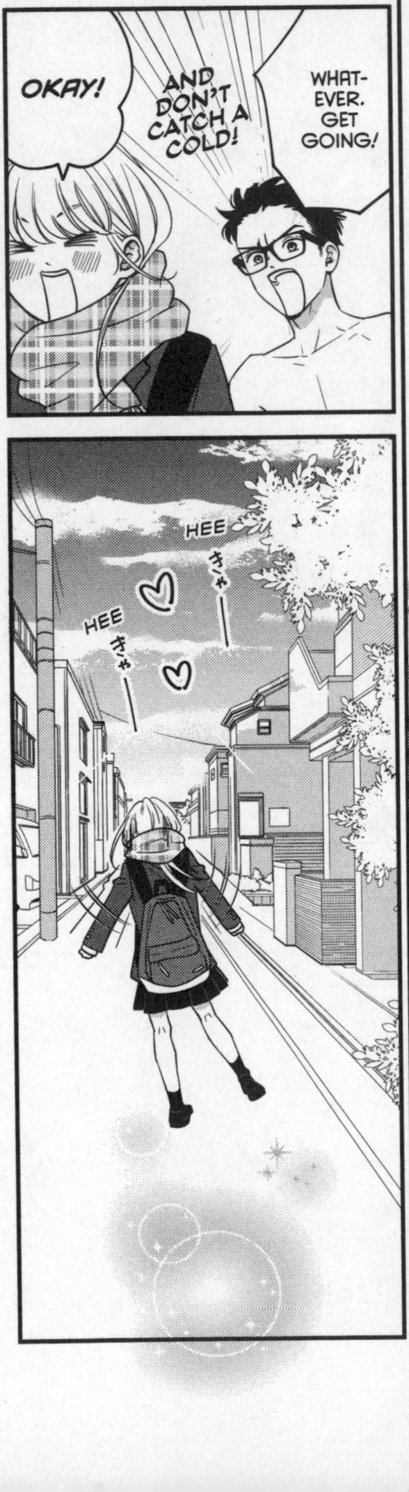
WHAT-EVER. GET GOING!
AND DON'T CATCH A COLD!
OKAY!
HEE
きゃー
HEE
きゃー

DUN-
DUN

Final Examination	
Uniforms/Advisory Week	
Results Day	
Parent-Teacher Conferences	

FINALS

PARENT-TEACHER CONFERENCES

HOW IS IT ALREADY DECEM-BER?!

SCHE-DULE

NO! HOW IS IT ALREADY FINALS AND PARENT-TEACHER CONFER-ENCES?!

YEAH, THE TESTS ARE IN, LIKE, FOUR DAYS.

HOW DID YOU NOT KNOW?

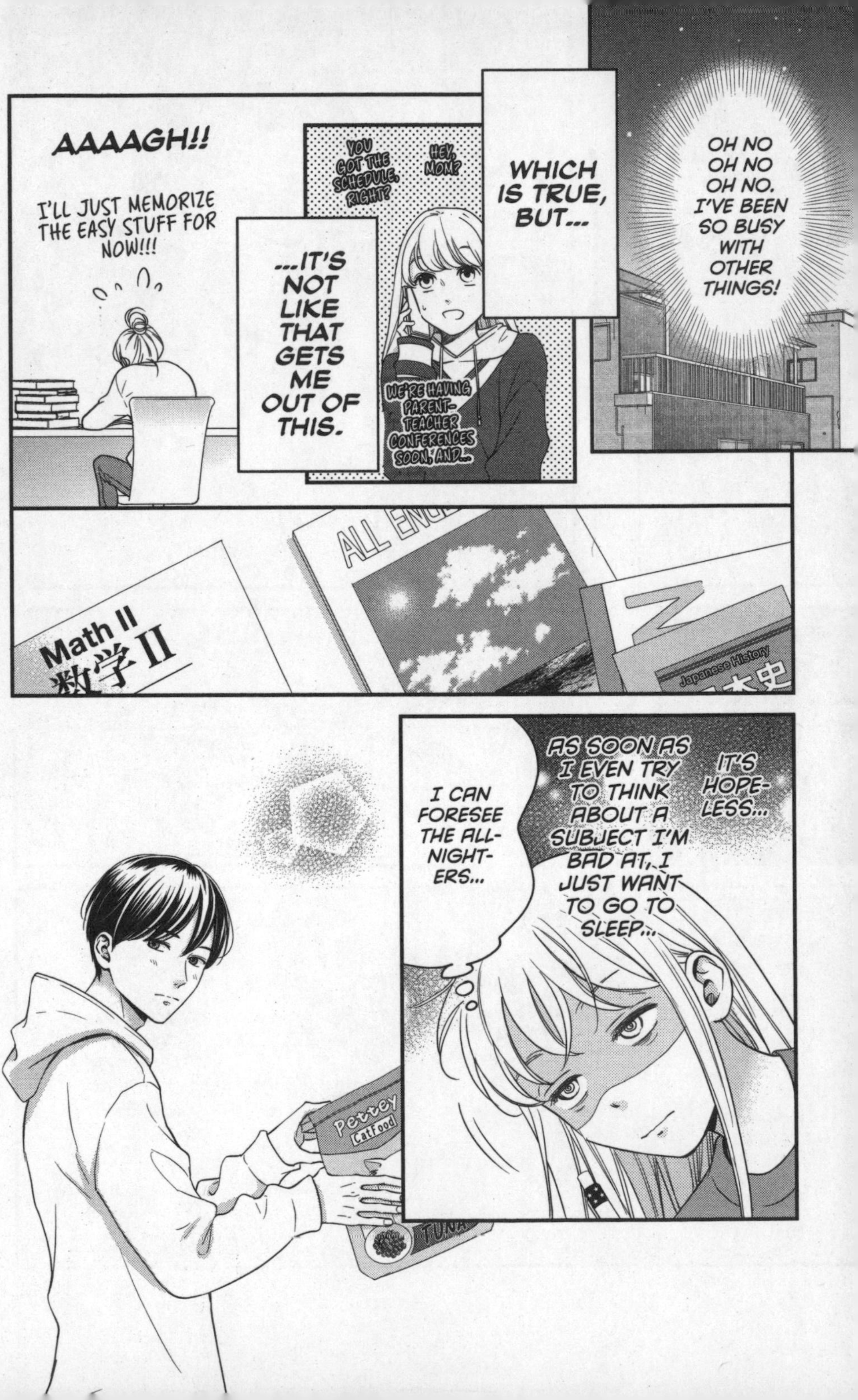

OH NO OH NO OH NO. I'VE BEEN SO BUSY WITH OTHER THINGS!
WHICH IS TRUE, BUT...
HEY, MOM?
YOU GOT THE SCHEDULE, RIGHT?
WE'RE HAVING PARENT-TEACHER CONFERENCES SOON, AND...
...IT'S NOT LIKE THAT GETS ME OUT OF THIS.
AAAAGH!!
I'LL JUST MEMORIZE THE EASY STUFF FOR NOW!!!
Japanese History
Math II
数学II
IT'S HOPE-LESS...
AS SOON AS I EVEN TRY TO THINK ABOUT A SUBJECT I'M BAD AT, I JUST WANT TO GO TO SLEEP...
I CAN FORESEE THE ALL-NIGHT-ERS...
Pettey
CatFood
TUNA

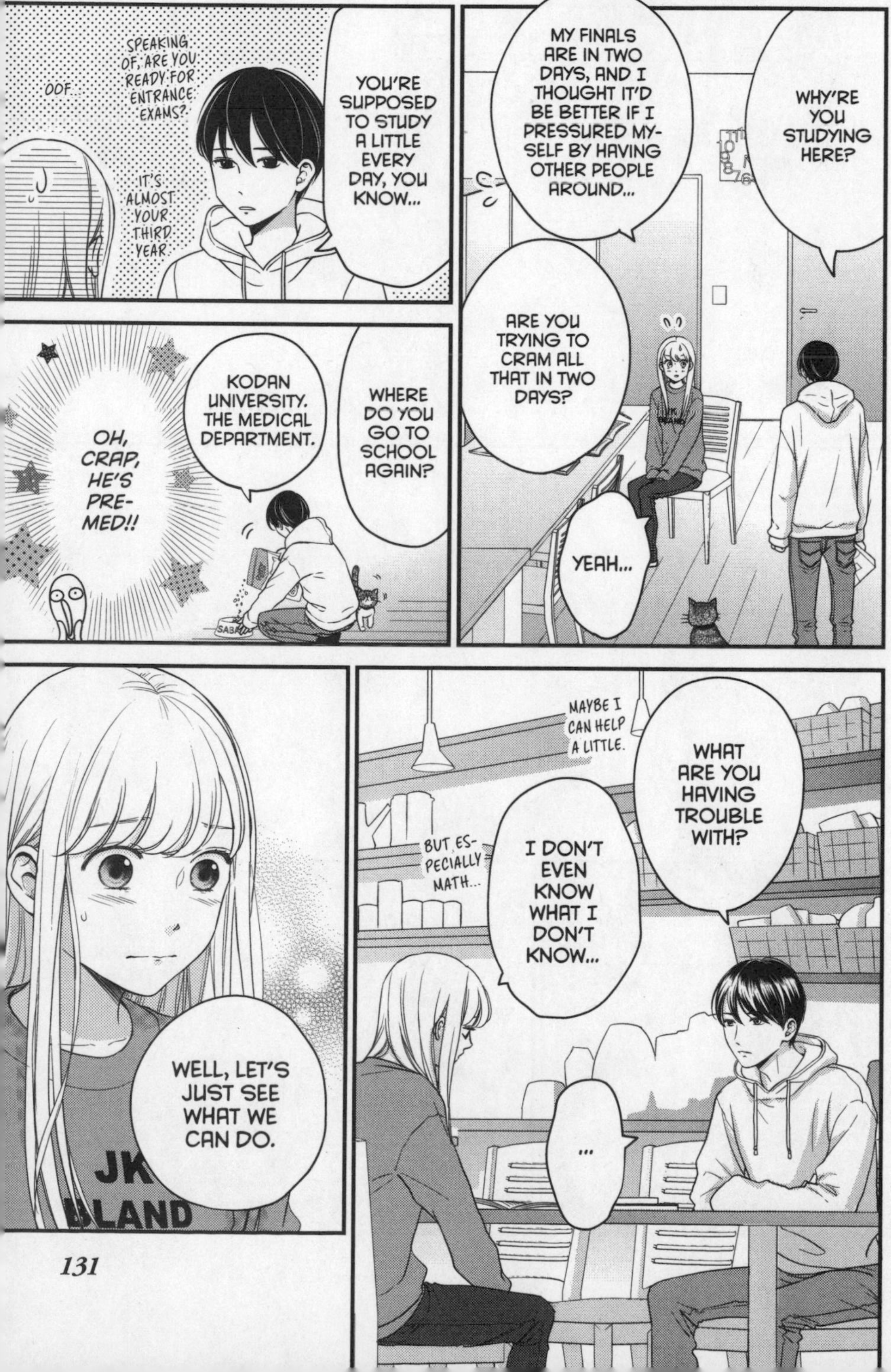
WHY'RE YOU STUDYING HERE?
MY FINALS ARE IN TWO DAYS, AND I THOUGHT IT'D BE BETTER IF I PRESSURED MY-SELF BY HAVING OTHER PEOPLE AROUND...
ARE YOU TRYING TO CRAM ALL THAT IN TWO DAYS?
YEAH...
YOU'RE SUPPOSED TO STUDY A LITTLE EVERY DAY, YOU KNOW...
SPEAKING OF, ARE YOU READY FOR ENTRANCE EXAMS?
IT'S ALMOST YOUR THIRD YEAR.
OOF
WHERE DO YOU GO TO SCHOOL AGAIN?
KODAN UNIVERSITY. THE MEDICAL DEPARTMENT.
OH, CRAP, HE'S PRE-MED!!
WHAT ARE YOU HAVING TROUBLE WITH?
MAYBE I CAN HELP A LITTLE.
I DON'T EVEN KNOW WHAT I DON'T KNOW...
BUT ES-PECIALLY MATH...
...
WELL, LET'S JUST SEE WHAT WE CAN DO.

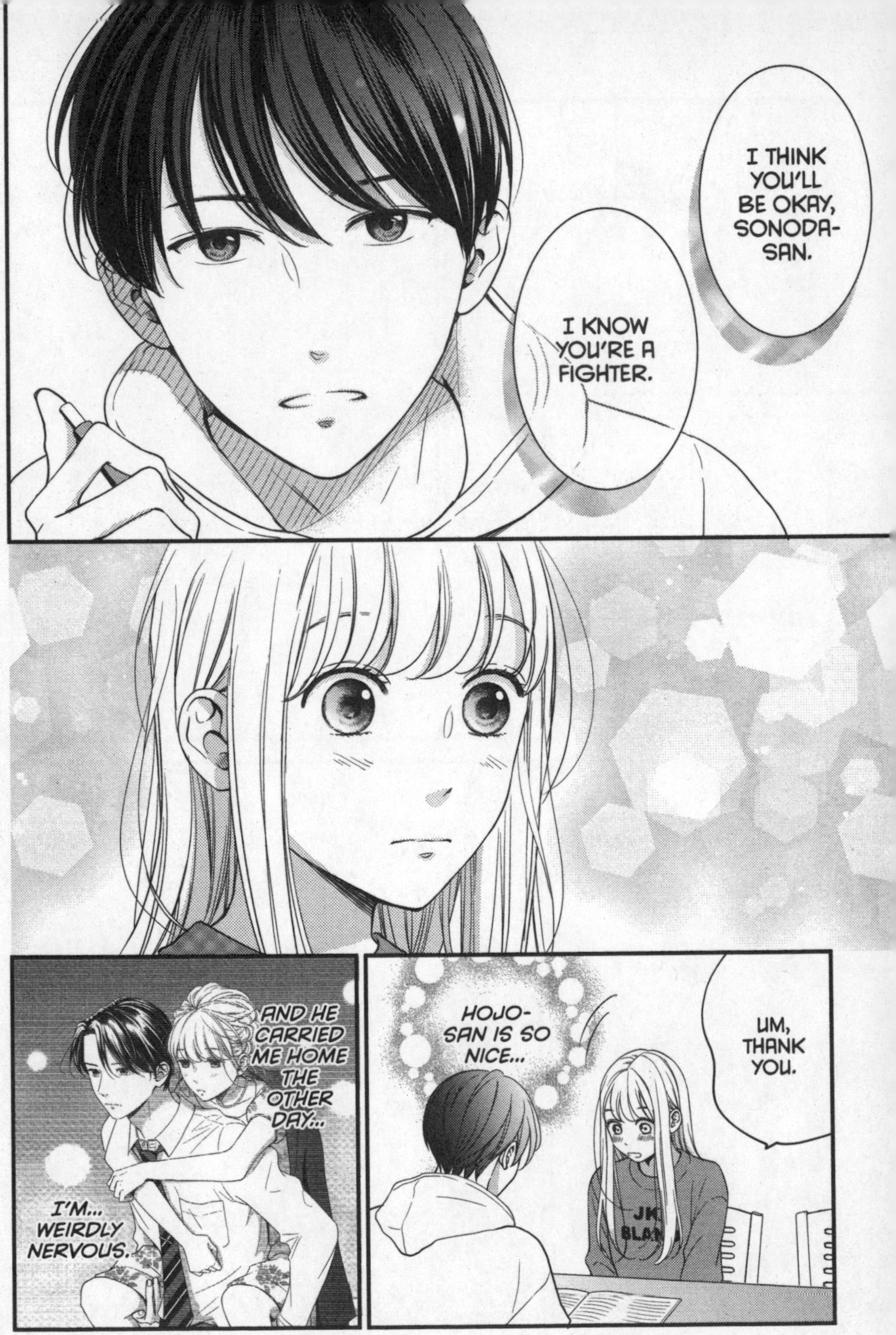
I THINK YOU'LL BE OKAY, SONODA-SAN.
I KNOW YOU'RE A FIGHTER.
UM, THANK YOU.
HOJO-SAN IS SO NICE...
AND HE CARRIED ME HOME THE OTHER DAY...
I'M... WEIRDLY NERVOUS.

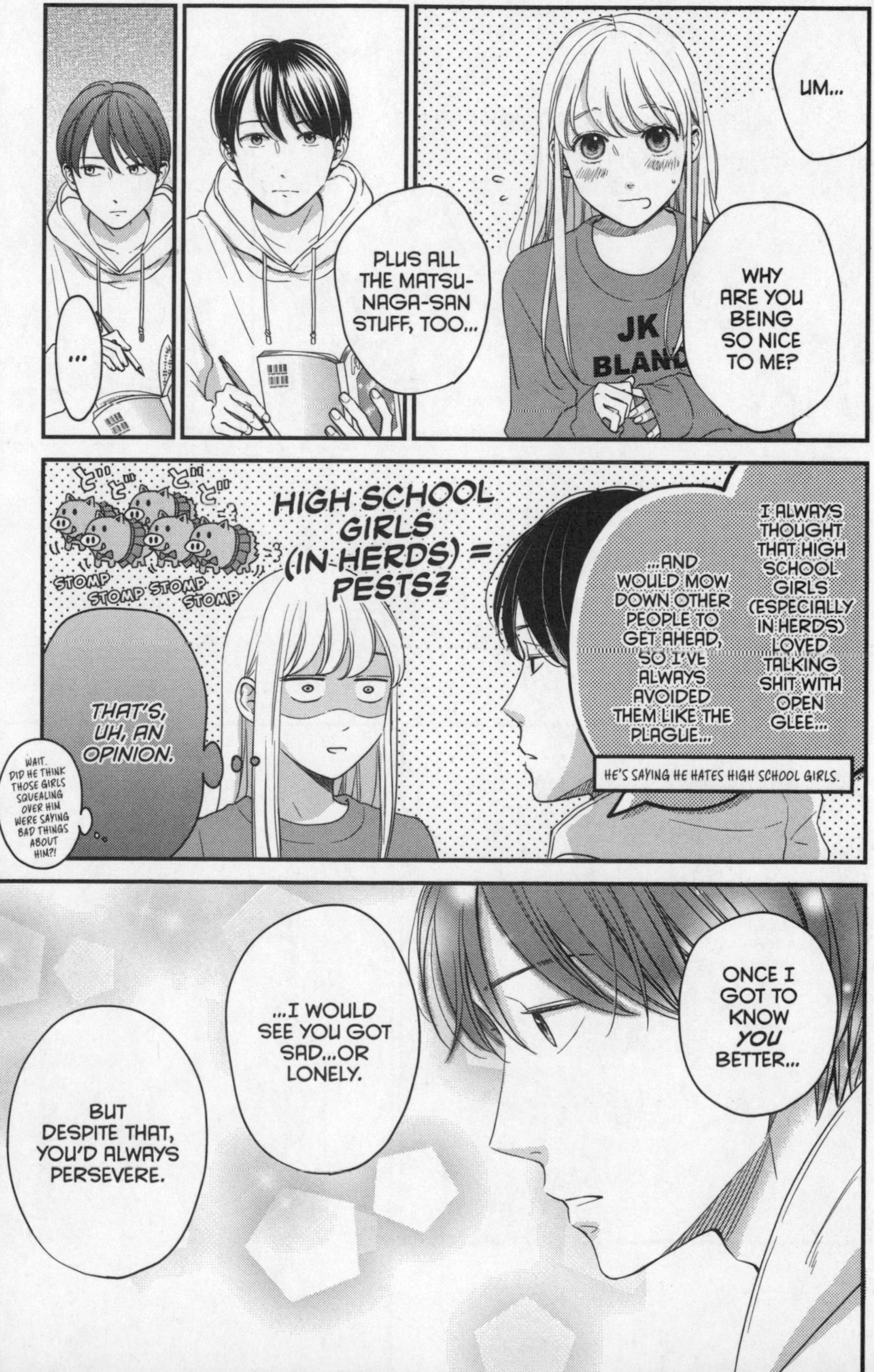
UM...
WHY ARE YOU BEING SO NICE TO ME?
PLUS ALL THE MATSU-NAGA-SAN STUFF, TOO...
...
I ALWAYS THOUGHT THAT HIGH SCHOOL GIRLS (ESPECIALLY IN HERDS) LOVED TALKING SHIT WITH OPEN GLEE...
...AND WOULD MOW DOWN OTHER PEOPLE TO GET AHEAD, SO I'VE ALWAYS AVOIDED THEM LIKE THE PLAGUE...
HE'S SAYING HE HATES HIGH SCHOOL GIRLS.
HIGH SCHOOL GIRLS (IN HERDS) = PESTS?
STOMP STOMP STOMP STOMP
THAT'S, UH, AN OPINION.
WAIT. DID HE THINK THOSE GIRLS SQUEALING OVER HIM WERE SAYING BAD THINGS ABOUT HIM?!
ONCE I GOT TO KNOW *YOU* BETTER...
...I WOULD SEE YOU GOT SAD...OR LONELY.
BUT DESPITE THAT, YOU'D ALWAYS PERSEVERE.

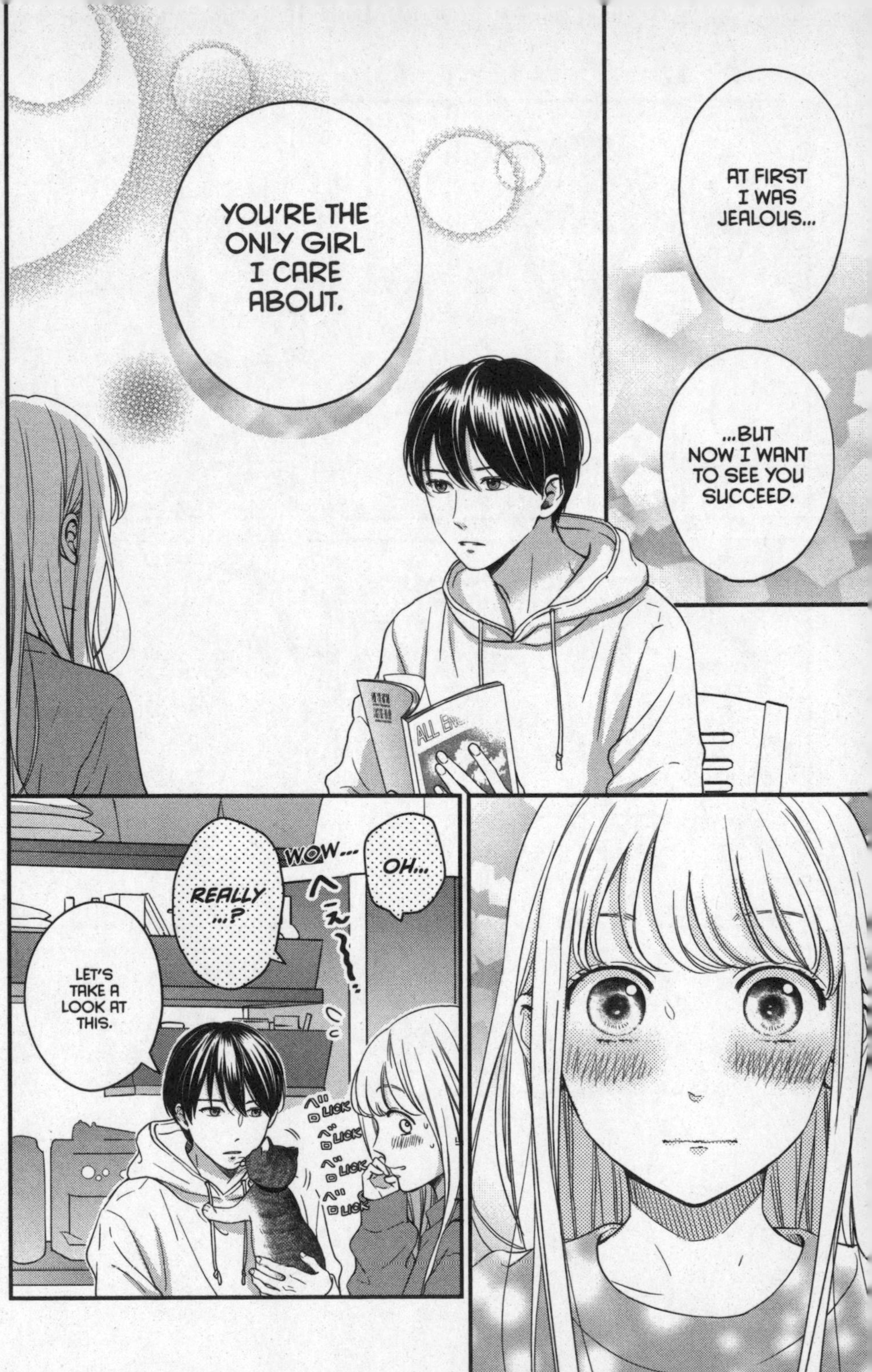
AT FIRST I WAS JEALOUS...
...BUT NOW I WANT TO SEE YOU SUCCEED.
YOU'RE THE ONLY GIRL I CARE ABOUT.
OH...
WOW...
REALLY ...?
LET'S TAKE A LOOK AT THIS.
LICK
LICK
LICK
LICK

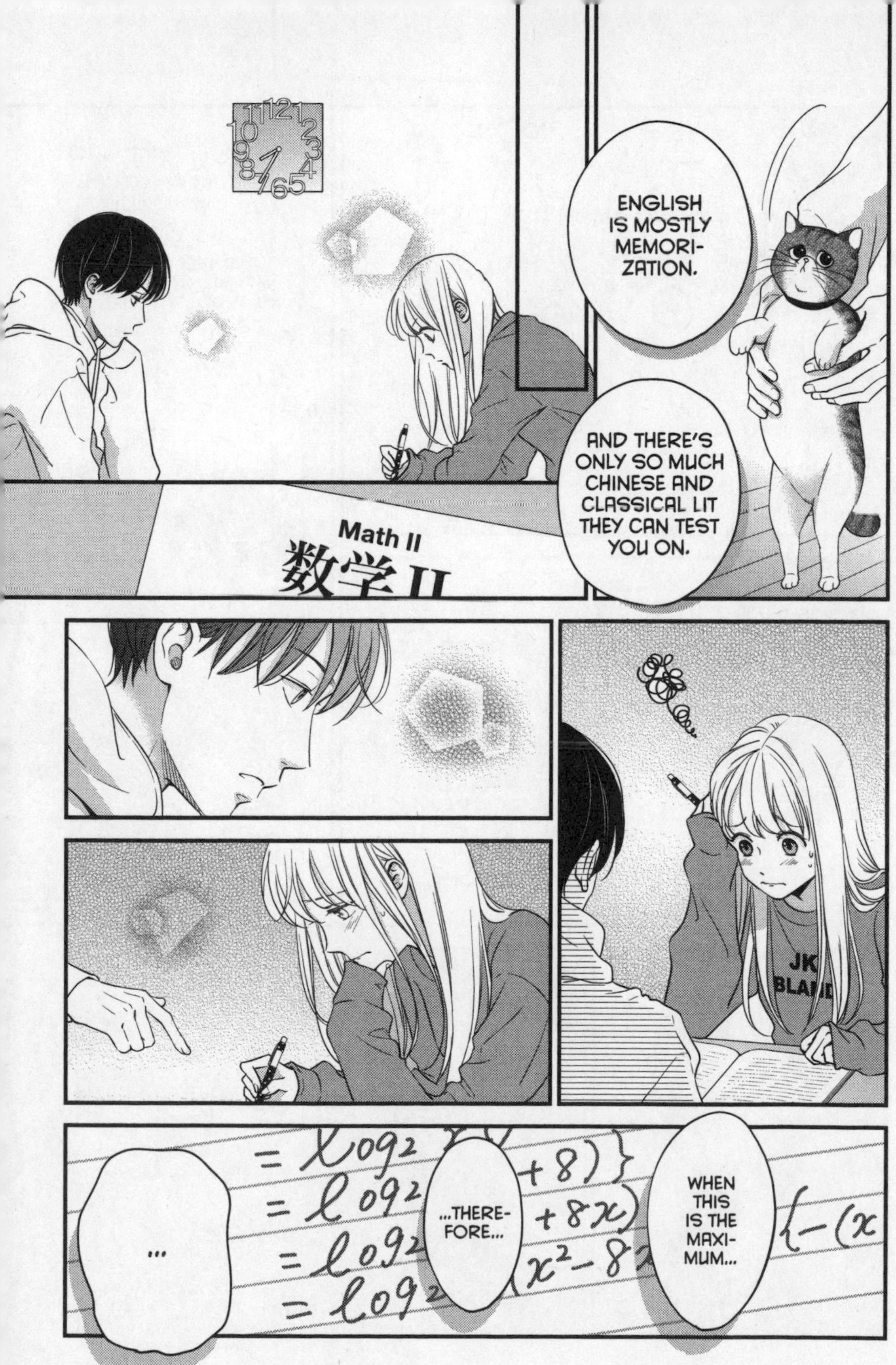
ENGLISH IS MOSTLY MEMORI-ZATION.
AND THERE'S ONLY SO MUCH CHINESE AND CLASSICAL LIT THEY CAN TEST YOU ON.
Math II
数学II
WHEN THIS IS THE MAXI-MUM...
...THERE-FORE...
...

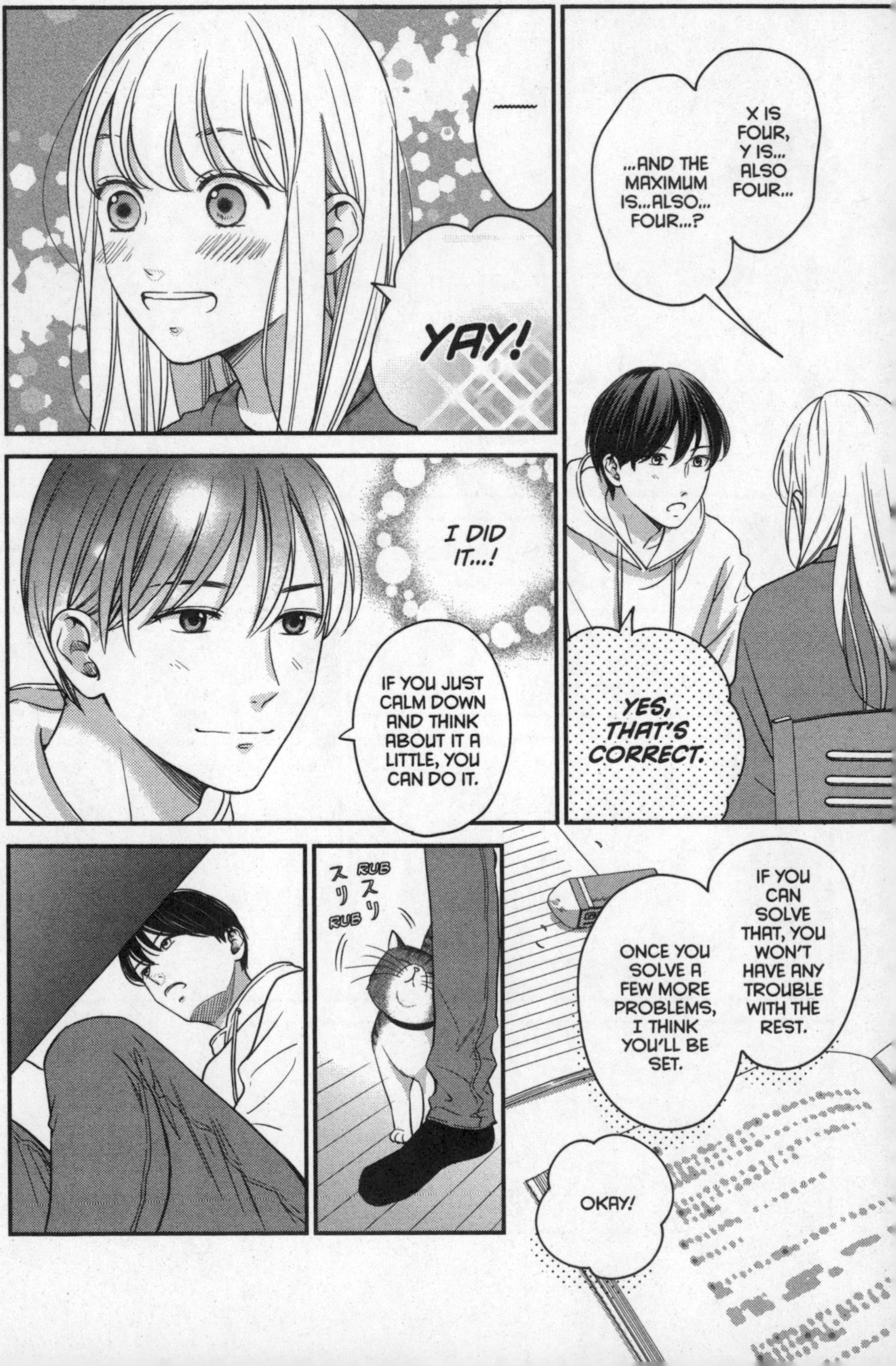

X IS FOUR, Y IS... ALSO FOUR...
...AND THE MAXIMUM IS...ALSO... FOUR...?
YES, THAT'S CORRECT.
~
YAY!
I DID IT...!
IF YOU JUST CALM DOWN AND THINK ABOUT IT A LITTLE, YOU CAN DO IT.
IF YOU CAN SOLVE THAT, YOU WON'T HAVE ANY TROUBLE WITH THE REST.
ONCE YOU SOLVE A FEW MORE PROBLEMS, I THINK YOU'LL BE SET.
OKAY!
スリ RUB
スリ RUB

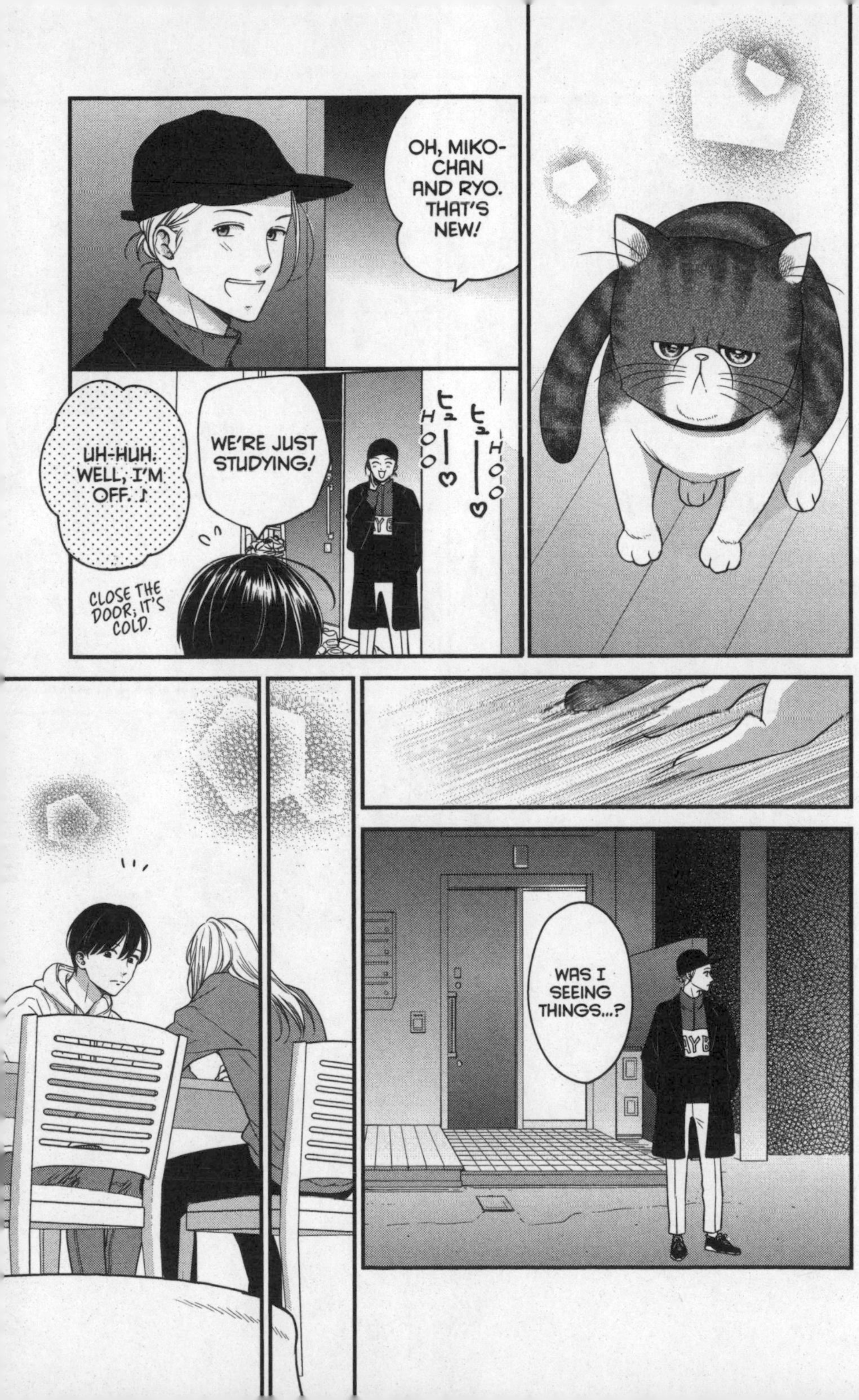
OH, MIKO-CHAN AND RYO. THAT'S NEW!
HOO ♥
HOO ♥
WE'RE JUST STUDYING!
UH-HUH. WELL, I'M OFF. ♪
CLOSE THE DOOR; IT'S COLD.
WAS I SEEING THINGS...?

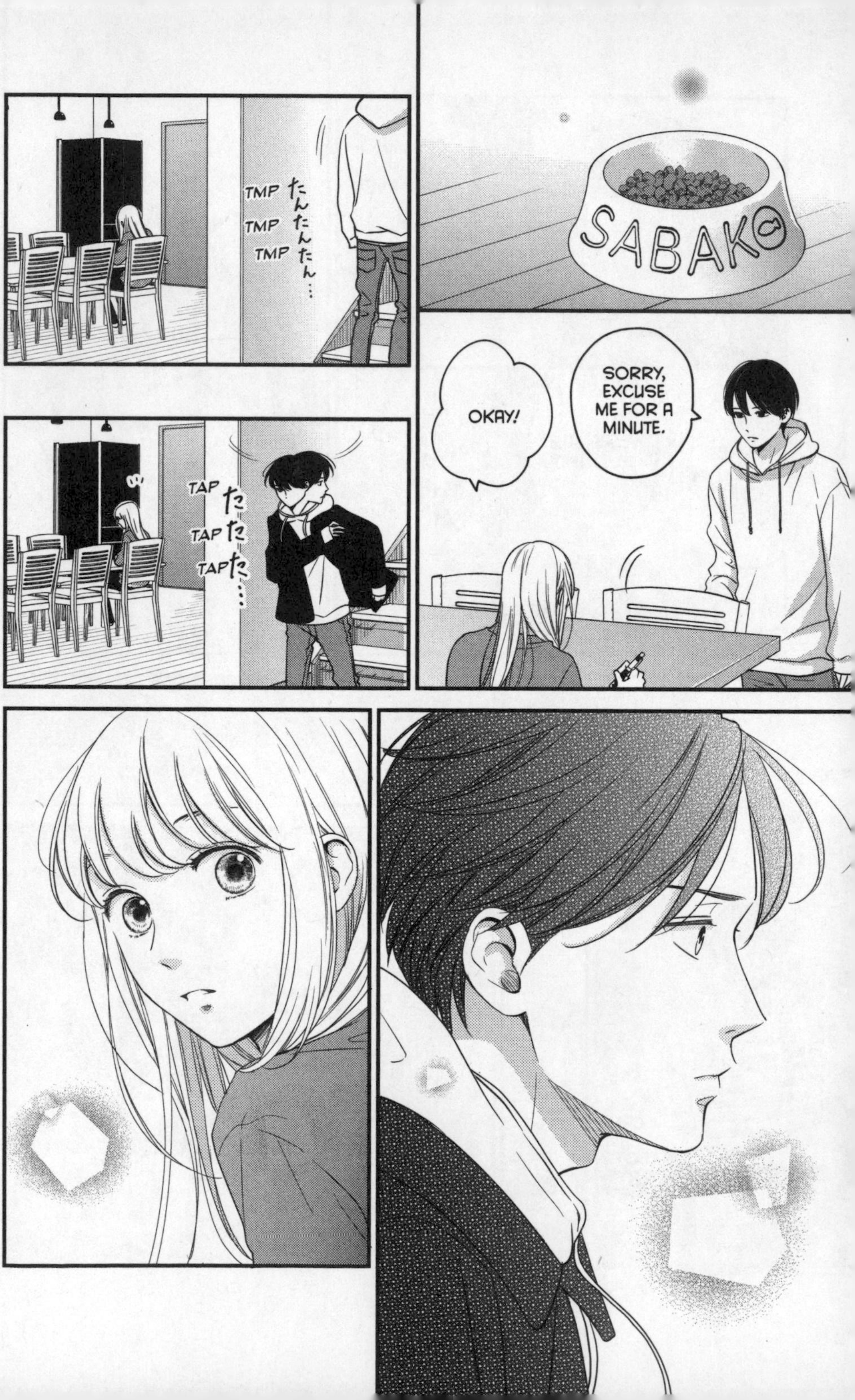
SABAKO
TMP TMP TMP たんたんたん…
SORRY, EXCUSE ME FOR A MINUTE.
OKAY!
TAP TAP TAP たたた…

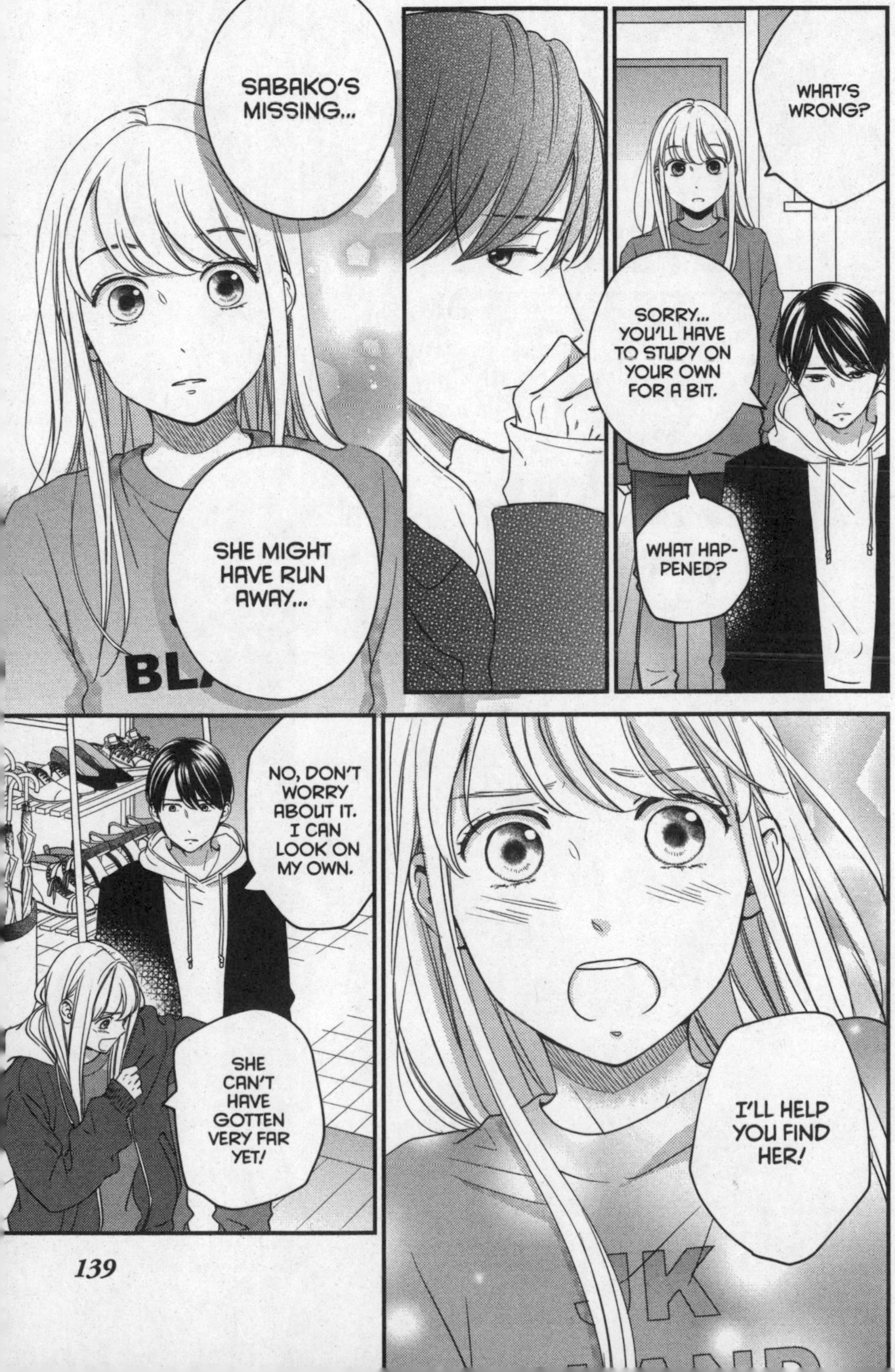
WHAT'S WRONG?
SORRY... YOU'LL HAVE TO STUDY ON YOUR OWN FOR A BIT.
WHAT HAP-PENED?
SABAKO'S MISSING...
SHE MIGHT HAVE RUN AWAY...
I'LL HELP YOU FIND HER!
NO, DON'T WORRY ABOUT IT. I CAN LOOK ON MY OWN.
SHE CAN'T HAVE GOTTEN VERY FAR YET!

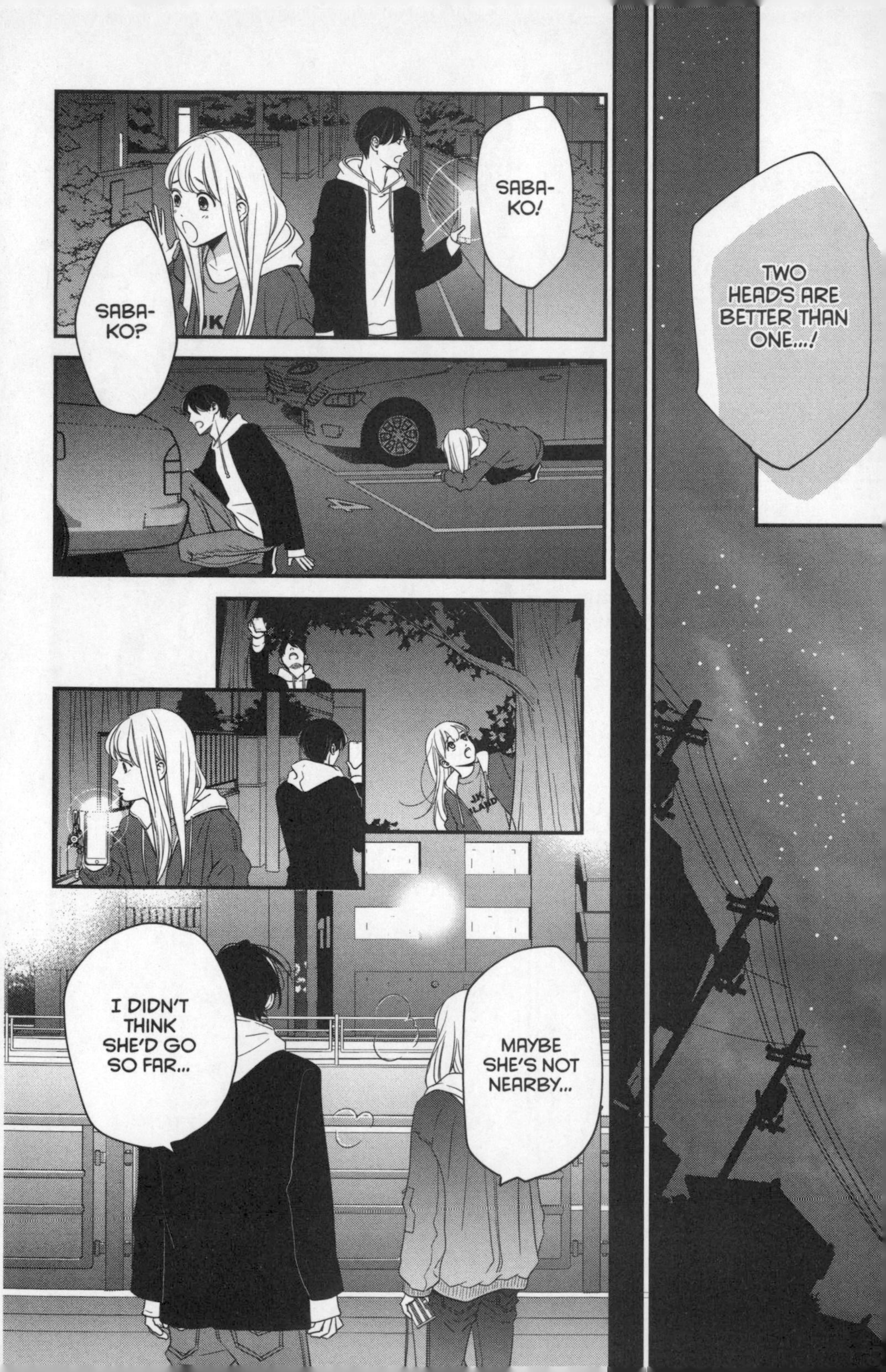
TWO HEADS ARE BETTER THAN ONE...!
SABA-KO!
SABA-KO?
MAYBE SHE'S NOT NEARBY...
I DIDN'T THINK SHE'D GO SO FAR...

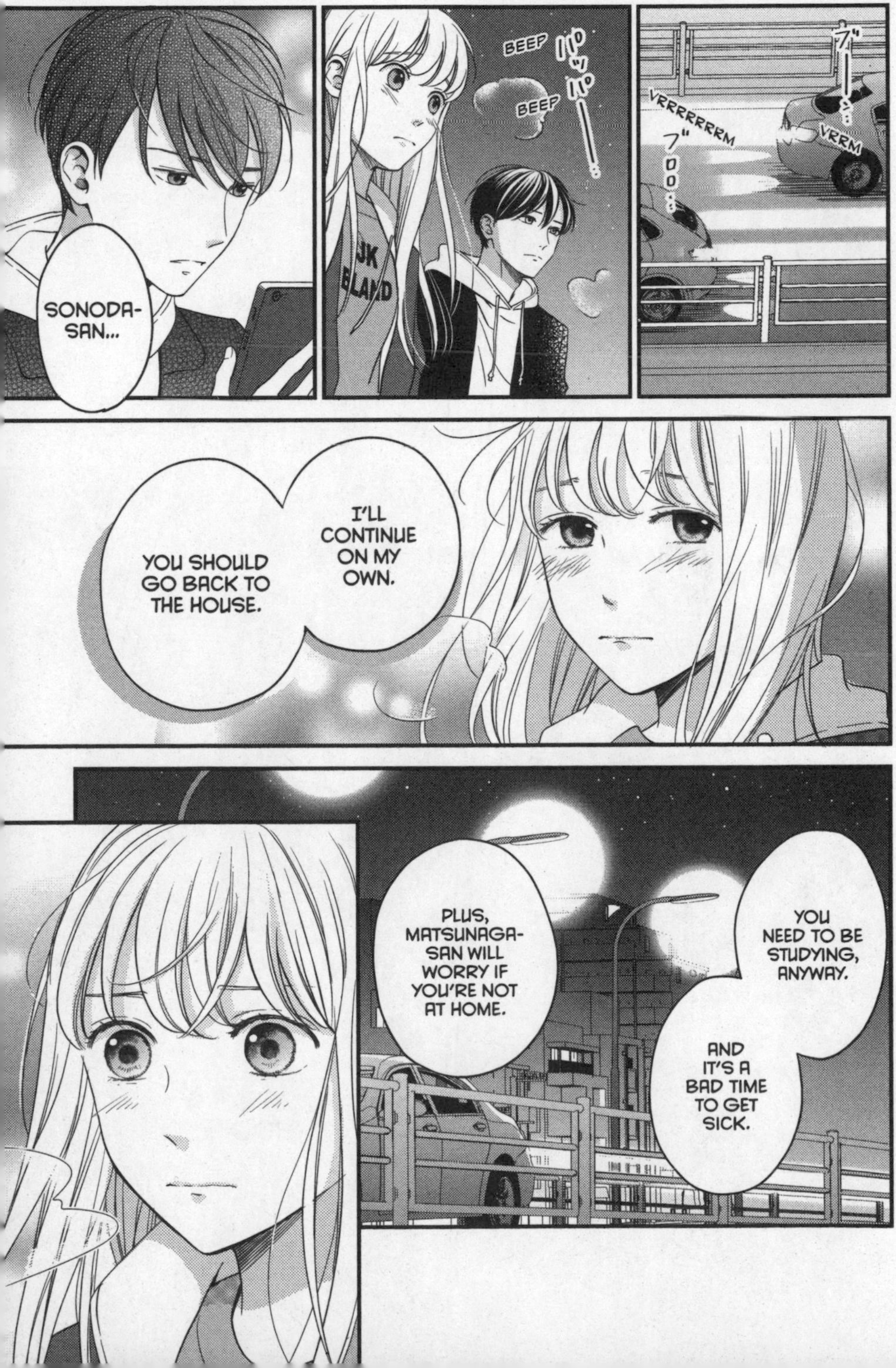
VRRRRRRRM
VRRM
BEEP
BEEP
SONODA-SAN...
I'LL CONTINUE ON MY OWN.
YOU SHOULD GO BACK TO THE HOUSE.
YOU NEED TO BE STUDYING, ANYWAY.
AND IT'S A BAD TIME TO GET SICK.
PLUS, MATSUNAGA-SAN WILL WORRY IF YOU'RE NOT AT HOME.

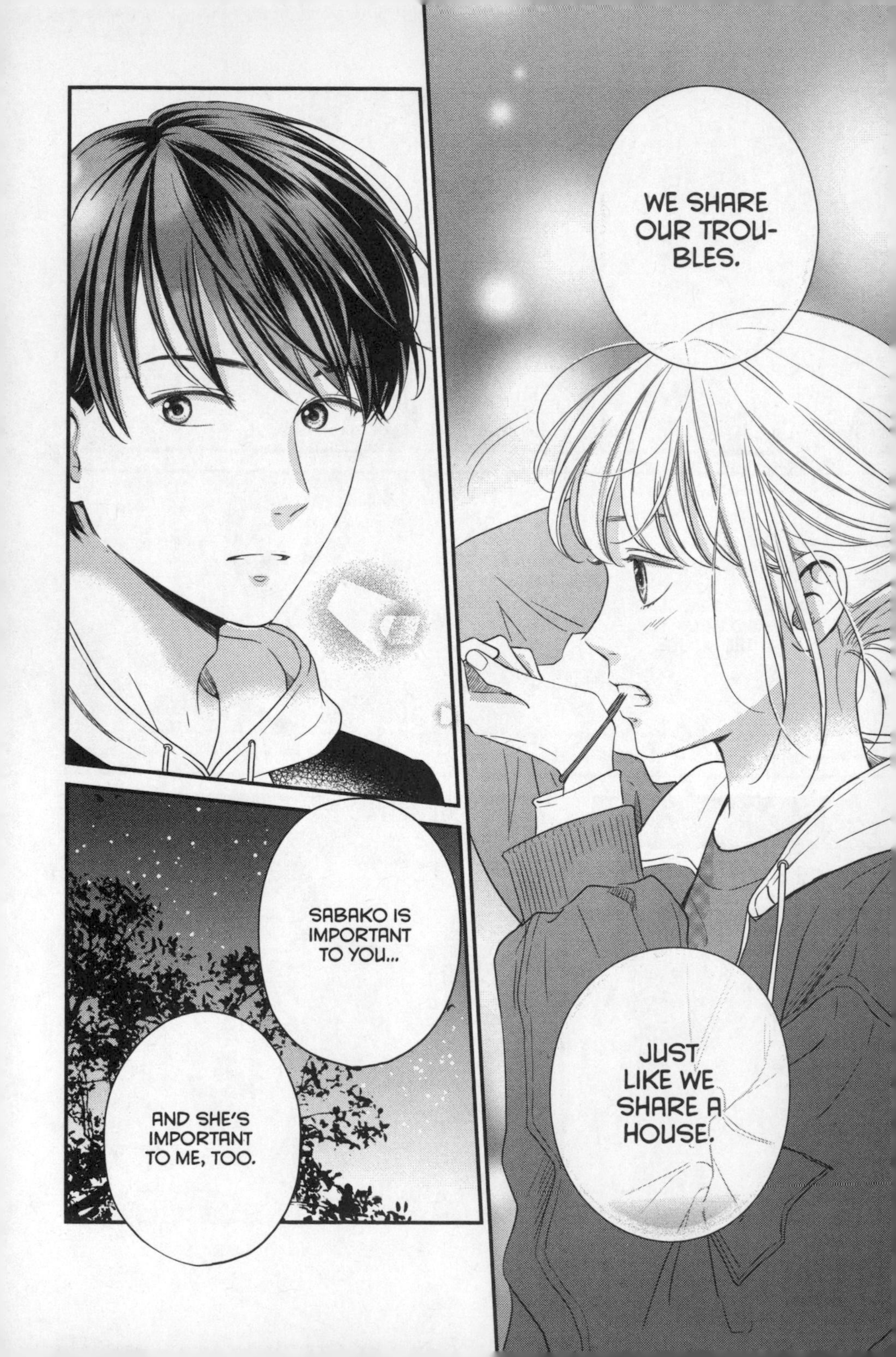
WE SHARE OUR TROU-BLES.
JUST LIKE WE SHARE A HOUSE.
SABAKO IS IMPORTANT TO YOU...
AND SHE'S IMPORTANT TO ME, TOO.

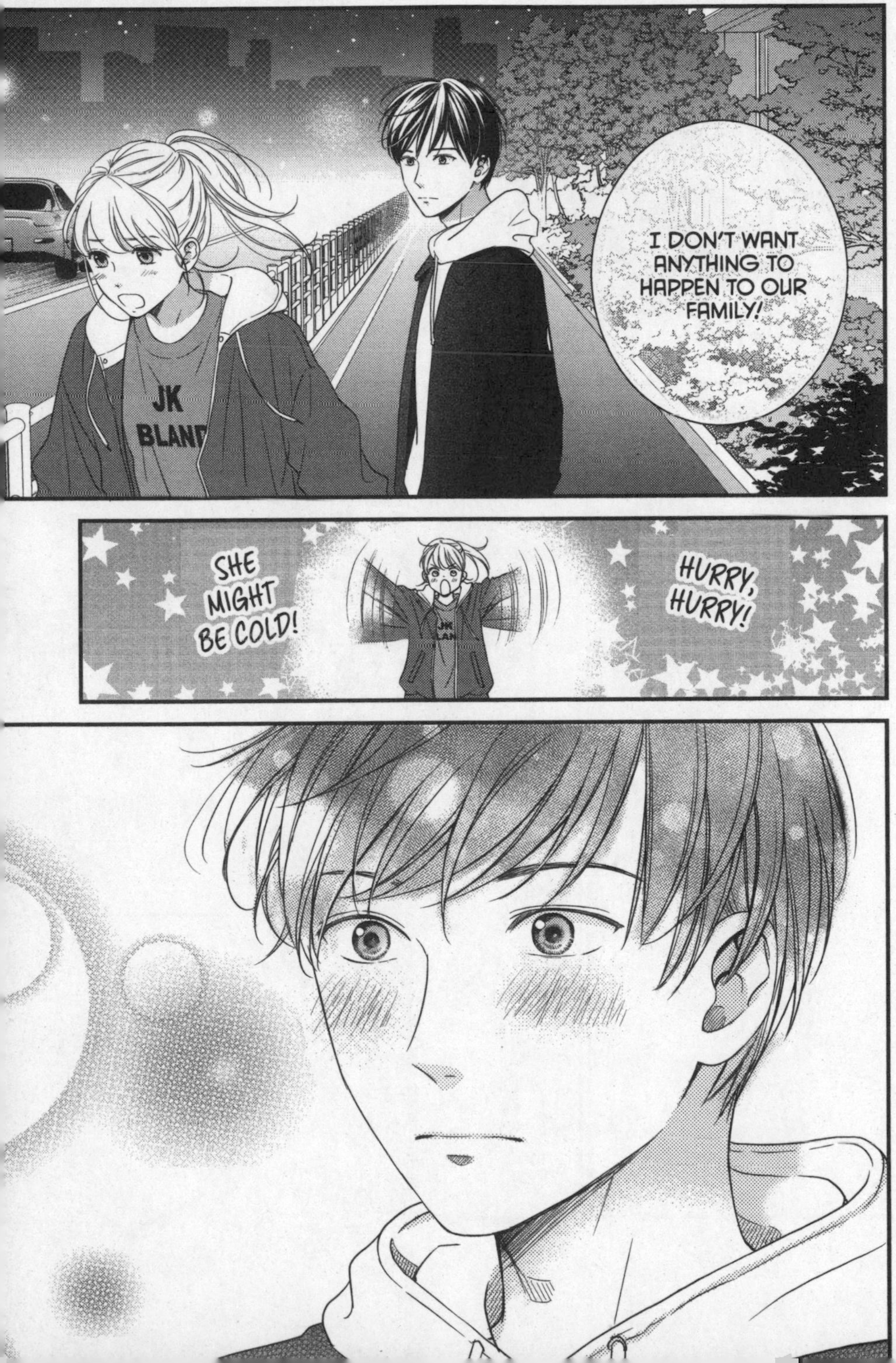
I DON'T WANT ANYTHING TO HAPPEN TO OUR FAMILY!
JK BLAND
HURRY, HURRY!
SHE MIGHT BE COLD!

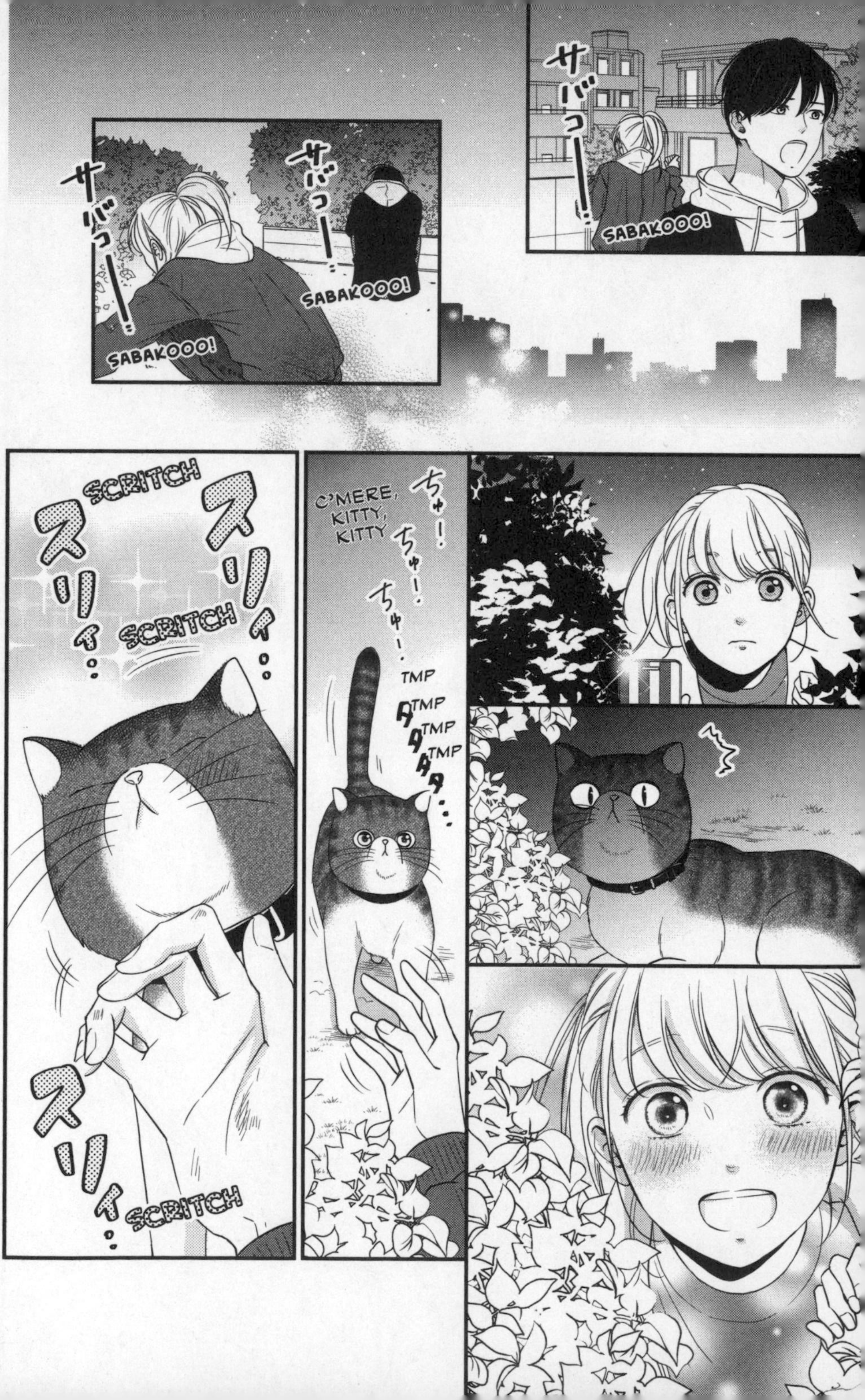

サバコー!
SABAKOOO!
サバコー!
SABAKOOO!
サバコー!
SABAKOOO!
ちゅ!ちゅ!ちゅ~!
C'MERE, KITTY, KITTY
TMP TMP TMP TMP
タタタタ...
スリィ...
SCRITCH
スリィ...
SCRITCH
スリィ...
SCRITCH

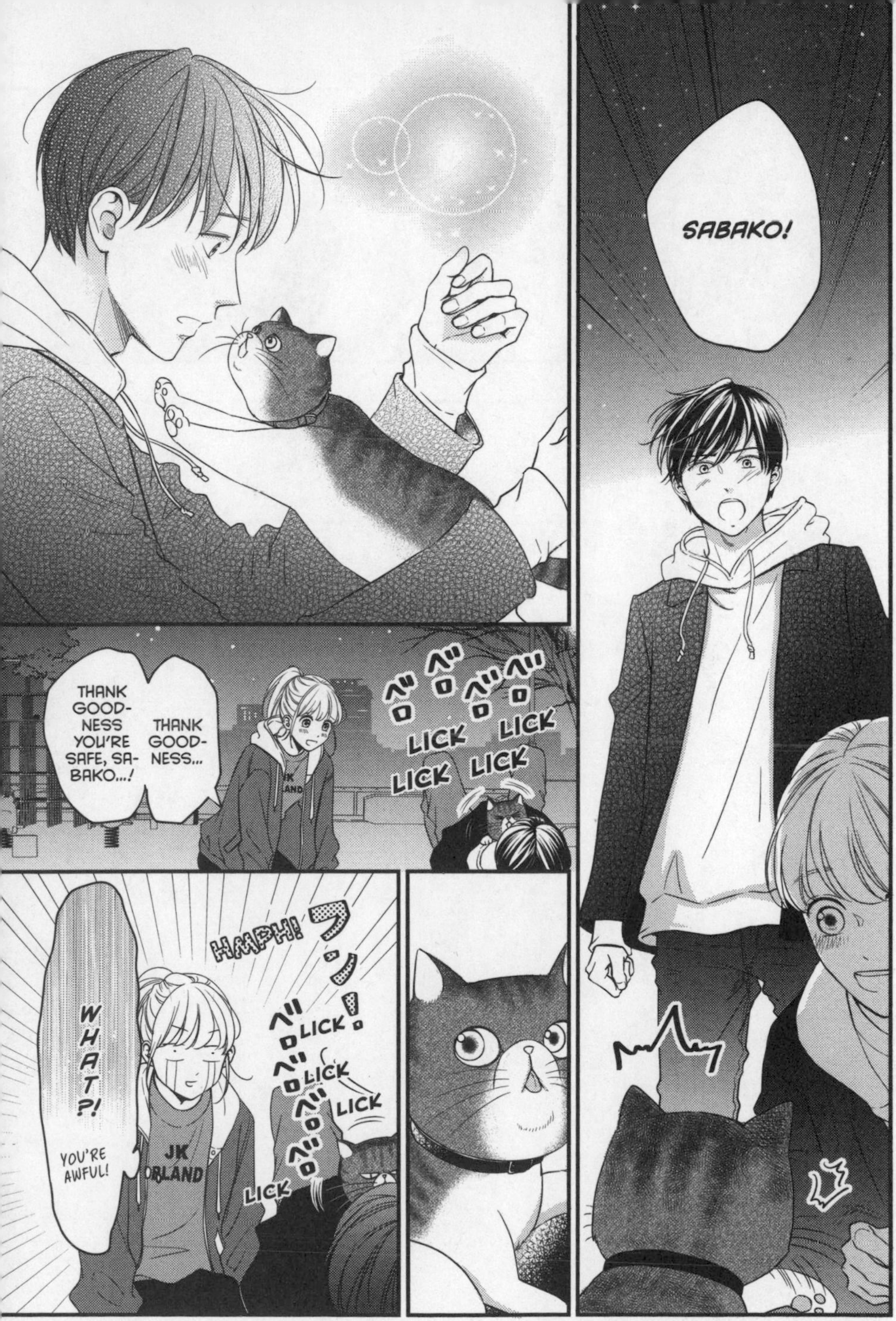
SABAKO!
LICK LICK
LICK LICK
THANK GOODNESS...
THANK GOODNESS YOU'RE SAFE, SABAKO...!
HMPH!
フン!
LICK
LICK
LICK
LICK
WHAT?!
YOU'RE AWFUL!

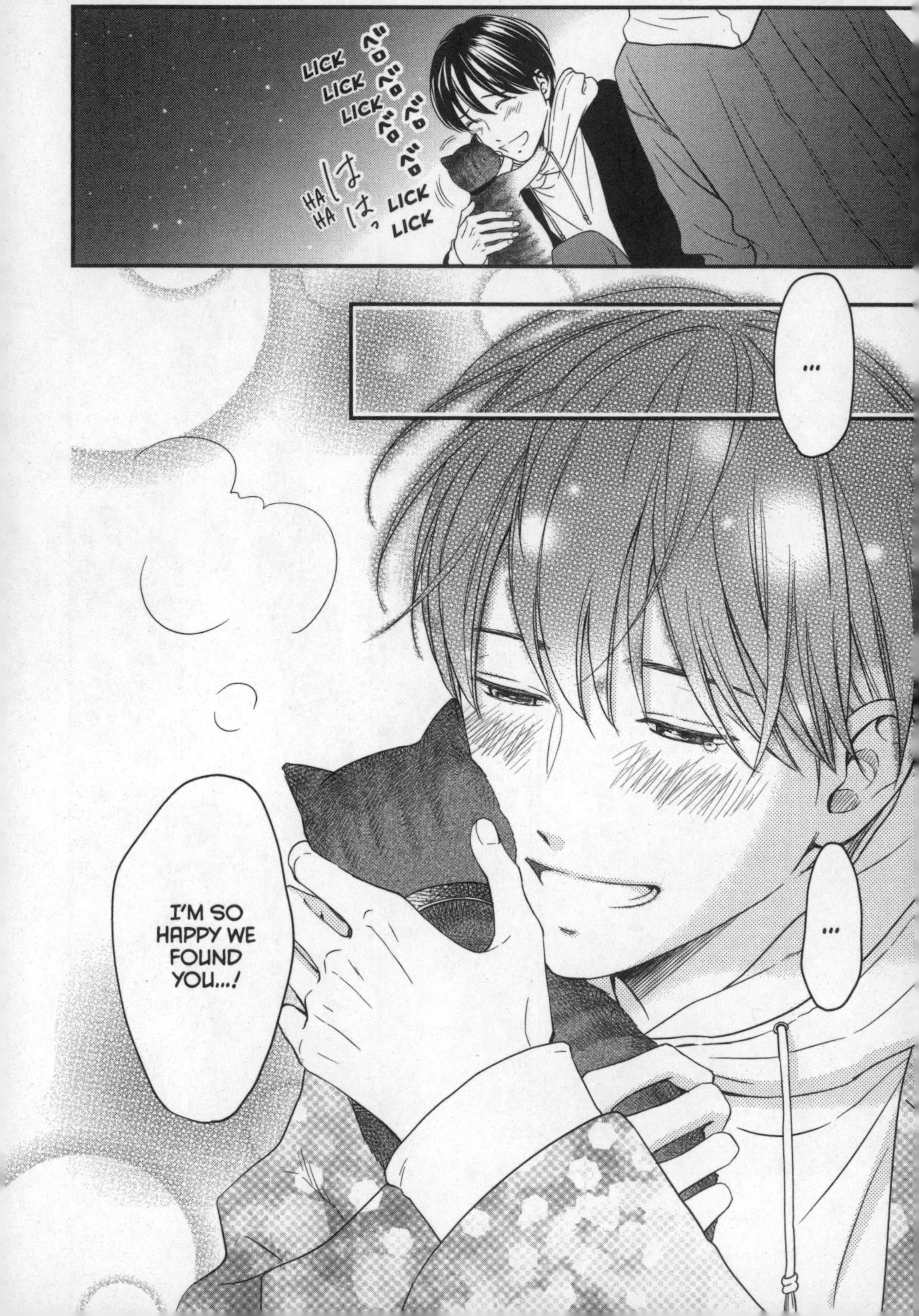
LICK LICK LICK
LICK LICK
HA HA
はは
...
...
I'M SO HAPPY WE FOUND YOU...!

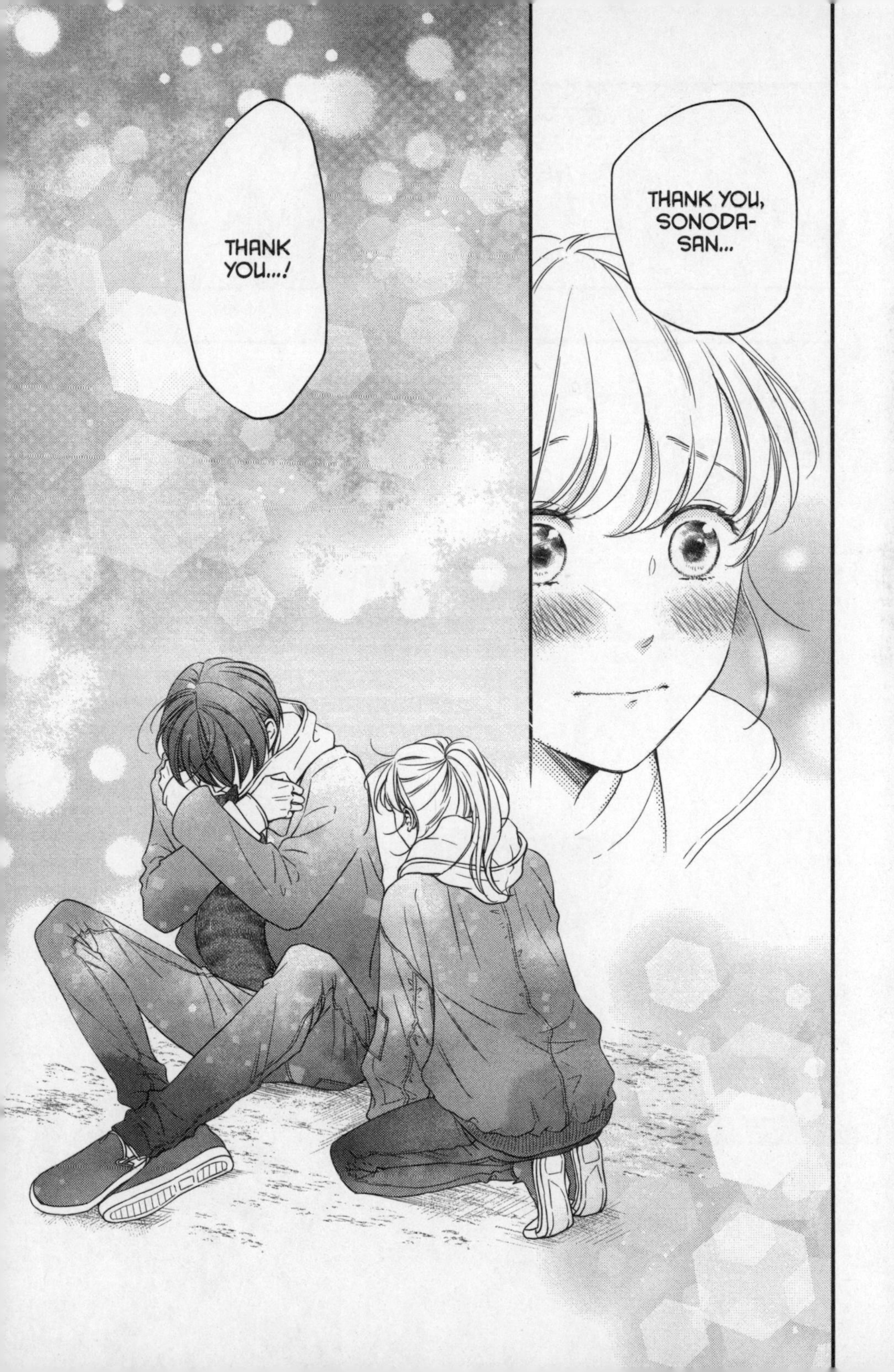
THANK YOU, SONODA-SAN...
THANK YOU...!

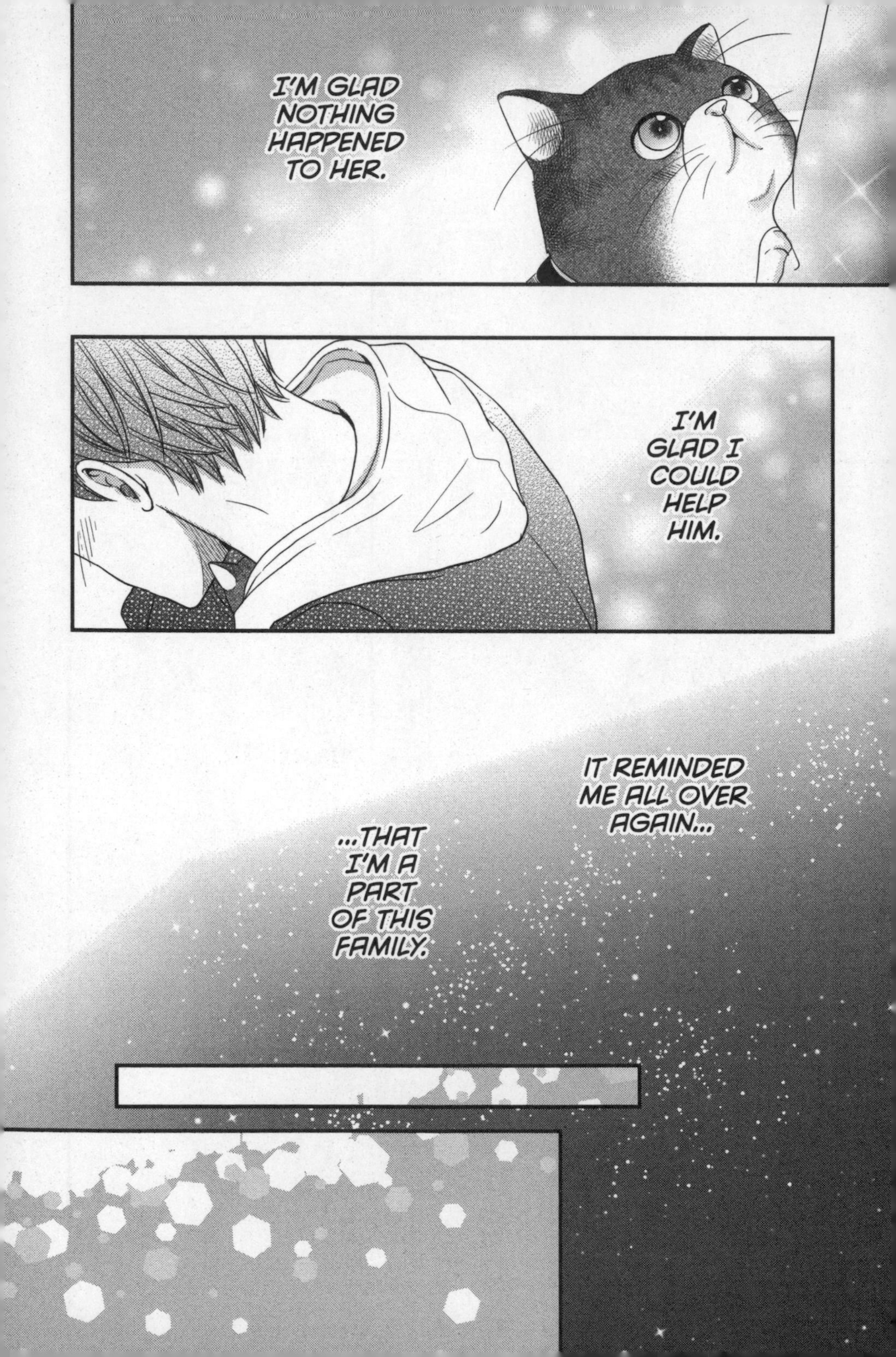
I'M GLAD NOTHING HAPPENED TO HER.
I'M GLAD I COULD HELP HIM.
IT REMINDED ME ALL OVER AGAIN...
...THAT I'M A PART OF THIS FAMILY.

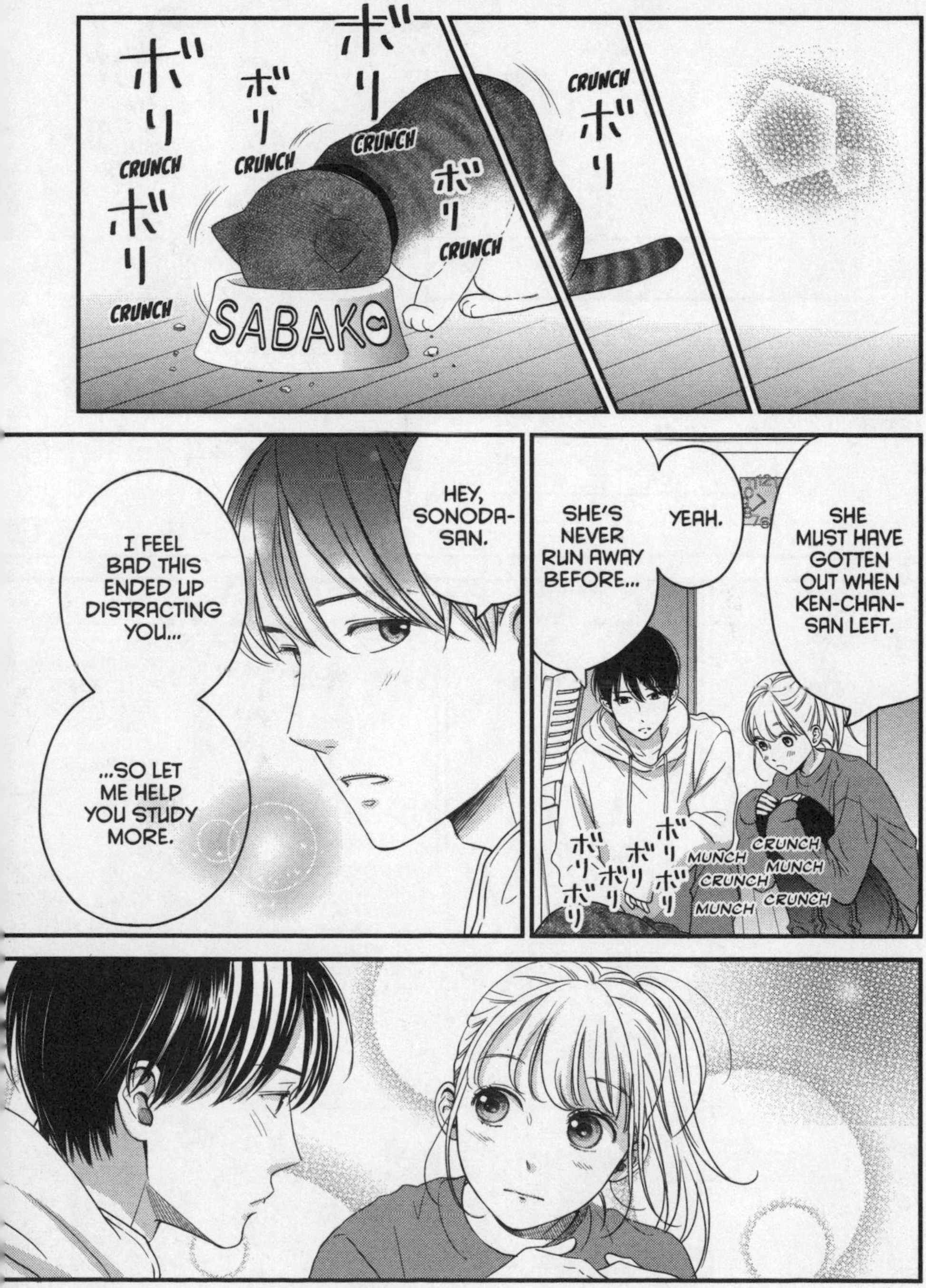
CRUNCH
ボリ
ボリ
CRUNCH
ボリ
CRUNCH
ボリ
CRUNCH
ボリ
CRUNCH
ボリ
CRUNCH
SABAKO
SHE MUST HAVE GOTTEN OUT WHEN KEN-CHAN-SAN LEFT.
YEAH.
SHE'S NEVER RUN AWAY BEFORE...
ボリボリ
ボリボリ
ボリボリ
MUNCH CRUNCH MUNCH CRUNCH MUNCH CRUNCH
HEY, SONODA-SAN.
I FEEL BAD THIS ENDED UP DISTRACTING YOU...
...SO LET ME HELP YOU STUDY MORE.

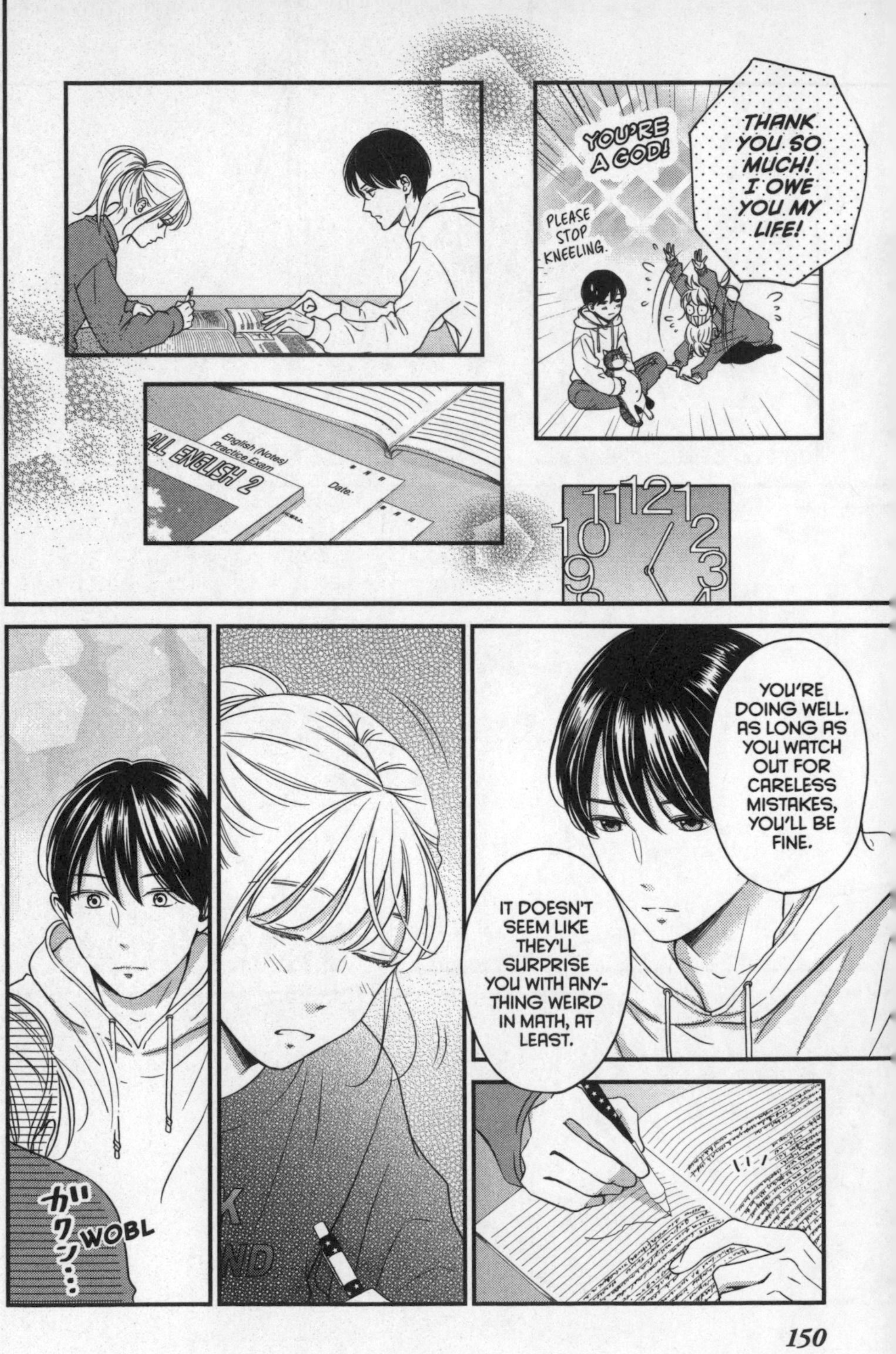
THANK YOU SO MUCH! I OWE YOU MY LIFE!
YOU'RE A GOD!
PLEASE STOP KNEELING.
English (Notes) Practice Exam
ALL ENGLISH 2
Date:
YOU'RE DOING WELL. AS LONG AS YOU WATCH OUT FOR CARELESS MISTAKES, YOU'LL BE FINE.
IT DOESN'T SEEM LIKE THEY'LL SURPRISE YOU WITH ANYTHING WEIRD IN MATH, AT LEAST.
ガクン…
WOBL

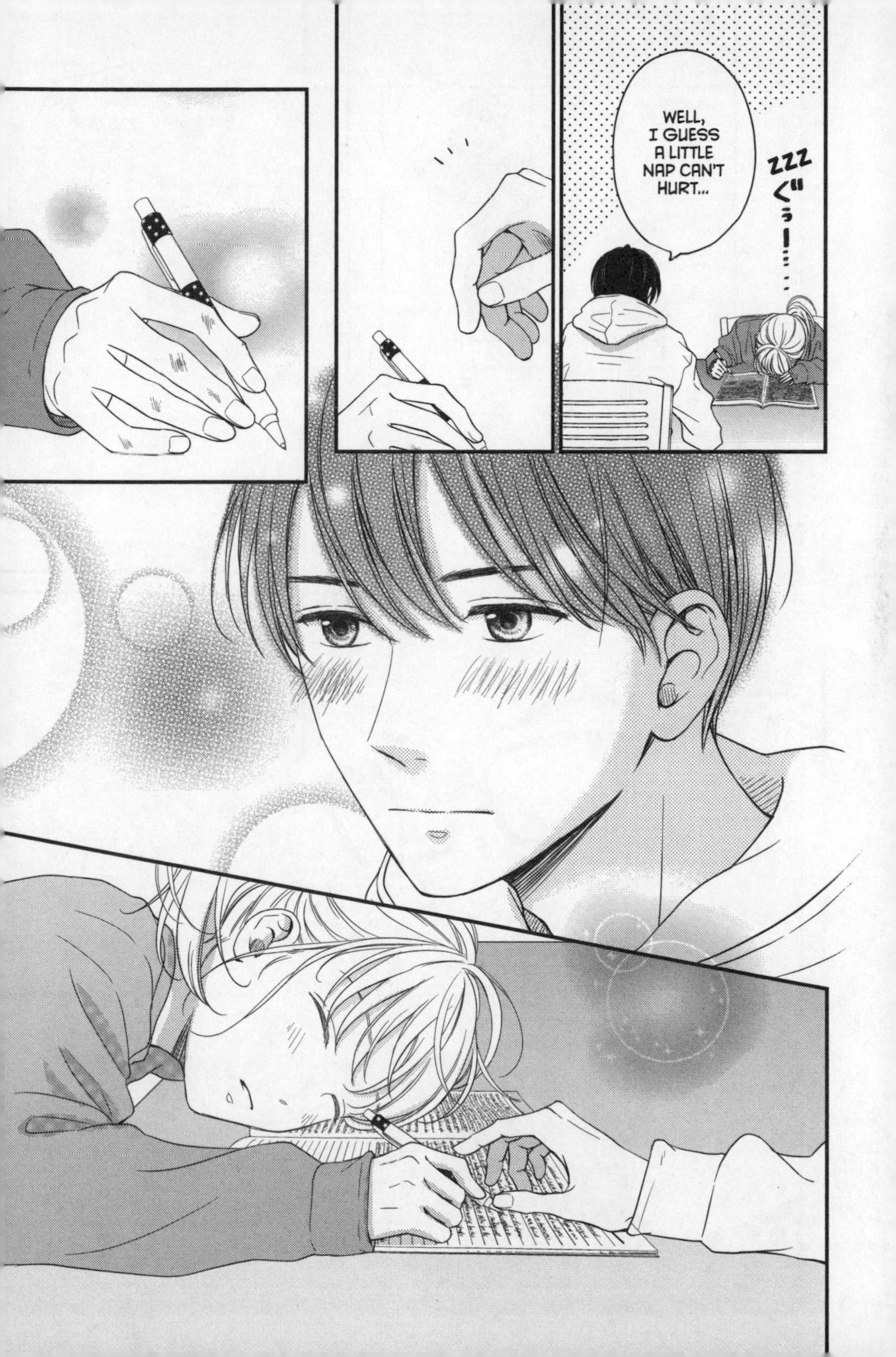
WELL, I GUESS A LITTLE NAP CAN'T HURT...
ZZZ
ぐぅー…

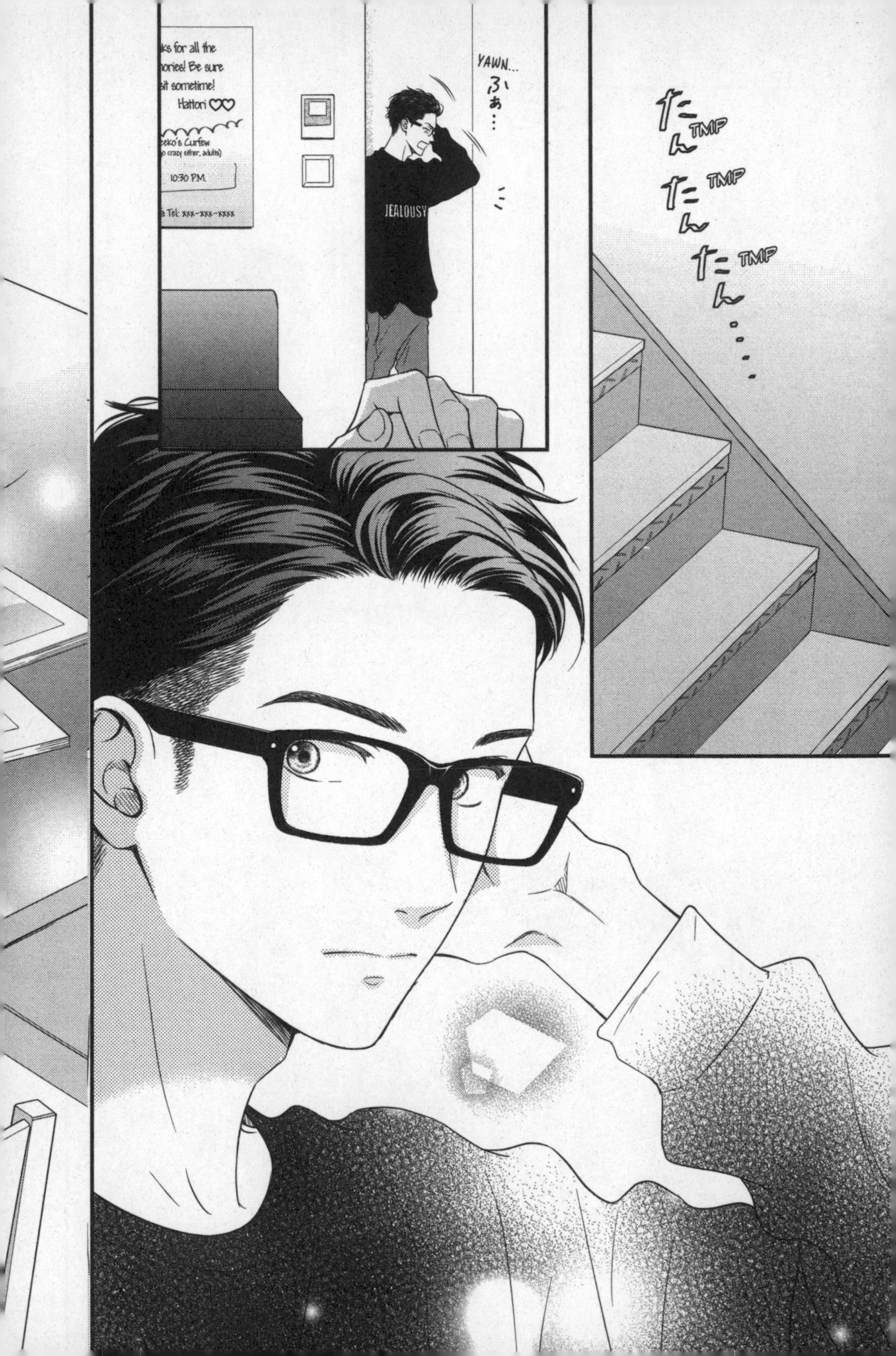
たん TMP
たん TMP
たん TMP...
ks for all the
mories! Be sure
sit sometime!
Hattori ♡♡
eeko's Curfew
10:30 P.M.
a Tel: xxx-xxx-xxxx
YAWN...
ふぁ...
JEALOUSY

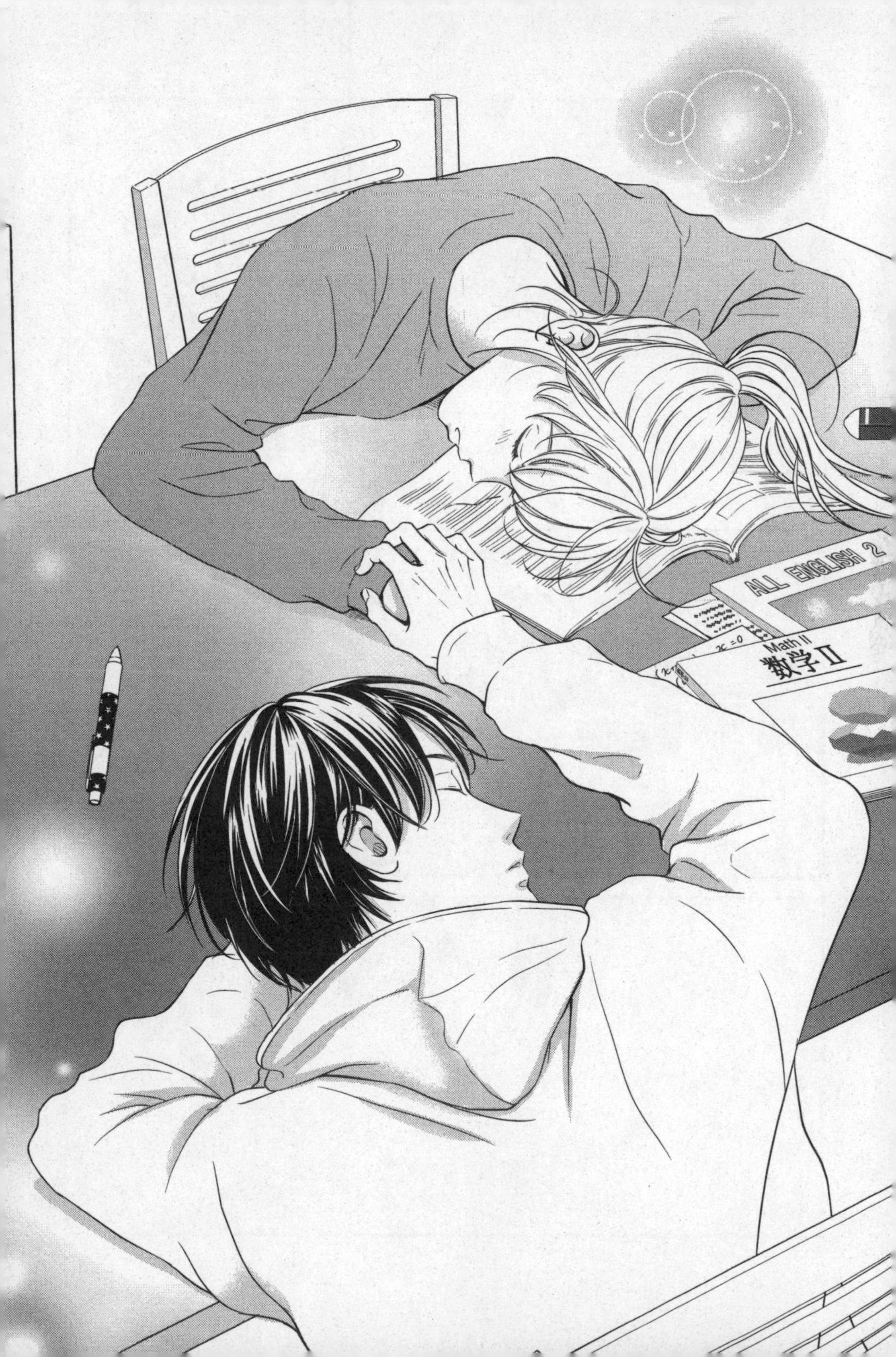
ALL ENGLISH 2
Math II
数学Ⅱ

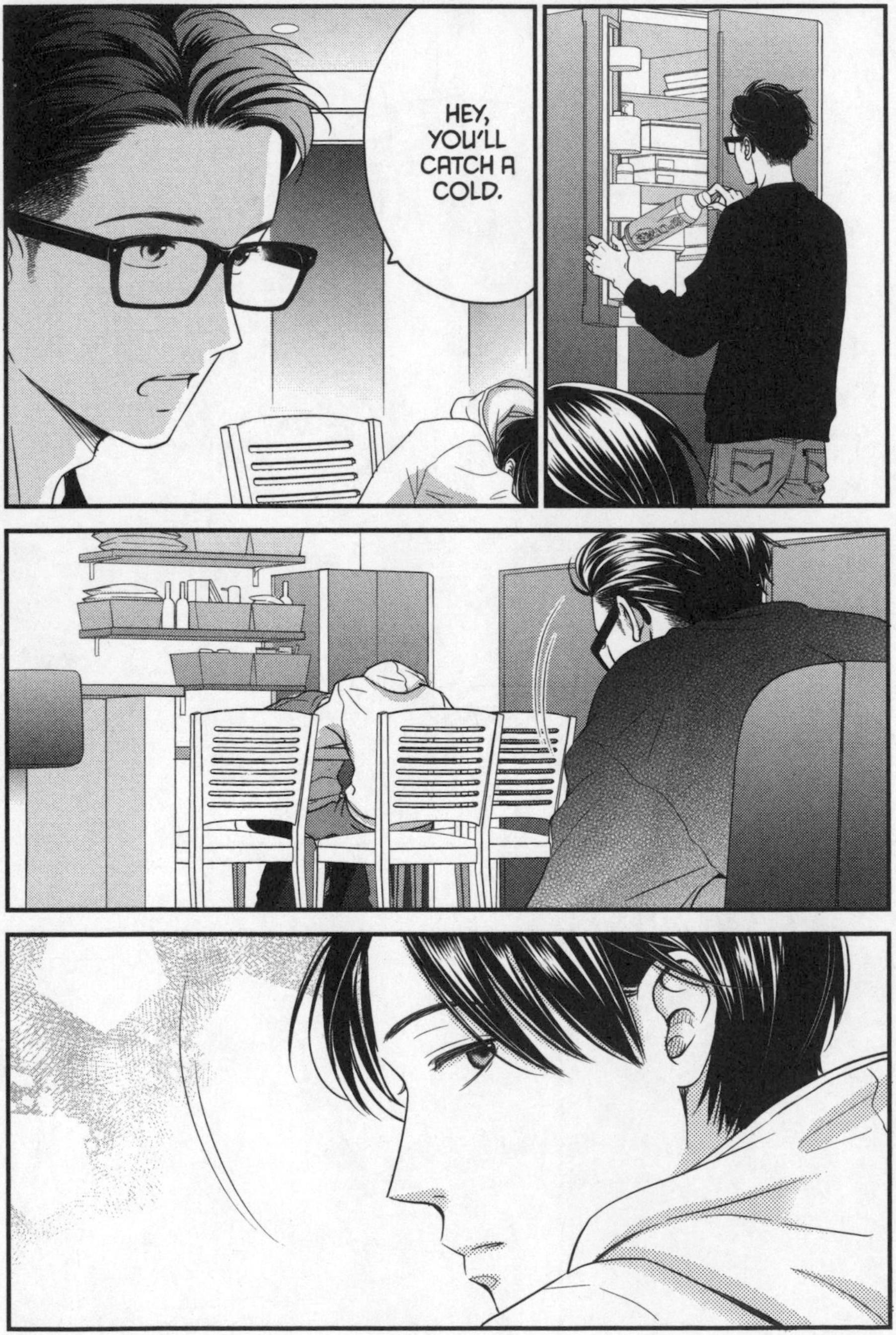
HEY, YOU'LL CATCH A COLD.

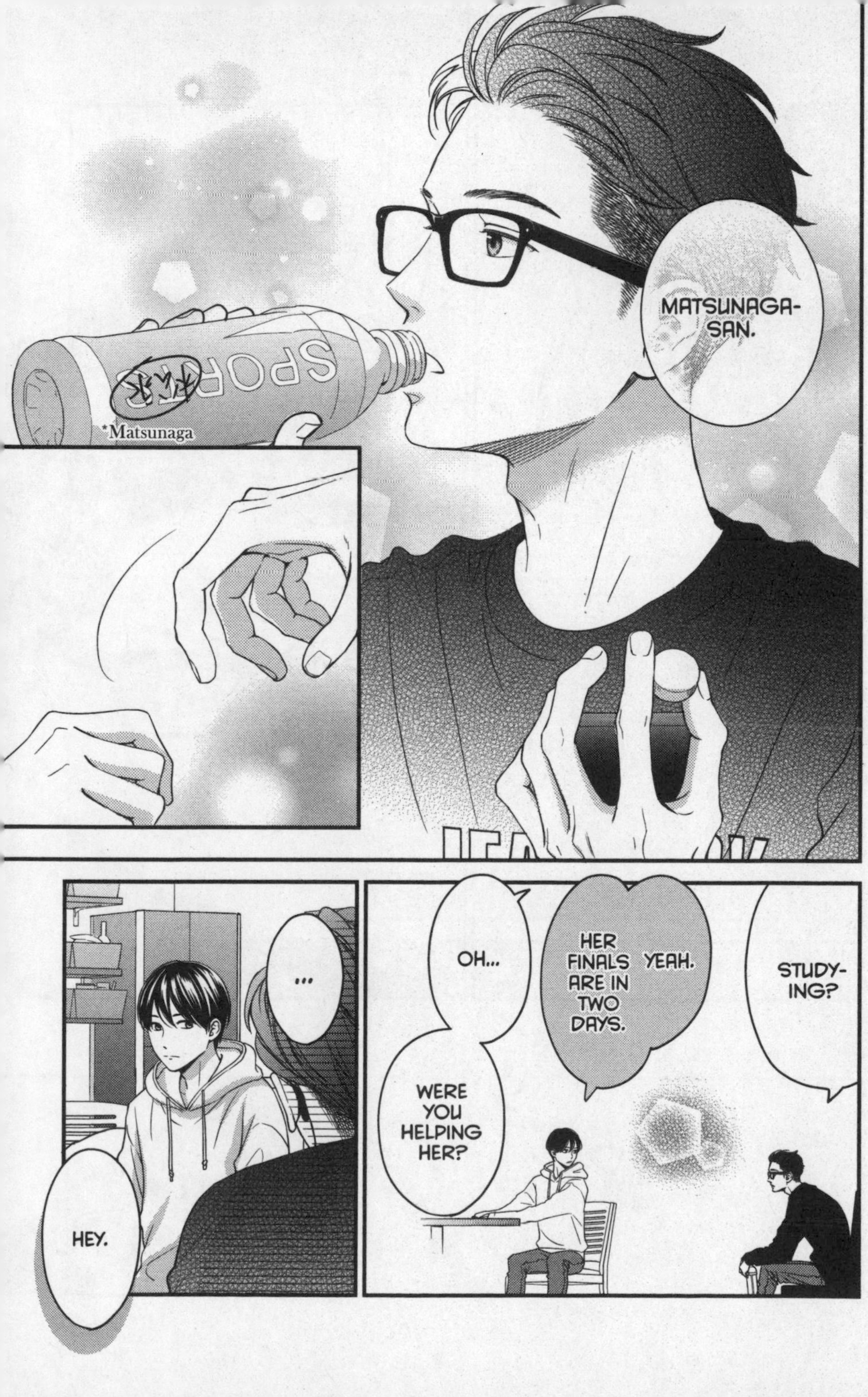
MATSUNAGA-SAN.
*Matsunaga
STUDYING?
YEAH.
HER FINALS ARE IN TWO DAYS.
OH...
WERE YOU HELPING HER?
...
HEY.

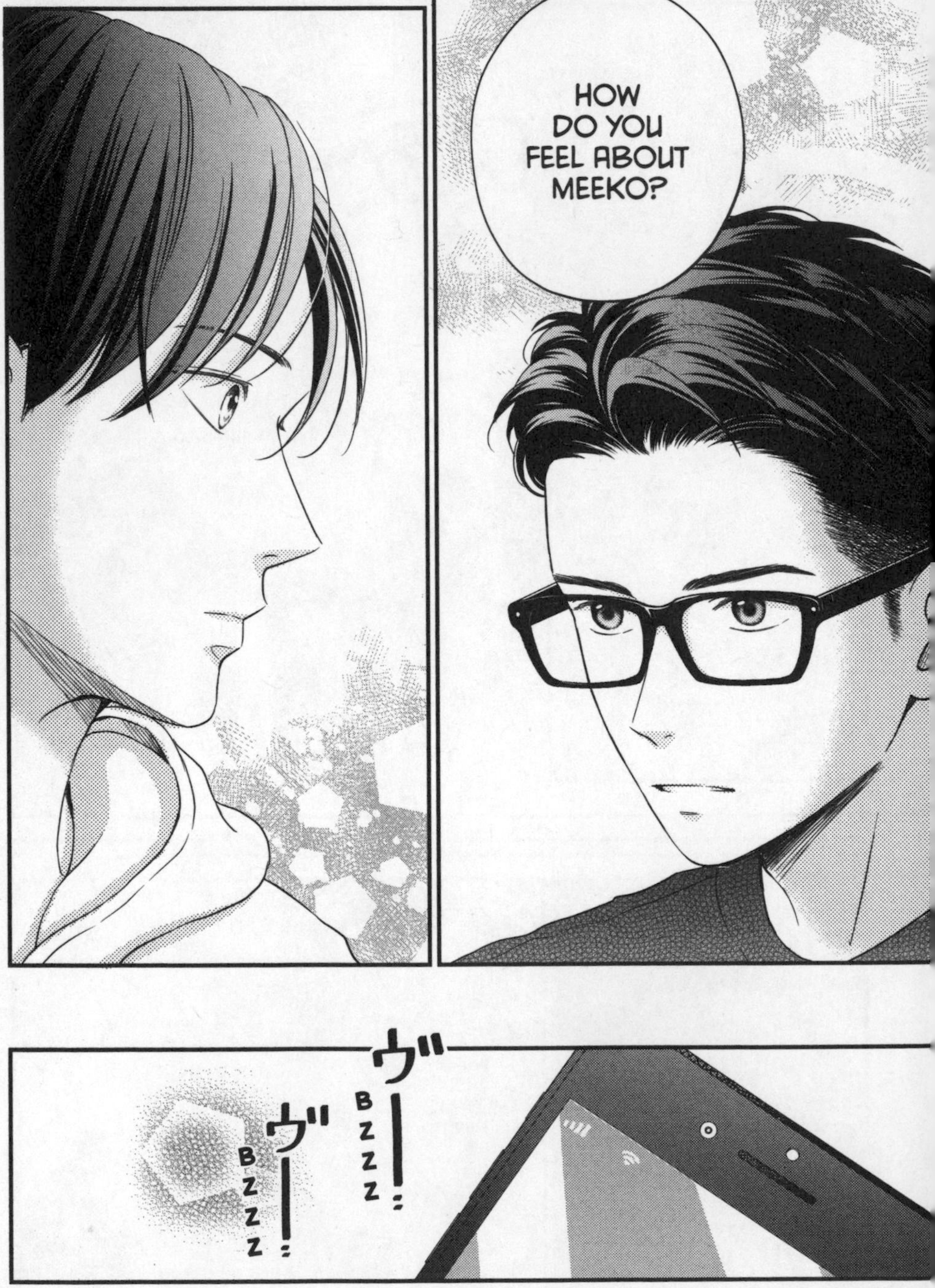
HOW DO YOU FEEL ABOUT MEEKO?
ヴー
BZZZ
ヴー
BZZZ

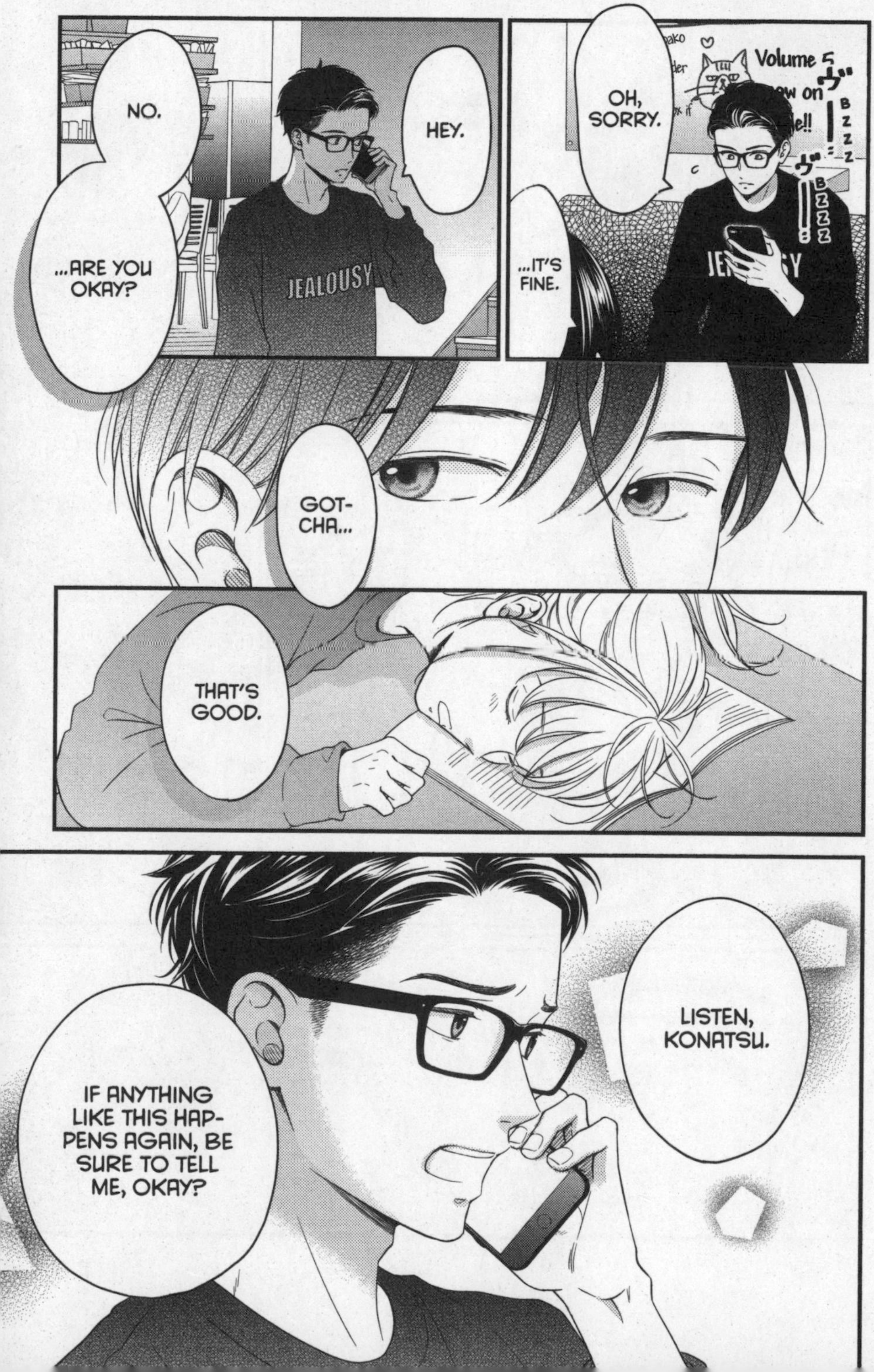
BZZZ
OH, SORRY.
BZZZ
...IT'S FINE.
HEY.
NO.
JEALOUSY
...ARE YOU OKAY?
GOT-CHA...
THAT'S GOOD.
LISTEN, KONATSU.
IF ANYTHING LIKE THIS HAP-PENS AGAIN, BE SURE TO TELL ME, OKAY?

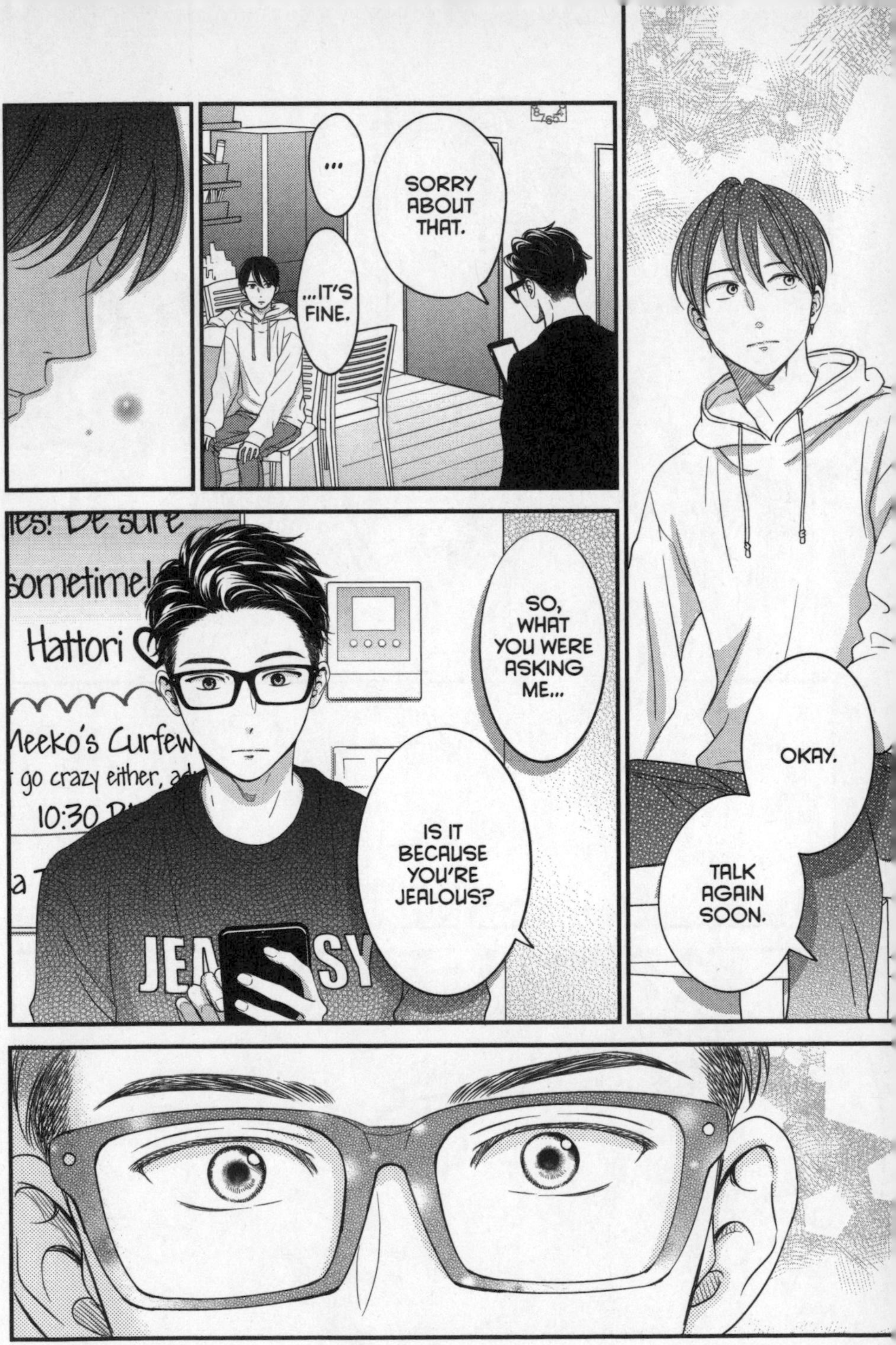
OKAY.
TALK AGAIN SOON.
SORRY ABOUT THAT.
...
...IT'S FINE.
sometime!
Hattori
Meeko's Curfew
SO, WHAT YOU WERE ASKING ME...
IS IT BECAUSE YOU'RE JEALOUS?

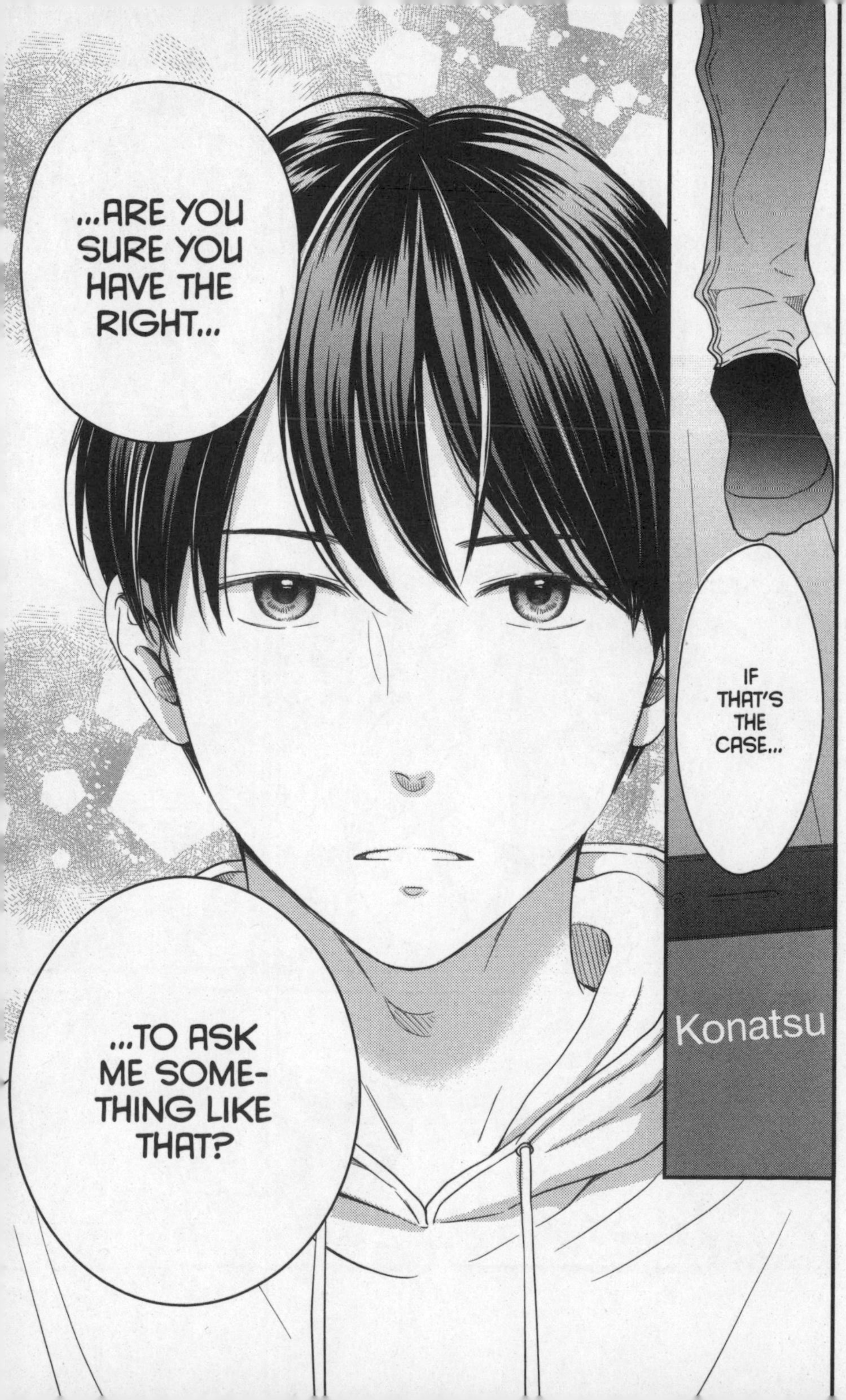
IF THAT'S THE CASE...
Konatsu
...ARE YOU SURE YOU HAVE THE RIGHT...
...TO ASK ME SOME-THING LIKE THAT?

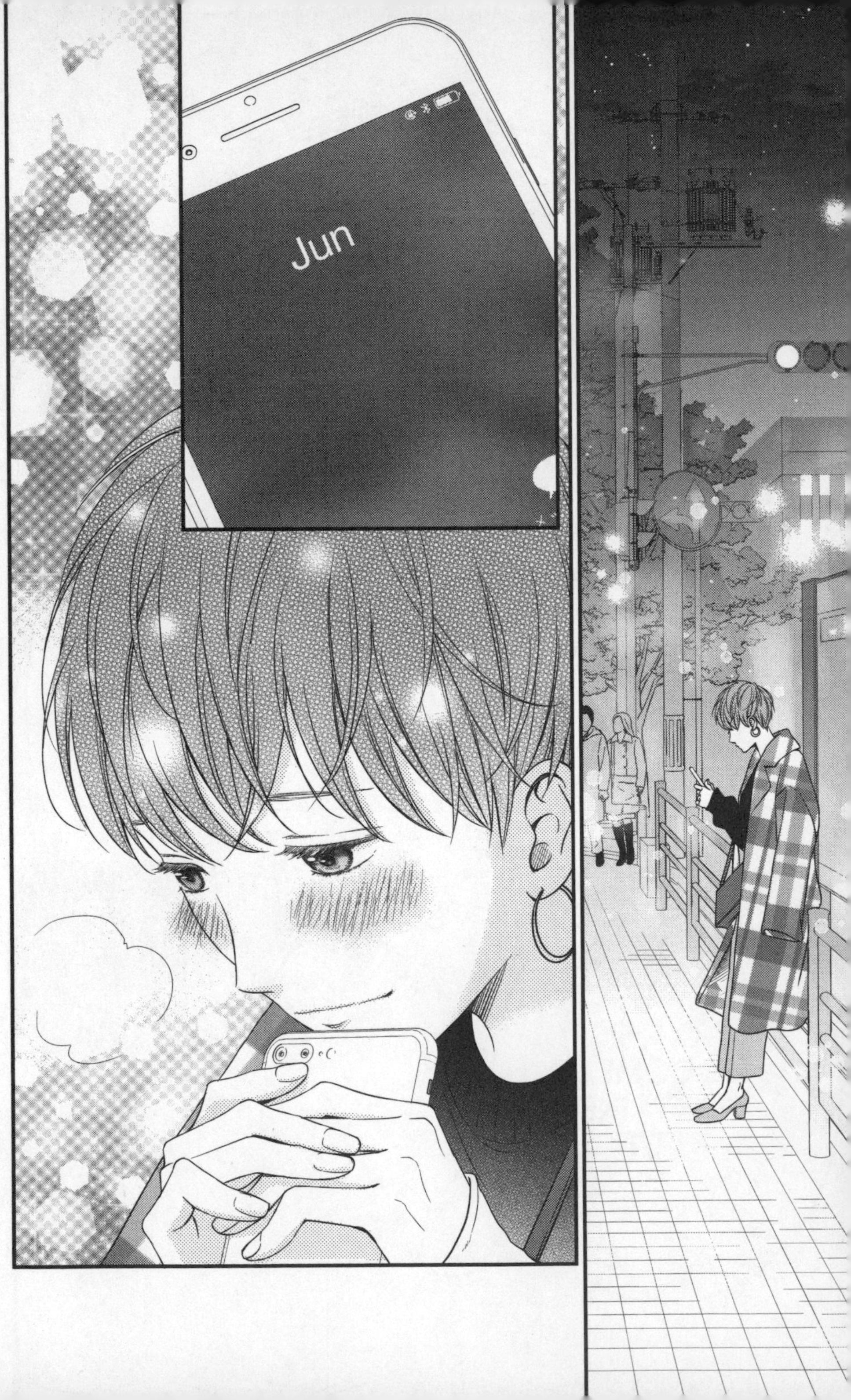
Jun

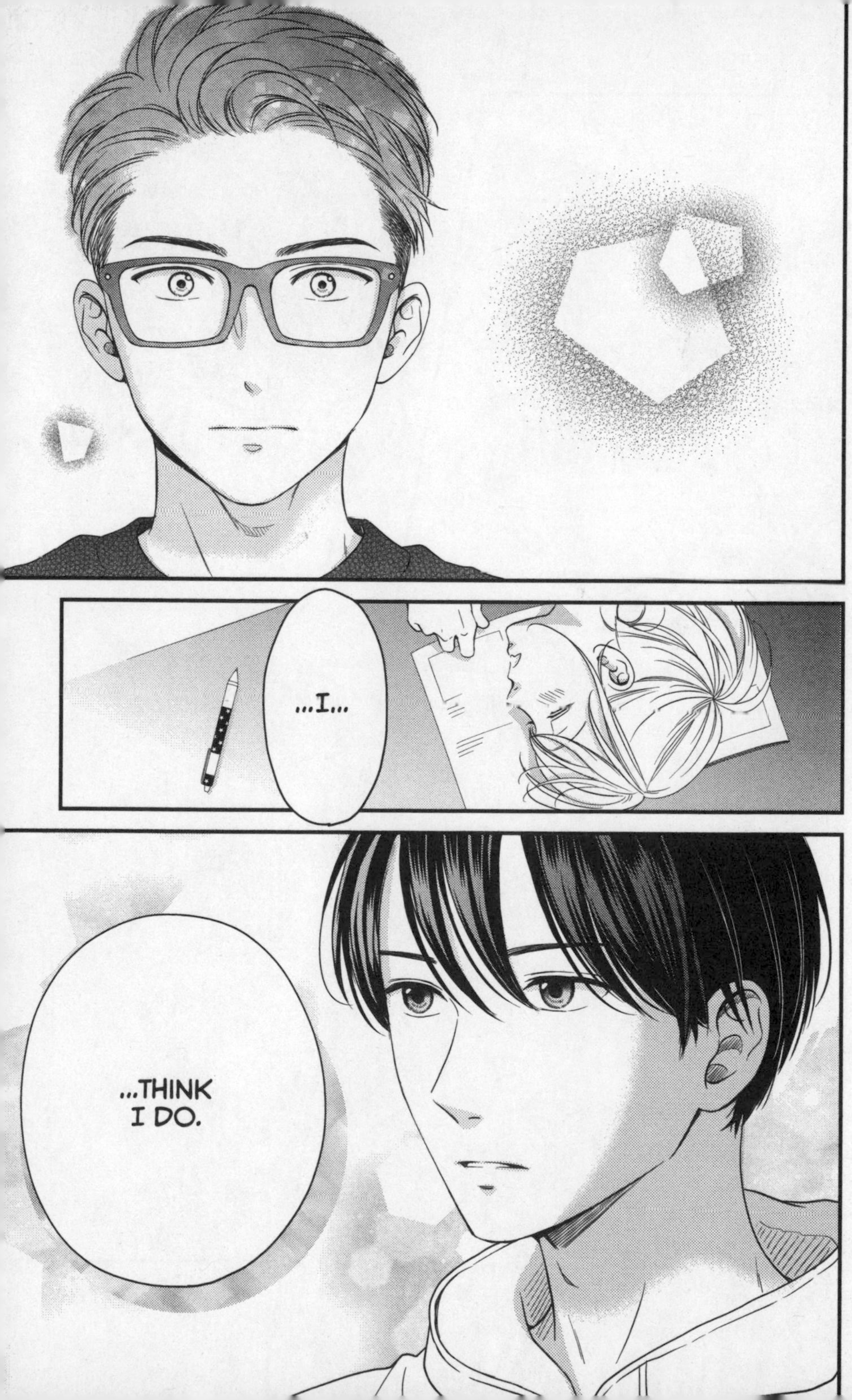
...I...
...THINK I DO.

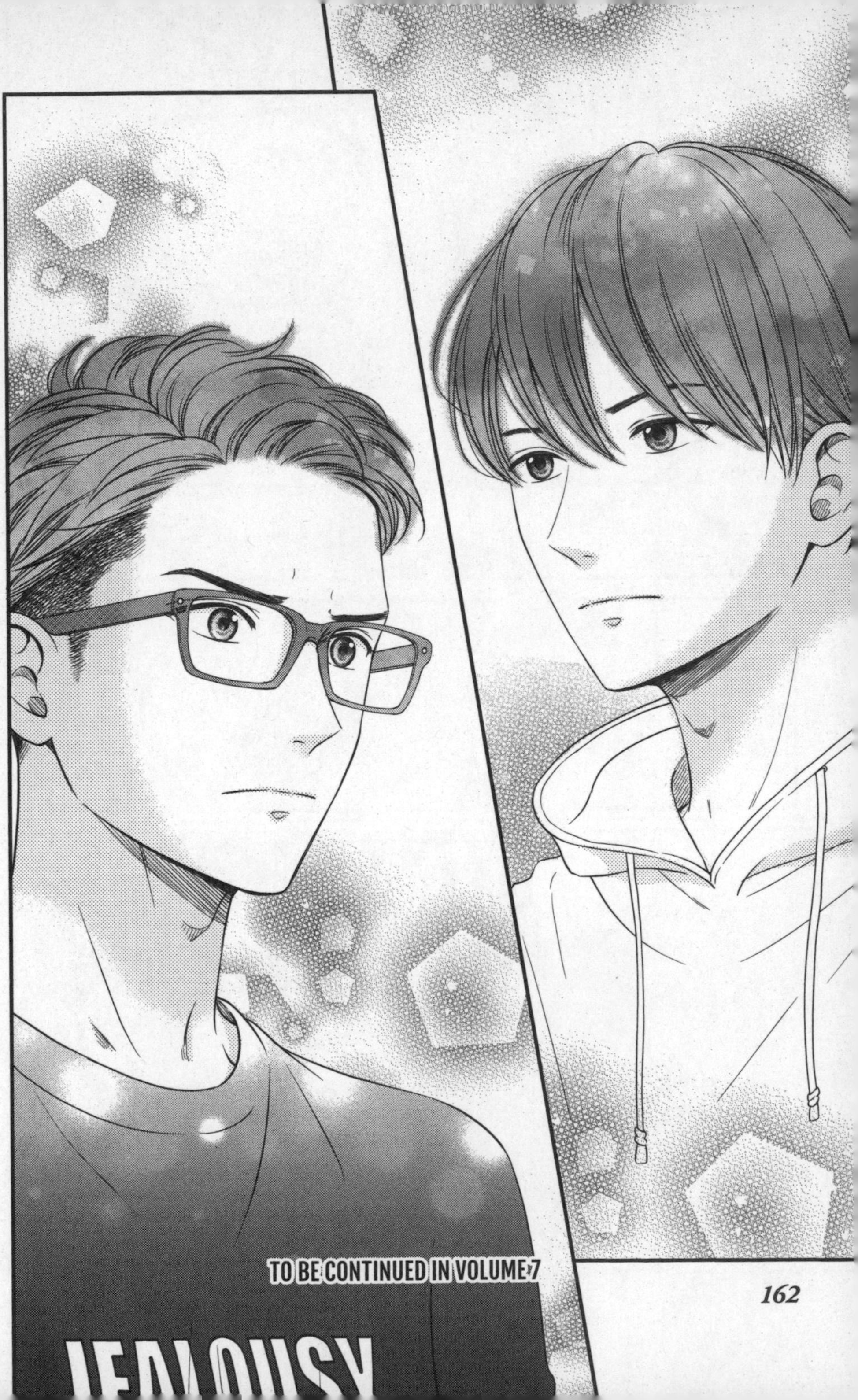
TO BE CONTINUED IN VOLUME 7

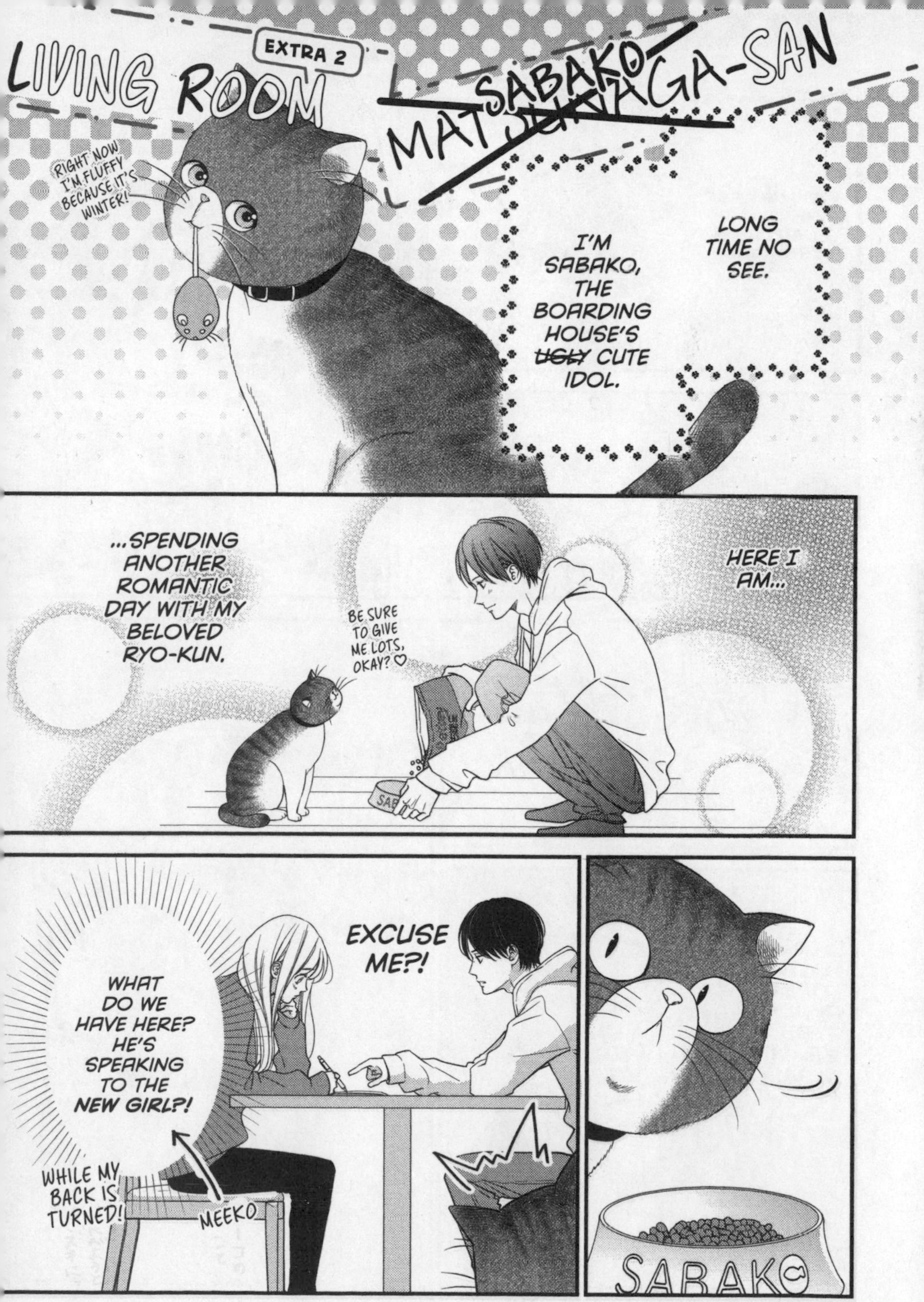

EXTRA 2
LIVING ROOM
SABAKO
MAT~~SUNA~~GA-SAN
LONG TIME NO SEE.
I'M SABAKO, THE BOARDING HOUSE'S ~~UGLY~~ CUTE IDOL.
RIGHT NOW I'M FLUFFY BECAUSE IT'S WINTER!
HERE I AM...
...SPENDING ANOTHER ROMANTIC DAY WITH MY BELOVED RYO-KUN.
BE SURE TO GIVE ME LOTS, OKAY? ♡
SABAKO
EXCUSE ME?!
WHAT DO WE HAVE HERE? HE'S SPEAKING TO THE NEW GIRL?!
WHILE MY BACK IS TURNED!
MEEKO

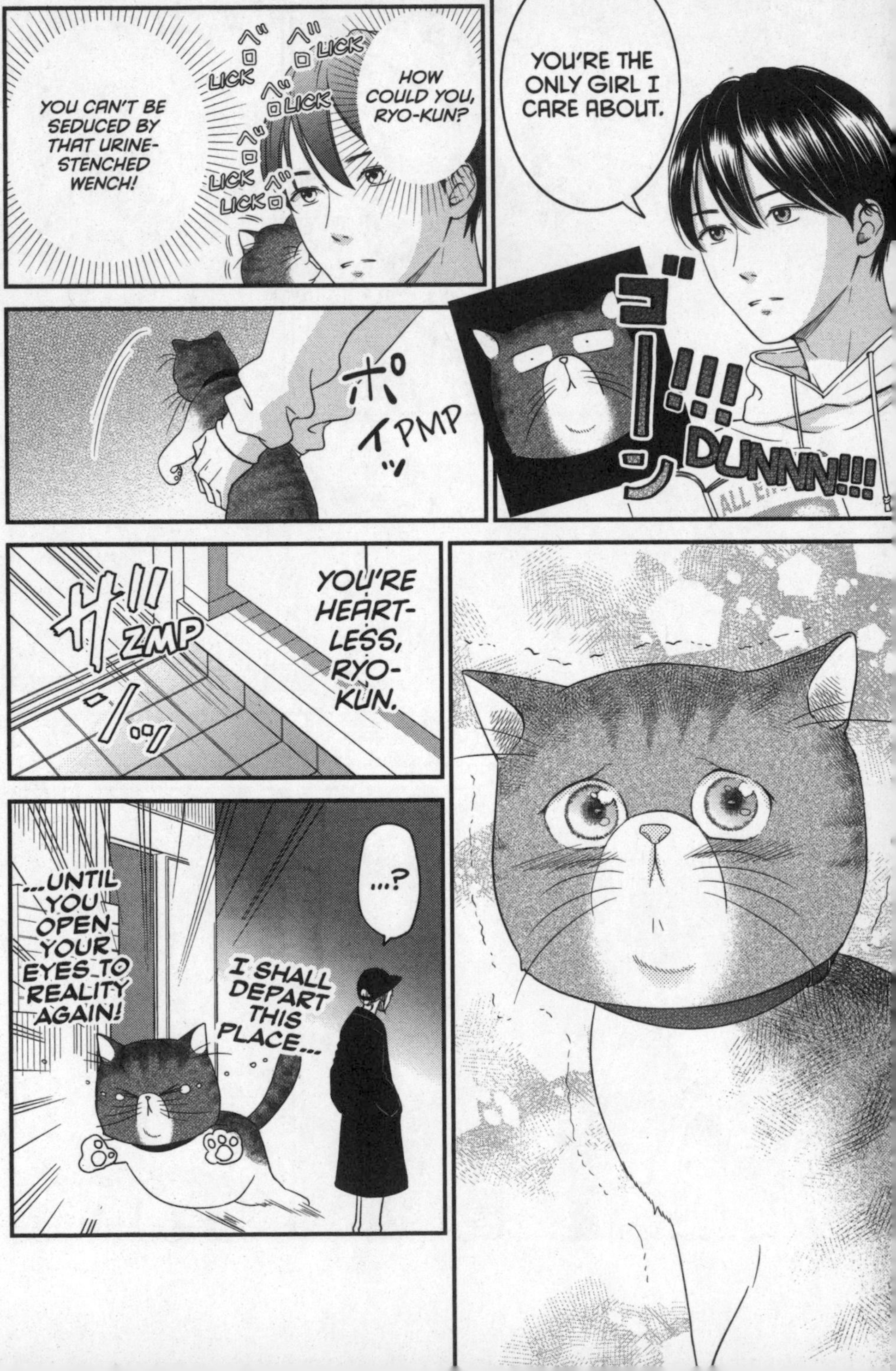
YOU'RE THE ONLY GIRL I CARE ABOUT.
DUNNN!!!
HOW COULD YOU, RYO-KUN?
LICK LICK LICK LICK LICK
YOU CAN'T BE SEDUCED BY THAT URINE-STENCHED WENCH!
PMP
YOU'RE HEARTLESS, RYO-KUN.
ZMP
...?
I SHALL DEPART THIS PLACE...
...UNTIL YOU OPEN YOUR EYES TO REALITY AGAIN!

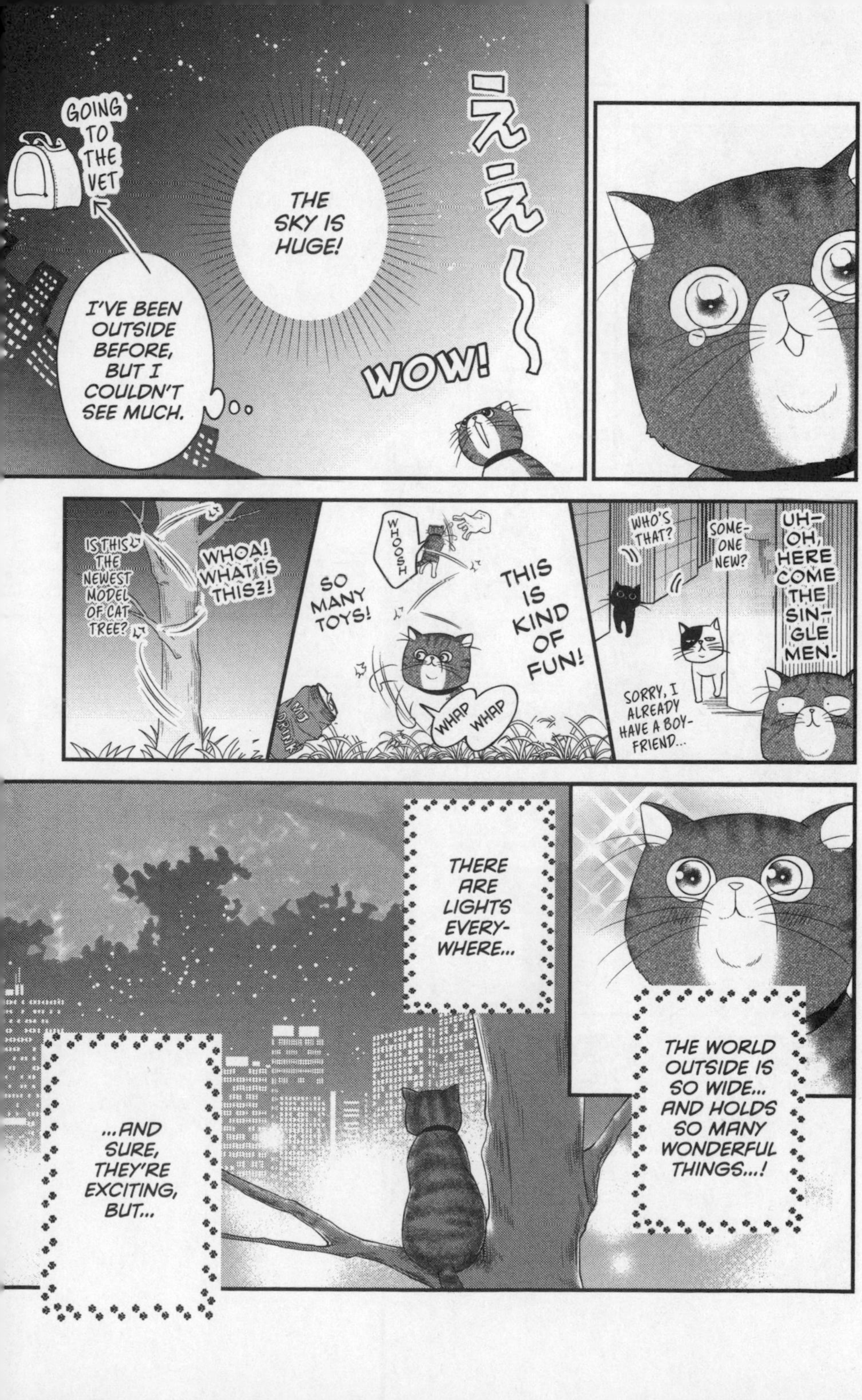
ええ〜
WOW!
THE SKY IS HUGE!
GOING TO THE VET
I'VE BEEN OUTSIDE BEFORE, BUT I COULDN'T SEE MUCH.
UH-OH, HERE COME THE SINGLE MEN.
SOME-ONE NEW?
WHO'S THAT?
SORRY, I ALREADY HAVE A BOY-FRIEND...
THIS IS KIND OF FUN!
WHOOSH
SO MANY TOYS!
WHAP WHAP
WHOA! WHAT IS THIS?!
IS THIS THE NEWEST MODEL OF CAT TREE?
THE WORLD OUTSIDE IS SO WIDE... AND HOLDS SO MANY WONDERFUL THINGS...!
THERE ARE LIGHTS EVERY-WHERE...
...AND SURE, THEY'RE EXCITING, BUT...

IT'S COLD...
I SHOULD HAVE AT LEAST EAT-EN BEFORE LEAVING...
OH, NO! I JUST REMEM-BERED!
I DON'T KNOW WHERE THE HOUSE IS...
IS...
...THIS WHERE I DIE...?
I SHOULD NEVER...
...HAVE LEFT HOME...
カサッ
RUSTLE

IN THE END...
...NOTH-ING BEATS SLEEPING ON RYO'S LAP.

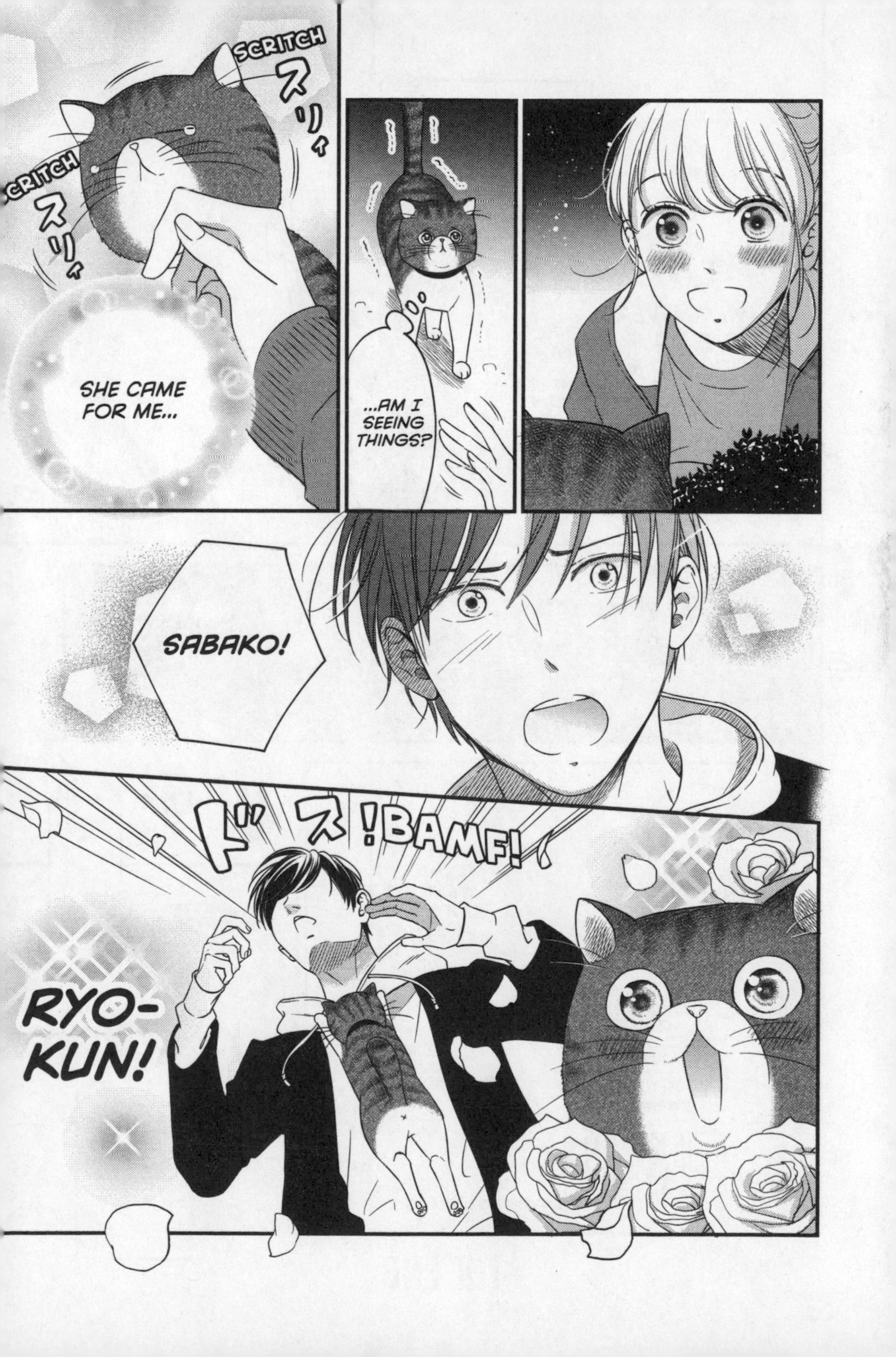
...AM I SEEING THINGS?
SCRITCH
スリィ
SCRITCH
スリィ
SHE CAME FOR ME...
SABAKO!
ドス
!BAMF!
RYO-KUN!

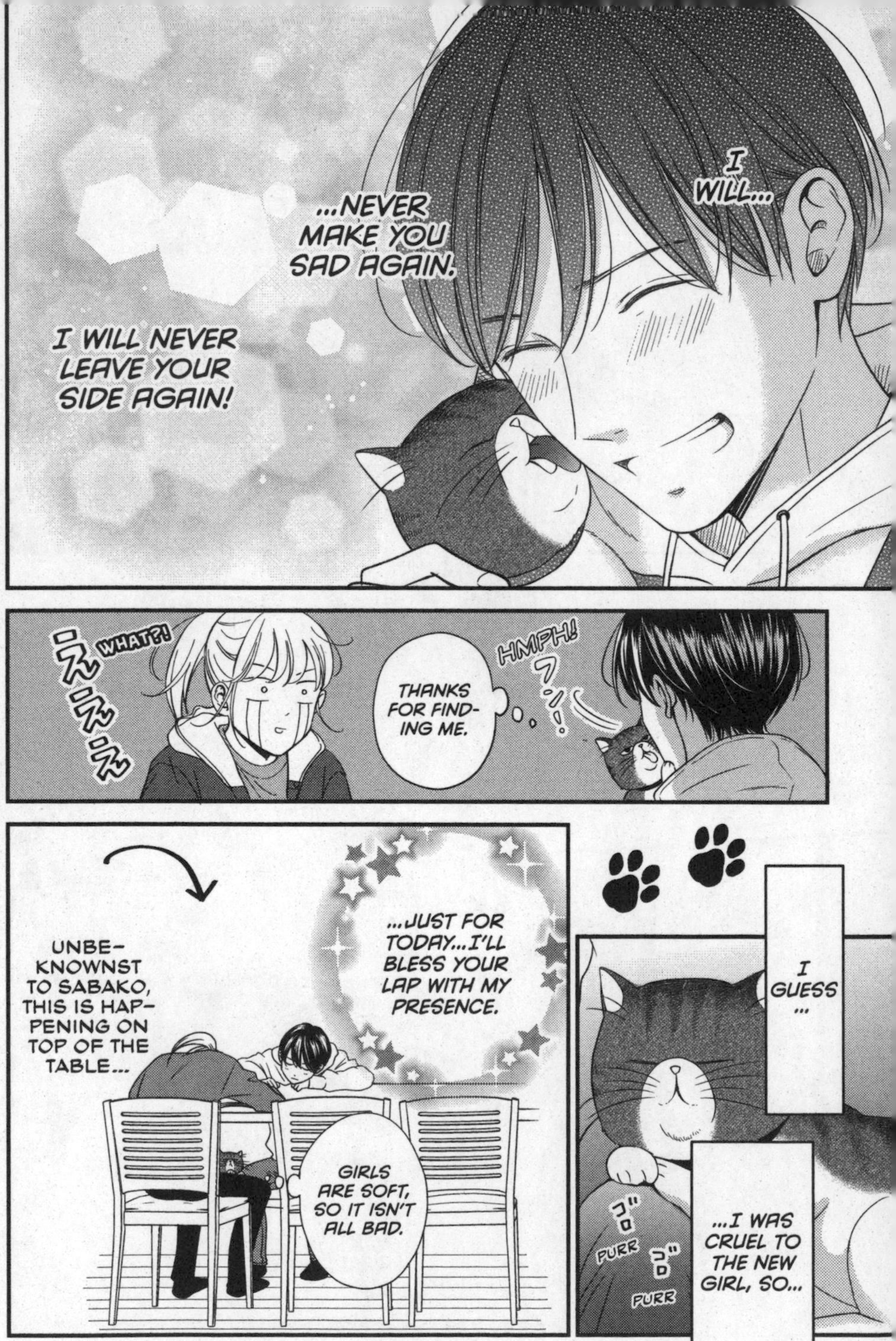
I WILL...
...NEVER MAKE YOU SAD AGAIN.
I WILL NEVER LEAVE YOUR SIDE AGAIN!
HMPH!
フン!
THANKS FOR FINDING ME.
WHAT?!
ええええ
I GUESS...
...I WAS CRUEL TO THE NEW GIRL, SO...
ゴロ
PURR
ゴロ
PURR
...JUST FOR TODAY...I'LL BLESS YOUR LAP WITH MY PRESENCE.
UNBEKNOWNST TO SABAKO, THIS IS HAPPENING ON TOP OF THE TABLE...
GIRLS ARE SOFT, SO IT ISN'T ALL BAD.

THE END

AFTERWORD

THANK YOU SO MUCH FOR READING LIVING-ROOM MATSUNAGA-SAN. THIS VOLUME CAME OUT RIGHT AROUND THE START OF THE REIWA ERA.

DID YOU ENJOY THE FIRST VOLUME OF THE REIWA ERA? HATTORI-SAN IS GONE, AND RYO-KUN IS STARTING TO STAND OUT... IT'S REALLY STARTING TO FEEL LIKE A CLASSIC BOARDING HOUSE STORY, RIGHT?

THE STORY HAS BEEN GAINING A MIND OF ITS OWN AS I DRAW IT, WHICH IS AT ONCE VERY EXCITING AND VERY FRUSTRATING. I THINK THE DEVELOPMENTS IN VOLUME 7 WILL BE EVEN MORE EXCITING! (THERE'S A LOT I'M LOOKING FORWARD TO DRAWING IN THERE!!!)

I'M GOING TO WORK HARD TO MAKE THE REST OF THIS THE BEST STORY I CAN, SO THANKS FOR READING! ♡

2019.5.13
2019.5.13

岩下慶子
KEIKO IWASHITA

I FINALLY GOT USED TO DRAWING MATSUNAGA-SAN'S HAIR, AND NOW IT'S RYO-KUN (AND HIS BANGS) I CAN'T DRAW...

THANK YOU SO MUCH FOR ALL YOUR FEEDBACK! ♡♡♡

I LOOK FORWARD TO HEARING YOUR SUGGESTIONS ABOUT T-SHIRTS (OR SWEATSHIRTS) FOR MATSUNAGA-SAN, THINGS FOR RYO-KUN TO DO, AND EVERYTHING ELSE!

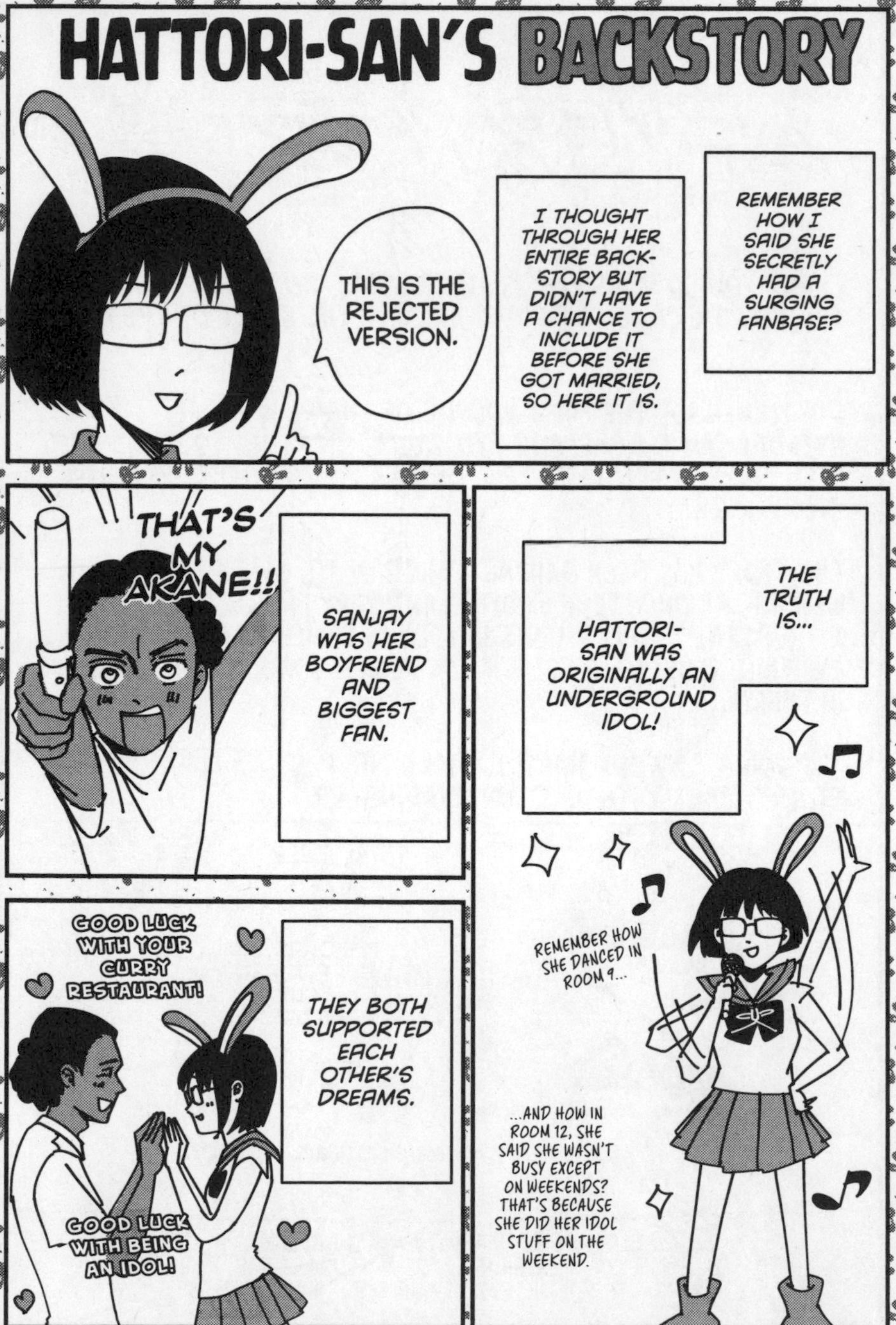
HATTORI-SAN'S BACKSTORY
REMEMBER HOW I SAID SHE SECRETLY HAD A SURGING FANBASE?
I THOUGHT THROUGH HER ENTIRE BACK-STORY BUT DIDN'T HAVE A CHANCE TO INCLUDE IT BEFORE SHE GOT MARRIED, SO HERE IT IS.
THIS IS THE REJECTED VERSION.
THE TRUTH IS...
HATTORI-SAN WAS ORIGINALLY AN UNDERGROUND IDOL!
REMEMBER HOW SHE DANCED IN ROOM 9...
...AND HOW IN ROOM 12, SHE SAID SHE WASN'T BUSY EXCEPT ON WEEKENDS? THAT'S BECAUSE SHE DID HER IDOL STUFF ON THE WEEKEND.
SANJAY WAS HER BOYFRIEND AND BIGGEST FAN.
THAT'S MY AKANE!!
THEY BOTH SUPPORTED EACH OTHER'S DREAMS.
GOOD LUCK WITH YOUR CURRY RESTAURANT!
GOOD LUCK WITH BEING AN IDOL!

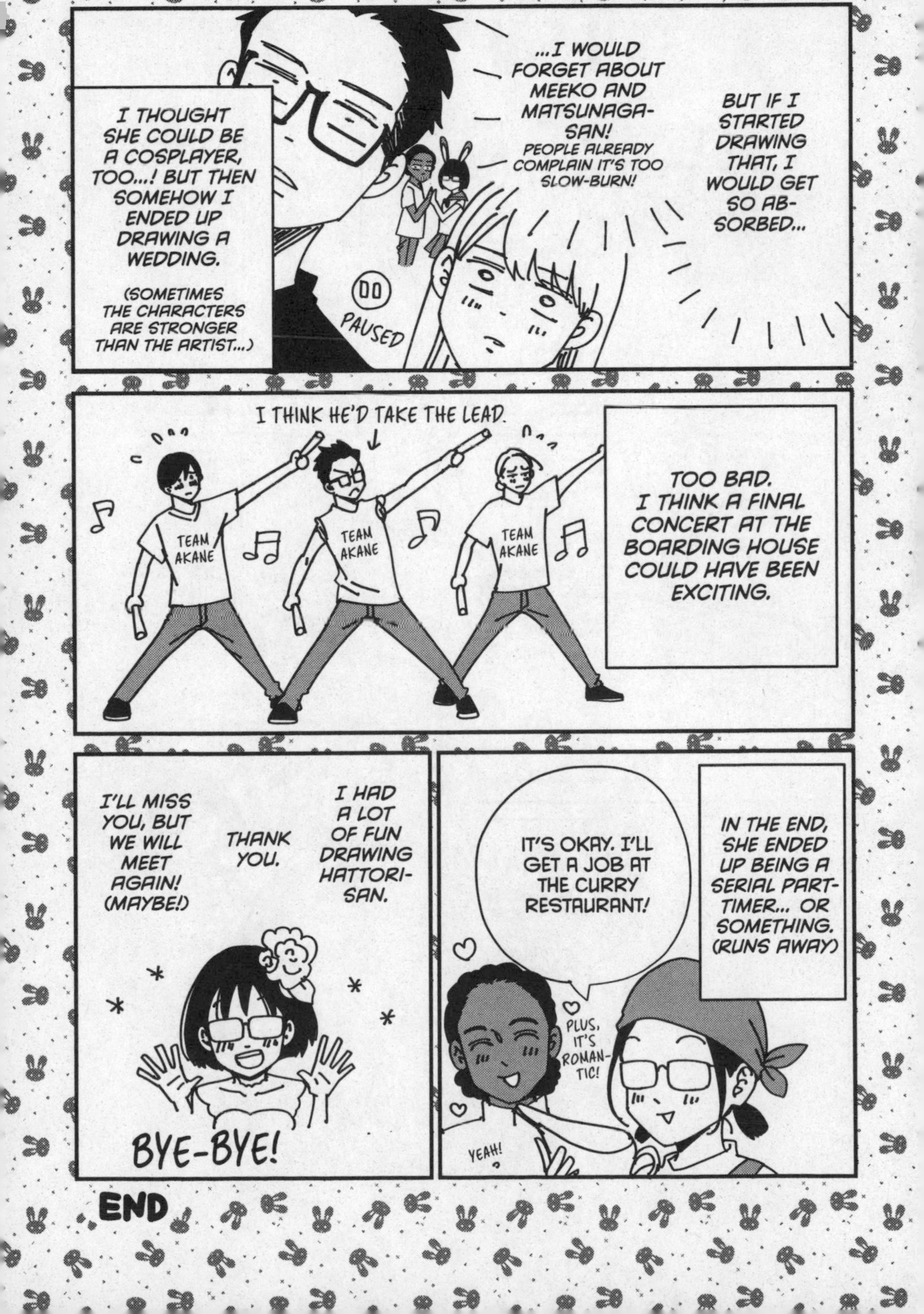
BUT IF I STARTED DRAWING THAT, I WOULD GET SO ABSORBED...
...I WOULD FORGET ABOUT MEEKO AND MATSUNAGA-SAN!
PEOPLE ALREADY COMPLAIN IT'S TOO SLOW-BURN!
I THOUGHT SHE COULD BE A COSPLAYER, TOO...! BUT THEN SOMEHOW I ENDED UP DRAWING A WEDDING.
(SOMETIMES THE CHARACTERS ARE STRONGER THAN THE ARTIST...)
PAUSED
TOO BAD. I THINK A FINAL CONCERT AT THE BOARDING HOUSE COULD HAVE BEEN EXCITING.
I THINK HE'D TAKE THE LEAD.
TEAM AKANE
TEAM AKANE
TEAM AKANE
IN THE END, SHE ENDED UP BEING A SERIAL PART-TIMER... OR SOMETHING. (RUNS AWAY)
IT'S OKAY. I'LL GET A JOB AT THE CURRY RESTAURANT!
PLUS, IT'S ROMANTIC!
YEAH!
I HAD A LOT OF FUN DRAWING HATTORI-SAN.
THANK YOU.
I'LL MISS YOU, BUT WE WILL MEET AGAIN! (MAYBE!)
BYE-BYE!

END

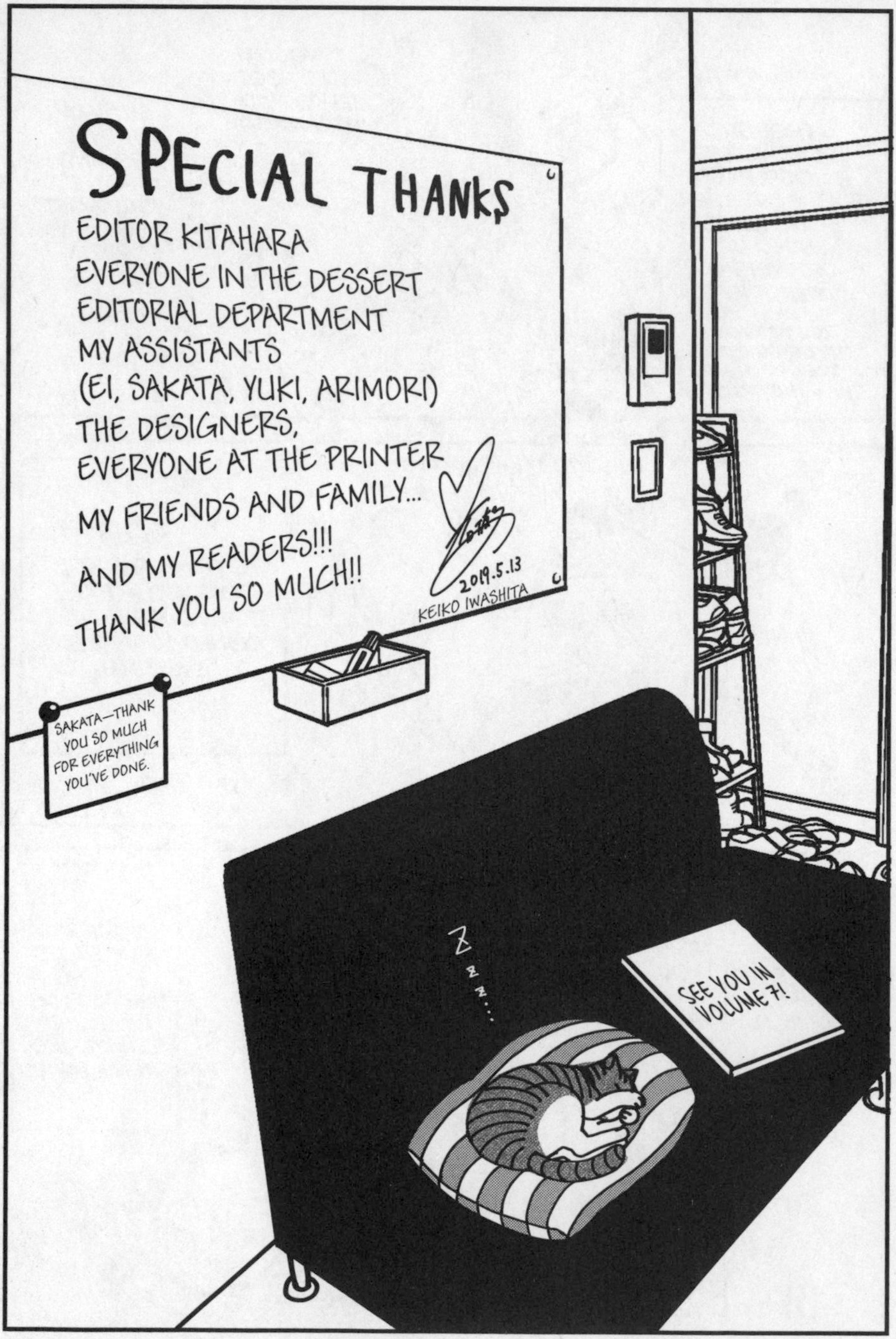
SPECIAL THANKS
EDITOR KITAHARA
EVERYONE IN THE DESSERT EDITORIAL DEPARTMENT
MY ASSISTANTS (EI, SAKATA, YUKI, ARIMORI)
THE DESIGNERS, EVERYONE AT THE PRINTER
MY FRIENDS AND FAMILY...
AND MY READERS!!!
THANK YOU SO MUCH!!
2019.5.13
KEIKO IWASHITA
SAKATA—THANK YOU SO MUCH FOR EVERYTHING YOU'VE DONE.
Z z z...
SEE YOU IN VOLUME 7!

LIVING·ROOM
MATSUNAGA·SAN

One of CLAMP's biggest hits returns
in this definitive, premium, hardcover
20th anniversary collector's edition!

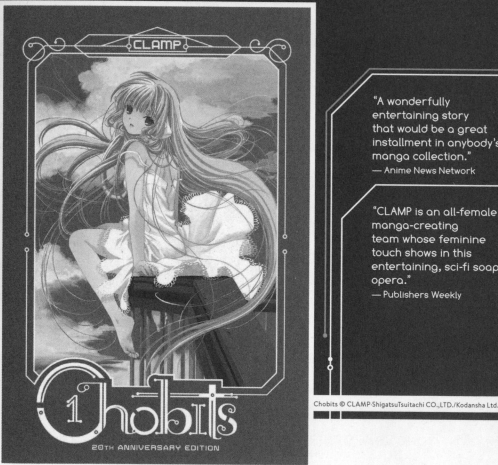

CLAMP

①Chobits
20TH ANNIVERSARY EDITION

"A wonderfully
entertaining story
that would be a great
installment in anybody's
manga collection."
— Anime News Network

"CLAMP is an all-female
manga-creating
team whose feminine
touch shows in this
entertaining, sci-fi soap
opera."
— Publishers Weekly

Chobits © CLAMP·ShigatsuTsuitachi CO.,LTD./Kodansha Ltd.

Poor college student Hideki is down on his luck. All he wants is a
good job, a girlfriend, and his very own "persocom"—the latest
and greatest in humanoid computer technology. Hideki's luck
changes one night when he finds Chi—a persocom thrown out in
a pile of trash. But Hideki soon discovers that there's much more
to his cute new persocom than meets the eye.

KC
KODANSHA
COMICS